Catholic Women's Rhetoric in the United States

Catholic Women's Rhetoric in the United States

Ethos, the Patriarchy, and Feminist Resistance

Edited by
Christina R. Pinkston
and Elizabethada A. Wright

LEXINGTON BOOKS
Lanham • Boulder • New York • London

Published by Lexington Books
An imprint of The Rowman & Littlefield Publishing Group, Inc.
4501 Forbes Boulevard, Suite 200, Lanham, Maryland 20706
www.rowman.com

86-90 Paul Street, London EC2A 4NE

British Library Cataloguing in Publication Information Available

Library of Congress Cataloging-in-Publication Data on File

ISBN 978-1-7936-3621-8 (cloth : alk. Paper)
ISBN 978-1-7936-3623-2 (pbk. : alk. Paper)
ISBN 978-1-7936-3622-5 (electronic)

∞™ The paper used in this publication meets the minimum requirements of American National Standard for Information Sciences—Permanence of Paper for Printed Library Materials, ANSI/NISO Z39.48-1992.

For Tracy Schier and Sister Mary Ryan, S.P.

Contents

Acknowledgments ix
Christina R. Pinkston and Elizabethada A. Wright

Introduction: Ethos, the Patriarchy, and Feminist Resistance 1
Elizabethada A. Wright

PART I: ETHOS WITHIN WOMEN'S RELIGIOUS ORDERS 23

1 "If We Are Always Your Cherished Daughters": Ethos, Parrhesia, and Two Nineteenth-Century European American Catholic Sisters 25
Elizabethada A. Wright

2 Remembering Mother McAuley: Epideictic Rhetoric, Ethos, and Memory 47
Amy Ferdinandt Stolley

3 The Habits and Dwelling Places of Sisters of Color: The New Orleans' Soeurs de Sainte-Famille's Reconstruction of Ethos 61
Elizabethada A. Wright and Christiana Ares-Christian

4 Corporeal, Confrontational Resistance: The Embodied Rhetoric of the Sisters of Loretto 79
Shana Scudder

PART II: INTERSECTIONS OF LAY AND CLERGY 97

5 Who Owns This Church? Feminist Methods of Protest and Lay Catholic Activism 99
Laura J. Panning Davies

6 Clergy Sex Abuse Scandals and the (Re)Making of Good Catholic Mothers 117
Allison Niebauer and Elisa Vogel

7 Ethos as Presence in Lay Catholic Women's Rhetorics of Accountability 139
Jamie White-Farnham

PART III: CATHOLIC LAY WOMEN'S ETHOS **153**

8 "A Leader and a Lady": Catholic Women's Use of Business Writing to Create an Ethos of Professionalism and Catholic Lay Womanhood 155
Jennifer Crosby Burgess

9 Mary Daly's Radical Ethos as Epistemic Voyage 173
Julianna Edmonds

10 Metanoic Faith: Living Rhetorically in Dorothy Day's *The Long Loneliness* 187
Jimmy Hamill

11 Word and Deed: Dolores Huerta, Chicana Feminism, and a Zurdo Ethos of Faith in Action 205
L Heidenreich

PART IV: WOMEN RELIGIOUS' NEGOTIATIONS OF ETHOS **227**

12 Sister Miriam Joseph's Rhetorical Advocacy: The Trivium and Renaissance Rhetoric at St. Mary's College, 1931–1960 229
Joseph Burzynski

13 "Holiness Is Not for Wimps": The Rhetoric of Mother Angelica 249
Jennifer L. Bay

14 A Time to Be Queer: Challenging the Rhetoric of Acceptance through the Works of Sister Joan Chittister 267
Beth Buyserie

15 Standing in the Eye of the Storm: The Eternal Habits of U.S. Women Religious 287
Jamie L. Downing

Index 311

About the Contributors 321

Acknowledgments

Christina R. Pinkston and Elizabethada A. Wright

This collection is the culmination of years of hard work and dedicated friendship.

We owe a huge "thank you" to numerous people, far too many to list, but we particularly thank Tracy Schier whose work on Catholic Women's Colleges and whose experiences led to the archives of St. Mary-of-the-Woods and made our exploration into Catholic Women's rhetoric possible. Additionally, we are enormously grateful to Sister Mary Ryan of the Sisters of Providence who made her archives feel like home. It is to them, especially, to whom we dedicate this book.

To our universities and supportive colleagues, namely, Désiré Baloubi, Annie Perkins, Karen Holmes, Suzanne Bordelon, Martha Cheng, and Virginia Ryan, we extend our tremendous appreciation.

With grateful hearts, we thank members of our family whose patience and encouragement kept us well motivated: Margaret Christian Pinkston, Christiana Patrice Ares-Christian (and husband, Isaiah), Shayla Élise Pinkston Betts (and fiancé, D'Won), Ariana Melita Pinkston Gallegos (and husband, Manu), Timothy Mark Pinkston, Harold Edward Pinkston Jr., Patricia Yvette Pinkston, George Segee-Wright, and James Segee-Wright. Most assuredly, Scott Segee deserves an enormous round of applause for his proofing skills as well as for his countless hours assisting both of us; he was the "liaison-in-chief" with our communications, most notably during the COVID quarantine.

Terrific thanks we offer to Lexington Books' Judith Lakamper whose quick responses to our frequent questions were crucial to the success of this book's publication.

Linda Bray and Barbara Lund have been wonderful with their friendship and encouragement. So, too, we thank our Tampa/Louisville/Daytona Beach comrades for their constant love and wonderful support: Marlo Belschner, Martha Davis, Carolyn Gebhard, Beth Knappenberger, Roberta Reavy, and Brenda Whitley.

Introduction

Ethos, the Patriarchy, and Feminist Resistance

Elizabethada A. Wright

In 1999, I was hired as an assistant professor at then Rivier College in New Hampshire. I was excited to begin this tenure-track position at a Catholic College, especially with its loudly proclaimed Catholic social justice agenda, despite the fact that I was not—and still am not—Catholic. Boasting my recent publication of a "short history" of rhetorical education in the United States that had I coauthored with my mentor S. Michael Halloran, I met one of my new colleagues, Tracy Schier, who told me about her recent publication, an edited collection of Catholic women's colleges. When I read this collection that Schier had coedited with Cynthia Russett, I was stunned at my own lack of awareness about the history of rhetorical education in the United States.[1]

Educating girls in North America since the seventeenth century, Catholic sisters have provided instruction in rhetoric and many other subjects to millions of Americans. Over 2 million Catholic and non-Catholic students in the United States were educated in Catholic schools in 2015 alone (36 percent of students in all private schools),[2] taught by both sisters and lay teachers, and this number is down significantly from that of the mid-twentieth century when, according to Thomas Landy, Catholic colleges outpaced others significantly.[3] What is little realized is that Catholic schools, usually run by women, were the engine of educating the masses of students—of all religions—for the early part of the United States' history.

While it is commonly believed that schooling was available to all in the early North American colonies, this myth is far from fact. Instead, there were numerous academies and institutes supported by various religions, and one of the most prolific supporters of education for all was the Catholic Church.[4] Girls were such a significant part of this group of educated children that Carol Coburn and Martha Smith note that, in the nineteenth and early twentieth centuries, more women attended secondary schools in the United States than did men because of the availability of education for girls via Catholic sisters.[5] Additionally, in the nineteenth century, so much education was supplied by Catholic institutions that political leaders such as Thomas Jefferson provided their daughters with Catholic education, while prominent religious leaders such as Lyman Beecher railed against Catholic schools and the need for the creation of non-Catholic ones.[6]

As Schier and Russett observe, most of the scholarship on Catholic education has been done by Catholic scholars who focus on "better-known institutions like Notre Dame and Georgetown, which were founded by and for men,"[7] while study of lesser-known institutions has been virtually ignored. Some of the responsibility for this disregard falls on Catholic scholars themselves. Quoting Catholic historian James Hennesey, Timothy Walch states that Catholic historiography "remains fairly set in its ways" and is "heavily parochial in regard to the journals and publishers it employs," resulting in general American historical scholarship's almost complete apathy concerning Catholicism's rich traditions.[8] In other words, no matter what the cause, the study of Catholic education—especially that created by and for women—has been held in low esteem outside of Catholic academic circles.

One reason for this state of affairs may very well be lack of interest. In a foreword to a book version of a catalog to the art museum exhibit "Krone und Schleier" (Crown and Veil) that presented art by cloistered women, Caroline Walker Bynum notes similar preconceptions found in the general public regarding Catholic women religious. Bynum comments that when she attended the show in Germany, many of the other audience members to the exhibit "were an overflow crowd from the Egyptian exhibit next door."[9] Listening to their discussion of the exhibit, Bynum learned that this audience expected the display to be on female patronage and art in the Middle Ages and that the audience was disappointed to learn that the exhibit, instead, focused, focused on Catholic women religious. Bynum heard one viewer expressing how dull they expected the exhibit to be: "Oh dear, it's nuns."[10] Showing how these preconceptions are often wrong, Bynum also observed that as the audience explored the exhibit, there was an increasing excitement.

This collection is intended to have a similar result: to create an increased interest in the rhetoric of a long marginalized group, Roman Catholic women.[11] What this collection is particularly concerned with is how this group, marginalized by an institution yet still seeking membership in the institution because of the institution's professed ideals, has used various elements of the group's positionality to develop ethē that provides means to make change. Building on Nedra Reynolds's and Krista Ratcliffe's critiques of reduced theories of ethos that understand ethos as only being gained by "the rugged white male individualist,"[12] Kathleen J. Ryan, Nancy Myers, and Rebecca Jones argue that many women think more ecologically to "craft a viable ethos" by using their "knowledge of their entire communicative landscape."[13]

Since ethos is such a "slippery" term,[14] such rethinking of ethos is much needed. Prior to this rethinking, most "classical" concepts of ethos reference the social context surrounding the solitary rhetor,[15] and these social contexts demand that the rhetor "manifest the virtues most valued by the culture to and for which one speaks."[16] Such a demand dooms women's rhetoric, as numerous late twentieth-century scholars comment. For example, Karlyn Kohrs Campbell observes that the ideal rhetor, a good woman speaking well, has long been "a violation of the female role"[17] because "the qualities associated with successful rhetorical action—cogent argument, expertise, and skill in rebuttal—are qualities associated with masculinity"; thus, women orators have faced a "double bind."[18] Such ecological thinking responds to Barbara Biesecker's 1992 question: "How do women effectively intervene in the space of the symbolic, given the conventional modes of the enterprise as such . . . have historically effected their silence and, thus, circumvented their force?"[19]

This rethinking of ethos through an ecological lens uses Lorraine Code's understandings of how a context's interwoven physical and social realities are constructed by a variety of "dominant social-political imaginaries."[20] Yes, the social context of the individual rhetor does matter but so, too, matter numerous other contexts that may not be initially identifiable. When an individual engages in ecological thinking, the knower "is cognizant of being part of and specifically located within a social-physical world that constraints and enables human practices, where knowing and acting always generate consequences. . . . [E]cological thinking relocates inquiry 'down on the ground' where knowledge is made, negotiate, circulated."[21] In other words, though ecological thinking may well be partial, it recognizes that there are no "transcendent truths or principles";[22] instead, ecological thinkers negotiate the physical and social realities surrounding them to create what is accepted in the world.

This collection, therefore, uses Ryan et al.'s concepts of ethos and Code's understandings of ecological thinking as foundations for insight into how Catholic women have influenced the dominant public, when such influence might, at first, seem to be a violation of their roles as good Catholic women. Considering such an ecological perspective, this book recognizes that while the Catholic Church has limited women's positionality based on gendered norms, it has, at the same time, provided means for women's power. Just as Ryan et al. observe regarding other women, the women rhetors who are the subjects of this book have always taken their understandings of their "'subordinate status,' relative to knowledge of the entire communicative landscape, and use[d] it to craft a viable ethos for participation in a dominate public."[23]

And, indeed, they have participated in the dominate public. For example, writing in 1896 one of the most important histories of religious women, Lina Eckenstein states:

> The right to self-development and social responsibility which the woman of to-day so persistently asks for, is in many ways analogous to the right which the convent secured to womankind a thousand years ago. The woman of to-day, who realizes that the home circle as at present constituted affords insufficient scope for her energies, had a precursor in the nun who sought a field of activity in the convent.[24]

Although Eckenstein writes in the late nineteenth century as she states that women religious are much like "the woman of to-day," we in the twenty-first century can appreciate much how the women religious whom Eckenstein discusses are *also* like twenty-first-century women. This collection, then, focuses on Catholic women in the United States, seeking to understand how the ecological thinking of these women, past and present, has influenced what Catholicism and American society are today.

ENDING THE IGNORANCE

Understandings of women's involvement in Catholicism has been too long ignored in academic circles for a variety of reasons, including attitudes similar to those held by the general public that are observed by Bynum. Some of these attitudes stem from American anti-Catholicism, as documented in Carol Mattingly's *Secret Habits*: people such as members of the Beecher family used anti-Catholic rhetoric to advocate for women's education.[25] The John F. Kennedy Library's archives also attest to similar discourse in the mid-twentieth century, with anti-Catholic pamphlets making up much of its section on religious literature.[26] Though scholars in the twenty-first century would probably like to think they are above such prejudicial attitudes, anti-Catholic sentiment within the United States may have made non-Catholic scholars hesitant to approach religion and may have made Protestantism an "unmarked category" in scholarship, unmarked as "white" has been unmarked in hegemonic discourses full of implicit racial bias.[27] Sometimes the work on women's discourse includes discussions of Catholic women, but it does not investigate how the Catholicity impacts the rhetoric. For example, Mari Boor Tonn's 2010 *Rhetoric Society Quarterly* article on Mary Harris "Mother" Jones treats her as a Burkean "representative anecdote" to probe how the ocular could promote movements, not mentioning how religion may have precipitated Jones's activism or perceptions.[28] Despite the facts, in the twenty-first century, a very large minority (45 percent) of the United States' population either is or is connected to Catholicism: within the women serving in the United States Congress in 2020, 20 percent are Catholic (including Nancy Pelosi and Alexandria Ocasio-Cortez); and on the Supreme Court, two of the three female justices are Catholic (as are four of the men).[29] Even with this large influence of Catholic women, few studies examine the influence of Catholicism on twenty-first-century rhetoric, policy, or decisions.

When Catholicism is recognized, if the general public does not have anti-Catholic views, it has many stereotyped ideas of Catholic women. For example, popular culture depicts Catholic women from religious orders with various clichés in works such as *The Sound of Music*, *The Flying Nun*, *Agnes of God*, *Nunsense*, *Sister Act*, as well as in various horror films (e.g., *The Nun* and *The Convent*). When the public does think about Catholicism and women, religious or lay, the common assumption is that the Church only limits women. For example, in his introduction to the collection exploring feminine identity in the Catholic tradition, Christopher M. Flavin writes that it is "commonplace" to read Catholic women's texts as responses to their "inherently limited position based on gendered norms."[30] As Kathleen Sprows Cummings states, scholars of feminism tend to ignore Catholic women as subjects of study because the scholars believe women within the Catholic Church do not have much agency, let alone power.[31] Similarly, Maureen Fitzgerald comments that there is an assumption that Catholic women have been "more oppressed by men in their group than [are] Protestant and secular women."[32] Feminists, though, have not seemed concerned with this assumed oppression: Rosemary Ruether and Eleanor McLaughlin opine that feminists have tended to ignore women within Catholicism, being "especially attracted to rejected groups—heretics and even witches—expecting to find among them subversive views expressing feminist rejection of patriarchal religion."[33]

Fortunately, there has been recent feminist rhetorical scholarship exploring the power within the discourse of Catholic women. Led by prominent rhetoricians such as Carol Mattingly and Nan Johnson,[34] this important work stresses the education that these Catholic sisters in the United States provided, an education that was far more significant than many other examinations of American rhetorical history appreciate. This book continues this scholarship by considering Catholic women, both religious and lay, as it acknowledges the limitations put on women by the Church and the many ways women find their involvement with the Church liberating.

The key question within this book is what rhetorical choices have Catholic women made to gain voice within a tradition that endeavors to exclude their voice. While scholars within the field have been increasingly focusing on the rhetoric of various marginalized groups, any work addressing the discourse of this group on the periphery of a powerful patriarchal institution tends to be related to the field of rhetoric and religion—if it is studied at all. As Joseph Burzynski indicates in chapter 12, publications that do exist on the intersections of Catholicism and rhetoric are most often concerned with the discourse of men and male religious orders (e.g., Mailloux, O'Donnell, as well as Gannett and Brereton).[35] This book builds on this recent feminist scholarship and attempts to bring study to Catholic women's rhetoric to the mainstream of rhetorical analysis.

While giving attention to the rhetorical choices made by Catholic women (both religious and lay), this book aims to contribute to feminist rhetorical theory by analyzing how these women attempt to uphold their beliefs in the Church, and how they help the Church itself maintain its tenets, while resisting the Church's exclusionary practices. In particular, this collection explores how these women have negotiated their ethē, while seeking goals that are often denied to them by an Institutional Catholic Church which, as Jamie White-Farnum discusses in chapter 7, has repeatedly demonstrated is not for women. At the center of these analyses are repeated emphases on how these women have continually and paradoxically used the rhetoric of the Church to provide themselves with power. As the book examines a marginalized group that has wielded enormous influence, its purpose is to inform the discipline about how people on the boundaries can use discourse of the center to reshape the resistant center. Discussing Catholic women in the United States from various periods, regions, races, ethnicities, sexualities, classes, and backgrounds, the authors in this book use various lenses to analyze these women's discourse—yet the book searches for commonalities in how these women employ ethos to strengthen their own words and resist a powerful institution's efforts to silence them.

"A WIDER AND MORE PURPOSEFUL LIFE"

Before introducing the work in this book, I want to give a brief overview of women and Catholicism, a history that is far from singular, unified, or complete. This overview focuses on women in religious orders, mostly because there is so little scholarship available about lay Catholic women before the beginning of the modern age. As Deirdre M. Moloney observes, identity for most American Catholics prior to the twentieth century was tied to ethnic nationalism more than it was to Catholicity, yet Catholicity was an implicit and essential element of this ethnic nationalism.[36] Though this brief overview employs broad strokes and relies primarily on the scholarship of Jo Ann Kay McNamara,[37] the overview nevertheless reveals that the boundaries between the women in and out of religious orders have been fluid. Despite the fact that these boundaries have not always been so distinct, this book follows the advice of many women in religious orders with whom I have talked. They ask that people use the terms "women religious" and "sisters" to reference those women in non-cloistered religious orders, using the term "nun" only for women in religious cloisters. Despite this twenty-first-century request, though, these terms and distinctions have not always been, nor do they continue to be, very clear—as Jennifer Bay illustrates with her analysis of Mother Angelica in chapter 13.

Women have been an integral part of Christianity since the lifetime of Christ, and after his death, they were essential to the new religion's promotion. Mentioned numerous times in the New Testament as preachers and evangelists, they established small house churches, often with men, and worshiped via this new religion.[38] According to McNamara, women eagerly adopted Christianity because it appeared to give them a "wider and more purposeful life,"[39] preaching and conducting clerical duties,[40] but it also afforded women a means to free themselves from sexual demands of men, as chaste "castimony" (self-imposed virginity) became an alternative to matrimony through the centuries.[41] Within early periods of Christianity, individuals practicing castimony in both women's and men's early Christian communities defined themselves as a third sex, "transformed and lifted beyond the constructions of the gender system."[42]

In these earliest forms of the Christian Church, people were valued for the work they put into the formation of the religion, so there were few hierarchies;[43] however, as the Church developed, that egalitarianism changed. When, in 313 CE, Roman emperor Constantine declared that Christianity was no longer a crime, the Church began a steady multi-millennium devaluation of women. Numerous Church Councils attempted to minimize women's influence. As the Roman Empire disintegrated, the many people who came into Rome also began to adopt Christianity and spread it throughout the continent. Women religious, instead of being a "third sex," became "brides of Christ" and were denied clerical roles: preaching was no longer possible for women.[44] Those women who were able to remain active in the Church had wealth,[45] especially as wealthy women became instrumental in establishing the early Church.[46] Additionally, as the medieval world became more dangerous and uncertain, wealthy families found contributions to monasteries to be a means to preserve their wealth and lineages. Similarly, many rich women and girls entered monasteries as temporary solutions to financial or security problems, with many royal women becoming founders, abbesses, and residents of women's communities.[47]

As such, in many religious communities during the first millennium of Christianity, some women never accepted castimony and, for those who did, castimony was unstable or temporary.[48] Even sisters who were in cloister continued to interact with their families and communities.[49] According to

McNamara, during the first millennium, nuns did not make careers in "broad reaches of an order as monks did."[50] Instead, they tended to enter houses close to home and maintain their role in their communities: "There is some reason to believe that the main purpose for the endowment for women's communities was to support their economic, social, and charitable activities within that tight local network of influence."[51] Certainly, there were attempts to demarcate the indeterminate boundaries: with the creation of monasteries also came various rules for women's orders, determining the processes under which the women who chose to live together would follow. However, these rules were clearly bent—sometimes by women and sometimes by the men around them, as attempts to contain and marginalize Catholic women were always moderately successful.[52]

In the second millennium of Christianity, women continued to maintain their communities, and they engaged in work such as writing and management that would not have been permitted outside monasteries. With the Great Schism of 1054 dividing the Christian Church in two, the Roman Catholic and Eastern Orthodox faiths, women in religious orders had to find means to negotiate the break.[53] Lina Eckenstein terms the period from 1100 to 1200 the "golden age of monasticism," with women finding opportunities to counter the many limitations that the Catholic patriarchy had attempted to impose on them over the previous centuries.[54] Additionally, new types of religious women began to develop. One, the ancre or recluse, was a kind of self-appointed nun who lived in purity and isolation without the supervision of an abbess.[55] Engaging in an embodied rhetoric, as Shana Scudder brings up in chapter 4, these women built on the aesthetic tradition that had first been part of Christian religious tradition in the fourth century, in which women and men lived extraordinarily disciplined lives, denying themselves food, water, rest, sex, and other aspects of most other people's lives.[56]

Another type consisted of women in community who cared for the poor and took their vows of poverty to heart. These "third orders" or "tertiaries," such as the beguines, developed around the thirteenth century while mendicant orders, such as the Dominican nuns, were founded to address the gaps between the rich and poor.[57] What was different about many of these third orders is that their members lived among the poor, even they lived in communities, and they had degrees of freedom denied to cloistered nuns, as the tertiaries cared for and worked to prevent homelessness, especially among women.[58] Unlike previous religious roles for women which had primarily been available only to wealthy women, these new organizations consisted of lay women from various classes, who gathered together without strict rules to do charitable works. Claiming divine missions, these women were outside formal monastic boundaries and, therefore, created their own rules, defying limitations on women preaching by teaching Christian values and practices.

Consistent with nuns' positions with the upper class, these women who served the poor and sick were generally denied by Rome the status as a nun.[59] Their status was challenged during and after the Plague. With the Plague vilifying the resultant poverty, many in the public associated poverty with crime, and wealth with virtue, consequently perceiving proponents of apostolic poverty as heretics.[60] Still, the freedom and purpose offered by tertiary orders was popular among women; for example, in 1451, more than 600,000 Franciscan Tertiaries lived in homes in Italy.[61] In the period of the Protestant Reformation, women filled the role as teachers, attempting to remedy the ills in the Catholic Church defined by the Reformation.

In the sixteenth century, Martin Luther's challenges to the norms of the Church and Henry VIII's dissolution of the Catholic Church brought about the end to numerous monasteries. Some women responded enthusiastically to these changes, especially because they perceived that they might have more opportunities in the reformed church that called for lessened clerical authority and for more non-clergy involvement in the Church.[62] One of Luther's main goals was to expand education for all. While convents and the Catholic Church had supplied much education for wealthy people before this period, people outside the wealth had possessed few educational opportunities. In response to Luther's challenges, various new orders came into being for the purpose of educating the public regarding lay responsibilities within the Church. Two significant new ones were the male Order—the Society of Jesus (the Jesuits) and the female Order—the Company of St. Ursula (the Ursulines). While the boundaries between preaching, which was forbidden to women, and teaching were murky, women's attempts to teach outside of the convent were constantly challenged.[63] For example, the sixteenth century's Council of Trent demanded that religious women remain cloistered, thus making the possibilities of their teaching extraordinarily difficult. Yet women's desire to teach, combined with the Church's need for their services, created compromises that established many orders and many new opportunities for women.[64] For example, many Catholic women formed "religious institutes" that subjected them to less Vatican regulation and allowed them to work in their communities.[65] As increasing numbers of other orders, as well as groupings of lay recluse women, began to play an important role in providing education to the public, the Church eventually accepted and came to rely on the teaching of religious women.

With Europe expanding its powers into the Americas in the sixteenth century, members of women's religious orders continued to play this role—with women traveling to Europe's previously unknown continents. Some of the earliest schools for girls in North America were the Ursulines, with one established in Quebec in 1639, and the other (still existing) in New Orleans, in 1727. With the confluence of the young United States' promises of freedom of religion and France's revolution and the Napoleonic Wars, changes in religion that spread across Europe brought many religious men and women to the young nation to convert the growing American population. The formula that existed most frequently for these European sisters to come was that American Catholic clergy and bishops bemoaned their abilities to reach people in their dioceses, so they convinced European orders to send sisters to establish convents and schools in the United States. It was this formula that brought many of the orders discussed in this book to the United States. When Archbishop John Hughes developed a parish system of education that took away much of the power of these teaching orders, women continued their work—and with less control.

Celebrating the impact of Catholic education in the United States and striving to convince non-Catholics of the important—and benign—nature of Catholic education, the Church held a major showcase of Catholic education as part of the 1893 Columbian World's Fair. With samples of student work from 1,258 schools in the United States, this Catholic Educational Exhibit showcased only a portion of Catholic schools in America and across the globe, and it acted as a "visible and positive refutation of the statements that the Catholic Church is opposed to intelligence; that she delights in the allegiance of the ignorant; that she represses study, and 'chains the intellect of her people to the wheel of the Pope's chariot.'"[66] This educational exhibit complemented the Columbian Catholic Congress, which was part of the Fair's World's Parliament of Religions. Though Catholic religious were involved in this Congress, it was organized by laypeople as they attempted to become a more significant influence on American Catholicity (Moloney 13–42).[67]

Catholic laywomen were certainly a part of this effort, and as the twentieth century dawned and progressed, American Catholic women began to develop their identities as social reformers, as Jennifer Burgess notes in chapter 8. Maureen Fitzgerald's book *Habits of Compassion* argues that much of the structure and movement of the United States' Progressive Era was prompted by activities of Catholic women who viewed the poor through a lens very different from that of nineteenth-century Protestant reformers. Focusing particularly on Irish American sisters, Fitzgerald contends Catholic women's involvement in nursing and charity organizations fundamentally shaped the structures of these organizations.

As White-Farnham reviews in chapter 7 and Scudder in chapter 4, during the mid-twentieth century, revisions to Church doctrine created in the 1960s by Vatican II provided women with hope that they would be recognized as co-participants with men in the work of the Church. Its directives encouraged religious women "to act based on [their] consciousnesses, to be bold in making changes in the church, to fulfill [their] mission to serve the poor."[68] Though Vatican II changed much of the face of the Church (allowing women religious to go beyond their sartorial habits dictated by their orders), these promises were never realized as women faced "backlashes" during the terms of Popes John Paul II and Benedict.

In the late twentieth and early twenty-first centuries, the Church itself faced a huge backlash as news reports revealed what the Church had kept hidden for decades, the sexual abuse of children by clergy. While the revelations of sexual abuses was in themselves horrific, reports of the Church patriarchy's cover-ups and enabling of the abuses were especially harmful to the Church. As Allison Niebauer and Elisa Vogel as well as Jamie White-Farnham discuss in chapters 6 and 7, this cover-up prompted many Catholic women to rhetorical action. The backlash against the Church also caused great financial pain to the Church, with its congregant numbers dwindling because of the scandals and with the Church paying for lawyers and lawsuits.

During this time, many orders of women religious continued their teaching and social reform, engaging as they always had in various forms of activist rhetoric. However, in 2012, despite the criticism it was facing because of the clergy sex abuse scandal, the Vatican issued a statement condemning the Leadership Conference of Women Religious (LCWR). Discussed by Jamie L. Downing in chapter 15, LCWR is an organization to which a majority of the United States' women religious belonged, for its "prevalence of certain radical feminist themes incompatible with the Catholic faith."[69] With its censure of women religious, lay Catholic women felt the sting, as the connections between lay and religious Catholics developed, especially with changing demographics limiting the number of potential future sisters "(LCWR Planning)."[70] Still, women have maintained their connections to the Catholic Church, and oftentimes found power for themselves and their purposes in the church.

OVERVIEW

As this book illustrates, in the United States, lay and religious women have played important roles both in the formation of Catholicism and of the United States, though the marginalizations of them and of their contributions have continued. What this book especially focuses on is the variety of ways in which Catholic women have thought ecologically to craft ethēs that have allowed them to reshape the realities in which they lived. To maintain this cynosure, this book divides itself into four parts.

The first considers the ethos of specific religious orders and how the members of these orders use their knowledge of the landscape around them to craft an ethos that provides them with freedom from patriarchal oversight. In the first chapter, I analyze the discourse of two remarkably similar, yet different, Mother Superiors who responded to the call from Catholic clergy to come to the United States. Considering their use of the rhetoric of blame (parrhesia), I demonstrate how their awarenesses of their environments impacted their abilities to succeed rhetorically. In chapter 2, Amy Ferdinandt Stolley explores how the Sisters of Mercy use the texts of their founder, Catherine McAuley, as a form of epideictic rhetoric. This form requires the Sisters change their behaviors with the challenges of their times in order to remain consistent with the values required of them by their founder. Christiana Ares-Christian's and my third chapter examines how the *Soeurs de Sainte-Famille*, New Orleans' African American Sisters of the Holy Family, embraced the ecological meaning of ethos, habits, and dwelling place to shift nineteenth-century prejudices against women of color as they demanded the garb of a religious sister and changed the meanings of the various locations that they inhabited. In Shana Scudder's chapter 4, she sees religious orders as gaining ethos via an embodied rhetoric. Examining the Sisters of Loretto's activism, Scudder shows how the Loretto Community gains credibility when its members immerse their whole selves in what they profess.

The second section overviews lay feminist interventions to "save" the Church by questioning the authority and ethos of the Catholic patriarchy. Laura Davis's chapter 5 asks, "Who Owns This Church?" as it uses the concept of feminist rhetorical resistance to understand a lay community's efforts to save a church building that the community's Catholic diocese wanted to shutter. Via this concept, Davies questions how transformation can occur, not radically, but more subtly. Both chapters 6 and 7 investigate the rhetoric within the Catholic Clergy Perpetrated Sex Abuse (CPSA) scandal. In their chapter, Allison Niebauer and Elisa Vogel consider how Catholic mothers who sued the Catholic patriarchy for the clergy sex abuse used their identities as Catholic mothers and as citizens of the United States to address the Church's crisis. In chapter 7, Jamie White-Farnham approaches the CPSA scandal with a different lens: she focuses on the definitions and uses of the term "accountability" in the rhetorical activity surrounding priest abuse and survivorship by mapping the particular instances of accountability rhetoric of three high-profile contemporary lay Catholic women.

The third section of this book examines the rhetoric of women outside of religious orders who, despite their "lay" status, have investments in the Church and work to shape the Church. This section begins with Jennifer Burgess's exploration of how late nineteenth-century Catholic lay women developed an ethos grounded in professionalism and Catholic identity. Looking at Catholic women's groups, Burgess investigates how Catholic women have navigated the conflicting ethē demanded of them in various situations. Terming these conflicting ethē "coexistent ethos," Burgess explores the ways in which Catholic women wrote and acted as professionals while maintaining their traditional religious and familial roles. In chapter 9, Juliana Edmonds examines radical theologian Mary Daly's scholarship to argue that Daly's radicalism was a direct response to her first failed attempt at negotiating a listening stance toward the Church. Drawing on two of Daly's works, Edmonds shows that Daly's radicalism was not a defining characteristic of her ethos, but instead was a part of her rhetorical progression from attempts at accommodation to an ethos of interruption. Jimmy Hamill's chapter 10 considers one of the most studied Catholic lay women, Dorothy Day. In this chapter, Hamill delves into Day's book *The Long Loneliness* to illustrate how Day employs *metanoia*, or a "change of heart," to negotiate an ethos that transforms both her self as an individual as well as the spaces and structures in which she existed. Chicanx Feminist Dolores Huerta is the focus of L Heidenreich's chapter 11. Echoing Scudder's chapter 4 discussion of embodied rhetoric, Heidenreich asks how the famous union leader and Catholic laywoman Dolores Huerta embraced the traditions of her Indigenous, Chicanx, and Catholic communities to create an "enfleshed" rhetoric that tied her to an ever-expanding community.

The fourth and final section returns to probe the discourse of women religious, as the women in these sections also challenge the credibility of the clergy and Catholic patriarchy. In chapter 12, Joseph Burzynski examines the impact of Sister Miriam Joseph on the discipline of rhetoric, asking why she is so marginalized in the narratives of rhetoric's twentieth-century resurgence. Comparing Sister Miriam Joseph's advocacy for rhetoric to that of the Jesuits, Burzynski concludes that it was her reliance on Aristotelian conceptions of ethos, rather than the environmental ones advocated by modern feminist scholars of rhetoric, that has led to her oversight, an oversight that twenty-first-century scholars need to remedy. Jennifer Bay's chapter 13 tells of the remarkably contradictory contemplative nun who launched a television station and challenged the Catholic patriarchy, Mother Angelica. Examining how Mother Angelica maintained conservative values while dismissing the patriarchal establishment, Bay illustrates Mother Angelica's cultivation of ethos through her populist style. In chapter 14, Beth Buyserie moves on to analyze the works of a very different Catholic sister, Joan Chittister, who advocates for LGBTQ peoples. Buyserie melds queer theory with rhetorical analysis to reveal how Joan Chittister redefines ethos as "authentic" and how Chittister compares this ever-fluid "authentic" ethos to the stable ethos espoused by the Church, an ethos contradicted by its practices. In this chapter, Buyserie analyzes the ways in which Chittister uses the language and values of the Church to challenge the ethos of the Church. In chapter 15, the book's final chapter, Jamie L. Downing examines the rhetorical strategies of the LCWR in response to the Vatican's investigations of the sisters' activities. Downing argues that members of LCWR used their ethē, developed from years of service, to illustrate publicly that they were beyond sanction of the Catholic patriarchy: they habitually practiced the teachings of the Gospel.

These sections and chapters highlight that women's experience in the Church has not been monolithic, yet there are many repeated themes in this book's analyses of how these women developed the influence to make change. One of these themes pertains to the way Catholic women have embodied ethos both literally and figuratively. Another theme that emerges from these chapters is how these Catholic women recognized their ever-fluctuating ethē and how they embraced these fluctuations to make change.

Ultimately, the goal of this book is twofold: first, it explores the various rhetorics and negotiations of ethos that these women have employed during the history of the United States, as the book also makes audiences more aware of the impact of their rhetorical action. Second, this book aims to encourage others to extend this exploration of Catholic women and to stop thinking, "Oh, dear, it's Catholic women." We need to start recognizing the rhetoric energy in Catholic women's strategies and discourses.

NOTES

1. Tracy Schier, and Cynthia Russett, *Catholic Women's Colleges in America* (Baltimore: Johns Hopkins UP, 2002).
2. NCES (National Center for Education Statistics), "School Choice in the United States: 2019," IES.NCES, accessed March 18, 2021, https://nces.ed.gov/programs/schoolchoice/ind_03.asp.
3. Thomas Landy, "The Colleges in Context," in *Catholic Women's Colleges in America*, eds. Schier and Russett (Baltimore: Johns Hopkins UP, 2002), 61–63.
4. Elizabethada A. Wright, Suzanne Bordelon, and S. Michael Halloran, "'Available Means' of Rhetorical Instruction: 'Broadening Perspectives' on Rhetorical Education Prior to 1900," in *A Short History of Writing Instruction: From Ancient Greece to the Modern United States*," 4th edition, eds. James J. Murphy and Christopher Thaiss (New York: Routledge, 2020), 253–255.
5. Carol K. Coburn and Martha Smith, *Spirited Lives: How Nuns Shaped Catholic Culture and American Life, 1836–1920* (Chapel Hill: University of North Carolina Press, 1999), 162.
6. Lyman Beecher, *A Plea for the West* (Cincinnati: Truman and Smith, 1835).
7. Tracy Schier and Cynthia Russett, "Introduction," in *Catholic Women's Colleges in America*, eds. Schier and Russett (Baltimore: Johns Hopkins UP, 2002), 3.
8. Timothy Walch, "New Tools for American Historical Research: A Review Essay," *U.S. Catholic Historian* 3, no. 3 (Fall-Winter 1983): 201, https://www.jstor.org/stable/25153698.

9. Caroline Walker Bynum, "Foreword," in *Crown and Veil: Female Monasticism from the Fifth to the Fifteenth Centuries*, eds. Jeffrey F. Hamburger and Susan Marti (New York: Columbia UP, 2008), xiii. Throughout the book, authors use the terms "sisters" or "women religious" to reference all Catholic women who have taken religious vows. The writers use the commonly used term "nun" only to reference woman in cloistered orders.

10. Bynum, "Foreword," xiii.

11. Throughout this book, when the authors reference "Catholic" or "Catholicism," they reference the Roman Catholic Church, not the Byzantine Catholic Church (also termed the Eastern Orthodox Churches). In this introduction, when I discuss the Catholic Church prior to the Great Schism of 1054, I am actually referencing all of Christianity before its division into the Eastern and Western Churches.

12. Nedra Reynolds, "Ethos as Location: New Sites for Understanding Discursive Authority," *Rhetoric Review* 11, no. 2 (Spring 1993): 325–338; Krista Ratcliffe, *Rhetorical Listening: Identification, Gender, Whiteness* (Carbondale: Southern Illinois UP, 2005), 124.

13. Kathleen Ryan, Nancy Myers, and Rebecca Jones, "Introduction: Identifying Feminist Ecological Ethē," in *Rethinking Ethos: A Feminist Ecological Approach to Rhetoric*, eds. Ryan, Myers, and Jones (Carbondale, IL: Southern Illinois UP, 2016), 4.

14. James S. Baumlin, "Introduction: Positioning *Ethos* in Historical and Contemporary Theory," in *Ethos: New Essays in Rhetorical and Critical Theory*, eds. Baumlin and Tita French Baumlin (Dallas: Southern Methodist University Press, 1994), xvii.

15. Reynolds, "Ethos as Location," 327.

16. S. Michael Halloran, "Aristotle's Concept of Ethos, Or If Not His, Somebody Else's," *Rhetoric Review* 1 (1982): 60, https://www.jstor.org/stable/465559.

17. Karlyn Kohrs Campbell, *Man Cannot Speak for Her: A Critical Study of Early Feminist Rhetoric*, Vol. 1 (New York: Greenwood, 1989), 75.

18. Karlyn Kohrs Campbell, "Gender and Genre: Loci of Invention and Contradiction," *Quarterly Journal of Speech* 81, no. 4 (1995): 479.

19. Barbara A. Biesecker, "Towards a Transactional View of Rhetorical and Feminist Theory: Rereading Helene Cixous's *The Laugh of the Medusa*," *Southern Communication Journal* 57, no. 2 (Winter 1992): 91.

20. Lorraine Code, *Ecological Thinking: The Politics of Epistemic Location* (Oxford: Oxford UP, 2006), 4–5.

21. Code, *Ecological Thinking*, 5.

22. Code, *Ecological Thinking*, 5.

23. Ryan et al., "Introduction," 4.

24. Lina Eckenstein, *Woman under Monasticism: Chapters on Saint-Lore and Convent Life Between A.D. 500 and A.D. 1500* (Cambridge: Cambridge UP, 1896), ix.

25. Carol Mattingly, *Secret Habits: Catholic Literacy Education for Women in the Early Nineteenth Century* (Southern Illinois UP, 2016), 56–57.

26. "Archives," John F. Kennedy Presidential Library and Museum, accessed March 18, 2021, https://www.jfklibrary.org/asset-viewer/archives/JFKCAMP1960/1017/JFKCAMP1960-1017-001.

27. Ann Braude, "Review of Anne M. Boyland's The Origins of Women's Activism: New York and Boston, 1794–1840," *Catholic Historical Review* 91, no. 1 (2005): 183.

28. Mari Boor Tonn, "'From the Eye to the Soul': Industrial Labor's Mary Harris 'Mother' Jones and the Rhetorics of Display," *Rhetoric Society Quarterly* 41, no. 3 (2011): 231–249. https://doi.org/10.1080/02773945.2011.575325.

29. "U.S. Catholics Open to Non-Traditional Families." Religion and Public Life. Pew Research Center. https://www.pewforum.org/2015/09/02/u-s-catholics-open-to-non-traditional-families/.

30. Christopher M. Flavin, *Constructions of Feminine Identity in the Catholic Tradition* (Lanham, MD: Lexington, 2020), 9.

31. Kathleen Sprows Cummings, *New Women of the Old Faith: Gender and American Catholicism in the Progressive Era* (Chapel Hill: University of North Carolina Press, 2009), 2–3.

32. Maureen Fitzgerald, *Habits of Compassion: Irish Catholic Nuns and the Origins of New York's Welfare System, 1830–1920* (Urbana: University of Illinois Press, 2006), 8.

33. Rosemary Ruether, and Eleanor McLaughlin, "Introduction," in *Women of Spirit: Female Leadership in the Jewish and Christian Traditions*, eds. Ruether and McLaughlin (New York: Simon and Schuster, 1979), 19.

34. Mattingly, *Secret Habits*; Nan Johnson, "Rhetorical Education at Catholic Colleges for Woman in Ohio, 1925–1940," in *Rhetoric and Writing Studies in the New Century: Historiography, Pedagogy, and Politics*, eds. Cheryl Glenn and Roxanne Mountford (Carbondale: Southern Illinois UP, 2017), 214–229.

35. Steven Mailloux, "Jesuit Eloquentia Perfecta and Theotropic Logology," in *Studies in Philosophy and Education* 34, no. 4 (2015): 403–412; James A. O'Donnell, "The Jesuit Ratio Studiorum," *Philippine Studies* 32, no. 4 (1984): 462–475; Cinthia Gannett and John Brereton, *Traditions of Eloquence: The Jesuits and Modern Rhetorical Studies* (New York: Fordham UP, 2016).

36. *American Catholic Lay Groups and Transatlantic Social Reform in the Progressive Era* (Chapel Hill: University of North Carolina Press, 2002), 1–3. George French Theriault's 1951 Harvard PhD dissertation and the work of Richard S. Sorrell provide insight into this division between Catholics of different ethnic nationalisms with their discussions of the literal battles between Catholic Irish Americans and Catholic Franco Americans (French Canadian Americans). The Franco Americans viewed their faith as essentially tied to their ability to speak French and felt Irish Americans were trying to assimilate them to an English-speaking religion, one they viewed as antithetical to their identity.

37. Jo Ann Kay McNamara, *Sisters in Arms: Catholic Nuns through Two Millennia* (Cambridge: Harvard UP, 1996).

38. Elisabeth Schüssler Fiorenza, "Word, Spirit, and Power: Women in Early Christian Communities," in *Women of Spirit: Female Leadership in the Jewish and Christian Traditions*, eds. Rosemary Ruether and Eleanor McLaughlin (New York: Simon and Schuster, 1979), 29–70; McNamara, *Sisters in Arms*, 9–34.

39. McNamara, *Sisters in Arms*, 13.

40. McNamara, *Sisters in Arms*, 37.

41. McNamara, *Sisters in Arms*, 15; Elizabeth Rapley, *The Dévotes: Women and Church in Seventeenth-Century France* (Montreal: McGill-Queens UP, 1990).

42. McNamara, *Sisters in Arms*, 43.

43. Fiorenza, "Word," 31.

44. McNamara, *Sisters in Arms*, 38–45.

45. Eileen Edna Power, *Medieval English Nunneries c. 1275–1535* (Cambridge: Cambridge UP, 1922), Project Gutenberg, 268, https://www.gutenberg.org/files/39537/39537-h/39537-h.htm.

46. Fiorenza, "Word," 32.

47. McNamara, *Sisters in Arms*, 104–108; Eckenstein, *Woman under Monasticism*, 151; Jan Gerchow, Katrinette Bodarwé, Susan Marti, and Hedwig Röckelein, "Early Monasteries and Foundations (500–1200): An Introduction," in *Crown and Veil: Female Monasticism from the Fifth to the Fifteenth Centuries*, eds. Jeffrey F. Hamburger and Susan Marti (New York: Columbia UP, 2008), 17.

48. McNamara, *Sisters in Arms*, 335–363.

49. McNamara, Sisters in Arms, 37–38, 279, 335, 363; Linda Lierheimer, *Female Eloquence and Maternal Ministry: The Apostolate of Ursuline Nuns in Seventeenth-Century France* (PhD diss., Princeton University, 1994), 14.

50. McNamara, *Sisters in Arms*, 279.

51. McNamara, *Sisters in Arms*, 279.

52. Gerchow et al., "Early Monasteries"; Bynum, "Foreword," xv.

53. Anna Campbell, "Contextualising Reform: Colette of Corbie's Relations with a Divided Church," *Franciscan Studies* 74 (2016): 353–373, https://www.jstor.org/stable/44652734. Campbell discusses an example of how one woman religious negotiated this schism.

54. Eckenstein, *Woman under Monasticism*, 185.

55. Eckenstein, *Woman under Monasticism*, 313.

56. McNamara, *Sisters in Arms*, 61–88.

57. Jeffrey F. Hamburger, Petra Marx, and Susan Marti, "The Time of the Orders, 1200–1500," in *Crown and Veil: Female Monasticism from the Fifth to the Fifteenth Centuries*, eds. Hamburger and Marti (New York: Columbia UP, 2008), 42–43.

58. Hamburger et al., "The Time of the Orders," 43; Eckenstein, *Women under Monasticism*, 331.

59. McNamara, *Sisters in Arms*, 235–255.

60. McNamara, *Sisters in Arms*, 452.

61. McNamara, *Sisters in Arms*, 392.

62. McNamara, *Sisters in Arms*, 417–422.

63. Lierheimer, *Female Eloquence*, 7.

64. Lierheimer, *Female Eloquence*, 15–17; Rapley, *The Dévotes*.

65. Fitzgerald, *Habits of Compassion*, 18.

66. John Lancaster Spaulding Maurelian [and Carola Milanis], *The Catholic Educational Exhibit at the World's Columbian Exposition*, 1893 (Chicago: J.S. Hyland, 1895), 244, 4.

67. Deirdre M. Moloney, *American Catholic Lay Groups and Transatlantic Social Reform in the Progressive Era* (Chapel Hill: University of North Carolina Press, 2002), 13–42.

68. Joann Malone, *Awake to Racism* (n.p.: QiPublishing, 2021), loc. 38 of 2626, Kindle.

69. Congregation for the Doctrine of the Faith, "Doctrinal Assessment of the Leadership Conference of Women Religious," April 18, 2012, http://www.vatican.va/roman_curia/congregations/cfaith/documents/rc_con_cfaith_doc_20120418_assessment-lcwr_en.html.

70. "LCWR Planning Process Bridges Religious Life Past to the Emerging Future," *Update: A Publication of the Leadership of Catholic Women Religious*. April 2019, https://lcwr.org/sites/default/files/publications/files/lcwr_newsletter_-april_2019_0.pdf.

BIBLIOGRAPHY

Baumlin, James S. "Introduction: Positioning *Ethos* in Historical and Contemporary Theory." In *Ethos: New Essays in Rhetorical and Critical Theory*, edited by Baumlin and Tita French Baumlin, xi–xxxi. Dallas: Southern Methodist University Press, 1994.

Beecher, Lyman. *A Plea for the West*. Cincinnati: Truman and Smith, 1835.

Biesecker, Barbara A. "Towards a Transactional View of Rhetorical and Feminist Theory: Rereading Helene Cixous's *The Laugh of the Medusa*." *Southern Communication Journal* 57, no. 2 (Winter 1992): 86–96. https://doi.org/10.1080/10417949209372856.

Braude, Ann. "Review of Anne M. Boyland's The Origins of Women's Activism: New York and Boston, 1794–1840." *Catholic Historical Review* 91, no. 1 (2005): 183–184. http://doi.org/10.1353/cat.2005.0091.

Bynum, Caroline Walker. "Foreword." In *Crown and Veil: Female Monasticism from the Fifth to the Fifteenth Centuries*, edited by Jeffrey F. Hamburger and Susan Marti, xiii–xviii. New York: Columbia UP, 2008.

Campbell, Anna. "Contextualising Reform: Colette of Corbie's Relations with a Divided Church." *Franciscan Studies* 74 (2016): 353–373. https://www.jstor.org/stable/44652734.

Campbell, Karlyn Kohrs. "Gender and Genre: Loci of Invention and Contradiction." *Quarterly Journal of Speech* 81, no. 4 (1995): 479–495. https://doi.org/10.1080/00335639509384130.

———. *Man Cannot Speak for Her: A Critical Study of Early Feminist Rhetoric*. Vol 1. New York: Greenwood, 1989.

Coburn, Carol K., and Martha Smith. *Spirited Lives: How Nuns Shaped Catholic Culture and American Life, 1836–1920*. Chapel Hill: University of North Carolina Press, 1999.

Code, Lorraine. *Ecological Thinking: The Politics of Epistemic Location*. Oxford: Oxford UP, 2006.

Congregation for the Doctrine of the Faith. Doctrinal Assessment of the Leadership Conference of Women Religious. April 18, 2012. http://www.vatican.va/roman_curia/congregations/cfaith/documents/rc_con_cfaith_doc_20120418_assessment-lcwr_en.html.

Cummings, Kathleen Sprows. *New Women of the Old Faith: Gender and American Catholicism in the Progressive Era.* Chapel Hill: University of North Carolina Press, 2009.

Eckenstein, Lina. *Woman under Monasticism: Chapters on Saint-Lore and Convent Life Between A.D. 500 and A.D. 1500.* Cambridge: Cambridge UP, 1896.

Fiorenza, Elisabeth Schüssler. "Word, Spirit, and Power: Women in Early Christian Communities." In *Women of Spirit: Female Leadership in the Jewish and Christian Traditions*, edited by Rosemary Ruether and Eleanor McLaughlin, 29–70. New York: Simon and Schuster, 1979.

Fitzgerald, Maureen. *Habits of Compassion: Irish Catholic Nuns and the Origins of New York's Welfare System, 1830–1920.* Urbana: University of Illinois Press, 2006.

Flavin, Christopher M. *Constructions of Feminine Identity in the Catholic Tradition.* Lanham, MD: Lexington, 2020.

Gannett, Cinthia, and John Brereton. *Traditions of Eloquence: The Jesuits and Modern Rhetorical Studies.* Fordham UP, 2016.

Gerchow, Jan, with Katrinette Bodarwé, Susan Marti, and Hedwig Röckelein. "Early Monasteries and Foundations (500–1200): An Introduction." In *Crown and Veil: Female Monasticism from the Fifth to the Fifteenth Centuries*, edited by Jeffrey F. Hamburger and Susan Marti, 13–40. Columbia UP, 2008.

Halloran, S. Michael. "Aristotle's Concept of Ethos, Or If Not His, Somebody Else's." *Rhetoric Review* 1 (1982): 58–63. https://www.jstor.org/stable/465559.

Hamburger, Jeffrey F., Petra Marx, and Susan Marti. "The Time of the Orders, 1200–1500." In *Crown and Veil: Female Monasticism from the Fifth to the Fifteenth Centuries*, edited by Hamburger and Marti, 41–75. New York: Columbia UP, 2008.

Johnson, Nan. "Rhetorical Education at Catholic Colleges for Women in Ohio: 1925–1940." In *Rhetoric and Writing Studies in the New Century: Historiography, Pedagogy and Politics*, edited by Cheryl Glenn and Roxanne Mountford, 214–229. Carbondale: Southern Illinois UP, 2017.

Landy, Thomas. "The Colleges in Context." In *Catholic Women's Colleges in America*, edited by Schier and Russett, 55–97. Baltimore: Johns Hopkins UP, 2002.

"LCWR Planning Process Bridges Religious Life Past to the Emerging Future." *Update: A Publication of the Leadership of Catholic Women Religious.* April 2019. https://lcwr.org/sites/default/files/publications/files/lcwr_newsletter_-april_2019_0.pdf.

Lierheimer, Linda. "Female Eloquence and Maternal Ministry: The Apostolate of Ursuline Nuns in Seventeenth-Century France." PhD diss., Princeton, 1994.

Luther, Martin. "To the Councilmen of All Cities in Germany: That They Establish and Maintain Christian Schools." Trinity Lutheran Church and School. Accessed January 19, 2021. http://trinitycheyenne.org/luther-on-the-establishment-of-schools/.

Mailloux, Steven. "Jesuit Eloquentia Perfecta and Theotropic Logology." *Studies in Philosophy and Education* 34, no. 4 (2015): 403–412.

Malone, Joann. *Awake to Racism*. n.p.: QiPublishing, 2021. Kindle.

Mattingly, Carol. *Secret Habits: Catholic Literacy Education for Women in the Early Nineteenth Century*. Carbondale: Southern Illinois UP, 2016.

Maurelian, John Lancaster Spaulding [and Carola Milanis]. *The Catholic Educational Exhibit at the World's Columbian Exposition, 1893*. Chicago: J.S. Hyland, 1895.

McNamara, Jo Ann Kay. *Sisters in Arms: Catholic Nuns through Two Millennia*. Cambridge: Harvard UP, 1996.

Moloney, Deirdre M. *American Catholic Lay Groups and Transatlantic Social Reform in the Progressive Era*. Chapel Hill: University of North Carolina Press, 2002.

NCES (National Center for Education Statistics). "School Choice in the United States: 2019," IES.NCES. Accessed March 18, 2021. https://nces.ed.gov/programs/schoolchoice/ind_03.asp.

Nuyen, A.T. "The Rhetoric of Feminist Writings." *Philosophy and Rhetoric* 28 (1995): 69–82.

O'Donnell, James A. "The Jesuit Ratio Studiorum." *Philippine Studies* 32, no. 4 (1984): 462–475. www.jstor.org/stable/42632739.

Power, Eileen Edna. *Medieval English Nunneries c. 1275–1535*. Cambridge: Cambridge UP, 1922. https://www.gutenberg.org/files/39537/39537-h/39537-h.htm.

Rapley, Elizabeth. *The Dévotes: Women and Church in Seventeenth-Century France*. Montreal: McGill-Queens UP, 1990.

Ratcliffe, Krista. *Rhetorical Listening: Identification, Gender, Whiteness*. Carbondale: Southern Illinois UP, 2005.

Reynolds,Nedra. "Ethos as Location: New Sites for Understanding Discursive Authority." *Rhetoric Review* 11, no. 2 (Spring 1993): 325–338.

Ruether, Rosemary, and Eleanor McLaughlin. "Introduction." In *Women of Spirit: Female Leadership in the Jewish and Christian Traditions*, edited by Ruether and McLaughlin, 15–28. New York: Simon and Schuster, 1979.

Ryan, Kathleen, Nancy Myers, and Rebecca Jones. "Introduction: Identifying Feminist Ecological Ethē." In *Rethinking Ethos: A Feminist Ecological Approach to Rhetoric*, edited by Ryan, Myers, and Jones, 1–25. Carbondale: Southern Illinois UP, 2016.

Schier, Tracy, and Cynthia Russett. *Catholic Women's Colleges in America*. Baltimore: Johns Hopkins UP, 2002.

Schier, Tracy, and Cynthia Russett. "Introduction." In *Catholic Women's Colleges in America*, edited by Schier and Russett, 1–10. Baltimore: Johns Hopkins UP, 2002.

Sorrell, Richard S. "The Sentinelle Affair: Religious and Militant Survivance in Woonsocket, Rhode Island." *Rhode Island History* 36, no. 3 (1977): 67–80.

Theriault, George French. "The Franco-Americans in a New English Community" PhD diss., Harvard University, 1951.

Tonn, Mari Boor. "'From the Eye to the Soul': Industrial Labor's Mary Harris 'Mother' Jones and the Rhetorics of Display." *Rhetoric Society Quarterly* 41, no. 3 (2011): 231–249. http://www.jstor.org/stable/23064465.

"U.S. Catholics Open to Non-Traditional Families." Religion and Public Life. Pew Research Center. https://www.pewforum.org/2015/09/02/u-s-catholics-open-to-non-traditional-families/.

Walch, Timothy. "New Tools for American Historical Research: A Review Essay." *U.S. Catholic Historian* 3, no. 3 (Fall-Winter 1983): 191–201, https://www.jstor.org/stable/25153698.

Wright, Elizabethada. "'The Caprices of an Undisciplined Fancy': Using Blame to Negotiate the 'betweens' of *Ethos* via the Epideictic." *Rhetoric Review* 38, no. 3 (2019): 271–284. http://doi.org/10.1080/07350198.2019.1618157.

———. "'Virtue and Knowledge Combined: French Catholic Tradition within a Nineteenth-Century American School for Women." *Rhetoric Review* 34, no. 4 (2015): 373–390. http://doi.org/10.1080/07350198.2015.1073555.

Wright, Elizabethada, Suzanne Bordelon, and S. Michael Halloran. "'Available Means' of Rhetorical Instruction: 'Broadening Perspectives' on Rhetorical Education Prior to 1900." In *A Short History of Writing Instruction: From Ancient Greece to the Modern United States*, 4th edition, edited by James J. Murphy and Christopher Thaiss, 244–271. New York: Routledge, 2020.

Part I

ETHOS WITHIN WOMEN'S RELIGIOUS ORDERS

Chapter 1

"If We Are Always Your Cherished Daughters"

Ethos, Parrhesia, and Two Nineteenth-Century European American Catholic Sisters

Elizabethada A. Wright

In discussing the nature of ethos, Risa Applegarth observes how ethos is a "fundamentally *located*, *situated*, and *social* act" that must be managed in all environments,[1] but this managing is extraordinarily difficult: "[a]ttending to rhetors' negotiations with (sometimes hostile) audience, (often limiting) social norms and scripts, and (frequently devalued forms of gendered, raced, and classed) embodiment reminds us forcefully that a rhetor is never fully in control of her ethos construction."[2] Despite this lack of full control, Applegarth illustrates how negotiations allow rhetors to somewhat manage their ethos, though such negotiations always involve "high stakes," within "the power-saturated nature of ethos."[3]

As feminist rhetoricians have commented for decades, the high stakes involved with ethos construction is something female rhetors have grappled with for centuries, as speaking and writing women have frequently encountered hostile audiences, limiting norms and scripts, and devalued embodiments. Kathleen J. Ryan, Nancy Myers, and Rebecca Jones's feminist ecological approach to ethos, in which Applegarth's article appears, provides an important expansion to understandings of ethos as it recognizes "interrelationality, materiality, and agency within ethos" practices.[4]

One situation in which a rhetor would want to have control over ethos would be within the enactment of parrhesia, a speaking truth to power in which rhetors—at their own risk—challenge more powerful individuals. In her study of parrhesia, Renea Carol Frey observes the importance of ethos but says little regarding how ethos might be negotiated within such a delicate situation. Frey notes that in parrhesia, "ethos is perhaps the strongest appeal that the parrhesiastic holds."[5] However, it is more probable that parrhesia lessens a rhetor's ethos, especially because the definition of the term "parrhesia" includes mention of risk; if parrhesia enhanced ethos, the likelihood of risk would be minimal. In fact, Frey acknowledges that not all audiences perceive parrhesiastics favorably since different audiences observe this parrhesiastic rhetoric, and the differing audiences have different positionalities.[6] Frey discerns that these differences explain "why some parrhesiastic rhetors are popular with some segments of society and others unpopular, and why some acts that may appear parrhesiastic can alienate an audience and turn public opinion against a rhetor."[7] To have control of ethos construction, then, rhetors would need to ensure that they only spoke truth to power within the segments of society where they were popular, a seemingly impossible task if the segments of society where they were unpopular had the means to change the rhetorical situations.

However, the nineteenth-century French American Catholic Sister Mother Theodore Guerin illustrates that this seemingly impossible task is not so impossible after all—when the environment in which the rhetoric appears is carefully managed. Guerin engaged in what could easily be termed parrhesiastic rhetoric within her letters and public diaries that discussed the conflict she faced with the bishop of Indiana, Célestine-Réne Guynemer de la Hailandière. Debating with Hailandière issues regarding who should make decisions regarding the schools and convents Guerin had founded, Guerin also wrote frequently to her family and religious colleagues in both France and the United States about the conflict.

To illustrate how the simultaneous negotiation of ethos with multiple audiences can be effective, this chapter considers both Guerin's rhetorical situation and that of another nineteenth-century Catholic mother superior who faced a very similar debate. While Guerin emigrated from France to Indiana in 1840 at the request of the man with whom she eventually had the conflict, Benedicta Riepp sailed from what is now Germany to Pennsylvania twelve years later at the request of a man with whom she had a similar conflict. Coming from different cultural contexts and settling in different Midwestern locations, the two women faced remarkably parallel situations and engaged in parrhesiastic rhetoric as they attempted to right what they perceived as a wrong. With their negotiations of ethos differing significantly, their negotiations also led to very different results: one overcame her difficulties with the patriarchy and is now revered by the Catholic Church as a saint; the other failed, disgraced and forgotten—except by a few American Sisters who tell conflicting tales about her.

Considering both Frey's definitions of parrhesiastic rhetoric and the lens of a feminist ecological approach to rhetoric, this chapter uses published and archived letters written by these two immigrant women to consider how they spoke truth to power within similar environments. Using an environmental approach to ethos, this chapter also considers how the different positionalities of each woman influenced the ways in which she constructed her identities and texts "in relation" to various audiences.[8] Riepp and Guerin both valued the community of women with whom they lived, and they used that community to assist them as they faced hostility from their communities and the Catholic patriarchy. However, coming from an Order that was accustomed to creating coalitions, Guerin was much more adept at negotiating across boundaries, so that when she encountered extreme vilification from her American bishop, she was able to use her environment to defend herself. On the other hand, Riepp maintained subservience to the patriarchy until she felt forced to speak out. While Riepp must have believed this approach would work, without a community that valued her for her outspokenness, the abbot with whom she debated used her direct manner as a means to undermine her. As this chapter illustrates, the difference between the two mother superiors' use of ethos appears to rely much on a distinction outlined by Roichi Okabe between ascribed and achieved ethos,[9] whether Riepp and Guerin relied on preexisting concepts of their virtue or worked to make their audiences appreciate their goodness.

Within the discussion of the rhetoric, this chapter focuses not so much on the rhetoric between the mother superiors and the male members of the patriarchy who created the problem, but on the communication between the women and their communities. Though both women did attempt to persuade the hostile male figures and to construct a positive ethos within their communication with them, both women also reached out to their more sympathetic communities to construct their ethē. However, with her background, Guerin proved to be more adept with the negotiation of ethos with these various communities, especially because, as these two examples illustrate, it is crucial to negotiate ethos with audiences other than the one(s) giving censure. With these sympathetic audiences, the rhetor must maintain a careful balance, adhering to limiting social norms and scripts. In the case of these sisters, they needed to recognize their devalued embodiment as chaste, poor, female, European American Catholic sisters. Any negation of their prescribed roles or bodies could sully their ethos, and the mere act of engaging in parrhesia might seem to be such a negation.

This analysis of these two women's discourse in very similar situations but from very different backgrounds reveals is that it is not parrhesia that allows marginalized people to succeed in challenging social structures; instead, it is the rhetoric that complements parrhesia that allows for such change. In fact, this analysis suggests parrhesia may be a remnant of Thomas Carlyle's "great man theory,"[10] and the success of speaking truth to power relies not on a single parrhesiastic speech but on a series of discourses that create an environment favorable to a rhetor's ability to speak truth to power.

WOMEN SCATTERED AND FULL OF SORROW

In 1840, Mother Theodore Guerin arrived in New York with four other Sisters of Providence on their way to Indiana to set up a convent and school at the request of Indiana's bishop, French American Hailandière. Newly ordained, Hailandière had traveled to France to persuade women religious to join him in establishing schools in the still wild state after several other orders had left. Part of Hailandière's promise to them was that he would welcome the Sisters when they arrived on the first step of their American journey, but neither he nor his representatives were there to greet the immigrants. Thus, Guerin and the other Sisters began their difficult journey from New York to Indiana with the help of other Catholic figures they met along the way.[11]

Twelve years later, Mother Benedicta Riepp and two other Benedictine Sisters similarly arrived in New York on their way to Pennsylvania to set up a convent and school at the request of Bavarian American Abbot Boniface Wimmer, who had arrived in the United States from Bavaria six years earlier. In the United States, Wimmer, like Hailandière, found it difficult to retain sisters to achieve his goals because of the harsh environment and "unfavorable soil conditions."[12] Therefore, he began corresponding with the Benedictine convent in Eichstätt, Bavaria, to persuade these women to join him, making promises similar to those made by Hailandière. And like Hailandière, Wimmer broke his first promise when he was not there to greet them when they arrived in New York.[13]

The similarities between the two European mother superiors' situations are remarkable. Both brought to the United States other sisters to engage in what they saw as their mission of educating American children and expanding their convents. Both accepted the difficulties and began teaching in their native languages because of their lack of English proficiency. Both women also recruited new sisters from Europe and the United States to help them with their work. Most significantly to this chapter, both women encountered similar difficulties: men in the Catholic patriarchy attempted to usurp their control of their order, though in both instances the men also did the same to male orders.[14] Both women believed they would maintain connections with the European convents from which they had come, having been promised by the men who recruited them that they would have some autonomy in making decisions regarding their convents, schools, and orders. Both found, shortly after they arrived, that the men who made these promises were quick to forget them.

Additionally, published histories of both Orders include sections discussing problems with the patriarchy. Sister Mary Borromeo Brown's history of the Sisters of Providence identifies 1841–1847 as their "years of sorrow" caused by quarrels with Hailandière over money and control.[15] During this time, the Sisters offered to leave Indiana, and Guerin traveled to France in search of financial and moral support. As the problems increased, Hailandière told Guerin to leave the Order, forbade communication between her and other Sisters of Providence, and attempted to excommunicate her. Sister Ephrem Hollermann's history of the Benedictine Sisters in America includes a chapter on the years 1856–1859, titled "Women Uprooted and Scattered," that discusses the series of events that continued until Riepp's death in 1862 during which Riepp and several other Sisters offered to leave Pennsylvania to go to Minnesota. Riepp traveled to the area of Germany in search of financial and moral support, and Wimmer forbade Riepp to return to either her Pennsylvania or Minnesota Order when she returned from the German area.[16]

Different Environments

Another similarity between these two women is that their Orders were both significantly impacted by the European unrest following the French Revolution—but this similarity belies their differences. The two women were from different countries and cultures, and not only did German and French Catholicism differ in their histories and practices, but also Riepp's convent had existed since 1035 C.E. while Guerin's Order had been founded only in the early nineteenth century.[17]

Riepp's St. Walburg Abby in Eichstätt, Bavaria, was founded to combine even Older orders of Benedictine Sisters with new recruits to care for the tomb of eighth-century Anglo-Saxon missionary to the Frankish empire, St. Walburga.[18] According to Lina Eckenstein, this time period immediately preceded what she terms the "golden age of monasticism," when the Church recognized monasticism as a means of securing a "foothold" for itself in various regions,[19] yet it was also the period in which the Church increasingly disempowered women's orders as society demonized women.[20] To add to their credibility and to gain a level of security, the women of St. Walburg were cloistered, meaning they were closed to the outside world. Though such closing off to society existed in various forms,[21] little is known about the early period of this convent. What is known is that these women lived in community with each other, had somewhat limited interaction with the world, came from wealthy families (as did a majority of the sisters in this era), and survived several intervals of decline.[22] While many women religious of the area that is now Germany were extraordinarily well educated and literate (Hroswitha of Gandersheim and Hildegard of Bingen being two notable examples), little is known of the educational prowess of the Sisters of St. Walburg. Though St. Walburg clearly survived it, how the abbey responded to Martin Luther's Reformation is also not known. Some German-area nuns embraced Luther's reforms, perceiving the Reformation as providing them more active roles in ministry.[23] Other German-area monasteries were destroyed.[24] Still some, such as St. Walburg, endured.

An even more damaging chapter for St. Walburg Abbey occurred centuries later, in the time following Napoleon's rise to power. In the earliest years of the nineteenth century, a leader of Eichstätt who was approved by Napoleon attempted to remove numerous convents from Catholic control. The mother superior of St. Walburg at the time ingratiated herself to Napoleon's wife; hence, St. Walburg was allowed to remain on the condition that it open a school for girls. The mother superior objected, noting the Sisters' lack of qualifications, but offered that they teach needlework and handicrafts. A compromise allowed the Abby to exist in a diminished form until the 1830s, when another government leader in the area told the Sisters their abbey would close unless they begin teaching a school for girls.[25] This time, the Sisters agreed and began teaching, living in a semi-cloistered format that had become increasingly common among orders of Catholic women.[26]

Eight years later, Benedicta Riepp entered St. Walburg. Though the convent had changed to accommodate the new charge of teaching, many nuns wished to retain the traditions of the old monastery.[27] The mother superior at St. Walburg during Riepp's time there wrote: "In a convent it is well to follow the old traditions, centuries-tried usages, since they have been established to serve all times and conditions. Each generation should esteem and hold fast to those customs which older Sisters, who conscientiously observe the Rule, practice."[28] With such guidance, Riepp and other new Sisters had little agency to affect any change, even with the new charge of teaching. Instead, they were told that their convent would "retain a firm footing" with adherence to the "old traditions."[29]

Guerin's French Sisters of Providence were also impacted by the French Revolution, but in very different ways. Prior to the Revolution, women religious were an important part of French society, less devastated by the Protestant Reformation than were nuns in German areas. Most significantly for French women religious, Luther's work with education prompted the Catholic Church also to educate its congregations, and it needed to find people to engage in this education. As Linda Lierheimer writes, "The Church's battle against heresy and unorthodoxy required an army of female catechists and teachers, and women rose to the challenge."[30] Numerous French orders were created to teach or took up teaching until the French Revolution put a temporary end to this teaching, as well as to Catholicism. Then, Napoleon's Concordat of 1801 allowed religious activity, and with this activity, former orders reactivated and new ones began.

One such new order was that of the Sisters of Providence, established in 1826, with a formal "Rule" created in 1835 providing that the purpose of the

Order was to "instruct children and to care for the sick."[31] Guerin had entered this Order in 1823 even before it was fully established and thus was influential in shaping its "definite frameworks" for education.[32] She was known for being able to take on "demoralized children" from "depraved sections of the city of Rennes, who laughed to scorn her efforts to control them and danced and sang about the classroom to annoy and disconcert her. How she disarmed and won them over was an oft-told tale to emphasize the dictum that love and interest, not force, are the prime educational factors."[33] Guerin illustrated a clear sense of knowing how to pragmatically build coalitions. She knew people, such as the children of Rennes, would not automatically do as she asked. Instead, she had to gain consensus by using "love and interest" to win over her audiences.

The different environments from which these two women came to the United States influenced their perspectives on communication. While Guerin arrived with vast experience negotiating a classroom and recognizing the power of discourse, Riepp arrived from a tradition that evolved from surveillance. As I have argued elsewhere, surveillance itself is not necessarily inhibiting to communication—but Riepp's Order appears not to have learned how to negotiate via relationships with various groups of people.[34]

For example, the archive of Guerin's correspondence that is maintained by her Order is well preserved and celebrated; the collection of Riepp's correspondence kept by her Order is slim. In addition, there are numerous histories of the founding of Guerin's Order just as there is a published, 463-page book full of her journals and diaries with added commentary. Riepp's work is published in a 227-page volume that provides correspondence surrounding the founding of her Order that includes letters and other texts from many other religious figures.[35] In sum, the book includes twelve of Riepp's texts. While this difference could be accounted for by numerous factors such as those articulated by Liz Rohan regarding the problems of archival research,[36] it seems that the difference also results from their varying traditions of communication. Guerin wrote frequently to her family and former colleagues in France as she also communicated with many people she had come to know in the United States. Guerin's correspondence was comprised of not only letters to friends but also of "letters circular," mass produced and sent to many in her community. Additionally, Guerin kept a very public journal, in which she had copies made and sent to her friends in Europe; even the students at Guerin's school used Mother Theodore's journal as a textbook to learn appropriate means of correspondence.[37] While there probably is material written by Riepp that is not available to the twenty-first-century researcher, Riepp wrote and promoted her texts to a significantly lesser degree.

CORRESPONDENCE

While Guerin spread her correspondence more widely than did Riepp, both wrote to others after they arrived in the United States and found that the men who had persuaded them to come to America did not keep their promises.[38] In her letter of November 27, 1852, Riepp corresponded with an archbishop she knew personally,[39] reminding this archbishop of their acquaintance as she repeatedly noted her unworthiness (e.g., "in spite of my unworthiness and weakness, I am encouraged by the thought that God often call the weak to do his work"[40]). In the letter, she tells the archbishop that the Sisters cannot maintain cloister's necessary enclosure, "which for us is the most important thing," because their house is too small, and that to build any structure "answering our greatest needs," she and the Sisters need money.[41] She says she knows she asks for much but, as she observes, the archbishop's mission "sends contributions to all parts of the Catholic world; may we not also receive a small contribution?"[42] In response to her request, Bavarian King Ludwig sent the requested funds via Wimmer, and in a letter dated January 8, 1853, Riepp thanks him, also telling him of the "poverty of the parish" she serves and of her "somewhat far-reaching" plans to educate the children of the poor parish.[43] The only hint she provides in her ingratiating letters to either of these men regarding her problems with Wimmer exists when she says, "I have had always been in the greatest dilemma to know from where we should draw the necessary funds to build the convent."[44]

Riepp's efforts to "draw the necessary funds" are certainly understandable. In a new land known for its poor soil and given the task of teaching while maintaining cloister, Riepp had few financial means. However, she frames her need by focusing on her inadequacies: she is "unworthy" and "weak"; the Sisters are poor and face dilemmas; the Sisters' ambitions are "far-reaching." Riepp never suggests Wimmer has anything to do with their poverty and dilemmas. While this framing did elicit funding, it also elicited patronizing comments such as this from her mother superior in St. Walburg: "The daughter-house founded at St. Mary's frequently comes with requests, as if the fashion of daughters, for more help."[45] While this comment may have been made in jest, it nevertheless foregrounds a needy and unrealistic nature of Riepp instead of her sacrifice.

Guerin framed her requests very differently. She was quick to share her concerns regarding her difficulties with the male Catholic leadership. Writing shortly after her arrival in the United States, Guerin tells her mother superior in France that the bishop does not want her to wear her a French habit, one she hoped "never to give . . . up."[46] Speaking of the bishop, she writes, "Monseigneur wishes to make one change today, another tomorrow, but we have held firm, and nothing, absolutely nothing has been changed. . . .

Monseigneur seems animated with the best intentions, but so busy, so poor, that truly he knows not what to do."[47] Like Riepp, Guerin shows her willingness to comply with social norms. Riepp wants to maintain cloister; Guerin wants to wear the habit. However, unlike Riepp, Guerin does not hesitate to identify the source of her inability to adhere to these norms. Yet even in saying that the bishop "knows not what to do," Guerin affirms her position as a dutiful daughter by offering that he has "the best of intentions."

Guerin wrote this letter one day after she had responded to a number of her lay and religious friends who wanted a copy of her journal describing her journey across the Atlantic. In the letter accompanying the requested copies, Guerin is, like Riepp, demure as she notes her journal's imperfections. Yet she says she sends the imperfect work because she thought her friends "would be very glad to know all about us as soon as possible":

> I want to do all in my power to draw closer and strengthen the double chain which must unite us. . . . If you will help, if you will not abandon us, if we are always your cherished daughters, and you give us proofs of it by writing to us, consoling us, helping us, we shall suffer with constancy and even with a sort of joy in the infinite and incalculable protections that the Lord is preparing for us here in His great mercy.[48]

Unlike Riepp, Guerin appears to have made great effort to maintain her relationships with her allies in France. What she specifically references with the term "double chain" is unclear: it could be ties of past and present, of familial and religious connections, of spiritual and secular. Nonetheless, with this letter, Guerin actively works to maintain relationships with those who admire her while, like Riepp, adhering to a script of social norms that demands her humbleness. Instead of immediately discussing her difficulties and need for aid, Guerin makes an offering of her journal as she requests not financial assistance—but texts, consolation, and help. Certainly, Guerin did frequently ask for financial assistance, but she first negotiated a relationship that built an ethos of goodwill. She used her physical and metaphorical embodied position as a Catholic sister to act as her allies' "daughter," not merely a weak woman needing assistance.

Riepp evidently also knew the potency of a public viewing of correspondence. In January 1855, Riepp sent a letter to the Munich archbishop for publication in the *Annalen der Verbreitung des Glaubens, the Annals of Spreading the Faith.*[49] Writing this letter three years after she had heard that she would receive funding from the king but not receiving it because of Wimmer's interception, Riepp says nothing of her problems with Wimmer though she does state that she is writing "to take advantage of the departure" of Wimmer.[50] After greeting the archbishop, Riepp tells of her accomplishments. Although she notes she has had to overcome obstacles, she does not indicate Wimmer is the source of any of them. Instead, she offers him praise, observing that it is Wimmer's "aim to spread the Order of St. Benedict" in the United States.[51] Stating that she does not "hesitate to accept novices at once to acquaint them with the Holy Rule,"[52] Riepp does allude to the problem she has with Wimmer regarding which and how many novices to accept into her new Order; however, she undermines this allusion. Giving the appearance that all is well, Riepp offers the archbishop "as a token of . . . respect and gratitude, send[s] . . . , through the courtesy of Rev. Boniface Wimmer, a photograph of St. Marys [*sic*]."[53] With this rosy closing, Riepp again credits Wimmer with much success, even though she was well aware of Wimmer's interception of money from the king and she was debating with Wimmer about issues of the Orders' control.

As the tensions between Riepp and Wimmer escalated, so too did the tensions between Guerin and Hailandière, and as these tensions mounted the two men felt little hesitation to attack the two women. Though much of these verbal attacks were not recorded in letters, traces of the attacks exist in the letters. Three years after Guerin arrived in Indiana, Hailandière states that her actions "would merit from your Bishop [Hailandière, himself] a severe judgment and Canonical censure."[54] A March 8, 1846, letter circular from Guerin to her "very dear sisters" notes that she had received "a letter of ten pages from the Bishop . . . full of accusations and reproaches which are personal, three-fourth of which are palpably untrue."[55]

Riepp also received her share of accusations from the man who had requested she come to America. In July 24, 1857, Wimmer wrote to the Court Chaplain of Ludwig I that he was "no longer pleased with the superior, because she is too self-willed, does not take advice, and still does not perform her duty satisfactorily," adding that Riepp's Sisters could "bring prejudice, disgrace and scandal upon my priest and brothers, the children of my parishes, the sisters themselves, and the Order, and in the end I would have to support a crowd of womenfolk, who would be good-for-nothing and would be for me a means of annoyance."[56]

PARRHESIA

Facing such damnation, both Sisters—like any other person—could choose from three rhetorical options: (1) silence; (2) a mollified discourse, attempting to negotiate a watered-down remedy; or (3) unapologetically speak truth despite the dangers of doing so. As the work of Gerard Hauser, Arthur Walzer, Gae Lyn Henderson, Michel Foucault, and many classical rhetoricians have discussed, sometimes this third choice, termed parrhesia, can be necessary.[57]

In fact, Renea Carol Frey writes that parrhesia can be particularly useful to women as it can "create an opening or crack in the conventional social practice that allows future actions."[58] The negotiation of ethos, however, in such circumstances would seem to be irrelevant, especially since, as Frey claims, parrhesiastic rhetoric cannot work to please an audience. Instead, the mere act of speaking out despite the dangers of so doing illustrates the parrhesiastic's goodwill, creating an ethos which—according to Frey—is "perhaps the strongest appeal that the parrhesiastic holds."[59] Still, as Frey also observes, not all audiences respond favorably to such speaking truth to power.

There is evidence of face-to-face discussion between both Sisters and the men with whom they quarreled, but this chapter naturally relies on the few existent letters from the Sisters as examples of the rhetoric in which they spoke their truths about male Catholic figures' behaviors and in so doing put themselves in very precarious positions. As this analysis shows, the two approached parrhesiastic rhetoric differently because they negotiated their ethē differently. In fact, the only existent letter between Riepp and Wimmer is clearly not an example of parrhesia: Riepp writes, first asking for apologies for "bothering" him, begging him to "listen graciously to [her] earnest request."[60] Riepp notes how difficult it is for the Sisters in their crowded Pennsylvania convent and asks for permission to go to Minnesota. If she cannot, she says, her health "will be considerably impaired" since she is so unhappy in Pennsylvania.[61] Undermining her ethos, she states "I can accomplish very little good under these circumstances."[62]

What response Riepp received is unclear. What is clear is that she had received an invitation from monks in Minnesota to go there, and she saw the move as a solution to the problems with crowded quarters and lack of food in Pennsylvania. It is also evident that she believed she had permission from Wimmer to travel, so she set out to do so, stopping at another convent she had founded further west in Pennsylvania. She did not continue to Minnesota; instead, a few other Sisters did. Riepp sailed for Europe instead to gain support.

In Europe, Riepp's indirect methods of communicating her complaints ended, and she instead wrote her truth in a list of "Six Points of Difference," articulating her complaints to the bishop of Eichstätt, who in turn sent her list to the archbishop of Munich and the German-area mission, who in turn corresponded with Rome.[63] Direct and detailed, the complaints include concerns regarding Wimmer usurping authority within the management of the Order and convent. Riepp also included accusations regarding Wimmer's taking money intended for the Sisters.

Riepp's use of bureaucratic parrhesia did not work well. Wimmer responded point by point to Riepp's complaints, accusing her of lying about particulars in the accusations and questioning how she could possibly know what she claimed to know. He communicated with many of his colleagues vilifying her. For example, in a letter to the mission that funded the American Benedictine efforts, Wimmer described Riepp as "a taciturn, inefficient woman."[64] According to Wimmer, "Sister Superior will dig a pit for herself and fall in, and so it happened!" ("grube graben und hinein stütze, et factum est ita!").[65] Eventually, many of the points Riepp argued were decided in her favor; however, by the time Rome came to the conclusion regarding Riepp's correctness in her assertions, her reputation had been ruined.[66] During her time in the area of Germany, Wimmer distanced her from her fellow Sisters, forbidding her to go to St. Walburg. When she returned to the United States, Wimmer prohibited her from going to Minnesota. Though she did go when the bishop of Erie gave her permission,[67] Wimmer made every effort to punish the Minnesota Order for defying his edict. Riepp died disgraced in 1862, and to this day Sisters in Pennsylvania believe she did not serve the Benedictine Order well.[68]

Like Riepp, Guerin appears to have communicated with Hailandière via face-to-face communication, but there is significantly more correspondence between them. Two of the most interesting correspondences are, first, to other Sisters of Providence from Guerin, and, a second, to Hailandière from Guerin and five Sisters. In the first of these, dated March 8, 1845, Guerin outlines her concerns with Hailandière and requests the Sisters' support. She tells the Sisters, though, that they "are not obliged to sign the letter I [Guerin] am sending, if it is contrary to your views."[69] Guerin also comments that, in signing, they may suffer repercussions. Nevertheless, five joined her. The second, dated the same day, makes clear the letter is "faithful to the spirit of candor which we have always followed," as it points out Hailandière's errors in thinking regarding his expectations of the Sisters, including his claim that the French American sisters cannot own American property.[70] This letter, signed by Guerin and five other Sisters, is dated the same day as a letter to the Sisters. In response, Hailandière demanded from the Sisters an "Act of Reparation," to which Guerin and three Sisters replied on April 6, 1846, outlining their evidence point by point "to prove" their correctness in their assertions.[71]

During this period of time, Guerin wrote extensively to many other people: bishops, priests, sisters, family in both France and the United States. Within this correspondence, she did not mince words regarding her concerns regarding Hailandière's behavior. For example, in 1844 she wrote to Bishop Bouvier in France detailing specific instances of Hailandière's poor management and deceit. In this letter, Guerin goes as far as stating that Hailandière suffered from "the caprices of an undisciplined fancy."[72] In another letter written closer to the time in which Guerin and her fellow Sisters detailed their complaints to Hailandière, Guerin wrote to a vicar in Mississippi, The Very Reverend A. Martin, who had just left for France. Mourning his departure to the European continent, Guerin praises Martin as her congregation's "venerated protector" and "devoted friend," asking "Who will now protect us?"[73] She tells him that she will "leave it to Father Corbe [an American priest] to tell you some particular things that are said to be going on in America since you left,"[74] but she also reminds him of previous conversations she had with Martin regarding these same issues. As she alludes to, but does not speak of, these concerns, she also asks him to "pray for your Daughters in Indiana. Get prayers said for them by pious and fervent souls, whose numbers are so great in our dear Brittany. You will not to have to go far to find them."[75] With Guerin reminding him of the many devout people who believed in her integrity, Martin seems to have heeded her commands; at least he wrote to Bishop Bouvier, telling the French bishop of his support for Guerin.[76] Later that July, Guerin herself wrote to Bouvier about the situation, making clear she expected that he had heard the same from other sources ("no doubt our good Mother Mary has informed you of the news that I imparted to her in my letter of last month"[77]). She details the specifics of her complaints, her approach to address them, and asks for prayers.

SPEAKING TRUTH TO POWER IN RELATION TO OTHERS

The rhetoric of Riepp and Guerin in their difficulties has two major differences. First, Guerin does not hesitate to place responsibility for her problems on Hailandière, while Riepp blames Wimmer only after all else fails. Second, Guerin continually makes attempts to reach as broad an audience as possible in discussing her conflict. These two differences are very intertwined, with the second's negotiation of ethos enabling the first. Using the terms of Ryan et al.'s feminist ecological approach to ethos, as Guerin sought this broad audience, she engaged in a "relation-relating" means to ethos.

Ryan et al. argue that as many women rhetors have recognized that their environments give them subordinate status, these women "craft a viable ethos for participation in a dominant public."[78] Building on Donna Haraway's "situated knowledges," Ryan et al. observe that rhetors' locations can not only give them authority to speak, but also the locations give rhetors "a concomitant responsibility to speak from that position with the knowledge conferred by that location."[79] In other words, ethos is not constant but alters with the movements in a rhetor's location and its rhetorical ecology. This ecological understanding of feminist ethē thus considers ethē's social, ethical, and special dimensions, noting that what is good is determined by a community.[80] Outlining three rhetorical strategies women rhetors have used "to enact feminist ethē," Ryan et al. identify the third as "relation-relating,"[81] a means of constructing "identities and texts in relation to others and their environments," via "collaboration, connection, and coalitions or alliances."[82]

With Guerin's "relation-relating" enactment of a feminist ethos, her discourse with her supporters does not seem to fit the definition of parrhesia, though it is a means of speaking truth to power. Unlike the correspondence to Hailandière, these letters to Martin and Bouvier do not seem to put Guerin in any danger: Guerin writes to friends; she asks for prayers, she tells of her appreciation of her correspondents, she thanks them for past favors. What this discourse does do is allow Guerin to negotiate her ethos via her relationships. She locates herself and her ethos within an alliance that shares values. While she performs obedience to norms, scripts, and appropriate forms of embodiment, she also makes clear that Hailandière has values other than those shared with her beloved allies. In other words, Guerin illustrates that she had earned, or achieved her credibility, while Hailandière relies on his status for his credibility.

Certainly, though, Hailandière's ascribed ethos provided him with enormous power. While my discussion of Guerin might present her as being perfectly safe, she was not. Like Riepp, she was roundly chastised by the man she criticized and was forbidden from the convent she had founded. She was also given the most horrific condemnation a religious woman could receive: excommunication, though Hailandière was never able to carry through with his threat because of Guerin's ability to negotiate her ethos via her relationships.

Coming from an order in which collaboration was essential, Guerin had experience working with various parties to achieve her ends. Seeming to recognize that a rhetor is never fully in control of her ethos construction, Guerin worked to construct her ethos in numerous environments so that if she engaged with a hostile audience, she could call upon another more sympathetic one to intervene. Always working within socially scripted norms, she stretched the norms' limitations by drawing attention to her embodiment (e.g., her habit, her subservience) and its value in the Catholic hierarchy. In so doing, she solidified her ethos with different audiences—and used their recognition of her value to challenge the power of the hostile audiences. Riepp, on the other hand, assumed her value was inherent. Coming from an order that crafted its sanctity behind walls, sometimes engaging with the public but only in modified forms, she abided by her mother superior's advice to "hold fast" to traditions. In these traditions, women strove for goodness and appeared to believe that those who valued goodness would recognize their ethos, believing that what was sacred was stable.

The difference between the two's negotiation of ethos could be explained by the differences in ascribed and achieved ethos. In discussing variances between rhetorics of Japan and the United States, Roichi Okabe defines and distinguishes between the two: ascribed ethos consists of one's possession of "such qualities as seniority, sex, and family status," while achieved ethos is promoted by "such qualities as intelligence, competence, and character."[83] Thus, it appears that the key distinctions between these two revolve around nuances of agency. While achieved ethos requires active agency, the agency required for ascribed ethos is more passive. As Okabe comments, "what matters in Japan [in contrast to what matters in the United States] is not what [an individual] has learned, but where he or she has learned it."[84] The manner in which one acts to earn ascribed ethos is very different from the way one acts to achieve ethos. With ascribed ethos, credibility is passively earned via the passage of time (as with the quality of seniority), the actions of others (as with family status), or choice of—or ability to attend—a school.

Though the two women were not negotiating differences between Japanese and American rhetorical norms, they did come from different cultures. The culture of St. Walburg from which Riepp came appears to have relied on ascribed ethos. Riepp was told at St. Walburg that she should rely on inherited traditions. She need not earn credibility; credibility was built into her position. Guerin, on the other hand, came from a new order that could rely on nothing. She had to negotiate, even with schoolchildren, for her credibility. Therefore, in the United States, Guerin was more prepared to negotiate, or achieve, ethos to counter the male patriarchy's more powerful traditional, or ascribed, ethos.

RETHINKING PARRHESIA THROUGH THE LENS OF ETHOS

As this discussion shows, Guerin spoke truth to power and negotiated her ethos, not with someone who was predisposed to view her unfavorably, but with audiences who would view the contest between her and the patriarchy. Guerin framed her parrhesia as a matter of ethos: her audience could see how her values aligned with her audiences more than did Hailandière's. Riepp spoke truth to power with people who ultimately made choices that recognized her truth over Wimmer's, but because she relied on ascribed ethos, Wimmer's constant denigration of her made various audiences see his truth as the valid one.

Looking at these two Sisters, then, it appears that the issue of ethos within parrhesia is not a matter of "some parrhesiastic rhetors [being] popular with some segments of society and others unpopular" but is much more complex.[85] If the person being addressed is unlikely, as Frey notes, to think favorably of the parrhesiastic, then the parrhesiastic needs to negotiate ethos with other audiences, those who are likely to influence the person being addressed. In other words, the parrhesiastic needs to develop relationships with "audience members of different positionalities" other than the audience the parrhesiastic quarrels with. Another way of considering this need is that just as Ryan et al. point out the inadequacy of traditional concepts of ethos stemming from conceptions of "a solitary individual crafting his or her character,"[86] so too is it inadequate to consider parrhesia to be a matter of one rhetor suddenly speaking truth to power and changing the status quo. Instead, for a rhetor to speak such truth to power and crack social conventions, the rhetor needs to negotiate ethos with the audiences who will witness the rhetoric. The rhetor needs to relate to the audience to show that the audience and the rhetor share the same values.

Coming from a tradition in which she was accustomed to negotiating ethos, Guerin knew she could not rely on any ascribed credibility; she had to connect with audiences to earn ethos. Riepp, on the other hand, was taught to follow old traditions based on women's community in isolation from much of the world. The most significant difference, then, between Guerin and Riepp (that likely resulted in the differences in their situations' outcomes) is that Guerin negotiated ethos with audiences across both material and abstract distances. Though Riepp wrote to friends and allies as she performed obedience to norms, scripts, and appropriate forms of embodiment, she relied too much on ascribed ethos. In other words, she saw little need to resituate or earn her ethos. Far from her homeland, she believed her ethos would remain constant, yet with her audiences it did not. Thus, as she engaged in what she believed were shared goals, she asked for aid and was treated as a child asking for something more than she was supposed to have. Similarly, when she complained of Wimmer, his narratives of her "taciturn, inefficient" behavior were given credence: it was her own fault she was having problems. When she engaged in parrhesia, her audience was predisposed to think critically of her. She had dug the pit into which she fell.

Guerin's situation clearly achieved the potential that Frey notes parrhesia can have: it cracked conventional social practice and created an enormous force "around which power must realign itself."[87] Hailandière was forced out of his position, and Guerin is now a celebrated American saint. Though Riepp's situation might have had the same potential, it did not turn out well for her. Because Riepp relied so much on an ascribed position and did not relate to others how much she had earned her credibility, Wimmer was able to continually mock and belittle her in his communication with others; thus, Riepp is forgotten and maligned by twenty-first-century Sisters of the Pennsylvania Order she founded.

This analysis of these two women's discourse in very similar situations suggests it is not parrhesia that cracks social practice and causes power structures to realign. Instead, it is this rhetoric that precedes and complements parrhesia; it is this rhetoric that cracks social practices and forces realignment of power structures. It is this rhetoric that negotiates the ethos that allows the parrhesiastic rhetor to succeed. In other words, it is what the parrhesiastic does with audiences other than the parties being addressed in parrhesia that matters most. While in some cases, an ascribed ethos may be sufficient, more often than not such an ethos is not. What is essential is that the rhetor negotiates strong relationships with the audiences witnessing parrhesia. With such negotiation and achieved ethos, the rhetor can succeed in speaking truth to power even if the person censured dislikes the truth; the audience bearing witness can be the agent in creating what Frey terms the "opening or crack in the conventional social practice that allows future actions."[88]

Thus, the differences between these two women illustrate that the difference in successful parrhesia is not a single act or that some parrhesiastics are "popular with some segments of society and others unpopular." Instead, rhetors who recognize parrhesia as a located, situated, and social act can best negotiate the ethos necessary to open audiences' eyes to the rhetor's truth.

NOTES

1. Risa Applegarth, "Working with and Working for: Ethos and Power in Women's Writing," in *Rethinking Ethos: A Feminist Ecological Approach to Rhetoric*, edited by Kathleen Ryan, Nancy Meyers, and Rebecca Jones (Carbondale: Southern Illinois UP, 2016), 219.
2. Applegarth, "Working," 219.
3. Applegarth, "Working," 219.
4. Kathleen Ryan, Nancy Meyers, and Rebecca Jones, "Introduction: Identifying Feminist Ecological Ethē," in *Rethinking Ethos: A Feminist Ecological Approach to Rhetoric*, eds. Kathleen Ryan, Nancy Meyers, and Rebecca Jones (Carbondale: Southern Illinois UP, 2016), viii.
5. Renea Carol Frey, "Speaking Truth to Power: Recovering a Rhetorical Theory of Parrhesia" (PhD Diss., Miami University, 2015), 99.
6. Frey, *Speaking*, 96.
7. Frey, *Speaking*, 97.
8. Kathleen J. Ryan, Nancy Meyers, and Rebecca Jones, "Ethē as Relation-Relating," in *Rethinking Ethos: A Feminist Ecological Approach to Rhetoric*, eds. Kathleen Ryan, Nancy Meyers, and Rebecca Jones (Carbondale: Southern Illinois UP, 2016), 195.
9. Roichi Okabe, "Cultural Assumptions of East and West: Japan and the United States," in *The Rhetoric of Western Thought*, 4th edition, eds. J.L. Golden, G.F. Berquist, and W.E. Coleman (Dubuque, IA: Kendall/Hunt, 1989), 546–565.

10. Thomas Carlyle, *On Heroes, Hero-Worship, and the Heroic in History*. Project Gutenberg, accessed August 9, 2020, https://www.gutenberg.org/files/1091/1091-h/1091-h.htm.

11. Mary Borromeo Brown, *History of the Sisters of Providence of Saint Mary-of-the-Woods* (New York: Benziger Brothers, 1949), 49–62.

12. Emmanuel Dray, *Spring and Harvest* (*Die Abtei St. Walburg (1035–1935): 900 Jahre in Wort und Bild*), trans. Gonzaga Engelhart (St. Meinrad, IN: The Grail, 1952), 42; M. Incarnata Girgen, *Behind the Beginnings: Benedictine Women in America* (St. Joseph, Minnesota: St. Benedict's Convent, 1981), 9–12.

13. Girgen, *Behind the Beginnings*, 15.

14. Jerome Oetgen, "Boniface Wimmer and the American Benedictines: 1856–1866," *American Benedictine Review* 23, no. 3 (1972): 300–304; Joseph M. White, *Worthy of the Gospel of Christ. A History of the Catholic Diocese of Fort Wayne-South Bend* (Fort Wayne, IN: Diocese of Fort Wayne-South Bend, 2007), 35–37.

15. Brown, *History*, 133–577.

16. *The Reshaping of a Tradition: American Benedictine Women 1852–1881* (St. Joseph, MN: Sisters of the Order of Saint Benedict, 1994), 91–202.

17. Ephrem Hollermann, *The Reshaping of a Tradition: American Benedictine Women 1852–1881* (St. Joseph, MN: Sisters of the Order of Saint Benedict, 1994), 10–11; Brown, *History*, 7–20.

18. Hollermann, *Reshaping of a Tradition*, 10–20.

19. Lina Eckenstein, *Woman under Monasticism: Chapters on Saint-Lore and Convent Life Between A.D. 500 and A.D. 1500* (Cambridge: Cambridge UP, 1896), 185.

20. Jo Ann Kay McNamara, *Sisters in Arms: Catholic Nuns through Two Millennia* (Cambridge: Harvard UP, 1996), 202–239.

21. Caroline Walker Brynum, "Foreword," in *Crown and Veil: Female Monasteries from the Fifth to Fifteenth Centuries*, eds. Jeffrey F. Hamburger and Susan Manti (New York: Columbia UP, 2008), xv.

22. Hollermann, *Reshaping of a Tradition*, 20–25.

23. McNamara, *Sisters in Arms*, 420.

24. McNamara, *Sisters in Arms*, 430, 438.

25. Dray, *Spring and Harvest*, 37.

26. Hollermann, *Reshaping of a Tradition*, 26–28.

27. Hollermann, *Reshaping of a Tradition*, 58–59; Dray, *Spring and Harvest*, 37.

28. Dray, *Spring and Harvest*, 36.

29. Dray, *Spring and Harvest*, 35.

30. Linda Lierheimer, "Eloquence and Maternal Ministry: The Apostolate of Ursuline Nuns in Seventeenth-Century France" (PhD Diss., Princeton University, 1994), 1.

31. Brown, *History*, 19.

32. Brown, *History*, 22, 158.

33. Brown, *History*, 159.

34. Elizabethada Wright, "'God Sees Me': Surveillance and Oratorical Training at St. Mary's-of-the-Woods in Indiana," in *Rhetoric, History, and Women's Oratorical*

Education: American Women Learn to Speak, eds. David Gold and Catherine Hobbs (New York: Routledge, 2013), 116–133.

35. Girgen, *Behind the Beginnings*.

36. Liz Rohan, "Stitching and Writing a Life," in *Beyond the Archives: Research as Lived Process*, eds. Gesa E. Kirsch and Rohan (Carbondale: Southern Illinois UP, 2008), 147–153. My experiences at the archives reflect the differences. At the archive of the Sisters of Providence, the archivist pulled anything I requested including scores of letters by Guerin. At the archive of the Benedictine Sisters, the archivist insisted the only letters of Riepp's that they held were in Girgen's book *Behind the Beginnings*. After a great deal of sleuthing as well as negotiating my *ethos* with the Sisters, they pulled from their archives some copies of the same letters from Girgen's book but in handwritten German.

37. Brown, *History*, 162.

38. Girgen, *Behind the Beginnings*, 18–19; Hollermann, *Reshaping a Tradition*, 66–67; Brown, *History*, 83–83.

39. Girgen, *Behind the Beginnings*, 23.

40. Girgen, *Behind the Beginnings*, 24.

41. Girgen, *Behind the Beginnings*, 24.

42. Girgen, *Behind the Beginnings*, 25.

43. Girgen, *Behind the Beginnings*, 26–27.

44. Girgen, *Behind the Beginnings*, 26.

45. Dray, *Spring and Harvest*, 44.

46. Brown, *History*, 75.

47. Brown, *History*, 75.

48. Brown, *History*, 88.

49. Girgen, *Behind the Beginnings*, 38.

50. Girgen, *Behind the Beginnings*, 38.

51. Girgen, *Behind the Beginnings*, 39.

52. Girgen, *Behind the Beginnings*, 38–39.

53. Girgen, *Behind the Beginnings*, 39.

54. Brown, *History*, 409.

55. Brown, *History*, 191.

56. Girgen, *Behind the Beginnings*, 86–87.

57. Gerard Hauser, *Prisoners of Conscience: Moral Vernaculars of Political Agency* (Columbia, SC: U of South Carolina P, 2012); Arthur Walzer, "*Parrēsia*, Foucault, and the Classical Rhetorical Tradition," *Rhetoric Society Quarterly* 43, no. 1 (2013): 1–21, http://doi.org/10.1080/02773945.2012.740130; Gae Lyn Henderson, "The 'Parrhesiastic Game': Textual Self-Justification in Spiritual Narratives of Early Modern Women," *Rhetoric Society Quarterly* 37, no. 4 (2007): 423–451, https://doi/10.1080/02773940601078072; Michel Foucault, *Fearless Speech* (Los Angeles, CA: Semiotext(e), 2001).

58. Frey, *Speaking*, 92.

59. Frey, *Speaking*, 99.

60. Girgen, *Behind the Beginnings*, 65.

61. Girgen, *Behind the Beginnings*, 66.

62. Girgen, *Behind the Beginnings*, 66.
63. Dray, *Spring and Harvest*.
64. Oetgen, "Boniface Wimmer," 297.
65. Girgen, *Behind the Beginnings*, 118; Boniface Wimmer, Letter to Obercamp, November 23, 1857 (St. Benedict's Convent Archives, St. Joseph, MN).
66. Oetgen, "Boniface Wimmer," 300.
67. Hollermann, *Reshaping a Tradition*, 164; Girgen, *Behind the Beginnings*, 135.
68. M. Incarnata Girgen, Personal Conversation, February 14, 2020 (Saint Benedict's Convent, St. Joseph, MN).
69. Theodore.Guerin, *Journals and Letters of Mother Theodore Guerin*, eds. Mary Theodosia Mug (Saint-Mary-of-the-Woods, IN: St. Mary-of-the-Woods, 1942), 190–192.
70. Guerin, *Journals and Letters*, 192–194.
71. Guerin, *Journals and Letters*, 194–196.
72. Elizabethada Wright, "'The Caprices of an Undisciplined Fancy': Using Blame to Negotiate the 'betweens' of Ethos via the Epideictic," *Rhetoric Review* 38, no. 3 (2019): 271–284, https://doi.org/10.1080/07350198.2019.1618157.
73. Guerin, *Journals and Letters*, 200.
74. Guerin, *Journals and Letters*, 200.
75. Guerin, *Journals and Letters*, 202.
76. Guerin, *Journals and Letters*, 204.
77. Guerin, *Journals and Letters*, 206.
78. Ryan et al., "Introduction," 4.
79. Ryan et al., "Introduction," 8.
80. Ryan et al., "Introduction," 6.
81. Ryan et al., "Introduction," 4.
82. Ryan et al., "Ethē," 195.
83. Okabe, "Cultural Assumptions of East and West," 555–556.
84. Okabe, "Cultural Assumptions of East and West," 555.
85. Frey, *Speaking*, 97.
86. Ryan et al., "Introduction," 5.
87. Frey, *Speaking*, 92–93.
88. Frey, *Speaking*, 92.

BIBLIOGRAPHY

Applegarth, Risa. "Working With and Working For: Ethos and Power in Women's Writing." In *Rethinking Ethos: A Feminist Ecological Approach to Rhetoric*, edited by Kathleen J. Ryan, Nancy Meyers, and Rebecca Jones, 216–236. Carbondale: Southern Illinois UP, 2016.

Brown, Mary Borromeo. *History of the Sisters of Providence of Saint Mary-of-the-Woods*. New York: Benziger Brothers, 1949.

Brynum, Caroline Walker. "Foreword." In *Crown and Veil: Female Monasteries from the Fifth to Fifteenth Centuries*, edited by Jeffrey F. Hamburger and Susan Manti, xiii–xviii. New York: Columbia UP, 2008.

Carlyle, Thomas. *On Heroes, Hero-Worship, and the Heroic in History.* Accessed August 9, 2020. https://www.gutenberg.org/files/1091/1091-h/1091-h.htm.

Dray, Emmanuel. *Spring and Harvest (Die Abtei St. Walburg (1035–1935): 900 Jahre in Wort und Bild).* Translated by Gonzago Engelhart. St. Meinrad, IN: The Grail, 1952.

Eckenstein, Lina. *Woman under Monasticism: Chapters on Saint-Lore and Convent Life Between A.D. 500 and A.D. 1500.* Cambridge: Cambridge UP, 1896.

Foucault. Michel. *Fearless Speech.* Los Angeles, CA: Semiotext(e), 2001.

Frey, Renea Carol. "Speaking Truth to Power: Recovering a Rhetorical Theory of Parrhesia." PhD Diss., Miami University, 2015.

Girgen, M. Incarnata. *Behind the Beginnings: Benedictine Women in America.* St. Joseph, MN: Saint Benedict's Convent, 1981.

Guerin, Theodore. *Journals and Letters of Mother Theodore Guerin.* Edited by Mary Theodosia Mug. St. Mary-of-the-Woods, IN: Sisters of Providence, 1942.

Hauser, Gerard. *Prisoners of Conscience: Moral Vernaculars of Political Agency.* Columbia, SC: U of South Carolina P, 2012.

Henderson, Gae Lyn. "The 'Parrhesiastic Game': Textual Self-Justification in Spiritual Narratives of Early Modern Women." *Rhetoric Society Quarterly* 37, no. 4 (September 2007): 423–451. https://doi.org/10.1080/02773940601078072.

Hollermann, Ephrem. *The Reshaping of a Tradition: American Benedictine Women 1852–1881.* St. Joseph, MN: *Sisters* of the Order of Saint Benedict, 1994.

Lierheimer, Linda. "Female Eloquence and Maternal Ministry: The Apostolate of Ursuline Nuns in Seventeenth-Century France." PhD Diss., Princeton University, 1994,

McNamara, Jo Ann Kay. *Sisters in Arms: Catholic Nuns through Two Millennia.* Cambridge: Harvard UP, 1996.

Oetgen, Jerome. "Boniface Wimmer and the American Benedictines: 1856–1866." *American Benedictine Review* 23, no. 3 (1972): 283–313.

Okabe, Roichi. "Cultural Assumptions of East and West: Japan and the United States." In *The Rhetoric of Western Thought*, 4th edition, edited by J.L. Golden, G.F. Berquist, and W.E. Coleman, 546–565. Dubuque, IA: Kendall/Hunt, 1989.

Rohan, Liz. "Stitching and Writing a Life." In *Beyond the Archives: Research as Lived Process*, edited by Gesa E. Kirsch and Liz Rohan, 147–153. Carbondale: Southern Illinois UP, 2008.

Ryan, Kathleen J., Nancy Meyers, and Rebecca Jones. *Rethinking Ethos: A Feminist Ecological Approach to Rhetoric.* Carbondale: Southern Illinois UP, 2016.

Walzer, Arthur. "*Parrēsia,* Foucault, and the Classical Rhetorical Tradition." *Rhetoric Society Quarterly* 43, no. 1 (January 2013): 1–21. https://doi.org/10.1080/02773945.2012.740130.

White, Joseph M. *Worthy of the Gospel of Christ. A History of the Catholic Diocese of Fort Wayne-South Bend*. Fort Wayne, IN: Diocese of Fort Wayne-South Bend, 2007.

Wimmer, Boniface. Letter to Obercamp, 23 November 1857, St. Benedict's Convent Archives, St. Joseph, MN.

Wright, Elizabethada. "'The Caprices of an Undisciplined Fancy': Using Blame to Negotiate the 'betweens' of Ethos via the Epideictic." *Rhetoric Review* 38, no. 3 (July 2019): 271–284. https://doi.org/10.1080/07350198.2019.1618157.

———. "'God Sees Me': Surveillance and Oratorical Training at St. Mary's-of-the-Woods in Indiana." In *Rhetoric, History, and Women's Oratorical Education: American Women Learn to Speak*, edited by David Gold and Catherine Hobbs, 116–133. New York: Routledge, 2013.

Chapter 2

Remembering Mother McAuley

Epideictic Rhetoric, Ethos, and Memory

Amy Ferdinandt Stolley

In 1827, Catherine McAuley (1778–1841) founded the Mercy Institute in Dublin, Ireland, with the inheritance from a Protestant benefactor. A single, Catholic woman, McAuley aimed to establish a religious organization to educate and provide lodging for poor young women and girls. In 1831, this organization was recognized by the Dublin archdiocese and the Vatican as the Catholic Order of the Sisters of Mercy.

The Sisters of Mercy welcomed women of good character who wished to pursue religious life while living in a convent, especially women whose lack of family wealth kept them from joining more established orders of religious women.[1] In the fourteen years between McAuley's founding of the first institute and her unexpected death in 1841, she and the Sisters of Mercy established fourteen institutes in cities around Ireland and England.

In the decades immediately following McAuley's death, the Sisters of Mercy continued to expand, following Irish immigrants to America and Australia where they established schools and hospitals to support the Irish diaspora. Today, the Sisters of Mercy continue to live and serve in over forty countries. The Sisters of Mercy of the Americas—those living and working in the Western Hemisphere—shape their work by what they call their "critical concerns," which prioritize five areas of social need: immigration, earth, nonviolence, women, and racism. The Sisters make these principles visible through prayer, communal life as a religious organization, education, advocacy with leaders, and corporate engagement. Simply put, the Sisters of Mercy advocate for those in need by engaging in public discourse using their religious and spiritual beliefs as a foundation for their arguments.

The Sisters of Mercy have become particularly vocal and visible in the new age of protest and demonstrations that has emerged since 2016. A few examples: On the day that Donald Trump was inaugurated President of the

United States, the Sisters joined other women religious in 100 days of prayer for the first 100 days of his presidency. The Sisters used social media to publish these prayers, which were clearly linked to their critical concerns but also responsive to the early Trump agenda. For example, on January 23, 2016, the Sisters tweeted, "This morning we pray for the political commitment to address the root causes of migration."[2] Four days later, the Trump administration signed the so-called Muslim ban, an executive order prohibiting the travel of refugees from the Middle East and northern Africa. Since then, the Sisters have organized followers to participate in marches and advocacy around issues aligned with their critical concerns, including Deferred Action for Childhood Arrivals and the Dream Act,[3] the March for Our Lives to protest gun violence,[4] and the Black Lives Matter movement after the killings of George Floyd, Ahmaud Arbery, and Breonna Taylor in 2020.[5]

In what could be seen by some as a surprising decision, the Sisters also joined in the Women's March in 2017 and 2018, stating in a press release that they were motivated "to act in solidarity with women seeking fullness of life and equality."[6] Many observers, both Catholic and non-Catholic, did not expect to see women religious at the Women's March, which had its roots in feminist activist communities. Catholicism, with its long history of marginalizing women and opposing reproductive freedom, does not always seem to align neatly with issues related to women's equality or feminist platforms, and those positioned within the church's hierarchy, including orders of religious women, are expected to maintain the church teachings on such issues.

Yet, for the Sisters of Mercy, actively participating in these types of public activism is a meaningful way for them to embody and promote the Order's critical concerns and Catherine McAuley's memory, which remain a guiding force for the Order. Although their activism may contradict others' expectations or assumptions of religious women, to the Sisters there seems to be no other choice than to advocate publicly for those suffering and in need. After the extrajudicial killing of George Floyd in May 2020, the Sisters declared, "We pray unceasingly, and we stand . . . in solidarity."[7] The Sisters do not pray in isolation; they pray in public and in community with others in an effort to "make Mercy real," a phrase they use often to articulate their desire to stand out publicly and make the values that undergird their faith tangible and visible to and for others.

So how do we get from habit-wearing Sisters of Mercy who taught and nursed women and children in nineteenth-century Ireland to the activist Sisters of Mercy today? To understand this evolution, we can look to how memories of Catherine McAuley coalesced shortly after her death through the epideictic writings of other women in the Order. Those writings became the founding documents of the McAuley archive and the primary sources for the first biographies of McAuley that would be written and circulated.

By describing three phases in McAuley's public memory—communicative, circulating, and cultural—we can see how the Sisters' memory of McAuley's life ultimately created a living, breathing Mercy ethos that could adapt and spread across time and space. More importantly, because this ethos was rooted in the Sisters' experience with McAuley in their religious community, rather than filtered through or for outside (male) influence, the Mercy ethos gives the members of the Order space and authority to function outside of the narrow space often reserved for women religious, empowering them to engage in contemporary social debates central to their community's critical concerns.

TRACING THE MERCY ETHOS THROUGH CATHERINE MCAULEY'S MEMORY

Phase One: Communicating Memory through Epideictic

After McAuley's unexpected death from tuberculosis in 1841 at the Institute in Dublin, the Sisters of Mercy living there began the process of preserving McAuley's memory. They immediately started collecting and storing her personal effects, including all of her religious writing and the letters she had received from church officials, family members, and other women in the Order. Simultaneously, the Sisters at institutes around Ireland and England began sharing recollections of McAuley over evening tea, building an oral history of what they knew of McAuley's early life, her work in the early days of the Order, and the knowledge she shared with young women who had joined the Mercy novitiate.

Those who knew McAuley best began writing down their memories of her, storing them in the records (referred to as the Annals) of the institutes at which the writers were stationed. By sharing their recollections of McAuley in these Annals, the Sisters recounted important moments in McAuley's—and the Order's—life, which not only served as an early biography of McAuley but also highlighted the more exemplary qualities they found in their mother superior. For example, Sister Mary Ann Doyle recalled that McAuley's call to form an institute to support women and girls consumed her nightly dreams: "Night after night she would see herself in some very large place where a number of young women were employed as laundresses or at plain-work, while she herself would be surrounded by a crowd of ragged children which she was washing and dressing very busily."[8] Sister Mary Clare Moore reflected on McAuley's character: "She was most careful to correct her faults, and to practice a genuine humility and patient forbearance; but charity was her characteristic virtue. She loved all, and sought to do good to all."[9]

In addition to the institutes' Annals, which stayed fixed in their location at each institute, the Sisters continued writing to one another, sharing their experiences from the communities where Orders had been established while reflecting on their memories of McAuley. These letters stand as examples of epideictic that was not delivered orally as it is traditionally understood, but through correspondence, illustrating Elizabethada A. Wright's claim that women use epideictic conveyed through letters to "[negotiate] values among people who literally dwell in different places."[10] Collectively, the Sisters' recorded memories and letters became the core elements of the original McAuley archive, but they were scattered across Ireland and England. They did not circulate beyond their fixed locations.

Unsurprisingly, the memories of McAuley recorded immediately following her death reflect the interests, experiences, and priorities of the writers; as Mary C. Sullivan notes, "Each narrator gives us the only Catherine she can give us: her version of her, as it were: the Catherine she perceived, treasured, and remembered."[11] Read separately, the recorded memories of McAuley seem similar to the gospels. Each writer wrote from her own perspective and in her own style, emphasizing the ideas most central to her understanding of who McAuley was. Read together, however, the memories of McAuley begin to coalesce around central characteristics the Sisters agreed were key to understanding McAuley: her unwavering devotion to women and children's education and safety; her steadfast faith in God's salvation; her humility, particularly when dealing with the church's patriarchy; and her desire to adapt herself (and by extension, the Order) to the communities she found herself in.

The first phase of McAuley's archive reflects Aristotle's classical understanding of epideictic, a genre that "achieves its rhetorical force through ethos, amplification, and narrative."[12] The stories the Sisters told of McAuley, read alongside the writings and correspondence of McAuley herself, served to highlight and amplify McAuley's character and ethos, while also strengthening the ethos of those who knew her well enough to contribute to the institutes' Annals. However, the years immediately following McAuley's unexpected death also precipitated the need for the Sisters of Mercy to articulate a shared understanding of their own community. As Celeste Michelle Condit explains, change within a community (such as a leader's death) creates the occasion for epideictic, and speakers from the community "will be called forth . . . to help discover what the event means to the community, and what the community will come to be in the face of the new event."[13] McAuley's death required the Sisters to decide who they would be without their foundress; the collection of memories that made up the original McAuley archive suggests that they decided to be a community driven by memory of her and her ethos of steadfast faith, self-sacrificing service, and humility.

In this stage of the Sisters of Mercy's collective memory of McAuley, the archive functioned as communicative memory, which Jan Assmann and John Czaplicka describe as a period when the memories of those who lived through events circulate and compete with each other through "everyday communication"[14] within "groups who conceive their unity and peculiarity through a common image of their past."[15] It seems there was little competition, however. Although there were some discrepancies in facts, the Sisters' narratives were remarkably consistent in the portrait of McAuley they created. Maurice Halbwachs explains that this kind of consistency is due, in part, to the fact that "individual memory is nevertheless a part or an aspect of group memory, since each impression and each fact, even if it apparently concerns a particular person exclusively, leaves a lasting memory only to the extent that . . . it is connected with the thoughts that come to us from the social milieu."[16] The Sisters experienced McAuley primarily through her leadership of the Order, so the principles and values the women shared in their community were woven into their memories of her and attached to McAuley herself. Through death, McAuley became the embodiment of the Mercy ethos, and the surviving Sisters dedicated themselves to preserving McAuley's memory by preserving and attaching her ethos to the ethos of the Order.

Phase Two: Circulating Memory

Within a few years of McAuley's death, the Sisters decided that their memories of McAuley needed to be collected in a more permanent, accessible form. In the mid-to-late 1800s, four manuscripts were published by women in the Order. The first was *Retreat Instructions*, published in 1844, which was a compilation of the novices' notes and memories from their time spent preparing to join the Order. *Retreat Instructions* was compiled and published specifically to circulate the ideas and spirit of McAuley to all women who were joining the Order after McAuley's death, which supports Eviatar Zerubavel's claim that "familiarizing new members with its past is an important part of a community's effort to incorporate them."[17] As Sister Mary Teresa Purcell writes in the original preface to *Retreat Instructions*, "We should study these unpretending instructions of our Mother Foundress [McAuley] to imbibe her humble, simple, hidden spirit and to imitate her virtues so that we may be Sisters of Mercy in deed and in heart."[18] The Sisters who recorded these instructions did so to instill McAuley's ethos into each member's understanding of herself and her role in their religious community, elevating McAuley to a model all other women in the Order should emulate. In Purcell's words, the instructions recorded in this volume "will tell us what we ought to be and will let us see whether we honestly follow her counsel. Perhaps they will show us how far we are from what our Mother Foundress wishes us to be."[19]

In addition to recording and circulating memories of McAuley within the Order, others sought to raise her profile beyond the confines of their religious community. In the 1860s, two biographies of McAuley were published, and they both used oral histories and written recollections from the institutes' Annals as their primary source material. Harnett's *Life of Mother Catherine McAuley* was published in 1864, and Carroll's *Life of Catherine McAuley* was published in 1866. In the 1880s, Carroll continued her work in chronicling Catherine's life by publishing selections from the Annals of the Irish, English, and American institutes in separate volumes, which included the Sisters' original written recollections of McAuley. These books were reprinted and further circulated in the mid-twentieth century, and they remained the primary sources of information about McAuley and the early days of the Order until the late twentieth century.

The biographies and collections published during this period served to make McAuley's memory more accessible to those outside the Order who otherwise might not have had access to this information. Moreover, through these circulating texts, memories of McAuley moved from communicative to cultural, collective memory; those who knew McAuley had long since died, and memories of McAuley were mediated through published media rather than firsthand experience. What is important to note, however, is that the primary source material for these texts was the original archive created upon McAuley's death, which consisted primarily of the Sisters' epideictic, written recollections of her. Thus, the epideictic elevating both McAuley's character and her ethos became solidified as *the* story of Catherine McAuley because they could circulate in ways the primary documents could not.

Through sharing and circulating texts that praised McAuley's character and ethos, the writers elevated the Order as well. McAuley was the author of the founding document of the Order, the Sisters of Mercy Rules and Constitution, which became another important lens through which McAuley was remembered. Because she wrote the foundational principles of the Order, readers tied the mission and values of the community to McAuley herself. "Mercy" and McAuley became inseparable and mobile symbols, following the Order as the Sisters moved around the world, which echoes Jacqueline Jones Royster and Gesa E. Kirsch's argument that social circulation creates "networks [that] are often civic in nature, rhetorical in function, and both activist and community-building in outcome, such that the circles of ideas created within such discourses have the capacity to compound effects across time and space."[20] In the Mercy community, epideictic memories of McAuley serve two important purposes: they link memories of McAuley to central tenets of the Order, and they provide a foundation from which religious memory can adapt and change.

Phase Three: Cultural Memory

From the mid-twentieth century to the early twenty-first century, members of the Order of the Sisters of Mercy continued to collect and publish biographical materials related to Catherine McAuley. In 1957, Mary Bertrand Degnan published *Mercy unto Thousands*, another biography. Others paid particular attention to McAuley's letters: Mary Ignatia Neumann published *The Letters of Catherine McAuley, 1827–1841* in 1969, and Mary Angela Bolster published *The Correspondence of Catherine McAuley, 1827–1841* in 1989, each including different letters from the McAuley archive. However, it is the historical research of Mary C. Sullivan, herself a member of the Order, that has offered the most comprehensive picture of Catherine McAuley, the Order itself, and the interrelated ethos of both. She accomplished this through her exhaustive and meticulous archival research, which resulted in a curated, synthesized, published, and accessible collection of materials.

Sullivan's work to build a contemporary biography of McAuley began with a critical edition of some of the original materials of the Mercy/McAuley archive (*Catherine McAuley and the Tradition of Mercy*, 1995), followed almost a decade later by a complete compilation of McAuley's archived correspondence (*The Correspondence of Catherine McAuley: 1818–1841*, 2004). In 2012, Sullivan published the most recent biography of McAuley, *The Path of Mercy: The Life of Catherine McAuley.* Relying on the archival research she had already completed, as well as the biographies written by her predecessors, Sullivan's biography offers a comprehensive narrative of McAuley's life. In the preface to this work, Sullivan makes clear that, although her biography of McAuley differs from those that came before, she also had the benefit of "a wealth of new published research in women's history, Irish history, and religious history [that] has now opened up in great detail the several contexts within which this woman lived and acted."[21] Sullivan aimed specifically to write a history of McAuley and the early days of the Order that was rooted in Ireland's unique, challenging historical context.

Through all of these works, Sullivan maintains and expands on the Mercy ethos established by the early McAuley archive, citing examples of how McAuley embodied the principles of humility, charity, and service from the primary sources of the women who knew McAuley personally. Although she uses the Sisters' epideictic memories as source material, Sullivan positions her work as historical in nature, a biography without agenda or purpose beyond writing an accurate history. She claims, "In this biography, I have tried to question assumptions and received information; to acknowledge areas where the data are not clear or available, and may never be; to avoid deliberately hagiographical style; and to rely, in general, in primary sources."[22] Based on this description of her methodology, it seems Sullivan is deliberately eschewing the epideictic for the rational, researched, and footnoted history she aimed to write. Yet she acknowledges that her biography "draws on a wide cast of characters . . . [McAuley's] immediate and extended family, her foster parents, her first companions, priests and bishops with whom she worked, women who helped or supported her, directly or indirectly."[23] While Sullivan aims to frame her biography as a factual depiction of McAuley's life, it is one that is rooted in the epideictic narratives recorded and stored in the institutes' archives in the years immediately following McAuley's death.

By no means do I wish to discredit Sullivan's work; on the contrary, the depth and scope of her historical research has made McAuley's and the Sisters' stories accessible to countless researchers interested in the history of Ireland's religious women. What remains clear, though, despite Sullivan's claims to the contrary, is that a history written with epideictic rhetoric as its "factual" source material will not be able to escape the narrative created by those original texts. We know that all history is rhetorical, told with a unique point of view and with an agenda, but it is difficult to break the molds established by the early narratives, rooted in memory and love, of those who knew McAuley best.

In this regard, Sullivan's work represents what Assmann and Czaplicka call the cultural stage in collective memory, a period when all those who knew the subject or lived through an experience have died and all that remains are stories told of the past. In this phase, collective memory positions the archive as a site of "working memory" that, as Ann Rigney explains, is "performed by individuals and groups as they recollect the past selectively through . . . media and become involved in various forms of memorial activity."[24] Thus, we can understand Sullivan's work as an act of remembering McAuley for her readers. A significant feature of the memorial activity that Rigney as well as Assmann and Czaplicka describe is that it has both a deliberate, stated purpose and a secondary, perhaps unintentional, outcome. Sullivan intended her work to create a historical record for those interested in learning about and researching McAuley and the early days of the Order, which she certainly accomplished. Yet, whether it was intended or not, Sullivan also reified the original epideictic memories shared by the women who knew and worked alongside Catherine McAuley.

THEORIZING PHASES OF MEMORY AND THE DEVELOPMENT OF THE MERCY ETHOS

Kathleen J. Ryan, Nancy Meyers, and Rebecca Jones maintain that ethos, when understood as qualities or characteristics that are valued by a community, can often be limiting to women who are "not recognized as worthy of public participation" in the larger culture.[25] Certainly in McAuley's time, and arguably still today, women religious are often expected to remain cloistered and remote, visible only through their acts of service in the classroom or hospital, so that whatever ethos they do have is rooted in their silence in and distance from public life. Although such historical sidelining of religious women has had negative effects on both women and communities for centuries, communities of religious women can function separately (to some degree) from the pressures of patriarchal systems that govern lay women. To be clear, the Sisters of Mercy would not exist without the permission and support of the church patriarchy. There are countless stories within the Order's history that illustrate the challenges the Sisters faced in dealing with men within the church who sought to limit or diminish their work and value.[26] I would argue that because the Order of the Sisters of Mercy was founded, organized, built, and developed by and for women, the development of their community's ethos had more room to grow, independent of some of the restrictions placed on other groups of women. Rather than relying on men or priests to tell the story of the Order, the women of the Order told their own story, and they chose to build that story around their communal memory of Catherine McAuley.

Fundamentally, the Mercy story is driven by the narratives written about McAuley immediately after her death that elevate her humility, charity, and self-sacrifice as her most defining characteristics and those most worthy of emulation by the surviving women of the Order. In this sense, these recorded memories of McAuley highlight her use of the rhetorical strategy Sean Barnette identifies as *kenosis*, which is achieved by "divesting oneself of any essential concept of self or preconstructed ethos, enabling oneself to enter more fully and responsively in relationship to others and with the material world."[27] Though Barnette explores the concept of *kenosis* in relation to hospitality modeled by Dorothy Day almost 100 years after McAuley's death, a similar self-emptying service was ascribed to McAuley through her Sisters' written reflections. For the Sisters of Mercy, it was McAuley's ability to diminish herself in service to others that defined who she was. By erasing a "preconstructed ethos," McAuley actually created a very clearly defined ethos centered on service and humility that would shape the Order for generations to come. In this sense, the Mercy ethos acknowledged what Ryan et al. identify as women rhetors' "subordinate status," but they managed to do so in a way that "[crafted] a viable ethos for participation in a dominant public."[28]

Sisters of Mercy are granted authority to speak and engage in public because they diminish their own preconstructed sense of self or individual ethos by adopting the communal Mercy ethos. The Sisters seem to believe that there is a transitive relationship between McAuley and themselves; McAuley's ethos has become their own. Their shared Mercy ethos drives the work of the Sisters of Mercy in two specific ways. First, the Sisters aim to elevate McAuley in the eyes of the public. Telling stories about McAuley and preserving her ethos has become central to the mission of the Order since her death; the sheer number of published works written by members of the Order (described above) demonstrates how important these stories are to the Order's sense of itself, and how much they want these stories to circulate. Second, the Order has worked to exalt McAuley in the eyes of the Catholic Church. In 2007, the Sisters of Mercy began working in earnest to make the case for McAuley's canonization, which would anoint her as a saint to whom Catholics might pray.[29] Although their primary motivation for seeking McAuley's canonization is their sincere belief in her holiness, it could be argued that the Sisters intuitively understand that their community's ethos and authority—not to mention their freedom to continue the public work of the Order—would be strengthened by McAuley's canonization and widespread public knowledge of the McAuley/Mercy ethos.

By elevating McAuley and, by extension, the Mercy ethos she inspired, the contemporary Sisters of Mercy have created an environment that allows them to enact their mission despite traditional understandings of women religious. There is a sort of symbiotic relationship that the Sisters preserve by circulating the memory of McAuley: by praising McAuley through epideictic, they also create space for and highlight all that flows from her memory, including her ethos, the Sisters' critical concerns, and their public work in support of those critical concerns. The Sisters' often justify their work within McAuley's memory by justifying their actions to themselves and others with the statement, "If Catherine were alive today, she would do the same as we."[30] Such interconnectedness between McAuley and the Sisters grants them authority to do work in McAuley's name, "making mercy real" through public protest and activism.

In that sense, the Sisters of Mercy have found a way to use the Mercy ethos to speak publicly in ways that other women, and perhaps even other orders of religious women, cannot. The Mercy/McAuley archive was constructed and evolved solely through the memories and interpretation of the women in the Order without outside influence from priests or community members. And because the ethos that emerged from those original epideictic acts of remembering became central to the Sisters' sense of themselves and their mission, they managed to grant themselves some level of self-determination and autonomy. They did so by using the memory of McAuley to justify their public, faithful actions and reinterpret their mission in the context of contemporary social issues. We know that ethos, like memory, "shifts and changes over time, across texts, and around competing spaces," so we cannot assume that the Mercy ethos or the work in which the Sisters engage will remain fixed and unchanged.[31] Instead, I would maintain that within their own community, the Sisters are enacting Assmann and Czaplicka's definition of "the concretion of identity," which occurs in the cultural stage of memory.[32] At this stage, members of a community say, "This is who we are," a statement of identity informed by their shared understanding of their history. But the Sisters' public work also reflects Rigney's modeling stage in memory's circulation: repeating, transforming, and appropriating what is remembered and how we remember in new situations.[33] As Ilon Lauer remarks, "epideictic rhetoric's temporal dynamism enables communities to anchor moral thought in the ever shifting present."[34] The Sisters root their work in the memory of McAuley, and, as such, they grant themselves the authority to respond in ways that are sensitive to both their beliefs and to the specific rhetorical situations in which they find themselves, adapting and changing over time.

As the number of women in the Order dwindles, the Sisters of Mercy believe it is incumbent on them to make Mercy meaningful to contemporary women and men. They do so by remembering and recontextualizing McAuley through the epideictic—both historical and contemporary—which has been made possible through the rich McAuley archive and the communal ethos it preserves. McAuley was only alive for the first fourteen years of the Order's 193-year history, but the force of her memory and the relevance of her mission have given shape and momentum to the continued circulation and spread of her ideals today.

NOTES

1. Mary C. Sullivan, *The Correspondence of Catherine McAuley: 1812–1841* (Baltimore: Four Courts Press, 2004), 41.
2. Sisters of Mercy (@sistersofmercy), "This Monday morning we pray for the political commitment to address the root causes of migration," Facebook photo, January 23, 2017, https://www.facebook.com/MercySisters/photos/a.10150217315057517/10154309602532517.
3. "Sisters of Mercy Condemn Trump Administration's Immoral and Unjust Ending of DACA for Young Immigrants," Sisters of Mercy, posted September 5, 2017, https://www.sistersofmercy.org/about-us/news-and-events/sisters-of-mercy-condemn-trump-administrations-immoral-and-unjust-ending-of-daca-for-young-immigrants/.
4. "Sisters of Mercy Mid-Atlantic Messages," Mid-Atlantic Community of the Sisters of Mercy, posted March 29, 2018, http://www.mercymidatlantic.org/Messages/Messages03292018.html.
5. "Mercy Responds to the Killings of George Floyd, Ahmaud Arbery, and Breonna Taylor," Sisters of Mercy, posted on May 29, 2020, https://www.sistersofmercy.org/about-us/news-and-events/mercy-responds-to-the-killings-of-george-floyd-ahmaud-arbery-breonna-taylor/.
6. "Mercy Participating in Women's March in Washington, DC," Sisters of Mercy, posted January 16, 2017, https://www.sistersofmercy.org/about-us/news-and-events/mercy-participating-in-womens-march-in-washington-dc/.

7. "Mercy Responds."

8. Mary Ann Doyle, "The Derry Large Manuscript: Notes on the Life of Mother Catherine McAuley by One of the First Sisters of Mercy," in *Catherine McAuley and the Tradition of Mercy*, ed. Mary C. Sullivan (South Bend: University of Notre Dame Press, 1995), 45.

9. Mary Clare Moore, "Excerpts from the from The Annals of the Convent of Our Lady of Mercy, Bermondsey," in *Catherine McAuley and the Tradition of Mercy*, ed. Mary C. Sullivan (South Bend: University of Notre Dame Press, 1995), 101.

10. Elizabethada A. Wright, "'The Caprices of an Undisciplined Fancy': Using Blame to Negotiate the 'betweens' of *Ethos* via the Epideictic," *Rhetoric Review* 38, no. 1 (2019): 274.

11. Mary C. Sullivan, *Catherine McAuley and the Tradition of Mercy* (South Bend: University of Notre Dame Press, 1995), 30.

12. Ilon Lauer, "Epideictic Rhetoric," *Communication Research Trends* 34, no. 2 (2015): 5.

13. Celeste Michelle Condit, "The Functions of Epideictic: The Boston Massacre Orations as Exemplar," *Communication Quarterly* 33, no. 4 (Fall 1985): 289.

14. Jan Assmann and John Czaplicka, "Collective Memory and Cultural Identity," *New German Critique* 65 (Spring–Summer 1995): 126, https://doi.org/10.2307/488538

15. Assmann and Czaplicka, "Collective Memory," 127.

16. Maurice Halbwachs, *On Collective Memory*, trans. and ed. Lewis A. Coser (Chicago: University of Chicago Press, 1992), 53.

17. Eviatar Zerubavel, "Social Memories: Steps towards a Sociology of the Past," in *The Collective Memory Reader*, eds. Jeffrey K. Olick, Vered Vinitzky-Seroussi, and Daniel Levy (Oxford: Oxford University Press, 2011), 224.

18. Mary Teresa Purcell, *Retreat Instructions of Mother Mary Catherine McAuley* (Westminster: The Newman Press, 1952), 17.

19. Purcell, *Retreat Instructions*, 23.

20. Jacqueline Jones Royster and Gesa E. Kirsch, *Feminist Rhetorical Practices: New Horizons for Rhetoric, Composition, and Literacy Studies* (Carbondale: Southern Illinois UP, 2012), 101.

21. Mary C. Sullivan, *The Path of Mercy: The Life of Catherine McAuley* (Baltimore: Four Courts Press, 2012), ix.

22. Sullivan, *Path*, xi.

23. Sullivan, *Path*, 14.

24. Ann Rigney, "Plenitude, Scarcity and the Circulation of Cultural Memory," *Journal of European Studies* 35, no. 1 (2005): 17, *Academic OneFile*.

25. Kathleen J. Ryan, Nancy Myers, and Rebecca Jones, "Introduction: Identifying Feminist Ecological Ethē," in *Rethinking Ethos: A Feminist Ecological Approach to Rhetoric*, eds. Kathleen J. Ryan, Nancy Myers, and Rebecca Jones (Carbondale: Southern Illinois UP, 2016), 7.

26. See Sullivan, *Catherine*.

27. Barnette, Sean, "Hospitality as Kenosis: Dorothy Day's Voluntary Poverty," in *Rethinking Ethos: A Feminist Ecological Approach to Rhetoric*, eds. Kathleen J. Ryan, Nancy Myers, and Rebecca Jones (Carbondale: Southern Illinois UP, 2016), 133.

28. Ryan, et al., "Introduction," 4.

29. "Canonisation Cause," Mercy International Association, updated 2021, https://www.mercyworld.org/catherine/canonisation-cause/canonisation-cause/.

30. Caitlin Conneelly, "Challenges from Our Tradition," Mercy International Association, posted March 20, 2012, https://web.archive.org/web/20120523083410/http://www.mercyworld.org/spirituality/view-reflection.cfm?uuid=2F75D50C-E09B-986F-96894BA92F3EC711.

31. Nedra Reynolds, "Ethos as Location: New Sites for Understanding Discursive Authority," *Rhetoric Review* 11, no. 2 (Spring 1993): 326, http://www.jstor.org/stable/465805.

32. Assmann and Czaplicka, "Collective Memory and Cultural Identity," 130.

33. Rigney, "Plenitude," 21–23.

34. Lauer, "Epideictic Rhetoric," 12.

BIBLIOGRAPHY

Assmann, Jan, and John Czaplicka. "Collective Memory and Cultural Identity." *New German Critique* 65 (Spring–Summer 1995): 125–133. https://doi.org/10.2307/488538.

Barnette, Sean. "Hospitality as Kenosis: Dorothy Day's Voluntary Poverty." In *Rethinking Ethos: A Feminist Ecological Approach to Rhetoric*, edited by Kathleen J. Ryan, Nancy Myers, and Rebecca Jones, 132–149. Carbondale: Southern Illinois UP, 2016.

"Canonisation Cause." Mercy International Association. Updated 2021. https://www.mercyworld.org/catherine/canonisation-cause/canonisation-cause/.

Condit, Celeste Michelle. "The Functions of Epideictic: The Boston Massacre Orations as Exemplar." *Communication Quarterly* 33, no. 4 (Fall 1985): 284–299. https://doi.org/10.1080/01463378509369608.

Conneelly, Caitlin. "Challenges from Our Tradition." Mercy International Association, posted March 20, 2012. https://web.archive.org/web/20120523083410/http://www.mercyworld.org/spirituality/view-reflection.cfm?uuid=2F75D50C-E09B-986F-96894BA92F3EC711.

Doyle, Mary Ann. "The Derry Large Manuscript: Notes on the Life of Mother Catherine McAuley by One of the First Sisters of Mercy." In *Catherine McAuley and the Tradition of Mercy*, edited by Mary C. Sullivan, 45–64. South Bend: University of Notre Dame Press, 1995.

Halbwachs, Maurice. *On Collective Memory*. Translated and edited by Lewis A. Coser. Chicago: University of Chicago Press, 1992.

Lauer, Ilon. "Epideictic Rhetoric." *Communication Research Trends* 34, no. 2 (2015): 4–18.

"Mercy Participating in Women's March in Washington, DC." Sisters of Mercy. Posted January 16, 2017. https://www.sistersofmercy.org/about-us/news-and-events/mercy-participating-in-womens-march-in-washington-dc/.

"Mercy Responds to the Killings of George Floyd, Ahmaud Arbery, and Breonna Taylor." Sisters of Mercy. Posted May 29, 2020. https://www.sistersofmercy.org/about-us/news-and-events/mercy-responds-to-the-killings-of-george-floyd-ahmaud-arbery-breonna-taylor/.

Moore, Mary Clare. "Excerpts from The Annals of the Convent of Our Lady of Mercy, Bermondsey." In *Catherine McAuley and the Tradition of Mercy*, edited by Mary C. Sullivan, 99–129. South Bend: University of Notre Dame Press, 1995.

Purcell, Mary Teresa. *Retreat Instructions of Mother Mary Catherine McAuley*. Westminster: The Newman Press, 1952.

Reynolds, Nedra. "Ethos as Location: New Sites for Understanding Discursive Authority." *Rhetoric Review* 11, no. 2 (Spring 1993): 325–338. http://www.jstor.org/stable/465805.

Rigney, Ann. "Plenitude, Scarcity and the Circulation of Cultural Memory." *Journal of European Studies* 35, no. 1 (2005): 11–28. *Academic OneFile*.

Royster, Jacqueline Jones, and Gesa E. Kirsch. *Feminist Rhetorical Practices: New Horizons for Rhetoric, Composition, and Literacy Studies*. Carbondale: Southern Illinois University Press, 2012.

Ryan, Kathleen J., Nancy Myers, and Rebecca Jones. "Introduction: Identifying Feminist Ecological Ethē." In *Rethinking Ethos: A Feminist Ecological Approach to Rhetoric*, edited by Kathleen J. Ryan, Nancy Myers, and Rebecca Jones, 1–22. Carbondale: Southern Illinois UP, 2016.

Sisters of Mercy (@sistersofmercy). "This Monday Morning We Pray for the Political Commitment to Address the Root Causes of Migration." Facebook photo. January 23, 2017. https://www.facebook.com/MercySisters/photos/a.10150217315057517/10154309602532517.

"Sisters of Mercy Condemn Trump Administration's Immoral and Unjust Ending of DACA for Young Immigrants." Sisters of Mercy. Posted September 5, 2017. https://www.sistersofmercy.org/about-us/news-and-events/sisters-of-mercy-condemn-trump-administrations-immoral-and-unjust-ending-of-daca-for-young-immigrants/.

"Sisters of Mercy Mid-Atlantic Messages." *Mid-Atlantic Community of the Sisters of Mercy*. Posted March 29, 2018. http://www.mercymidatlantic.org/Messages/Messages03292018.html.

Sullivan, Mary C. *Catherine McAuley and the Tradition of Mercy*. South Bend: University of Notre Dame Press, 1995.

Sullivan, Mary C., ed. *The Correspondence of Catherine McAuley: 1818–1841*. Baltimore: Four Courts Press, 2004.

Sullivan, Mary C. *The Path of Mercy: The Life of Catherine McAuley*. Baltimore: Four Courts Press, 2012.

Wright, Elizabethada A. "'The Caprices of an Undisciplined Fancy': Using Blame to Negotiate the 'betweens' of *Ethos* via the Epideictic." *Rhetoric Review* 38, no. 3 (2019): 271–284.

Zerubavel, Eviatar. "Social Memories: Steps towards a Sociology of the Past." In *The Collective Memory Reader*, edited by Jeffrey K. Olick, Vered Vinitzky-Seroussi, and Daniel Levy, 221–224. Oxford: Oxford University Press, 2011.

Chapter 3

The Habits and Dwelling Places of Sisters of Color

The New Orleans' Soeurs de Sainte-Famille's Reconstruction of Ethos

Elizabethada A. Wright and
Christiana Ares-Christian

In their introduction to their edited collection on a feminist rhetorical approach to rethinking ethos, Kathleen J. Ryan, Nancy Myers, and Rebecca Jones cite the efforts of Terry Tempest Williams to change the status quo via her activism and writing, as they note that many women, like Williams, "find that there is no comfortable ethos to employ if they want to shift the dominant discourse on a particular topic."[1] For women who have established Catholic religious orders, such a problem might seem outside their scope of need or experience. After all, their efforts to establish communities of religious sisters would seem to affirm the dominant discourse of Catholicism. However, as numerous founding narratives of these orders attest, such affirmation is not always the case. As in the nineteenth-century American Sisters of Providence's narratives cited in chapter 1, many orders attempted to shift Catholic misogynistic perspectives to gain legitimacy.

Another nineteenth-century order that had to shift dominant discourses with their attempts to found and establish themselves was the New Orleans' Soeurs de Sainte-Famille (SSF), that is, Sisters of the Holy Family. One of the first orders of women of color in the United States, SSF not only had to combat misogyny but also had to contend with racist perspectives that attempted to limit their religious ambitions. As Sister Mary Bernard Deggs's late nineteenth-century history of SSF illustrates, SSF had to contend with many obstacles in their efforts to do the work of the Church, including ones created by the Church itself.[2] Though Deggs is rarely explicit regarding racist obstacles that the SSF faced in New Orleans, race was an obvious catalyst for many of those obstacles facing all people of color in the United States.

In nineteenth-century New Orleans, though racism took very different forms than those in other parts of the United States, it existed, nonetheless. Before settlers arrived in the Americas, the area was inhabited by Indigenous people who lived in the area mostly temporarily because of the vicissitudes of the Mississippi.[3] As soon as the land became colonialized, it was claimed and inhabited by free and enslaved people from many nations, as well as mixes of all.[4] Unlike many cities throughout the United States, New Orleans had a large population of free African Americans and peoples of mixed races, yet race was very stratified in and out of black communities. As light-skinned women of color who came from free and propertied families, the founders of SSF had far more privilege than did many people of color of different (darker) shades and from different regions. They had access to education and resources. Additionally, unlike many enslaved people of color who were bound to their enslavers' property, these women had freedom to move throughout their culturally rich city. However, this freedom was limited.

As Deggs's history of the Order shows, the SSF were aware of these limitations to their freedom, especially as they attempted to replicate white women's ability to join and found Catholic religious orders. While some scholars contend that the SSF managed the bias from white hegemonic forces by working "in a low-keyed manner . . . . steer[ing] clear of controversial issues,"[5] this chapter suggests the SSF employed a kind of feminist ecological thinking. Recognizing that their bodies and the material places associated with light-skinned women of color tarnished their ethē, the SSF worked to change the meanings of the materialities they inhabited. Following the work of Nedra Reynolds and others who consider the interconnections of material place and ethos,[6] this chapter explores how these women's recognition of their practices contrasted with their community's perceptions of their habits and how they used their access to materiality to change their publicly understood identities. Focusing primarily on one of the three founders of the Order, Henriette Delille, this chapter uses feminist ecological understandings of ethos as location to examine how the SSF used such ecological approaches of ethos to use place as a means both to gain status and to restructure New Orleans' understandings of mixed-race women in New Orleans. Within this examination, this chapter illustrates Ryan et al.'s assertion that "[f]eminist ecological thinking is a habit of mind that . . . describes what many women rhetors have always believed and done."[7]

In the following sections, this chapter first overviews the history of Delille and the SSF before shifting to discuss how the materiality of these women shaped their identities. Though the sisters certainly never termed what they did as a form of "feminist ecological thinking" and may or may not have been explicit in their use of such thinking, the chapter posits that Deggs's history, and her lamentations of how a neighbor undermined the sanctity of the area, suggests such thinking among the sisters was possible. Framing this discussion within feminist ecological understandings of ethos as material location, the chapter then argues the SSF worked to reshape their identities via reshapings of their material world.

HENRIETTE DELILLE AND THE SSF

Although three women of color are credited with founding SSF—Delille, Juliette Gaudin, and Josephine Charles—Delille is the most well known and is currently considered a likely prospect for canonization, potentially becoming the first black saint from the United States.[8] Born in 1812, Delille was the great-great-granddaughter of a woman, Nannette, who was brought to the New Orleans area from Africa via the Middle Passage and who was enslaved in the early eighteenth century.[9] Baptized with another name, Nannette bore several of her enslaver's children; she managed to purchase not only her own freedom but also her daughter's (Delille's great grandmother's) and two of her grandchildren's freedom before her enslaver's death. Nannette's family subsequently became property owners in New Orleans.[10]

As such, Delille was educated within the Catholic Church, as were many of her relatives before her. However, unlike her family members, Delille decided she wanted to remain in the Church as a religious woman, despite her family's objections.[11] In 1836, Delille formed a "social club" with twenty-seven other women called the "Sisters of the Presentation," guided by *Regles et Règlements*, which included regularly practiced religious exercises.[12] At first unacknowledged by the Church, the "colored sisterhood" was finally recognized by the archdiocese two years later, and, in 1842, Delille and Gaudin received word that the Church was recognizing a "racially segregated congregation of women of color" with the new name Soeurs de Sainte-Famille.[13]

Delille was able to achieve this feat as a light-skinned woman of color, who was four generations removed from the Middle Passage and who was from a relatively well-off family that owned both property and their own freedom. Significantly, Delille gained a fair amount of her privilege as someone who would have been included in one of the descriptive categories delineating the amount of black blood she possessed—especially with her family listed as white on the 1830 New Orleans census.[14] The editors of Deggs's published history, Virginia Meacham Gould and Charles E. Nolan, observe that such privilege is what probably allowed Delille and her other cofounders to succeed "where other women of color would have failed."[15]

Yet this privilege was limited. As was true elsewhere in the nineteenth-century United States, whites were the most powerful in this city over peoples of many shades of color. As Tracy Fessenden notes, free people of color with financial means "remained in a limbo zone of 'quasi-citizenship,'" in part because New Orleans' antebellum laws required people of color to "place the words homme (or femme) de couleur next to their names on all business and legal documents," they could not vote, they were limited in what they could inherit from their white fathers, and they were often forced to remain in New Orleans (and if they did leave, they could be captured and sold into slavery if they could not produce manumission papers).[16]

Delille's privilege was also constricted because her light skin announced to many in the city that she was a child of an extralegal system that produced many of the mixed-race population in New Orleans: plaçage. According to M. Shawn Copeland, this system, common throughout the lower Southern United States, created

> a more or less permanent sexual agreement between a white man of financial substance . . . and a free woman of color. By the European aesthetic standards of the time, les femmes de couleur were beautiful, poised, and refined. Some were well educated, many were astute in the conduct of business, but all were resourceful, particularly with regard to their children, for plaçage could serve as an avenue for their freedom.[17]

In the eighteenth and early nineteenth centuries, plaçage allowed women of color to gain some respectability but, simultaneously, negated it. According to Caryn Cosse Bell, "In plaçage a *représentant* (the young woman's mother or a close relative) would investigate the financial stability and social standing of the white suitor. If the man was found acceptable, the representative would then negotiate a contract with the parents of the young woman of color."[18] Despite these potential benefits and that this extralegal institution was often romanticized, Kenneth Aslakson points out that, within plaçage, women subjected themselves, often for their children's sake, to the sexual whims of these most often married men and were never completely free. Within plaçage, black and mixed-race women were perceived as "commodified, fungible, and . . . lascivious . . . something less than human."[19] Additionally, the potential respectability of plaçage waned as the nineteenth century progressed and the extralegal system was increasingly equated to prostitution.[20]

Such waning of respectability matched with its waxing, as well. People of color knew that racial "privilege" was often ranked visually by the shade of a black person's skin; for instance, the brown paper bag test (wherein a person was allowed into certain social circles if his or her skin was lighter than a brown paper bag) originated in New Orleans,[21] as did numerous castes that included many with descriptive designations for the amount of black blood a person possessed (i.e., quadroon, mulatto, griffe, octoroon, etc.).[22] People of color also knew that identity was far from fixed. As Powell states,

> It could change between baptism and marriage and other points of intersection with the state. . . . People played the system. They jumped categories, changed nomenclatures, slipped into the cracks. The greater your acculturation to Spanish norms, the easier it was to manipulate labels and change identities. . . . Economic success also simplified socio-racial promotion. Money may not have whitened, but it did lighten. So did marriage to a person of lighter complexion. The crown even made it possible to purchase whiteness for a fee.[23]

With Delille's family counted as white in the 1830 census, they clearly knew how to alter materiality's meaning, as they tried to achieve the benefits of whiteness in a white hegemonic society. The maintenance of certain codes of behavior that fit white norms—what Michelle Smith terms "respectability politics"—may also have been a means to credibility.[24] So, too, was place.

MATERIALITY SHAPES IDENTITY

Despite claims that, as a heterogeneously inhabited place, New Orleans was "an unusual cultural interstice where [many] . . . peoples interacted in a power vacuum, a space without a hegemon," the city clearly had hegemonic forces at work, and places were associated with those forces.[25] After the United States' acquisition of New Orleans, the sections of the city where a majority of the white residents lived became the more prosperous and prestigious ones, and the people of color were increasingly marginalized.[26] Lynnell Thomas observes that black New Orleanians had long sought to control the public space in order to resist these forces (611).[27] Quoting urbanist Edward Soja, Thomas states, "Space is actively involved in generating and sustaining inequality, injustice, economic exploitation, racism, sexism, and other forms of oppression and discrimination."[28]

David Sibley's work on geographies of exclusion observes that people's feelings about others are often associated with material place.[29] The practices of space connect material places with certain groups of people and often mark place as "different"; for example, people associate certain parts of their cities with certain behaviors. Then, via the construction of self, individuals relate to space in various contexts: they often avoid those city regions to avoid behaviors that they believe are antithetical to their identities. The various oppressions and discriminations of which Soja speaks stem from these associations.

These associations between identity and place help Ryan et al. to "disrupt" traditional understandings of ethos as being constructed by an individual rhetor in solitude and to argue that "a feminist ecological imaginary . . . better accounts for the diverse concerns and experiences of women rhetors and feminist rhetoricians" (5).[30] Using Ulric Neisser's understandings of the "ecological" as the understanding of self as embedded and interacting with the environment, Ryan et al. explore how people develop subjectivity via location's material influence on people's ways of being, knowing, and communicating. Such an ecological imaginary is what Lorraine Code terms the "conditions for the very possibility of knowledge and action."[31]

Such an ecological imaginary is particularly relevant to conceptions of ethos (as Ryan et al. reference and S. Michael Halloran shows) because "the most concrete meaning given for the term [ethos] in the Greek is 'habitual gathering place,'"[32] or the ethical location one returns to again and again. Though Halloran may speak of this location metaphorically, other scholars suggest that ethos' connection with location can be concrete. For example, Nedra Reynolds agrees with Halloran that character is formed by habit, but she observes that if "[o]ne identified an individual's character . . . by looking to the community," then "[a]n individual's ethos cannot be determined outside of the space in which it was created or without a sense of the cultural context."[33]

Certainly, Reynolds's use of the word "space" could reference deCerteau's *espace*, something that is not a physical reality.[34] However, as Sibley thoroughly demonstrates, the associations of spaces' practices manifest themselves in the physicality of materialities—the smells, sounds, affective responses of the material places—especially from humans' early lives.[35] These feelings become imprinted in our heads and bodies: I hear the orchestra finding the common note on the scale and feel I belong; I smell the burning trash and want to escape. Phil Hubbard, Rob Kitchin, and Gill Valentine discuss scholarship that shows how material place not only provides people with a sense of belonging but also provides a "locus of identity."[36] Such a "locus of identity" is not much different from ethos' connection with location. Where a person literally resides can impact either an individual's habits or what a community perceives an individual's habits to be. However, Hubbard et al. are quick to observe, also, that place's meaning is not absolute but always created via humans: "Places are thus constituted of multiple, intersecting social, political, and economic relations, giving rise to a myriad of spacialities. Places and the social relations within and between them are the results of particular arrangements of power, whether is it individual and institutional, or imaginative and material."[37]

For women like Delille and the other sisters in her early Order, the practices of plaçage and the places associated with it were not the ones they chose.

For example, according to all histories of Delille, she had no interest in the practices of plaçage, even though it was expected that she would follow her mother's route, as her sister Cecile Bonille had.[38] So, too, did her fellow founder, Josephine Charles, resist the training her family tried to instill in her to prepare her for the extralegal practice. For example, Deggs tells of how SSF founder Josephine Charles resisted her family's encouragement of her taking dancing lessons—presumably to prepare her for plaçage. According to Deggs, Charles's family was very displeased at Josephine Charles's refusal, but Josephine Charles responded by showing her willingness to dance if not for social and sinful reasons. Deggs writes, "[D]ear Josephine preferred to go to [King] David's dancing master, that is to dance before the altar of Christ. I say, to dance with Christ, for one hour in the chapel in the presence of the dear Lord in the blessed sacrament is far sweeter than a whole life of vanity in the ballroom."[39]

As did Charles by associating her dancing with David's psalms, the SSF worked to escape plaçage's shadow via the Church, finding its practices more appropriate for where they wanted to be. Additionally, unlike many other spaces in New Orleans and Catholic Churches in many other cities, the New Orleans Catholic Church not only welcomed people of color but was also not segregated. For example, it was a place where many people of color could not only practice their devotion to God, but also where they could announce their respectability via their purchase of prominent pews in the sanctuaries.[40] Recognizing how the practices and associated materialities of the place fed her identity, Delille created the Order to provide similar practices and identities for others like her.

VISIBLE HABITS

Delille and her cofounders faced many obstacles because of their race. For example, after Delille joined with others to form the Sisters of the Presentation, she faced much resistance from the Church just to have the group recognized.[41] One response to this racism appears to be that the Sisters attempted to deny their bodies' blackness. For instance, while the Sisters of the Presentation was considered a "colored sisterhood," it was more of an interracial convent, for it was organized by several other women of color and a white woman.[42] Additionally, after establishing her interracial "colored sisterhood," Delille and one of her cofounders, Gaudin, attempted to become novitiates in the white Order the Religious of Sacred Heart in 1851.[43] Although her Order taught and cared for people of color, it (like many other orders of the period) possessed enslaved people, and it was attentive to issues of colorism.[44] For example, in describing the founder

Josephine Charles (a woman of color), Deggs writes, "Everyone who knew her and saw her remarked 'what a fresh complexion.' She was a blonde and had blue eyes and a naturally fat and rosy face."[45] In commenting on the community's early metrics for accepting postulants, Deggs writes, "The rule of the old first motherhouse state [*sic*] that we accept only those of free and well-known families. The only one who was refused was an Indian, red skinned."[46]

The prejudice the SSF faced may have been a result of colorism as much as binary racism. While light-skinned people of color had more prestige in nineteenth-century New Orleans, they were also reminders to the city of its system of plaçage, a system whose practices were in opposition to the Church's. Delille and the other SSF went to great lengths to show that they shared the practices of the Church, as did Deggs's retelling of Charles's rejection of ballroom dancing in favor of dancing to David's psalms. Still, the color of their skin reminded others of their difference and told people they were part of practices beyond the Church; as Wendy Dasler Johnson illustrates can often occur, bodies themselves can be rhetorically suggestive of "difficult material context, historical contingencies, political and biological and racial pressures, and gender."[47] With the presence of plaçage throughout the city, the Sisters' bodies reminded people of the extralegal system, not God's work.

To gain credibility, the religious Order needed to somehow counter its bodies as physical emblems of what was seen as black women's sexuality, and the religious habit was one of these means.[48] With traditional religious garb usually adopted by young orders, the SSF began wearing percale dresses with black bonnets as soon as they were first accepted into the Sisters of the Presentation.[49] When they became the SSF, New Orleans' diocesan vicar general and the SSF's advisor-chaplain would not permit them to adopt a more traditional habit.[50] Finally relenting, the vicar general died before he could provide the habit to the SSF. In 1872, cofounder Josephine Charles designed her own version of an SSF habit and gave it to one of the SSF to wear when serving at the New Orleans' new archbishop's residence.[51] As Sister Francis Borgia Hart wrote in an unpublished history seventy-eight years later, when that light-skinned Sister revealed to the archbishop that she was not a white religious sister but one of color, he exclaimed, "Go take that off! Who do you think you are? You are too proud, too proud! That dress is not for you."[52] To the Sisters, however, the habit was as essential as were their practices. The habit and the practice were one. Both countered the associations people had with light-skinned women and plaçage. As Fessenden notes, the SSF's connection to their habit was so important to the Sisters that even after Vatican II's permission for religious to eliminate the habit, the SSF keep theirs.[53]

DWELLING PLACES

Associations with their material bodies were not the only relationship between materiality and credibility that the SSF needed to change. They also worked to change the meaning of places associated with plaçage and, therefore, with them. Yet, as Sibley shows, people associate places with behaviors, and these associations are not absolute. Expanding the idea that geography both constructs difference and can change, Danielle Endres and Samantha Senda-Cook build on the work of Hubbard et al. to argue that, while place can itself act as rhetoric, individuals can also modify preexisting meanings to enact the rhetorical power of place. By repeatedly creating fissures in the dominant meanings of places, rhetors can create new meanings of places.[54] What was once a "bad" section of town becomes regentrified and the wealthy move in, or vice versa. As Reynolds cites bell hooks, people can use their inhabitation of place, or "dwelling," as a form of resistance.[55] One's dwelling is not necessarily stable; travelers dwell: "learning to dwell, can only begin with an understanding of how geography constructs difference and how differences become inscribed geographically."[56]

Such modifications of meaning, like those discussed by Endres and Senda-Cook, appear to have been a practice for the SSF. Creating a similar inversion of meaning but with material place, Deggs's history describes the Sisters' purchase of a New Orleans property for the Sisters' use:

> A house that had been used for a trader's yard in the time of slavery. After the late war, many in this city looked on the old house as a disgraceful place and it was abandoned. No one would think of buying it for the very reason that it had previously been a traders' yard and many sins had been committed at that place, not only sins, but the most horrible crimes. It must have been the will of God that our sisters should buy the place to expiate the crimes that had been committed there.[57]

In this passage, Deggs outlines the Sisters' intent to turn what had been "a disgraceful place," abandoned because of the sins and crimes that had occurred in its location, into a place of good repute. With the Sisters' purchase of the former trader's yard, it would become a place of holiness and good works. However, the most spectacular of SSF's inversions of meaning for place involved a building on Orleans Street, behind the St. Louis Cathedral, a property known throughout the city as The Quadroon Ballroom.

Quadroon ballrooms were one of the reminders of plaçage's existence in New Orleans. Named using terminology referencing people (most often women) who were one-quarter or less of African descent, these buildings gave place to "quadroon balls," regularly occurring public events in several sections of the southern United States. Often held in locations specifically designed for the affair, these balls provided opportunities for white men to meet and choose their partners for plaçage or much shorter-term relationships.[58] Coming to New Orleans from Haiti in the late eighteenth century, the balls provided men, who were often married, a chance to meet women of color for various types of sexual relationships. The myth of the romantic nature of the quadroon ball has been perpetuated by white residents who claimed it provided women of color the opportunity to meet loving partners who would care for them romantically and financially. For example, Stephen Longstreet describes the balls as full of "color and candle-light, fine wines and romantic music"—yet even Longstreet acknowledges that they were "little more than high-grade pimping and soliciting" as well as "flesh markets."[59] Aslakson goes further with his disposal of the myth, contending that the frequency of these "balls" shows that they often created very temporary relationships.

In 1881, using money mortgaged from two of their founders' (Delille's and Gaudin's) previously acquired properties, the SSF went against the advice of some of the New Orleanian Catholic patriarchy to purchase one of the most prominent quadroon ballrooms for the exorbitant sum of over a quarter of a million dollars.[60] In her history of SSF, Deggs states that the Sisters purchased the Orleans Street property to be their motherhouse because such a large space was necessary, yet the Sisters' purpose appears to have been more complex.[61] Located behind the Cathedral in one of the few non-Anglo sections of the city that was primarily white,[62] the location was one that demonstrated the Sisters must have been aware that whiteness equaled respectability. With their motherhouse so close to the Cathedral, it was literally not in the margins and had to be confronted by the white population regularly. However, this aspect seems to be less significant than the fact that this place was associated with plaçage, as were the light-skinned Sisters: it was for a ball at such a place that Charles's family encouraged her to take dancing lessons. However, just as Charles inverted the meaning of dance, the Sisters changed the meaning of the physical place.

As Delille and her Sisters understood the physical Catholic Church as a place that enacted an ethos of respectability, the SSF also seemed to have been aware of "the myriad of spacialities" in their city and how these places "were the results of particular arrangements of power." With the Sisters' ability to purchase a building in such a prominent section of town for a quarter million dollars, the arrangements of power had shifted to some degree, but the Sisters wanted the places people passed to remind them of the shifts and for passers-by to become viscerally aware of the Sisters' habits of holiness. With their purchase, instead of ignoring the place's past, they announced it—as well as the changing meaning of the place. With their establishment in the building, they placed a plaque outside the building stating: "I have chosen rather to be an abject in the house of the Lord than to dwell in the temple with sinners."[63] What the Sisters appear to have been doing is redefining the place associated with black women. No longer could New Orleanians point to the building and tell tales of plaçage and black women's sexuality. Instead, the building had become the chosen dwelling of these women and their holy habits. Like the Catholic Church itself, the place of this convent acted rhetorically to tell of the Sisters' respectability.

RECONSTRUCTION OF MEANING, INTERRUPTED

While the Sisters are silent on any explicit reference to such a strategy for changing the meaning of place, such a strategy appears to have been on their minds, considering Deggs's history's extensive discussion of their Orleans Street neighbor, Frederick William Stempel, who arrived shortly after their move to the street with his circus/theater. Within eleven of the 169-page history published by Gould and Nolan, or 6.5 percent, Deggs relates the difficulties brought by the circus and its owner.

Having spent so much money on this large and symbolically significant building, the SSF found their efforts to change the meaning of the material place were usurped by this man, originally from New York, who was better known as Signor Faranta and was the purveyor of a popular theater—Faranta's Iron Circus. When Stempel moved his shows into the building close to the SSF's new building in 1883, he was a much traveled and accomplished showman, known for his feats as a contortionist.[64] Most immediately before coming to New Orleans, Stempel had managed and performed with a troupe on a failed tour of Central and South America that had left him without financial resources.[65] Even without money, he managed to "borrow" a pavilion next to the Sisters and began the six-year legacy of what became known as "Faranta's Iron Circus." Providing inexpensive entertainment to all New Orleans' residents, the circus theater had, at one point, 5,000 seats which it most often filled; ticket prices started at ten cents. With performing animals; "flying horses"; side shows; legitimate theater; minstrel shows; music, bicycle, and lantern performances; and most anything imaginable at various times, the theater practices ran counter to that which the SSF wanted to be associated. Regardless, the Iron Circus' popularity made their section of Orleans Street more linked with carnal physicality and sinfulness than with the Sisters' holiness. In addition to the infamy of their section of this street, the theater suffered two major fires before it finally closed; this was after a celebrated performer, J. B. Peynaud, dove to his death during one of his "death defying stunts" that happened to occur on a date on which any sports were prohibited by the Catholic Church.[66] While Peynaud lay dying after his fall, the SSF mother superior sat with him at his request, giving him a Bible and scapular and listening to his confessions.[67]

This contrast between the dying exhibitionist and the mother superior listening to confessions illustrates the divergence in the presentation of habits. The drunkenness, disruptiveness, sexual liaisons, and murder that occurred outside the Sisters' door undermined the Sisters' attempts to redefine the space of Orleans Street.[68] As its external plaque told passersby, the black residents of this place chose their vows of poverty over possibilities of wealth via sinfulness. However, with Faranta sharing the street, the Sisters seemed to fail in their ministry; the place continued to be associated with the imaginary sinfulness of New Orleans' people of color.

Deggs bemoaned the practices of Faranta's theater, its broad appeal, and its close proximity to their motherhouse. Indeed, Deggs tells of a time when a Jesuit priest came to preach at the convent when "it seemed that the old man himself, Faranta, had been waiting to see who would appear so he could make his noises."[69] She also writes that "he was the cause of many a one missing holy mass on Sunday."[70] Most importantly, though, the SSF were concerned that black performers and audiences, whom the Sisters had worked to redeem, would be lulled into sinful ways. Expressing her concern, Deggs wrote that Faranta and his troupe

> broke so many poor mothers' hearts when they saw their dear sons and daughters going to destruction. We saw so many other disorders that were caused by the wicked amusement. . . . Many said these things cause no harm, that they were simple pastimes for young people in the evenings when their work was completed. . . . Those amusements plunged many a poor girl and boy into ruin for life and they never saw it until it was too late. There were two or three nice girls who ran away from their mothers and homes to follow Faranta's stage troupe to ruin.[71]

Such narratives demonstrate that the SSF's attempts to redefine the location of Orleans Street from one of sinfulness to one of virtue were failing. Stempel's disruption of the SSF's plan resulted in her order's inability to make Orleans Avenue a "habitual gathering place" of good; the reality outside their doors betrayed their intentions.

With Peynaud's death in 1889, Stempel and his circus left New Orleans. After his departure, SSF continued their practice of renovating the meaning of places by buying the location of the Iron Circus with the purpose of making it into an orphanage for girls. This time, the SSF appear to have succeeded, remaining in that location—continually building their reputation—until the 1960s when they moved to another location in New Orleans. Still in existence, the location on Orleans Street continues to note the goodness of these women. In its current incarnation as the Bourbon Orleans Hotel, it still boasts a plaque telling of the Sisters' good work. Additionally, with the efforts to canonize Delille, the habitual character of the black women of New Orleans seems to be clearly established.

REDEFINING THE CHARACTER OF NEW ORLEANS

In a city where the credibility of the light-skinned women of color who made up the SSF was often lessened because of associations with their materiality and material places linked to them, the SSF utilized a form of feminist ecological thinking by working to redefine their own materiality as well as the material places in which they dwelled. Prominently wearing their religious habit, they announced to the New Orleans public that their customs were holy ones. With their spectacular acquisition of a building that was not only in a predominantly white section of New Orleans, but also that had been associated with the romanticized and devastating tradition of plaçage, the SSF attempted to change the material place's habits—from a place for white men to choose women of color for sex to a place of worship, education, and possibility. With Stempel's arrival near this place and with his circus' success in drawing thousands to his various entertainments, the SSF were flummoxed in their efforts. Even though Deggs writes little of the racial strife and violence that occurred near the Sisters, she writes at length about the problems Stempel brought the Order.

Looking closely at Deggs's history highlights that these women (while not directly stating it) were well aware of the importance of feminist ecological thinking as they used material place to redefine the character of New Orleans' black citizens.

NOTES

1. Kathleen J. Ryan, Nancy Myers, and Rebecca Jones. *Rethinking Ethos: A Feminist Ecological Approach to Rhetoric* (Carbondale: Southern Illinois UP, 2016), 2.
2. Mary Bernard Deggs, *No Cross, No Crown: Black Nuns in Nineteenth-Century New Orleans*, eds. Virginia Meacham Gould and Charles E. Nolan (Bloomington: Indiana UP, 2001).
3. Lawrence N Powell, *The Accidental City: Improvising New Orleans* (Cambridge: Harvard UP, 2012), 7.
4. Lynnell L Thomas, "Neutral Ground or Battleground? Hidden History, Tourism, and Spatial (In)Justice in the New Orleans French Quarter," *Journal of African American History* 103, no. 4 (Fall 2018): 609–636, doi: 10.1086/699953.

5. Edward T. Brett, "Race Issues and Conflict in Nineteenth- and Early Twentieth-Century Religious Life: The New Orleans Sisters of the Holy Family," *U.S. Catholic Historian* 29, no. 1 (2011): 122. www.jstor.org/stable/41289624.

6. Nedra Reynolds, "Ethos as Location. New Sites for Understanding Discursive Authority," *Rhetoric Review* 11, no. 2 (Spring 1993): 325–338. https://www.jstor.org/stable/465805.

7. Ryan et al., *Rethinking Ethos*, 13.

8. Deggs, *No Cross*, 8; Aprille Hanson, "Possible healing could advance Mother Delille's Sainthood Cause," *The National Catholic Reporter*. National Catholic Reporter Online. September 6, 2019. https://www.ncronline.org/news/global-sisters-report/possible-healing-could-advance-mother-delilles-sainthood-cause. Accessed June 30, 2020.

9. M. Shawn Copeland, *The Subversive Power of Love: The Vision of Henriette Delille* (New York: Paulist Press, 2007), loc. 291 of 2206, Kindle.

10. Copeland, *The Subversive Power of Love*, 291.

11. Caryn Cossé Bell, *Revolution, Romanticism, and the Afro-Creole Protest Tradition in Louisiana* (Baton Rouge: Louisiana State UP, 1997), 129.

12. Donna Marie Porche-Frilot, "Propelled by Faith: Henriette Delille and the Literacy Practices of Black Women Religious in Antebellum New Orleans" (PhD diss, Louisiana State University, 2005), 106–115, 139.

13. Bell, *Revolution*, 128, 131; Tracy Fessenden, "The Sisters of the Holy Family and the Veil of Race," *Religion and American Culture: A Journal of Interpretation* 10, no. 2 (Summer 2000): 193–194, https://www.jstor.org/stable/1123946.

14. Fessenden, "Sisters," 193.

15. Virginia Meacham Gould and Charles E. Nolan, "Mother Marie Cecilia Capla," in *No Cross, No Crown: Black Nuns in Nineteenth-Century New Orleans*, by Deggs (Bloomington: Indiana UP, 2001), 134.

16. Fessenden, "Sisters," 200; see also Poche-Frilot, *Propelled by Faith*, 52.

17. Copeland, *Subversive Power of Love*, loc. 95 of 2206.

18. Bell, *Revolution*, 112.

19. Copeland, *Subversive Power of Love*, loc. 498 of 2206.

20. Bell, *Revolution*, 112–117.

21. Michael Eric Dyson, *Come Hell or High Water: Hurricane Katrina and the Color of Disaster* (New York: Basic Books, 2006), 292–297.

22. Powell, *Accidental City*, 293–297.

23. Powell, *Accidental City*, 295.

24. Michelle Smith, "Affect and Respectability Politics," *Theory & Event*, no. 3 (Supplement 2014), muse.jhu.edu/article/559376.

25. Richard Campanella, "'Neutral Ground,'" *64 Parishes*, http://www.knowlouisiana.org/neutral-ground. Accessed August 10, 2020.

26. Amy R. Sumpter, "Segregation of the Free People of Color and the Construction of Race in Antebellum New Orleans," *Southeastern Geographer* 48, no. 1 (May 2008): 19–37, www.jstor.org/stable/10.2307/26225504.

27. Thomas, "Neutral Ground," 611.

28. Thomas, "Neutral Ground," 611–612.

29. David Sibley, *Geographies of Exclusion: Society and Difference in the West* (London: Routledge, 1995), 3.

30. Ryan et al., *Rethinking Ethos*, 5.

31. Ulric Neisser, "Five Kinds of Self-knowledge," *Philosophical Psychology* 1, no. 1 (1988): 36–41; Lorraine Code, *Ecological Thinking: The Politics of Epistemic Location* (Oxford: Oxford UP, 2006), 20.

32. S. Michael Halloran, "Aristotle's Concept of *Ethos*, or If Not His Somebody Else's," *Rhetoric Review* 1, no. 1 (September 1982): 58–63, http://www.jstor.com/stable/465559.

33. Reynolds, "Ethos as Location," 329.

34. Michel deCerteau. *The Practice of Everyday Life*, trans. Steven Rendall (Berkeley: University of California Press, 1984), 117–118.

35. Sibley, *Geographies of Exclusion*, 3.

36. Phil Hubbard and Rob Kitchin, "Introduction: Why Key Thinkers," in *Key Thinkers on Space and Place* (Thousand Oaks, CA: Sage, 2004), 1–17, 5.

37. Hubbard and Kitchin, "Introduction," 6.

38. Fessenden, "Sisters," 193; Copeland, *The Subversive Power of Love*, loc. 312 of 2206.

39. Deggs, *No Cross*, 42.

40. Bell, *Revolution*, 65–75; Fesssenden, "Sisters," 197–198.

41. Bell, *Revolution*, 128; Fesssenden, "Sisters," 193–194; Edward T. Brett, "Race Issues and Conflict in Nineteenth- and Early Twentieth-Century Religious Life: The New Orleans Sisters of the Holy Family," *U.S. Catholic Historian* 29, no. 1 (2011): 116, www.jstor.org/stable/41289624.

42. Bell, *Revolution*, 131; Fessenden, "Sisters," 191.

43. Fessenden, "Sisters," 190.

44. Fessenden, "Sisters," 196.

45. Deggs, *No Cross*, 52.

46. It appears such a strategy—if it were a strategy at all—failed. Bell (*Revolution*, 131) argues that one reason for Delille's Order was that the increasingly conservative New Orleans Church leadership wanted to erase the community's interracial origins.

47. Wendy Dasler Johnson, "Cultural Rhetorics of Women's Corsets," *Rhetoric Review* 20, no. 3/4 (Autumn, 2001), 205. https://www.jstor.org/stable/466067.

48. Fessenden, "Sisters," 188. Fessenden notes that the SSF's battle for their habit is so important to the Sisters that even after Vatican II's permission for religious to eliminate the habit, the SSF keep theirs.

49. Brett, "Race Issues," 121.

50. Brett, "Race Issues," 121.

51. Fessenden, "Sisters," 187–189.

52. Fessenden, "Sisters," 187–188; Brett, "Race Issues," 122.

53. Fessenden, "Sisters," 188.

54. Danielle Endres and Samantha Senda-Cook, "Location Matters: The Rhetoric of Place in Protest," *Quarterly Journal of Speech* 97, no. 3 (2011): 259, doi:10.1080/00335630.2011.585167.

55. Reynolds, "Ethos as Location," 141.

56. Reynolds, "Ethos as Location," 143.

57. Deggs, *No Cross*, 46.

58. Kenneth Aslakson, "The 'Quadroon-*Plaçage*' Myth of Antebellum New Orleans: Anglo-American (Mis)interpretations of a French-Caribbean Phenomenon," *Journal of Social History* 45, no. 3 (Spring 2012): 720–721, https://www.jstor.org/stable/41678906.

59. Stephen Longstreet, *Sportin' House: New Orleans and the Jazz Story* (Los Angeles: Sherbourne, 1965), 109–111.

60. Deggs, *No Cross*, 153–157; Fessenden, "Sisters," 195.

61. Deggs, *No Cross*, 26.

62. Sumpter, "Segregation," 29.

63. LaKisha Michelle Simmons, *Crescent City Girls: The Lives of Young Black Women in Segregated New Orleans* (Chapel Hill: University of North Carolina Press, 2015), 35.

64. Boyd Cruise and Merle Harton, *Signor Faranta's Iron Theatre* (New Orleans: Historic New Orleans Collection, 1982), 3.

65. Cruise and Harton, *Signor Faranta's Iron Theatre*, 12.

66. Deggs, *No Cross*, 67.

67. Deggs, *No Cross*, 72.

68. Cruise and Harton, *Signor Faranta's Iron Theatre*, 74–75.

69. Deggs, *No Cross*, 67.

70. Deggs, *No Cross*, 71.

71. Deggs, *No Cross*, 69–70.

BIBLIOGRAPHY

Aslakson, Kenneth. "The 'Quadroon-*Plaçage*' Myth of Antebellum New Orleans: Anglo-American (Mis)interpretations of a French-Caribbean Phenomenon." *Journal of Social History* 45, no. 3 (Spring 2012): 709–734, https://www.jstor.org/stable/41678906.

Bell, Caryn Cossé. *Revolution, Romanticism, and the Afro-Creole Protest Tradition in Louisiana*. Baton Rouge: Louisiana State UP, 1997.

Brett, Edward T. "Race Issues and Conflict in Nineteenth- and Early Twentieth-Century Religious Life: The New Orleans Sisters of the Holy Family." *U.S. Catholic Historian* 29, no. 1 (2011): 113–127, www.jstor.org/stable/41289624.

Campanella, Richard. "Neutral Ground." *64 Parishes*, http://www.knowlouisiana.org/neutral-ground. Accessed August 10, 2020.

Code, Lorraine. *Ecological Thinking: The Politics of Epistemic Location*. Oxford: Oxford UP, 2006.

Copeland, M. Shawn. *The Subversive Power of Love: The Vision of Henriette Delille*. New York: Paulist Press, 2007. Kindle.

Cruise, Boyd, and Merle Harton. *Signor Faranta's Iron Theatre*. Historic New Orleans Collection, 1982.

DeCerteau, Michel. *The Practice of Everyday Life*. Trans. Steven Rendall. Berkeley: University of California Press, 1984.

Deggs, Sister Mary Bernard. *No Cross, No Crown: Black Nuns in Nineteenth-Century New Orleans*. Edited by Virginia Meacham Gould and Charles E. Nolan. Bloomington: Indiana UP, 2001.

Dyson, Michael Eric. *Come Hell or High Water: Hurricane Katrina and the Color of Disaster*. New York: Basic Books, 2006.

Endres, Danielle, and Samantha Senda-Cook. "Location Matters: The Rhetoric of Place in Protest." *Quarterly Journal of Speech* 97, no. 3 (2011): 257–282, doi:10.1080/00335630.2011.585167.

Fessenden, Tracy. "The Sisters of the Holy Family and the Veil of Race." *Religion and American Culture: A Journal of Interpretation* 10, no. 2 (2000): 187–224, https://www.jstor.org/stable/1123946.

Gould, Virginia Meacham, and Charles E. Nolan. "Mother Marie Cecilia Capla." In *No Cross, No Crown: Black Nuns in Nineteenth-Century New Orleans*, by Deggs, 131–135. Bloomington: Indiana UP, 2001.

Halloran, S. Michael. "Aristotle's Concept of *Ethos*, or If Not His Somebody Else's." *Rhetoric Review* 1, no. 1 (September 1982): 58–63, http://www.jstor.com/stable/465559.

Hanson, Aprille. "Possible healing could advance Mother Delille's Sainthood Cause." *National Catholic Reporter*. National Catholic Reporter Online. September 6, 2019. https://www.ncronline.org/news/global-sisters-report/possible-healing-could-advance-mother-delilles-sainthood-cause. Accessed June 30, 2020.

Hubbard, Phil, and Rob Kitchin "Introduction: Why Key Thinkers." In *Key Thinkers on Space and Place*, 1–17. Thousand Oaks, CA: Sage, 2004.

Johnson, Wendy Dasler. "Cultural Rhetorics of Women's Corsets." *Rhetoric Review* 20, no. 3/4 (Autumn 2001): 203–233, https://www.jstor.org/stable/466067.

Longstreet, Stephen. *Sportin' House: New Orleans and the Jazz Story*. Los Angeles: Sherbourne, 1965.

Neisser, Ulric. "Five Kinds of Self-knowledge." *Philosophical Psychology* 1, no. 1 (1988): 35–59.

Porche-Frilot, Donna Marie. *Propelled by Faith: Henriette Delille and the Literacy Practices of Black Women Religious in Antebellum New Orleans*. PhD Diss., Louisiana State University, 2005.

Powell, Lawrence N. *The Accidental City: Improvising New Orleans*. Cambridge: Harvard UP, 2012.

Reynolds, Nedra. "Ethos as Location. New Sites for Understanding Discursive Authority." *Rhetoric Review* 11, no. 2 (1993): 325–338, https://www.jstor.org/stable/465805.

Ryan, Kathleen J., Nancy Myers, and Rebecca Jones. *Rethinking Ethos: A Feminist Ecological Approach to Rhetoric*. Carbondale: Southern Illinois UP, 2016.

Sibley, David. *Geographies of Exclusion: Society and Difference in the West*. London: Routledge, 1995.

Simmons, LaKisha Michelle. *Crescent City Girls: The Lives of Young Black Women in Segregated New Orleans*. Chapel Hill: University of North Carolina Press, 2015.

Smith, Michelle. "Affect and Respectability Politics." *Theory & Event* 17, no. 3 (2014). Project Muse, muse.jhu.edu/article/559376.

Sumpter, Amy R. "Segregation of the Free People of Color and the Construction of Race in Antebellum New Orleans." *Southeastern Geographer* 48, no. 1 (2008): 19–37, www.jstor.org/stable/10.2307/26225504.

Thomas, Lynnell L. "Neutral Ground or Battleground? Hidden History, Tourism, and Spatial (In)Justice in the New Orleans French Quarter." *Journal of African American History* (Fall 2018): 609–636. doi: 10.1086/699953.

Chapter 4

Corporeal, Confrontational Resistance

The Embodied Rhetoric of the Sisters of Loretto

Shana Scudder

In her work illustrating how Andrea Dworkin "invents a productive, confrontational ethos for women," Valerie Palmer-Mehta details the radical approaches Dworkin takes when speaking to her audiences. Palmer-Mehta comments that Dworkin's approach to constructing ethos is very different from that of many other women: "Historically female rhetors have coyly maneuvered around a host of frustrations and obstacles, making conciliatory gestures and accentuating those elements that connect rhetor and audience."[1] Dworkin does not do any of that; instead, she often makes her audiences uncomfortable, abandoning any "politics of manners" and "forcing her audience into a position where they need to edify" their ethos.[2] One way in which she does this is by citing her experiences as a prostitute, using her embodied experiences to challenge the abstract feminism of these audiences.[3] In many ways, she takes Nedra Reynolds's claims that "the sex of the knower is epistemologically significant"[4] several steps further; Dworkin conveys that the specific experiences of the knower are what grant her legitimacy to speak.

Such a confrontational ethos would seem impossible for Catholic women religious. For sisters who are vowed religious, embedded not only in the patriarchy that is Western society but also within the Vatican, rhetorical acts of resistance and the formation and dissemination of new ways of knowing would seem nothing less than revolutionary. Yet such radical acts and formations of new epistemologies are the work of many Catholic women's orders as they, like Dworkin, use their embodied experiences as forms of rhetoric that speaks to their purposes. Many Catholic women's orders pride themselves on their radical activism. These sisters' acts of resistance and ways of knowing often work both within and against the Church, especially for sisters who identify as feminist or those who work for LGBTQI inclusion and rights.[5] Often, these women work with a single-minded devotion to their causes, and, in this way, the vows they originally made when joining their order become embodied and redefined as their lives become transformed into gifts of service to the people and, thus, to God.

All women religious, whether cloistered or not, initially speak their vows to join their orders, pledging to commit their whole selves to the work of God. This promise, then, becomes embodied when the women live the vows they speak (vows of poverty, chastity, and obedience). This embodied rhetoric, like that described by A. Abby Knoblauch, is "the purposeful effort by an author to represent aspects of embodiment within the text he or she is shaping."[6] As this chapter shows, the embodied rhetoric of some orders takes place at two levels: (1) involvement, going out into the world and "doing," most notably physically "crossing the line," and (2) as a corporate body, which encompasses not only their community but also the body of Christ as unified in baptism. To better illustrate how some women religious use such embodied rhetoric, this chapter focuses on one particular community: the Sisters of Loretto, using examples of such embodied rhetoric from Cecily Jones's essay "Crossing the Line: Loretto and Social Protest" as well as a detailed discussion of one example provided by Jones, that of Joann Malone—one of the "D.C. Nine," a group who ransacked Dow Chemical's offices in Washington, DC, to protest the Vietnam War. With these various instances of embodied rhetoric, I will demonstrate how Catholic sisters redefine their vows to reflect lives lived truly in service of the people and, therefore, of God.

EMBODIED ETHOS

Embodied rhetoric among women religious has been a long-standing tradition. For example, in the Middle Ages, several well-known women and men used their bodies as tools for service and canvases upon which to display their devotion to God. This tradition, known as asceticism, is a type of embodied rhetoric which involves an individual's extreme deprivation, physical discipline, and even self-harm to demonstrate their devotion and commitment to God. This tradition was not considered an oddity by the Catholic Church; instead, many in the Church embraced the tradition. Jo Ann Kay McNamara writes, "Sharpened and perfected through rigorous training, ascetics became mediators between God and the world, frontier guards posted in the desert to ward off the forces of evil."[7] The ascetic practices of female mystics drew attention to the vocation and also attracted converts who wanted to embody this level of devotion to God.

However, ascetic practices went much deeper than simply being an advertisement for religious life, particularly for women. Rebecca Lester writes that "for some women, the cultural symbols of food, piety, and devotion took on special and individualized significance, perhaps serving as a liaison between individual and cultural concerns regarding independence, womanhood, and identity."[8] In this context, women religious expressed their devotion to God and their rejection of the values of the world through the ways in which they navigated their corporeality: through food restriction, self-flagellation and torture, and constant selfless service to others. Caroline Walker Bynum argues that "medieval piety, especially female medieval piety, was also deeply somatic with the body serving as a conduit and opportunity for the soul's ascent."[9] As Bynum makes clear, the ascetic practices of the medieval mystics went far beyond the performative and served as a clear example of an embodied rhetoric of devotion.

Catherine of Siena was one such woman who used her body as a tool not only to display her devotion but also to purify herself and make her body into a vehicle of transcendence. By showing that she had not only moved beyond desires of the flesh but also past any resistance to physical pain, Catherine built rhetorical authority with her mortal witnesses, the church hierarchy, and God. Fleckenstein argues in "Incarnate Word" that this embodied rhetoric enhanced Catherine's ability to persuade those in the Church. The creation of rhetorical identification is imperative in generating rhetorical authority, especially in social justice work.[10] An activist uses her body to make her audience identify with both her as the rhetor and with the constituents for whom she is advocating, thus generating empathy (pathos), and if the audience contains persons in power, change can thus occur.

Such a use of her body fits what Knoblauch terms embodied language—that which "draws attention to the body itself"—just as it is also embodied knowledge because it is perception from the "generative force of the body."[11] So, too, it is what Knoblauch terms embodied rhetoric: "a purposeful decision to include embodied knowledge and social positionalities as forms of meaning making."[12] The entreaties that Catherine made to the papacy were always on behalf of the people. She drew attention to her body's force and her positionality to make meaning. Catherine's use of her body as a tool showed how her devotion to God exceeded normal human limitations, and, therefore, the Vatican needed to heed her entreaties because her devotion was not any usual devotion. It was inspired.

In this way, Catherine's embodied rhetoric connects with that of modern sisters. While modern sisters largely reject ascetic practices tied to food and self-injury, selfless service and activism still play a prominent role in building an embodied ethos of devotion to God. Lester writes that, for many ascetic women, a union with God and Christ was their central concern, "and they were willing to sacrifice anything and everything to attain it."[13] Such sacrifice is not too dissimilar from more modern forms of embodied rhetoric. Citing Gesa Kirsch and Joy Ritchie as well as Adrienne Rich, Knoblauch asserts that when engaging in embodied rhetoric, feminists must rigorously engage in that for which they advocate. They need to connect their thinking to their "particular bodies, understanding that knowledge comes from the body."[14] Janice Chernekoff expands on Knoblauch's understanding of embodied rhetoric by analyzing ride reports, news reports written by long-distance cyclists detailing the specifics of the ride.[15] Chernekoff maintains that the genre provides "concrete instances of embodied rhetoric," in which the intelligence of the body takes over the mind in a "quasi-religious experience."[16] The experience Knoblauch chronicles describes a faith—not to any deity—but to "the ability of the body and mind to overcome hardship" as "[b]odily questions inspire rhetorical responses that inform and create intelligence." The reports make evident the "rhetorical intelligence of the body," the way the body can often seem "to take the lead."[17] Struggling to explain this experience, Chernekoff writes, "I am trying to pinpoint a practice, a form of moving-thinking-feeling-*languaging* that engages the whole body—body, mind, spirit—and is . . . in related forms of writing about other kinds of life-intensifying challenges."[18]

Such bodily connection, such "moving-thinking-feeling-languaging that engages the whole body" is repeatedly performed by many Catholic sisters. These women religious recognize that if they are to persuade political leaders to act on behalf of the people, whether it be for immigration reform, nuclear disarmament, or an end to war, they need to use their bodies to make the meanings. As this chapter demonstrates, this willingness to sacrifice is a commonality activist sisters share with ascetics. Whereas ascetics sacrificed food and physical comforts, modern sisters have sacrificed their freedom and sometimes their very lives in order to serve God through promoting causes of justice and peace.

As this chapter illustrates, not only do sisters construct embodied ethos through service and activism, but also they construct an embodied ethos via their attachment to a corporate body: the body of Christ as lived in their religious communities and in community with the world and those they serve. As sisters, they are called to act as one in support of each other's actions of "crossing the line," even if they intellectually disagree with the other sisters' decision to cross the line. In this way, sisters embody a "feminist ecological ethos," where "ethos is negotiated and renegotiated, embodied and communal."[19] As Nedra Reynolds suggests, "*ethos* is not measurable traits displayed by an individual; rather, it is a complex set of characteristics constructed by a group, sanctioned by that group, and more readily recognizable to others who belong or who share similar values or experiences."[20] The Sisters of Loretto, the Order on which this chapter focuses, engage in a formation of ethos that fits Reynolds's words: the members of this Order communally construct and sanction the characteristics of this group, making these characteristics not only readily recognizable but also a means of communicating the importance of their shared values.

CASE STUDY: THE SISTERS OF LORETTO

Who They Are

One community that embodies this notion of feminist ecological ethos and carries this way of being into their communal life and social justice advocacy is the Order of the Sisters of Loretto. The first women's religious order founded in the United States and the only order of sisters to have a representative at Vatican II,[21] the Sisters of Loretto have always possessed a pioneer spirit and desire for activism. With the Belgian priest, Charles Nerinckx, who had come to rural America because his Catholic activism in Europe made him persona non grata in the French/Belgian regions during the period following the French Revolution, a group of pioneer Kentucky women founded the Sisters of Loretto in 1812 in order to educate the youth around them.[22] Quickly, the Order spread throughout the region and country, eventually creating numerous schools and colleges.[23] While the original mission of the Loretto Community was to open schools, they have added to their mission an activism for social justice. As their Loretto Community website reads, "We work for justice and act for peace because the Gospel urges us."[24]

Like the Sisters of Providence and the Benedictine Sisters discussed in chapter 1, the Sisters of Loretto had their confrontations with the Catholic patriarchy. For example, Mother Praxedes joined Loretto in the nineteenth century, serving throughout the American West as well as Kentucky. Like chapter 2's Mothers Guerin and Riepp, Mother Praxedes faced a conflict with a member of the Catholic hierarchy, sailing to Rome to get a "special dispensation from the Pope so the Order could ignore the bishop's demands."[25] What is especially important about this narrative is that it has been taught to young novices in the Order to "set the tone" for the group to which the novices were about to join.[26] The success of the Order was made clear when one of their own, Sister Luke Tobin, was the only woman invited to Vatican II, where many of the limitations for women religious were curtailed.[27] In particular, with Vatican II, the Church issued a statement on "race and poverty, hunger, peace, unity and alienated youth . . . [expressing] deep concern, as well as a suggestion for actions which . . . members of the congregation could take."[28] Knowing that such actions might create conflict within her own Order, Sister Luke Tobin led the Loretto Community to adopt an

"Individual Support Statement": "The courage of a Sister of Loretto to act on her Christian conviction deserves the support of her sisters. A common application of the Gospel to any public issue may never be reached by us, but respect for another's integrity and conscience is a value we affirm and pledge ourselves to preserve."[29] Thus, with this call for action as well as for support for Sisters who respond to the call, even if consensus on the action has not been reached, the Sisters of Loretto immerse their entire selves in their work via bodily involvement and commitment to their corporate body. They create an embodied ethos.

Cecily Jones

The exemplary article this chapter uses to demonstrate the Sisters of Loretto's communal embodiment of ethos, "Crossing the Line: Loretto and Social Protest," is a chronicle of Loretto's social activism across three different social issues: the United Farm Workers Movement, the Vietnam War, and Nuclear Disarmament. The article is a testament to the Sisters of Loretto's direct physical actions against injustice.[30] Written by Cecily Jones who is herself a Sister of Loretto, "Crossing the Line" was published in the 1995 collection *Naming Our Truth: Stories of Loretto Women* which chronicles the social activism of the Sisters of Loretto from 1923 through the collection's publication. Both the chapter and book are celebrations of the lives and work of the Sisters and demonstrate the Sisters' tireless witnessing for peace and social justice. I chose Jones's essay in particular because of its scope and focus on some of the more controversial actions and stances that Jones and her fellow Sisters have taken on social issues from the 1960s through the 1990s.

Joann Malone

One of the more infamous protests in which a member of the Sisters of Loretto engaged was the protest at a Washington, DC, Dow Chemical building in 1969. With eight other people, including an ex-nun and five priests, Sister of Loretto Joann Malone stole and destroyed files from the building and splattered her own blood all over the offices the group entered. Protesting the profits made by Dow on the Vietnam War, the group made headlines throughout the nation for their actions. This chapter uses various retrospectives on the event, including interviews and a recorded personal conversation with Joann Malone, to explore how her action was characteristic of the embodied rhetoric of the Loretto Community.

CROSSING THE LINE

Jones opens the essay by introducing the metaphor of "crossing the line," then she echoes the metaphor throughout her chapter as she depicts the many ways the Sisters invest their entire bodies in their social movements. The metaphor is derived from a statement by an organizer of a protest at a Nevada Test Site: "Now some of you may choose to cross this line [referring to a cattle guard on a gravel road]. If so, you will face arrest. But all of you, just by your presence here, have already crossed the line."[31] Intending for her readers to understand that these women are "crossing the line" literally and figuratively, Jones defines this phrase as meaning "that a significant change has occurred in one's position."[32] I, too, echo Jones's metaphor to demonstrate how such a change in literal and metaphorical positions creates an embodied rhetoric. Jones's examples of crossing the line show the Sisters using their bodies as tools: as members of the Loretto Community, their bodies are implements used to carry out various missions just as they are devices of a sort that demonstrate their solidarity.

Jones's first example of the Sisters' embodied actions involves Loretto's work with the United Farm Workers (UFW). This organization, also discussed by L Heidenreich in chapter 11, has supported the unionization, living wages, and fair working conditions of farm workers since the 1960s. Within this example, Jones shows how the Sisters demonstrate solidarity with those for whom they advocate. Jones quotes Sister of Loretto Ruth Shy about her participation in a highly publicized march with the UFW in 1970: "As religious women, we think it is our mission to help spread the good news."[33] However, Shy recognizes that the farmworkers with whom she marches have lives that do not appear to reflect this "good news." To create solidarity, the Sisters of Loretto not only "join the march" with the UFW, but also they participate with the strikers for a week, under the "hot Colorado sun"; they boycott the products maligned with the workers' farms; and they encourage everyone they encounter to similarly boycott the products. Their involvement is not slight; it is entire. It both taxes their bodies and incorporates what they put into their bodies.

The Sisters were also heavily involved in domestic actions of embodied ethos during Vietnam War. As Jones points out, the Sisters of Loretto opposed the Vietnam War before such opposition became commonplace in the general public. In 1967, they circulated nationally a petition and "Statement of Social Concern" that called for new initiatives to end the war.[34] In 1968, they wrote a Statement of Peace that "supported a legal provision for selective conscientious objections on the part of draft-age men" in the United States.[35] Jones also details how "a few Loretto members crossed the line in a new way by crossing oceans on missions for peace."[36] In July 1970, Sister Mary Luke Tobin, then the president of the Sisters of Loretto,[37] traveled to Saigon with the Catholic Peace Fellowship. During the course of her actions in Saigon, Mary Luke became directly involved with the protest of Vietnamese students who were marching to the U.S. Embassy to petition the U.S. Government. With the Vietnamese protesters, Mary Luke was tear gassed. Joining with the Vietnamese people in their protests and sufferings, she perceived this experience as giving her direct connection "with people so immediately affected by the war and by a repressive American-supported government."[38] This connection and suffering with them strengthened her resolve, as she said the experience "continued to sharpen my determination to work for peace."[39] When Tobin suffered with the Vietnamese people in their protest of the war and experienced the devastation of war firsthand, she established a greater solidarity with those most deeply affected by American foreign policy. Therefore, part of the ethos of action is rooted in the Sisters' ethos of solidarity and community.

On November 17, 1971, seven Sisters of Loretto were participating in a "silent witness" demonstration near the Colorado Springs' United States Air Force Academy when they were subsequently arrested.[40] Their collective statement in their community newsletter explained that their purpose was active participation,[41] providing another example of their ethos constructed by the rhetoric of the body: the Sisters continued to use their physical bodies as instruments of protest, in the hopes that such protests could save lives and build a corporate body.

There were several other instances in which the Sisters participated in the embodied rhetoric of protest stateside. One such major action occurred on November 24, 1971, in Washington, D.C. Mary Frances Lottes, a Sister of Loretto, participated in a "lie-in" where she and thirty-four other people impersonated the dead in Vietnam who were part of the cost of the war. Mary Frances describes reading the Eight Beatitudes in the Rotunda of the Capitol, demonstrating the scriptural ethos that was a part of this action.[42] On May 12, 1972, three Sisters of Loretto were arrested for praying in the Capitol Rotunda. Repeatedly, the Sisters of Loretto disregarded their physical comfort and needs to allow their bodies to interfere with actions to which they objected. This defense of human dignity and safety continued after the Vietnam War ended, morphing into a movement for global disarmament.

The Sisters of Loretto also engaged in embodied rhetorics in other protests. For example, they became involved in the Anti-Nuclear Movement. Most of the Sisters' actions in this movement centered around Rocky Flats, a nuclear test site near Denver where one of Loretto's three major centers is located.[43] From 1978 to 1983, the Sisters of Loretto held a weekly prayer service at Rocky Flats, near property lines they were forbidden to cross because the lines guarded a “plutonium-trigger manufacturing and reprocessing plant.”[44] In April 1978 and March 1983, several Sisters of Loretto joined others disrespecting these property lines, literally crossing the line onto forbidden property to pray for peace.[45] Additionally, in 1986, Sister Mary Beth (Buffy) Boesen participated in the Great Peace March for Global Disarmament from California to Washington, DC, a distance of 3,701 miles.[46] This action was a powerful display of embodied rhetoric, as Sister Buffy carried her march of protest across the entire country, witnessing for peace over this incredible distance. Of this act, Cecily Jones writes, “‘Walking so that all beings may be peaceful,’ in the words of the Buddhist monk Thich Nhat Hanh, offered an important way for some in Loretto to cross the line in protesting nuclear arms.”[47]

Continually, the evils against which they are subjecting their bodies to ascetic-like suffering are forces such as war, environmental destruction, and human rights abuses. Loretto tends to show up whenever and wherever these atrocities are taking place. But they do not condemn individuals, only actions conducted by individuals that cause harm to others, including the planet as a whole.

CORPORATE BODY

The corporate body of the religious community features prominently in the lives of women religious, as the corporate body has since women started forming religious communities in the Middle Ages.[48] As Nedra Reynolds states, “Character is formed by habit, not engendered by nature, and those habits come from the community or culture. One identifies an individual’s character, then, by looking to the community.”[49] Sometimes Sisters act on their own in the interest of social justice, but even if they are physically alone at the time of a protest action, they are always acting in solidarity with their community and thus with Christ.

Not all of the Sisters “crossed the line” in a physical sense. For some, “Crossing the line meant that some members moved from a nonpolitical or an apolitical stance to citizen lobbying to end the war.”[50] Jones cites that during the Vietnam War era, each issue of Loretto’s monthly newsletter contained concrete suggestions for actions, both large and small. A frequent headline of the newsletter was “What *You* Can Do to End the War.”[51] The emphasis of the word “you” suggests that the individual affects the collective: the collective body of the Sisters of Loretto, the collective Body of Christ as Christians, and the collective world. This ethos of the collective, and of the common good, is one that appears and reappears frequently in writings of the Sisters. This demonstrates that the Sisters seek not only to be an order but also a community, and not just with each other, but with everyone, and also with Christ.

Jones's section about Loretto's actions of Vietnam War protest begins with the collective community statement: "As dedicated Christian women, we can no longer afford to ignore the moral implications of such a war."[52] Throughout their involvement in the antiwar movement, the Loretto Community issued many such official and collective statements, statements that reflect the ethos of the community. One of these statements eventually became one of the official Loretto community guidelines: "The courage of a Sister of Loretto to act on her Christian conviction deserves the support of her Sisters. A common application of the Gospel to any public issue may never be reached by us, but respect for another's integrity and conscience is a value we affirm and pledge ourselves to preserve."[53] This statement is rich with clues about the collective, corporate embodied ethos of the Sisters of Loretto. Several key words and phrases include "courage," "Christian conviction," "support of her Sisters," "application of the Gospel," as well as "respect for another's integrity and conscience is a value we affirm and pledge ourselves to preserve." All of these words and phrases can be taken as statements of ethos by the community. Loretto values courage, and this courage is derived from the Sisters' faith as Christian women. They live by Gospel values and believe in applying those values to the world around them through concrete action. They hold in high esteem the individual conscience of each member, and vow to support each other whether or not they agree, because they understand that each is living the Gospel values in the way that she understands them, and they affirm their common purpose even if individual interpretations, actions, and opinions vary. In a sense, this statement summarizes the core ethical principles of the Sisters of Loretto, and its inclusion in this piece about their activism is quite effective in succinctly naming the corporate embodied ethos of this community.

In March 1971, four Sisters participated in an international peace conference in Paris and returned with a vow to travel and speak widely of what they learned from peace workers in other nations upon their return.[54] At this point, Sisters were involved in every level of the movement: (internationally, locally, and within their community) through simply conversing with others about their beliefs. In this way, Sisters of Loretto were able to take what they learned from the world, bringing it back to the States, then back to the community. Even through casual conversation, each community member then became educated, and they converted, in some cases, to the antiwar efforts and the gleanings of those who had actually traveled to see the effects of the war firsthand.

D.C. NINE

One of the most controversial actions carried out by an individual Sister of Loretto was by Joann Malone, who was part of the "D.C. Nine," a group that ransacked Dow Chemical Company, a manufacturer of napalm. Malone had wanted to participate in the Civil Rights March in Selma, crossing the Pettus Bridge; however, she had not been given permission to go because of her teaching obligations.[55] After that, Malone had looked for opportunities to become fully involved in the protests against the Vietnam War. As a teacher, she had seen many of her students head off to the war only to return in caskets, and she felt a call to do whatever she could to stop the war. On March 22, 1969, with permission from the Order to miss teaching her Friday class,[56] Malone joined to prepare for the action with the eight others,[57] knowing that the "decision to do the action really was that I was willing to give my life to stop the war."[58]

The group planned their action for a "date the office was closed so there were no people in the office."[59] The inexperienced criminals, however, were a bit flummoxed by how they would actually break-in, but what they had planned for were witnesses to their crime, having called photographers and journalists to observe the break-in across the street from the *Washington Post* building.[60] Carefully tapping at the windows to break the glass so it would fall inside and not on supporters below,[61] Malone and her colleagues threw Dow files out of the broken windows for their supporters to gather, in order to make certain that the information from the files "got published in the *New York Times*, the *Washington Post*."[62]

Dow was the target of the D.C. Nine's protest because Dow not only produced napalm nerve gas and defoliants, but also that it enjoyed an enormous profit from these sales. As a statement from the D.C. Nine articulated

> We are outraged by the death-dealing exploitation of people of the Third World, and of all the poor and powerless who are victimized by your profit seeking ventures. Considering it our responsibility to respond, we deny the right of your faceless and inhuman corporations to exist. . . . You, corporations, who under the cover of stockholder and executive anonymity, exploit, deprive, dehumanize and kill in search of profit. . . . In your mad pursuit of profit, you, and others like you, are causing the psychological and physical destruction of mankind. We urge you all to join us as we say no to this madness.[63]

As the D.C. Nine protested the dehumanization promoted by Dow Chemical, they depict their own bodily humanness, continually demonstrating what Knoblauch defines as embodied knowledge, with the attention drawn to the body becoming a message in itself. This illustration continued throughout and after the "action."

Once inside, the D.C. Nine poured blood they had extracted from their own bodies, "and it was poured on some of the office equipment and files and then we threw files out the window."[64] This was not just pig's blood. According to Malone, "We thought it was more authentic . . . it was maybe part of that commitment."[65] While Malone and the others ransacked the building, they took their time, "purposely stay[ing] around to be arrested."[66] Then, placed in jail, they continued their protests, fasting the whole time and learning how to deal with prison crab lice.[67]

As a sister breaking and entering onto Dow Chemical Property, Malone may very well have crossed the line into "illegal" activity, but, as she herself says, she was "not a rebel against the Sisters of Loretto."[68] After all, even though she committed felonious crimes, she had sought permissions from the Sisters to leave her class on the day she needed to prepare for the felony. Instead of being a misfit with the Sisters of Loretto, Malone was "not that different"[69] from the other Sisters of Loretto as she embodied their call to serve God. As Malone repeatedly states in her 2017 interview, the Sisters of Loretto believed they should be "able to act according to their consciences," and the Sisters always stood by this promise, despite the fact that many Sisters "were probably horrified" by her action.[70] A high school teacher at Nerinx Hall, a Sisters of Loretto school, Malone returned from her DC action to find that many parents and administrators called for her dismissal from her job at the school. Contrarily, the Sisters, even those who disagreed with Malone's action, supported her and refused to dismiss her from her job.[71] They held true to their "Individual Support Statement" they had issued after Vatican II. As Malone articulates in the 2017 interview, "The Sisters of Loretto were amazing, phenomenal. The statements they had issued about a sister being able to act according to her conscience, they stood by that." They were one body, living in communion, believing "the courage of a Sister of Loretto to act on her Christian conviction deserves the support of her Sisters."[72] Unlike the Dow Chemical Corporation, the corporate body of the Sisters of Loretto never hid "under covers of stockholder or executive anonymity"; instead, the Loretto Community very publicly acknowledged their full support for a member who had crossed the line, accepting fallout from this support. When the school at which Malone taught had parents, students, and the community calling for her firing, the leader of the Order responded: "We have been petitioned by some . . . to immediately suspend Sister Joann Malone as a teacher at Nerinx Hall as a punishment for her anti-war act in Washington, DC. This we refuse to do. We hereby reassert our support of Sister Joann as a member of the Sisters of Loretto and as a faculty member at Nerinx Hall."[73]

In a 2017 interview, Malone was asked "how a nice girl from Kansas City, Missouri become a radical nun and Federal felon?" Malone replied, "It really starts with the Sisters of Loretto." According to Malone, the Loretto Community "took the basic Christian values . . . to a whole new level of teaching us that love is not an abstraction but something that really has to be lived in our daily lives and all our actions and extend to all people in the world."[74] For the women of this Order, love is not an abstraction, but something to embody as risk of life or public support. The body speaks, and the mind will follow.

Malone's action depicts both Jones's metaphor of "crossing the line" and how the Sisters embody a corporate ethos. Just as the many Sisters whom Jones discusses use their bodies as implements to achieve their end, Malone literally and figuratively utilized her body as a tool. Her blood is the paint that smears the walls; she thinks about crossing the line from life to death, from "good girl" to "Federal felon" who had to deal with prison crab lice. If that physical movement across the barrier will achieve what she has vowed to do, her body will endure it. In each aspect of Malone's involvement with the vandalization of the Dow Chemical act, she engaged in an aspect of embodied rhetoric. From her willingness to put her life at risk to her utilization of her own blood to spray the Dow building, from her connections between her conscience calling for her action and her bodily responses to action, to her participation in a corporate body of women "not that much different" from her, Malone wielded an embodied language, knowledge, and rhetoric. Knoblauch contends that while employing an embodied rhetoric, feminists must rigorously engage in that for which they advocate. That is what Malone—and the Sisters of Loretto—do: they connect their thinking to their "particular bodies"; they accept their callings of conscience, or what Knoblauch terms "gut reactions"; then they "cross the line" together—as a corporate body—manifesting Knoblauch's definition of embodied knowledge: "a purposeful decision to include embodied knowledge and social positionalities as forms of meaning making."[75] With these challenging actions, Malone and her sisters also employ the embodied rhetoric described by Chernekoff: they rigorously involve themselves in that for which they advocate, using their bodies in what Chernekoff terms "moving-thinking-feeling-*languaging*." They commit their entire selves, and the selves of the other Sisters, in making meaning that embodies their consciousnesses. The mind and body come together.[76]

CONCLUSION

Malone ended up having the federal felony conspiracy charges against her dropped, but she did serve four years in jail for lesser charges. No longer a Sister of Loretto in the twenty-first century, Malone has retained her relationship with her former Sisters. Though she has gone on to conduct her activism in other areas, she still embodies the Loretto corporate ethos and would be welcomed by the Sisters to join as a lay associate.

As they cross the line, the Sisters of Loretto challenge and intensify their lives—but more importantly, they hope to better the lives of others. They live their vows with their embodied actions. Actions such as these exemplify the Sisters' embodied rhetoric. They believe not only that it is crucial to be physically present and represented at major political actions, but also that it is crucial that members of their congregation participate physically, verbally, and spiritually in the actions. They believe in an ethos of total involvement, and with different individual sisters in each facet of action, they ensure that their total collective body is represented and fully immersed in all aspects of political action.

Ethos is built through the body in embodied acts of service and activism that enable women religious to build their credibility and redefine their vows, which then further strengthens their ethos recursively. This embodied ethos is clearly displayed in the activism of the Sisters of Loretto. According to Palczewski, Ice, and Fritch, "*Who* says a message and *how* a body is made present communicate as much as *what* is said. Body rhetoric, then, is *rhetoric that foregrounds the body as part of the symbolic act*."[77] Since ethos is "*the character of a rhetor performed in the rhetorical act and known by the audience because of prior interactions*,"[78] its relationship to body rhetoric would seem to be inherent in its very definition. Palczewski, Ice, and Fritch also write that "body rhetoric is often used by those who are denied access to more traditional forms of verbal address and of proof. In some cases, your own body may be your only available proof for a point you want to make."[79] As women working within the ultimate patriarchy, women religious have very much been historically forced to leverage their "only available proof," their bodies, to demonstrate their faith and to build credibility to bring attention to the various social justice causes for which they fight. Ultimately, they are constantly employing their bodies as tools of discipleship: to serve, to fight for justice, and to demonstrate to the world, to God, and to themselves their willingness to act tirelessly on behalf of God's people.

Like Andrea Dworkin, these sisters care little about the comfort of their audience as they, like Dworkin, "subvert[] a politics of manners" in their fight for justice.[80] Instead, they embody an ethos that they share with both their communities as well as with the Body of Christ.

NOTES

1. Valerie Palmer-Mehta, "Andrea Dworkin's Radical Ethos," in *Rethinking Ethos: A Feminist Ecological Approach to Rhetoric*, eds. Kathleen J. Ryan, Nancy Myers, and Rebecca Jones (Carbondale, IL: Southern Illinois UP, 2016), 63.
2. Palmer-Mehta, "Andrea Dworkin's Radical Ethos," 62.
3. Palmer-Mehta, "Andrea Dworkin's Radical Ethos," 65.

4. Nedra Reynolds, "*Ethos* as Location: New Sites for Understanding Discursive Authority," *Rhetoric Review* 11, no. 2 (1993): 330.

5. The Catholic Church still does not support ordination for women, access to abortion, or birth control, and considers all homosexual sexual activity a sin.

6. A. Abby Knoblauch, "Bodies of Knowledge: Definitions, Delineations, and Implications of Embodied Writing in the Academy," *Composition Studies* 40, no. 2 (Fall 2012): 58, http://www.compositionstudies.uwinnipeg.ca.

7. Jo Ann Kay McNamara, *Sisters in Arms: Catholic Nuns through Two Millennia* (Cambridge: Harvard UP, 1996), 62.

8. Rebecca J. Lester, "Embodied Voices: Women's Food Asceticism and the Negotiation of Identity," *Ethos* 23, no. 2 (1995): 197.

9. Caroline Walker Bynum, "The Female Body and Religious Practice in the Later Middle Ages," in *Fragmentation and Redemption: Essays on Gender and the Human Body in Medieval Religion*, ed. Bynum (New York: Zone Books, 1992), 182.

10. Kristine S. Fleckenstein, "Out of Wonderful Silence Come Sweet Words:The Rhetorical Authority of St. Catherine of Siena," in *Silence and Listening as Rhetorical Arts*, eds. Cheryl Glenn and Krista Ratcliffe (Carbondale, IL: Southern Illinois University Press, 2011), 48.

11. Knoblauch, "Bodies of Knowledge," 57.

12. Knoblauch, "Bodies of Knowledge," 52.

13. Lester, "Embodied Voices," 210.

14. Knoblauch, "Bodies of Knowledge," 60.

15. Janice Chernekoff, "Embodied Rhetorics: Writing Rides from the Seat o a Bike," *Kenneth Burke Journal* 13, no. 2 (Summer 2018). https://kbjournal.org/chernekoff_embodied_rhetorics.

16. Chernekoff, "Embodied Rhetorics."

17. Chernekoff, "Embodied Rhetorics."

18. Chernekoff, "Embodied Rhetorics," 5.

19. Kathleen J. Ryan, Nancy Myers, and Rebecca Jones, "Introduction: Identifying Feminist Ecological Ethē," in *Rethinking Ethos: A Feminist Ecological Approach to Rhetoric*, eds. Kathleen J. Ryan, Nancy Myers, and Rebecca Jones (Carbondale, IL: Southern Illinois University Press, 2016), 11.

20. Reynolds, "Ethos as Location," 327.

21. "Joann Malone—Interview 01-15-2016—Final," Youtube, https://www.youtube.com/watch?v=pGnBS-W0i6k; Helen Sanders, *More Than a Renewal: Loretto Before and After Vatican II: 1952–1977* (Nerinx, KY: Sisters of Loretto, 1982).

22. "Charles Nerinckx," *Catholic Online*, accessed May 22, 2021, https://www.catholic.org/encyclopedia/view.php?id=8393.

23. Mary Rhodes Buckler, "And the Learning is Mutual," *Naming our Truth: Stories of Loretto Women*, ed. Ann Patrick Ware (Nerinx, KY: Chardon Press, 1995), 1–23.

24. "Loretto Community," Loretto Community, accessed May 20, 2021, https://www.lorettocommunity.org.

25. Joann Malone, Zoom conversation, June 4, 2021. See also Patricia Jean, *Only One Heart: The Story of a Pioneer Nun in America* (Garden City, NY: Doubleday, 1963), 271–284.

26. Joann Malone, Zoom conversation, June 4, 2021.

27. Joann Malone, Zoom conversation, June 4, 2021; Sanders, "More than a Renewal."

28. Sanders, *More than a Renewal*, 183.

29. Sanders, *More than a Renewal*, 184.

30. Cecily Jones, "Crossing the Line: Loretto and Social Protest," in *Naming Our Truth: Stories of Loretto Women*, ed. Ann Patrick Ware (Nerinx, KY: Chardon Press, 1995), 161–197.

31. Jones, "Crossing the Line," 161.

32. Jones, "Crossing the Line," 161.

33. Jones, "Crossing the Line," 162–163.

34. Jones, "Crossing the Line," 168–169.

35. Jones, "Crossing the Line," 168.

36. Jones, "Crossing the Line," 171.

37. Religious orders no longer have "Mother Superiors"; they now have a governing body that is elected and functions in a democratic structure.

38. Jones, "Crossing the Line," 171.

39. Jones, "Crossing the Line," 171.

40. Jones, "Crossing the Line," 173–174.

41. Jones, "Crossing the Line," 174.

42. The Beatitudes are a famous blessing given by Christ.

43. The Loretto Motherhouse is located in Nerinx, Kentucky. Loretto formerly had centers in Denver and St. Louis, and still operate schools in Denver and El Paso, TX.

44. Jones, "Crossing the Line," 180.

45. Jones, "Crossing the Line,"180–181.

46. Jones, "Crossing the Line," 185.

47. Jones, "Crossing the Line," 186.

48. McNamara, *Sisters in Arms*, 239.

49. Reynolds, "*Ethos* as Location," 329.

50. Jones, "Crossing the Line," 170.

51. Jones, "Crossing the Line," 170.

52. Jones, "Crossing the Line," 168.

53. Jones, "Crossing the Line," 169.

54. Jones, "Crossing the Line," 172.

55. Joann Malone, *Awake to Racism* (N.P: QiPublishing, 2021): loc. 28 or 2626. Kindle.

56. Sanders, *More than a Renewal*, 185.

57. Originally, there had been another group that planned a separate action on the same day but the other group was thwarted by the FBI before their protest; Frank Carroll, "'Dow Shalt Not Kill': The Story of the D.C. Nine," Boundary Stones: WETA's Washington DC History Blog, January 23, 2020, accessed May 29, 2021, https://boundarystones.weta.org/2020/02/23/dow-shalt-not-kill-story-dc-nine.

58. "Joann Malone—Interview 01-15-2016—Final," YouTube, https://www.youtube.com/watch?v=pGnBS-W0i6k.
59. Joann Malone, Zoom conversation, June 4, 2021.
60. Carroll, "Dow Shalt No Kill."
61. Joann Malone, Zoom conversation, June 4, 2021.
62. "Joann Malone," YouTube.
63. Statement of the DC-9, "AN OPEN LETTER TO THE CORPORATIONS OF AMERICA," accessed November 13, 2021, http://www-personal.umd.umich.edu/~ppennock/doc-Letter%20to%20Dow%20Chemical.htm.
64. "Joann Malone," YouTube.
65. Joann Malone, Zoom conversation, June 4, 2021.
66. Joann Malone, Zoom conversation, June 4, 2021.
67. Malone, *Awake to Racism*, loc. 59 of 2626.
68. Joann Malone, Zoom conversation, June 4, 2021
69. Joann Malone, Zoom conversation, June 4, 2021.
70. Joann Malone, Zoom conversation, June 4, 2021.
71. Jones, "Crossing the Line," 169–170.
72. Joann Malone, Zoom conversation, June 4, 2021.
73. Sanders, *More than a Renewal*, 191–192.
74. "Joann Malone," YouTube.
75. Knoblauch, "Bodies of Knowledge," 52.
76. Knoblauch, "Bodies of Knowledge."
77. Catherine Helen Palczewski, Richard Ice, and John Fritch, *Rhetoric in Civic Life*, 2nd edition (State College, PA: Strata, 2016), 77.
78. Palczewski et al., *Rhetoric in Civic Life,* 167.
79. Palczewski et al., *Rhetoric in Civic Life*, 77.
80. Palmer-Mehta, "Andrea Dworkin's Radical Ethos," 62

BIBLIOGRAPHY

Buckler, Mary Rhodes. "And the Learning is Mutual." *Naming our Truth: Stories of Loretto Women*, edited by Ann Patrick Ware, 1–23. Nerinx, KY: Chardon Press, 1995.

Bynum, Caroline Walker. "The Female Body and Religious Practice in the Later Middle Ages." In *Fragmentation and Redemption: Essays on Gender and the Human Body in Medieval Religion*, edited by Bynum, 181–238. New York: Zone Books, 1992.

Carroll, Frank. "'Dow Shalt Not Kill': The Story of the D.C. Nine." Boundary Stones: WETA's Washington DC History Blog. January 23, 2020. Accessed May 29, 2021, https://boundarystones.weta.org/2020/02/23/dow-shalt-not-kill-story-dc-nine.

"Charles Nerinckx." *Catholic Online*. Accessed May 22, 2021. https://www.catholic.org/encyclopedia/view.php?id=8393.

Chernekoff, Janice. "Embodied Rhetorics: Writing Rides from the Seat of a Bike." *Kenneth Burke Journal* 13, no. 2 (Summer 2018), https://kbjournal.org/chernekoff_embodied_rhetorics.

Fleckenstein, Kristine. "Incarnate Word: Verbal Image, Body Image, and the Rhetorical Authority of Saint Catherine of Siena." *Enculturation*, no. 6.2 (2009), http://enculturation.net/6.2/fleckenstein.

———. "Out of 'Wonderful Silence' Come 'Sweet Words': The Rhetorical Authority of St. Catherine of Siena." In *Silence and Listening as Rhetorical Arts*, edited by Cheryl Glenn and Krista Ratcliffe, 37–55. Carbondale, IL: Southern Illinois University Press, 2011.

Jean, Patricia. *Only One Heart: The Story of a Pioneer Nun in America.* Garden City, NY: Doubleday, 1963.

"Joann Malone—Interview 01-15-2016—Final," YouTube. https://www.youtube.com/watch?v=pGnBS-W0i6k.

Jones, Cecily. "Crossing the Line: Loretto and Social Protest." In *Naming Our Truth: Stories of Loretto Women*, edited by Ann Patrick Ware, 161–197. Nerinx, KY: Chardon Press, 1995.

Knoblauch, A. Abby. "Bodies of Knowledge: Definitions, Delineations, and Implications of Embodied Writing in the Academy." *Composition Studies* 40, no. 2 (Fall 2012): 50–65, http://www.compositionstudies.uwinnipeg.ca.

Lester, Rebecca J. "Embodied Voices: Women's Food Asceticism and the Negotiation of Identity." *Ethos* 23, no. 2 (1995): 187–222, https://www.jstor.org/stable/640423.

Loretto Community. "Remembrance of the Life of Sister M. Cecily Jones SL." Last modified July 31, 2017. https://www.lorettocommunity.org/remembrance-of-the-life-of-sister-m-cecily-jones-sl/.

Malone, Joann. *Awake to Racism.* N.P: QiPublishing, 2021. Kindle.

McNamara, Jo Ann Kay. *Sisters in Arms: Catholic Nuns through Two Millennia.* Cambridge, MA: Harvard University Press, 1996.

Palczewski, Catherine Helen, Richard Ice, and John Fritch. *Rhetoric in Civic Life*, 2nd edition. State College, PA: Strata Publishing, 2016.

Palmer-Mehta, Valerie. "Andrea Dworkin's Radical Ethos." In *Rethinking Ethos: A Feminist Ecological Approach to Rhetoric*, edited by Kathleen J. Ryan, Nancy Myers, and Rebecca Jones, 50–70. Carbondale, IL: Southern Illinois UP, 2016.

Reynolds, Nedra. "*Ethos* as Location: New Sites for Understanding Discursive Authority." *Rhetoric Review* 11, no. 2 (1993): 325–338.

Ryan, Kathleen J., Nancy Myers, and Rebeca Jones. "Introduction: Identifying Feminist Ecological Ethē." In *Rethinking Ethos: A Feminist Ecological Approach to Rhetoric*, edited by Kathleen J. Ryan, Nancy Myers, and Rebecca Jones. Southern Illinois UP, 2016.

Sanders, Helen, *More Than a Renewal: Loretto Before and After Vatican II: 1952–1977.* Nerinx, KY: Sisters of Loretto, 1982.

Statement of the DC-9. "AN OPEN LETTER TO THE CORPORATIONS OF AMERICA" Accessed November 13, 2021. http://www-personal.umd.umich.edu/~ppennock/doc-Letter%20to%20Dow%20Chemical.htm.

Part II

INTERSECTIONS OF LAY AND CLERGY

Chapter 5

Who Owns This Church?

Feminist Methods of Protest and Lay Catholic Activism

Laura J. Panning Davies

Cars zipped by, the early morning January sun glinting off windshields. I grabbed my four-year-old's mittened hand, pulling him away from the curb and toward the spider-cracked concrete steps of the church, which has stood in the heart of the upstate village of Jamesville, New York since 1899. We were gathered together with two dozen others, holding a Sunday morning sidewalk service in front of the locked doors of St. Mary's Catholic Church. A layer of icy snow covered the plaster feet of St. Mary tucked away behind us in a small grove of spruce.

The story of St. Mary's Catholic Church in Jamesville, New York detailed here in this chapter, is an important site of research for rhetorical studies scholars not only because it is representative of the rhetorical work done by hundreds of small, local urban and rural Catholic churches in the United States who have faced closure since 2000, but also because it is a critically important example of the rhetoric of lay Catholic activism, particularly the work of lay Catholic women. The term "lay" here is one familiar within the Catholic community, and it refers to all people who do not belong to an ordained religious order and, thus, exists outside the dominant power structure inherent in Catholic hierarchy. When the Catholic Diocese of Syracuse in upstate New York removed the lay parishioners keeping vigil inside the church with police force in January 2008 and subsequently locked the doors of the church, the lay members of the church developed several initiatives both to reverse the Diocese's decision and also to keep the church community alive. I contend that these plans—from pursuing a canonical appeal at the Vatican and collaborating with other local parishes at risk of closure to holding weekly Sunday morning sidewalk services and reimagining the parish's beloved community traditions—are all the work of twenty-first-century lay Catholic rhetorical activism in the United States. This activism takes seriously the empowerment of the laity enshrined by Vatican II and seeks to address the tension between American ideals of democracy and the fundamental patriarchal hierarchy of the Catholic Church.

In this chapter, I argue that *feminist* rhetorical advocacy practices lay at the heart of the St. Mary's story. This distinction is important because, on the surface, it may seem odd to name the work of the St. Mary's lay community as feminist. Many of the resistance paths followed by the lay community still adhere to the traditional hierarchal and patriarchal structures of the Catholic Church, including filing appeals with the Congregation of the Clergy and the Apostolic Signatura and the community's deference shown by their reluctance to pursue civil suits against the Catholic Diocese of Syracuse, New York. However, it is important to note that feminist practices and resistance to the Church's patriarchal structure have been alive and well in the Catholic Church for centuries, including well-organized and well-published U.S. Catholic women's movements that argued for women's ordination and full integration in liturgical life in the mid-twentieth century, a movement that was dealt a tremendous blow when the Vatican issued a declaration prohibiting women's ordination in 1977.[1] What I highlight in this chapter is how the St. Mary's lay community used perpetual vigils and weekly protests to call attention to the power differentials between the Diocese and the lay community as well as how they built relationships with each other and in their local community to collectively strategize how to reverse the closing of their church and other churches facing a similar fate in the Dioceses. St. Mary's lay community quickly became attuned to the inherent conflicts of their activism, experiencing, like other feminist activists, an "overt and frustrated recognition of the disjunction between stated ideas and lived realities," or between their faith and the powerful forces of their local diocese.[2] Working together—meeting in a community member's living room and drafting documents late in the night, huddling together on the sidewalk on a wintery morning, holding parish meetings in the local fire hall, fundraising to send representatives to the Vatican to plead their case—clarified their goals, deepened their reliance on one another, and reinforced the idea among them that they needed to act as a community to achieve their purposes.

Specifically, I rely on the concept of feminist rhetorical resilience as a lens through which to understand this collective rhetorical work of St. Mary's lay community from 2006 to 2016. The concept of feminist rhetorical resilience is defined by Elizabeth Flynn, Patricia Sotirin, and Ann Brady in the introduction to their 2012 collection, *Feminist Rhetorical Resilience*.

Flynn, Sotirin, and Brady argue that the term *resilience* is a useful metaphor for feminist rhetoricians and trace its relationship to other organizing metaphors used in the field, such as *borderlands*, *stream*, *silence*, and *motion*. In contrast to these, resilience "places greater emphasis on agency, change, and hope in the daily lives of individuals or groups of individuals. Resilience suggests attention to choices made in the face of difficult or even impossible challenges."[3] Though the term "resilience" is used in other fields—psychology, education, and sociology come to mind, especially through the concept of "grit" recently popularized by Angela Duckworth—Flynn, Sotirin, and Brady clarify what *resilience* offers for feminist rhetorical studies.[4] They state, "a feminist conception of resilience is best seen not as fundamentally psychological but as rhetorical, relational, and contextual."[5] Resilience, then, is not an individual trait or characteristic that allows a single person to overcome tremendous odds, independent of others. Rather, feminist rhetorical resilience happens among people and within local communities. Importantly for me and for this project, feminist rhetorical resilience resists neat happy-ending narratives. It underscores that the transformation that can happen through resilience might not result in radically changed circumstances but, instead, more subtly changed relationships, communities, and outlooks. Flynn, Sotirin, and Brady explain three key attributes of feminist rhetorical resilience—agency, metis, and relationality. In this chapter, I demonstrate how these concepts help us understand the rhetorical work within the lay community of St. Mary's Catholic Church in Jamesville, New York.

I want to make clear my own stakes in this project and the ways in which my own identity and emotions have created a "passionate attachment," a concept articulated in depth by Jacqueline Jones Royster.[6] I am a lifelong Catholic and was a member of St. Mary's Catholic Church in Jamesville, when it was closed by the Syracuse Diocese in 2006. My son Gilbert was the last child baptized at St. Mary's Catholic Church, just two months before the doors were locked. I participated and continue to be involved in the lay community that still works to appeal the church's closure. My positionality obviously biases my project, but it also gives me access and insight into the rhetorical work happening at the heart of this controversy. This community's rhetorical work, put in context with the rhetorical work of other lay communities who protested U.S. Catholic church closures in the early twenty-first century, illustrates how lay communities can operate subversively to challenge dominant, hierarchal Catholic church structures. How St. Mary's lay community responded to their church closure is a valuable case study which invites rhetoricians to consider the democratic and feminist possibilities of Catholic lay church communities.

LAY RESISTANCE TO U.S. CATHOLIC CHURCH CLOSURES IN THE EARLY TWENTY-FIRST CENTURY

The Catholic Church in the United States today looks far different than it did even a generation ago. Although the raw number of Catholics has increased since 1965—from 48.5 million then to 81.6 million today—fewer of these Catholics are active in their church communities and attend Mass regularly.[7] The recent priest sexual abuse scandals have rocked people's trust in the Church and its leaders, and there is increasing pressure from the laity for the Church to be more inclusive, including ordaining women, fully welcoming members of LGBTQ communities, and promoting activism for economic, environmental, and political social justice.[8] The Catholic Church in the United States is far less white than it was fifty years ago, in part due to an increase in Catholic immigrants from Central and South America, and almost half of all young Catholics today between the ages of eighteen and twenty-nine identify as Hispanic.[9] Fewer priests and donations to the Church have contributed to a number of church closings since 2000.[10] Many of the churches that were closed by their dioceses were urban and rural churches that struggled to fill their pews and their coffers. These closures, which are canonically called "suppressions," happened across the United States in the past twenty years: the Diocese of Cleveland, Ohio, closed fifty-two parishes in 2008 and 2009; the Diocese of Youngstown, Ohio, reduced its parishes from 113 to 87 in 2010; the Archdiocese of New York announced the suppression of thirty-one churches in 2014.[11]

In some cases, these church closures were met by sustained resistance from their lay communities. When the Catholic Archdiocese of Boston announced, in 2004, the closure of 82 of its 357 parishes in response to the demographic shifts outlined above, several lay communities responded by holding "perpetual vigils" in which parishioners stayed in the church building after the last official Mass, thus continuously occupying the church building to prevent the Archdiocese from permanently locking the church doors.[12] These perpetual vigils at nine parishes in the Catholic Archdiocese of Boston were an active resistance to the Church hierarchy.[13] Furthermore, in Boston, the lay community's distrust of the Catholic Church was compounded by the *Boston Globe*'s 2002 extensive investigative reports that exposed decades of clergy sexual abuse that had been covered up by the Archdiocese, scandals that created a financial crisis that in part led to the Archdiocese's plan to close churches and consolidate parishes.[14] These scandals created a financial crisis, which the Archdiocese of Boston tried to solve by consolidating parishes. In New Orleans, the parishioners of St. Augustine Church reacted similarly when their Archdiocese announced the church's closure in 2006, in the months after the devastation wrecked by Hurricane Katrina.[15] St. Augustine Church, founded in 1824 and the oldest African American church in the Archdiocese, was slated to merge with a primarily white suburban church. St. Augustine Church's lay community pursued several avenues to protest their closure, including leading a nineteen-day perpetual vigil in March 2006.[16]

In addition to holding these perpetual vigils at individual churches, many lay communities in suppressed Catholic churches sought out and created networks with other churches that were closed or faced closures. For example, the parishioners holding perpetual vigils at their churches in the Archdiocese of Boston were supported by the Voice of the Faithful organization, a group started by lay activists in 2002.[17] Although the Voice of the Faithful was founded in response to the clergy sexual abuse scandals, one of its larger goals is to call for structural change within the Catholic Church in part by strengthening the "rights of the laity."[18] In the Catholic Diocese of Syracuse, New York, lay activists founded the group "Preserve Our Parishes" in 2009, after the Diocese of Syracuse announced that it would be closing forty-four churches, consolidating them into larger "Pastoral Care Areas."[19] This group, which also drew on the support of the local Jesuit community that operated outside the diocesan structure, "quickly gained members from across the diocese," researchers Matthew T. Loveland and Margret Ksander explain, "and came together to oppose the official process of reconfiguration, to defend parishes that had yet to close, and to support parishes that chose to appeal their closure."[20] The Preserve Our Parishes group claimed that the Diocese of Syracuse's plans amounted to "abandonment" of poorer rural and urban churches, as the "hurried" church mergers were arranged in favor of keeping the wealthier suburban churches open.[21]

The lay activists wrote letters and signed petitions, centering their argument on two key points. First, they stated that the Diocese's reconfiguration plan was executed without adequate input from the laity, calling for a more modern, Vatican II-inspired democratic understanding of the Church, where the Church's power and authority derived from the lay people, not the priest.[22] Second, the Preserve Our Parishes group contended that the closures would have negative long-term implications on the Diocese's rural and urban communities. A church is more than a place of worship, they contended, and it has value for the community even when a priest is not present. The church buildings, the lay activists maintained, are places "that should be protected from change because of [their] sacredness, [their] culture, and [their] place in personal biography and Catholic history."[23] From a rhetorical perspective, lay networks like Preserve Our Parishes and the Voice of the Faithful are crucial pieces to understanding the lay resistance to U.S. Catholic Church closures in the early twenty-first century. What they demonstrate is how lay communities, once relatively isolated in their own parishes, came together to share resources and strategies and to collectively advocate, through perpetual vigils, petitions, appeals, and demonstrations, for the rights of lay communities in the Catholic Church.

ST. MARY'S CATHOLIC CHURCH IN JAMESVILLE, NEW YORK: FROM CLOSURE TO A CANONICAL FIRST

The lay resistance to the closure of St. Mary's Catholic Church in Jamesville, New York, is an important site of study for rhetorical scholars because its closure and the subsequent lay response is unusual for two reasons. First, the church did not fit the profile of most U.S. Catholic churches slated for suppression since 2000. In 2006, the year St. Mary's parish was suppressed, the parish had 350 registered families and was still growing.[24] The church's location in Jamesville, a desirable and expanding suburb of Syracuse, New York, made it different from many of the rural and urban churches that were closed by their dioceses across the United States since 2000. Unlike the majority of these churches, St. Mary's was fiscally healthy, donating a substantial amount each year to the Diocese's Hope Appeal, which assisted less-resourced parishes.[25] St. Mary's story is also distinct because its lay community resisted the closure on two fronts: at home, through perpetual vigils, protests, petitions, and sidewalk services; and abroad, through a years-long canonical appeal that ultimately ruled in favor of the lay community over the Diocese of Syracuse. Lay representatives from St. Mary's Catholic Church attended many of the Preserve Our Parishes meetings and worked on their collective advocacy projects, yet its pursuit of a successful canonical appeal—the first-ever lay appeal that reached the Apostolic Signatura, the Vatican's highest court, that decided in favor of the lay community over the Diocese—sets this case apart.

In 2001, the Catholic Diocese divided its parishes into new administrative units called "Pastoral Care Area" (PCA). The PCAs were asked to create detailed plans that explained how they could work with each other to share resources. The plans included reconfiguring how neighboring parishes could offer services and serve their communities in response to an upcoming diocesan priest shortage.[26] All parishes, regardless of size or fiscal stability, were assigned to a PCA. Using these plans, the Diocese of Syracuse announced the closure of nearly 40 of its 171 parishes a few years later.[27] One of these parishes was St. Mary's. In early 2006, the St. Mary's Parish Council agreed to a merger between St. Mary's and a parish 4 miles away, Holy Cross Church in the suburb of DeWitt, New York. The merger plan that the St. Mary's Parish Council agreed upon stated that St. Mary's would become a "mission" of Holy Cross, yet the two churches would remain open and share one priest.[28] The St. Mary's community was disheartened by the decision; however, they rallied and created a "Mission Possible" taskforce to develop plans to work with the Holy Cross Church Parish Council to share resources, develop community building events, and offer religious education to the parish's children.[29]

However, in April 2006, the Diocese of Syracuse decided to permanently suppress, or close, St. Mary's Catholic Church without any further discussion with the St. Mary's lay community, a reversal of the diocesan process promised when the PCAs were created in 2001. At the time of St. Mary's suppression, Holy Cross Church took ownership of St. Mary's financial accounts, including the $60,000 St. Mary's received early that year from selling their baseball field to the town's Little League organization, money that was earmarked to fix St. Mary's aging roof.[30] Holy Cross was in substantial debt, over 1 million dollars, because of a recent renovation and expansion to its church building, while St. Mary's had no debt.[31] As the St. Mary's lay parishioners scrambled to develop a canonical appeal to protest their closure, the Diocese of Syracuse and Holy Cross Church moved fast to acquire St. Mary's assets, including pursuing plans to sell St. Mary's church building to the local school district for one dollar, even when the closure was under an active appeal process.[32]

In response to the sudden closure, a group of lay St. Mary's parishioners decided to act on multiple fronts, an act of resistance sustained for more than a decade. At the heart of this resistance is rhetorical advocacy work: public demonstrations, sit-ins, op-eds, articles, and interviews published in local newspapers and larger media outlets, including the *New York Times*, a local civil appeal process, and a Catholic canonical appeal process, which required them to make their case at the Vatican's highest court, the Apostolic Signatura, in Rome.

I argue that these rhetorical acts, especially when taken together, are a case of *feminist rhetorical resilience* as they rely on the concepts of agency, metis, and relationality.[33] The deeper warrants shaping St. Mary's rhetorical work are tied to the existential question at the core of twenty-first-century U.S. Catholicism: who owns this church? Ownership of a church can mean vastly different things to the laity than to those in the Catholic hierarchy. One way to establish ownership is to point to a church's civil or canonical jurisdiction. For some individuals, though, ownership is tied up with their lifetime relationship to a church building.

I want to reiterate here the importance of putting the story of St. Mary's appeal process in conversation with feminist theory and feminist rhetorical practices. As Eileen E. Schell wrote in 2010, feminist rhetorical studies is a field that brings together diverse methodological practices and inquiries, from historical archival recovery work to performance studies.[34] Schell contends that *motion* is at the heart of feminist rhetorical studies—moving across sites, cobbling together a *bricolage* of methods and methodologies, traversing through and across spaces, cultures, and identities, all attuned to the power structures that dictate how people access and use their available means of persuasion. This spirit of "mobility, flexibility, adaptability" central to feminist rhetorical work forms the undercurrent of how the St. Mary's lay community responded to their church closure, a canonical and literal act of suppression that silenced the community by seizing their space and removing the traditional avenues of persuasion available to lay people within a church parish.[35] What I have always seen in the story of St. Mary's is a lay community wayfinding through a crisis, inventing on the fly, using a range of rhetorical strategies to challenge the hierarchal power structure of the Catholic Church.

The concept of feminist rhetorical resilience described by Elizabeth A. Flynn, Patricia Sotirin, and Ann Brady offers a particularly productive lens through which to understand the rhetorical advocacy work of St. Mary's lay community. At first, the suppression of St. Mary's church seemed immutable. The first Vatican court that heard the case, the Congregation for the Clergy, sided with the Diocese, citing that the parishioners did not file a formal appeal until after the stated statute of limitations, thirty days.[36] The lay parishioners persisted despite this "difficult or even impossible challenge," marshaling resources among the local community to fund an appeal to the Vatican's highest court, the Apostolic Signatura, whose decision sided with the lay community in a historic first.[37] Feminist rhetorical resilience—Flynn, Sotirin, and Brady write—prioritizes the work of the community over the actions of an individual rhetor and emphasizes a community's continued invention and resourcefulness in response to "significant adversity."[38] Feminist rhetorical resilience is marked by how it construes *agency* as relational, its reliance on the resourceful improvisational spirit of *metis*, and the way the community cares for each other in mutuality and *relationality*. In the next section, I use this tripartite definition of feminist rhetorical resilience to read and more deeply understand the rhetorical advocacy work of St. Mary's lay community from 2006 onward.

THE FEMINIST RHETORICAL RESILIENCE OF ST. MARY'S LAY COMMUNITY

Agency

Flynn, Sotirin, and Brady define the rhetorical agency within resilience as fluid, inventive, pragmatic, and networked. Agency is not individual; instead, fellow actors work together to creatively find and use whatever rhetorical "resource" might be available to them in order to do their work.[39] This collective rhetorical agency is apparent through the perpetual vigils and sidewalk service protests led by the lay community of St. Mary's Catholic Church. When the Diocese of Syracuse changed the locks on the doors of St. Mary's church, the lay activists started a perpetual vigil, much like the vigils held across the Catholic Archdiocese of Boston in 2004. The vigil lasted for 217 days, the lay activists quickly creating shifts and schedules for over 100 members to ensure that there was always someone present inside the church.[40] The St. Mary's community members were able to "derive social and material support" through the quickly constituted relations that arose inside the occupied church: saying the rosary, sharing meals, and making sure their neighbor had a comfortable spot to sleep on the pews under the church's historic stained glass windows.[41] Although the situation was tense and confrontational with representatives from the Diocese, the affective atmosphere inside the church during the perpetual vigils was one of "determination, perseverance, hope, and imagination," hallmarks of the collective agency that Flynn, Sotirin, and Brady attribute to the work of feminist rhetorical resilience.[42]

In January 2008, Holy Cross Church asked the town police to end the perpetual vigil at St. Mary's by evicting all the protesters through a show of force. In response, the lay community of St. Mary's decided to continue their demonstration outside, a pragmatic shift that allowed the St. Mary's community to quickly and strategically "reinvent" both their identity and the rhetorical nature of their protest.[43] Inside the church, the parishioner's perpetual vigil was private, contained within the church building and its contentious relationship to the Diocese. On the sidewalk in front of the church steps, the protest became visible and public. The lay activists gathered every Sunday morning at 9:00 a.m. on the steps of St. Mary's church, regardless of weather.[44] Their collective protest shows the power of relational agency in feminist rhetorical resilience. Instead of one person persevering against a monolithic force, the St. Mary's community came together using whatever it was that they had—all their available means—to make their argument known to their newly expanded public audience.

The lay activists recognized, in both the perpetual vigil and the sidewalk services, the rhetorical power of "shaping and enacting relationships among selves and others, speakers and audiences, things and dreams, bodies and needs."[45] Of note is the way the St. Mary's community leveraged their bodies and their presence to rhetorical effect. During the perpetual vigils, the community members' bodies present inside the church rendered the new locks ineffective and denied the Diocese their desire to quickly and quietly shut down and sell the church. When they were evicted under the threat of violence to their bodies, this community showed its agency and its resourcefulness by laying claim to what space was available to them: the sidewalk and the front steps of their locked church. In their weekly sidewalk services and larger demonstrations, the community members come together to use the resources they have available: amps and microphones, voices and signs, donated hymnals, and even local priests who do not agree with the Diocese's decision. The lay community of St. Mary's enacts resilience through creating this collective agency, reinventing their strategy by drawing on the resources they are able to bring together as a community.

Metis

Metis, as Flynn, Sotirin, and Brady explain, is a Classical Greek rhetorical term, and it can be understood as "contextualized intelligence."[46] Metis, as they describe, "combines forethought, resourcefulness, opportunism, even deceit, to create circumstances where opportunities can be seized and possibilities explored."[47] Flynn, Sotirin, and Brady tell us that the Greek goddess Metis was a shape-shifter whose shape changed depending on the needs of the current situation. Metis is clearly at work in the St. Mary's story. Very early on, during the perpetual vigil, the lay community decided to pursue a canonical appeal, which meant they would protest the closure of St. Mary's to the Vatican itself. They realized that because the decisions of the Church lay outside New York State civil law, perhaps the only effective way to stop the closure and the sale of their church was to appeal to the higher levels of the Church hierarchy. They were able to do this—and, eventually, after five years of work, they became the only lay group of parishioners ever to succeed at the Apostolic Signatura, the Vatican's equivalent of the Supreme Court.[48] The St. Mary's lay community received two historic decrees that both prevented the Diocese from selling the St. Mary's church building and stated that St. Mary's must remain open.[49] This canonical appeal required the group to quickly develop an understanding of canon law. The first appeal was rejected by the lower Vatican court, the Congregation of the Clergy, because of procedural errors.[50] St. Mary's lay activists then made contacts with other Catholic communities in the United States who were also protesting their church closings, and these contacts helped them draft their subsequent appeals and translate the correspondence and decrees which were written in Latin.

Another element of metis is luck, and that luck was apparent in the resources individual people brought to the lay activist community: there were lawyers who could draft affidavits, bank tellers who reported that St. Mary's funds were being transferred to other accounts, prominent community members who could intervene with zoning boards that were under pressure to declare the church building unfit for occupancy, and a State Department employee with access to the Vatican who secured the group an audience and contacts with highly sought-after Vatican lawyers. The group was pragmatic and resourceful; it raised money in the community to send representatives to Rome to meet with the lawyers who would take the case all the way to the Apostolic Signatura.

Often, the group met at the local fire station until late in the night, shifting their ideas to meet the pressures and the opportunities presented to them, weighing the benefits of local action against a slower, quieter canonical appeal.

Relationality

The third concept Flynn, Sotirin, and Brady highlight as central to the idea of feminist rhetorical resilience is the concept of relationality, or the idea of "mutual empathy and empowerment," especially in situations where people are vulnerable.[51] St. Mary's lay activists recognized their vulnerability, as they were challenged not only by the local Church hierarchy in the Diocese but also by their friends and relatives, who named them "bad Catholics" for questioning the decision to close St. Mary's church. Working together—in the sidewalk services, during the perpetual vigil, on the canonical appeal—gave them security, confidence, and a sense of deep connection and community. There were real costs to this decade-long (and continuing) resistance: families stopped coming to the sidewalk services because they wanted their children to have the sacraments and belong to a larger church community. People central to the group in the beginning became ill or burned out, especially women who took on high-profile leadership roles. Members of the community disagreed about the group's methods, and some people left the community and left the Church completely. But there were also unexpected relationships built. When the doors to St. Mary's were locked, many local non-Catholic community members came to stand with and work with the lay activists, because what they saw was an outside power trying to damage an important local community. An important element of relationality is how the rhetorical act makes room for growth. In the story of St. Mary's, the lay community grew by deepening their relationships with one another, reshaping a more critical understanding of what it means to be part of the Catholic Church.

IN LIMBO: RESISTING HAPPY-ENDING STORIES

Flynn, Sotirin, and Brady caution against using big, sweeping change to measure the success of feminist rhetorical action, in particular action that resists dominant power structures. They acknowledge that there may be "little latitude for change in material and historical circumstances" for the activists.[52] Still, there is movement, even if it is "provisional," as the rhetors use their collective rhetorical resilience to engage in "ongoing refashionings of identity."[53] The change is underground seismic shifts: imperceptible, perhaps, but nevertheless present and, over time, consequential.

The story of St. Mary's does not have a satisfying happy ending. Despite over a decade of rhetorical advocacy work and two historic Vatican decrees, St. Mary's Church in Jamesville remains locked, open only for one or two Masses each year.[54] In response to the Vatican decrees that prevented the Diocese of Syracuse from selling the church building, the Diocese has decided to pursue the minimal requirements for keeping St. Mary's church a sacred space. Although the lay activists have not yet achieved what they organized to do over decade ago, their rhetorical resilience has had other positive effects. More churches in the Syracuse Diocese were slated for closure in 2007, and St. Mary's canonical appeal, along with lay activist groups like Preserve Our Parishes, nudged the Syracuse Diocese to consider other less drastic options, such as sharing a priest among several churches, thus preventing the same drastic closure that St. Mary's faced.[55] St. Mary's lay activists also demonstrate an ongoing vitalism and motion within the contemporary U.S. Catholic Church, highlighting how lay communities can assert their agency within the Catholic Church's patriarchal structure and use feminist rhetorical practices to form communities and challenge this powerful hierarchy.

Yet although there is much to celebrate within the resilience in the St. Mary's community, it is also crucial to pay attention to the cumulative corrosive effects of years of argument, petitioning against the Catholic Church's intransigent hierarchal and patriarchal power structures. This strife and the long years of resistance splintered and scattered the community: children grew too old to bring every Sunday, students went to college, families sought religious education and community elsewhere, couples divorced, families moved, people got sick and injured, lifelong community members died. The years without a physical space to gather gradually fragmented the community.

Flynn, Sotirin, and Brady argue, "There is a riskiness to resilient rhetorical action."[56] That risk is palpable in the St. Mary's story. When the lay community members decided to appeal their closure in 2006, they did not know that this action would lead to years of rhetorical advocacy work that stretched from the sidewalks in Jamesville to the highest court at the Vatican. The appeal was a risk: no other lay community had successfully overturned a diocesan closure before St. Mary's received their decrees from the Apostolic Signatura in 2011. Beyond the appeal, though, the lay community of St. Mary's risked the more subtle, yet perhaps more significant, "refashioning" of their identities. The rhetorical advocacy work the lay community did together led them to question their identities as Catholics and realize their mutual reliance on the people within their lay Catholic community. The rhetorical work of their appeal against the Diocese's decision fundamentally changed this community, weaving new networks of identity and community as, together, they wrote and researched appeals, prayed the rosary in their perpetual vigils, and met together, every week, on the front steps of St. Mary's Church.

NOTES

1. Mary J. Henold, "'A Matter of Conversion': American Catholic Feminism in Transition, 1975–1978," *American Catholic Studies* 116, no. 4 (2005): 2.

2. Kristin McGuire, Abigail J. Stewart, and Nicola Curtin, "Becoming Feminist Activists: Comparing Narratives," *Feminist Studies* 36, no. 1 (2010): 122.

3. Elizabeth A. Flynn, Patricia Sotirin, and Ann Brady, *Feminist Rhetorical Resilience* (Logan: Utah State University Press, 2012), 1.

4. Angela Duckworth, *Grit: The Power of Passion and Perseverance* (New York: Scribner, 2016), 1.

5. Flynn, Sotirin, and Brady, *Feminist Rhetorical Resilience*, 1.

6. Jacqueline Jones Royster, *Traces of a Stream: Literacy and Social Change among African American Women* (Pittsburgh: University of Pittsburgh Press, 2000), 276.

7. Alan Cooperman, et al., "America's Changing Religious Landscape," *Pew Research Center*, May 12, 2015, https://www.pewforum.org/2015/05/12/americas-changing-religious-landscape/; Michael Lipka, "The Number of U.S. Catholics Has Grown, So Why Are There Fewer Parishes?" *Pew Research Center*, November 6, 2014, https://www.pewresearch.org/fact-tank/2014/11/06/the-number-of-u-s-catholics-has-grown-so-why-are-there-fewer-parishes/; Brian McGill, "Catholicism in the U.S.," *The Wall Street Journal*, September 18, 2015, http://graphics.wsj.com/catholics-us/; Lydia Saad, "Catholics' Church Attendance Resumes Downward Slide," *Gallup*, April 9, 2018, https://news.gallup.com/poll/232226/church-attendance-among-catholics-resumes-downward-slide.aspx.

8. Claire Gecewicz and Gregory A. Smith, "Americans See Catholic Clergy Abuse as an Ongoing Problem," *Pew Research Center*, June 11, 2019, https://www.pewforum.org/2019/06/11/americans-see-catholic-clergy-sex-abuse-as-an-ongoing-problem/; David Masci and Gregory A. Smith, "7 Facts about American Catholics," *Pew Research Center*, October 10, 2018, https://www.pewresearch.org/fact-tank/2018/10/10/7-facts-about-american-catholics/.

9. McGill, "Catholicism in the U.S."

10. Lipka, "The Number of U.S. Catholics."

11. Marye Cathryn Goldsmith, "Changing Community in a Changing Landscape: Catholic Church Closings in the Illinois River Valley" (MA thesis. University of Wyoming, May 2011), 4; Maciej J. Mankowski, "Journeying Together in Christ as a Viable Parish Community: Pastoral Recommendations for Merging, Closing, and Collaborating of Catholic Parishes Based on Selected Case Studies from the Diocese of Youngstown, Ohio" (PhD diss., St. Mary Seminary and Graduate School of Theology, May 2016), 2; Sharon Otterman, "Heartache for New York's Catholics as Church Closings Are Announced," *The New York Times*, November 2, 2014, https://www.nytimes.com/2014/11/03/nyregion/new-york-catholics-are-set-to-learn-fate-of-their-parishes.html.

12. John C. Seitz, *No Closure: Catholic Practice and Boston's Parish Shutdowns* (Boston: Harvard University Press, 2011), 3, 10.

13. Seitz, *No Closure*, 15.

14. Seitz, *No Closure*, 6, 15.

15. Trushna Parekh, "Of Armed Guards and Kente Cloth: Afro-Creole Catholics and the Battle for St. Augustine Parish in Post-Katrina New Orleans," *American Quarterly* 61, no. 3 (2009): 577.

16. Parekh, "Of Armed Guards," 557.

17. Seitz, *No Closure*, 9.

18. "Responsibilities and Rights of the Laity," Voice of the Faithful, accessed February 1, 2021, http://votf.org/Voice_of_Renewal/Rights_of_the_Laity.pdf.

19. Matthew T. Loveland and Margret Ksander, "Shepherds and Sheep: Parish Reconfiguration, Authority, and Activism in a Catholic Diocese," *Review of Religious Research* 56, no. 3, (2014): 444.

20. Loveland and Ksander, "Shepherds and Sheep," 448.

21. Loveland and Ksander, "Shepherds and Sheep," 449.

22. Loveland and Ksander, "Shepherds and Sheep," 450.

23. Loveland and Ksander, "Shepherds and Sheep," 453.

24. Dick Case, "Refusing to Let Their Church Die," *Syracuse Post-Standard*, November 18, 2007, accessed February 1, 2021, http://stbartsnorwichny.com/closed-churches.htm#Refusing.

25. "Letter of Clarification in Response to 6-12-07 Letter from Bishop Moynihan," letter from Parishioners and Parish of St. Mary's to His Eminence Claudio Hummus, Congregation for the Clergy, June 12, 2007.

26. James J. Moynihan, "Equipping the Saints for the Work of Ministry: A Pastoral Letter," Roman Catholic Diocese of Syracuse, New York, November 1, 2001, https://syracusediocese.org/assets/Uploads/pdfs/pastoralletter-moynihan.pdf.

27. Loveland and Ksander, "Shepherds and Sheep," 444.

28. "Hierarchical Recourse in Response to Decree Of Suppression and Confiscation," appeal from Parishioners and Parish of St. Mary's to Congregation for the Clergy, May 26, 2007.

29. "Hierarchical Recourse."

30. "Letter of Clarification."

31. "Hierarchical Recourse."

32. "Letter of Clarification."

33. Flynn, Sotirin, and Brady, *Feminist Rhetorical Resilience.*

34. Eileen E. Schell, "Introduction," in *Rhetorica in Motion*, eds. by Eileen E. Schell, K.J. Rawson, and Kate Ronald (Pittsburgh: University of Pittsburgh Press, 2010), 7.

35. Schell, "Introduction," 6.

36. "Letter of Clarification."

37. Flynn, Sotirin, and Brady, *Feminist Rhetorical Resilience*, 1; "Jurisprudence of the Supreme Tribunal of the Apostolic Signatura," *The Jurist* 73 (2013): 597.

38. Flynn, Sotirin, and Brady, *Feminist Rhetorical Resilience*, 1.

39. Flynn, Sotirin, and Brady, *Feminist Rhetorical Resilience*, 7.

40. Case, "Refusing"; Fernanda Santos, "Upstate, Drop in Catholics Lead to Drop in Churches," *The New York Times*, February 10, 2008, https://www.nytimes.com/2008/02/10/nyregion/10church.html.

41. Flynn, Sotirin, and Brady, *Feminist Rhetorical Resilience*, 8.

42. Flynn, Sotirin, and Brady, *Feminist Rhetorical Resilience*, 8; Case, "Refusing."
43. Flynn, Sotirin, and Brady, *Feminist Rhetorical Resilience*, 8.
44. Santos, "Upstate."
45. Flynn, Sotirin, and Brady, *Feminist Rhetorical Resilience*, 8.
46. Flynn, Sotirin, and Brady, *Feminist Rhetorical Resilience*, 8.
47. Flynn, Sotirin, and Brady, *Feminist Rhetorical Resilience*, 9.
48. "Jurisprudence;" Maren Guse, "Vatican Says No Reason to Close Jamesville's St. Mary's Church," *CNY Central*, December 11, 2011, https://cnycentral.com/news/local/vatican-says-no-reason-to-close-jamesvilles-st-marys-church.
49. "Definitive Sentence: Suppression of the Parish of St. Mary in 'Jamesville' and Reduction of the Church to Profane Use," College of Judges of the Supreme Tribunal of the Apostolic Signatura. Rome, August 11, 2011; Guse, "Vatican Says."
50. "Decree," Statement from the Congregation for the Clergy to Ms. Colleen LaTray, August 5, 2008.
51. Flynn, Sotirin, and Brady, *Feminist Rhetorical Resilience*, 11.
52. Flynn, Sotirin, and Brady, *Feminist Rhetorical Resilience*, 8.
53. Flynn, Sotirin, and Brady, *Feminist Rhetorical Resilience*, 8.
54. Maureen Nolan, "Mass Will Be Held at Shuttered St. Mary's Church in Jamesville," *Syracuse Post-Standard*, August 13, 2012, https://www.syracuse.com/news/2012/08/mass_will_be_held_at_shuttered.html.
55. Loveland and Ksander, "Shepherds and Sheep."
56. Flynn, Sotirin, and Brady, *Feminist Rhetorical Resilience*, 8.

BIBLIOGRAPHY

Case, Dick. "Refusing to Let Their Church Die." *Syracuse Post-Standard*, November 18, 2007. Accessed February 1, 2021. http://stbartsnorwichny.com/closedchurches.htm#Refusing.

Cooperman, Alan, et al, eds. "America's Changing Religious Landscape." *Pew Research Center*, May 12, 2015. https://www.pewforum.org/2015/05/12/americas-changing-religious-landscape/.

"Decree." Statement from the Congregation for the Clergy to Ms. Colleen LaTray. August 5, 2008.

"Definitive Sentence: Suppression of the Parish of St. Mary in 'Jamesville' and Reduction of the Church to Profane Use." College of Judges of the Supreme Tribunal of the Apostolic Signatura. August 11, 2011.

Duckworth, Angela. *Grit: The Power of Passion and Perseverance*. New York: Scribner, 2016.

Flynn, Elizabeth A., Patricia Sotirin, and Ann Brady. *Feminist Rhetorical Resilience*. Logan: Utah State University Press, 2012.

Gadoua, Renee K. "CNY Congregations Appeal to Vatican to Save Churches." *Syracuse Post-Standard*, June 25, 2007.

Gecewicz, Claire, and Gregory A. Smith. "Americans See Catholic Clergy Abuse as an Ongoing Problem." *Pew Research Center*, June 11, 2019. https://www.pewforum.org/2019/06/11/americans-see-catholic-clergy-sex-abuse-as-an-ongoing-problem/.

Goldsmith, Marye Cathryn. "Changing Community in a Changing Landscape: Catholic Church Closings in the Illinois River Valley." MA thesis. University of Wyoming, May 2011.

Guse, Maren. "Vatican Says No Reason to Close Jamesville's St. Mary's Church." *CNY Central*, December 11, 2011. https://cnycentral.com/news/local/vatican-says-no-reason-to-close-jamesvilles-st-marys-church.

Henold, Mary J. "'A Matter of Conversion': American Catholic Feminism in Transition, 1975–1978." *American Catholic Studies* 116, no. 4 (2005): 1–23.

"Hierarchical Recourse in Response to Decree of Suppression and Confiscation." Appeal from Parishioners and Parish of St. Mary's to Congregation for the Clergy. May 26, 2007.

"Jurisprudence of the Supreme Tribunal of the Apostolic Signatura." *The Jurist* 73 (2013): 597–643.

"Letter of Clarification in Response to 6-12-07 Letter from Bishop Moynihan." Letter from Parishioners and Parish of St. Mary's to His Eminence Claudio Hummus, Congregation for the Clergy. June 12, 2007.

Lipka, Michael. "The Number of U.S. Catholics Has Grown, So Why Are There Fewer Parishes?" *Pew Research Center*, November 6, 2014. https://www.pewresearch.org/fact-tank/2014/11/06/the-number-of-u-s-catholics-has-grown-so-why-are-there-fewer-parishes/.

Loveland, Matthew T. and Margret Ksander. "Shepherds and Sheep: Parish Reconfiguration, Authority, and Activism in a Catholic Diocese." *Review of Religious Research* 56, no. 3 (2014): 443–465.

Mankowski, Maciej J. "Journeying Together in Christ as a Viable Parish Community: Pastoral Recommendations for Merging, Closing, and Collaborating of Catholic Parishes Based on Selected Case Studies from the Diocese of Youngstown, Ohio." PhD diss., St. Mary Seminary and Graduate School of Theology, May 2016.

Masci, David, and Gregory A. Smith. "7 Facts about American Catholics." *Pew Research Center*, October 10, 2018. https://www.pewresearch.org/fact-tank/2018/10/10/7-facts-about-american-catholics/.

McGill, Brian. "Catholicism in the U.S." *The Wall Street Journal*, September 18, 2015. http://graphics.wsj.com/catholics-us/.

McGuire, Kristin, Abigail J. Stewart, and Nicola Curtin. "Becoming Feminist Activists: Comparing Narratives." *Feminist Studies* 36, no. 1 (2010): 99–125.

Moynihan, James J. "Equipping the Saints for the Work of Ministry: A Pastoral Letter." Roman Catholic Diocese of Syracuse, New York. November 1, 2001. https://syracusediocese.org/assets/Uploads/pdfs/pastoralletter-moynihan.pdf.

Nolan, Maureen. "Mass Will Be Held at Shuttered St. Mary's Church in Jamesville." *Syracuse Post-Standard*. August 13, 2012. https://www.syracuse.com/news/2012/08/mass_will_be_held_at_shuttered.html.

Otterman, Sharon. "Heartache for New York's Catholics as Church Closings Are Announced." *The New York Times*, November 2, 2014. https://www.nytimes.com

/2014/11/03/nyregion/new-york-catholics-are-set-to-learn-fate-of-their-parishes .html.

Parekh, Trushna. "Of Armed Guards and Kente Cloth: Afro-Creole Catholics and the Battle for St. Augustine Parish in Post-Katrina New Orleans." *American Quarterly* 61, no. 3 (2009): 557–581.

Royster, Jacqueline Jones. *Traces of a Stream: Literacy and Social Change among African American Women*. Pittsburgh: University of Pittsburgh Press, 2000.

Saad, Lydia. "Catholics' Church Attendance Resumes Downward Slide." *Gallup*, April 9, 2018. https://news.gallup.com/poll/232226/church-attendance-among -catholics-resumes-downward-slide.aspx.

Santos, Fernanda. "Upstate, Drop in Catholics Lead to Drop in Churches." *The New York Times*, February 10, 2008. https://www.nytimes.com/2008/02/10/nyregion /10church.html.

Schell, Eileen E. "Introduction." In *Rhetorica in Motion*, edited by Eileen E. Schell, K.J. Rawson, and Kate Ronald, 1–20. Pittsburgh: University of Pittsburgh Press, 2010.

Seitz, John C. *No Closure: Catholic Practice and Boston's Parish Shutdowns*. Boston: Harvard University Press, 2011.

Voice of the Faithful. "Responsibilities and Rights of the Laity." Accessed February 1, 2021. http://votf.org/Voice_of_Renewal/Rights_of_the_Laity.pdf.

Chapter 6

Clergy Sex Abuse Scandals and the (Re)Making of Good Catholic Mothers

Allison Niebauer and Elisa Vogel

In 2019, the Catholic Women's Forum, an international network of Catholic women, were invited to assist with preparations for the Vatican's summit on preventing clergy perpetrated sexual abuse (CPSA). They chose to submit a survey of 5,038 Catholic lay women reporting attitudes toward the sexual abuse crisis; a personal testimony from Letitia Peyton, a mother whose child had been victimized by CPSA; and recommendations from five female seminary professors. The director of the Catholic Women's Forum, Mary Rice Hasson, summarized the sentiments that prompted the creation of the documents thusly:

> These are faithful, Catholic women. . . . Average women are frustrated by their inability to share the pain and bring forth suggestions or even get a response from bishops. There is no mechanism for them to be heard, and yet, women are the most active in the Church. We are mothers; our children are at risk, and serve the Church, and become the future priests.[1]

Hasson's statement highlights a collection of individuals who are seeking to speak *as* Catholic mothers. They are defined by their position as mothers, the constraints they face in terms of publicity and status, and the role they play within the Church. They utilize their position as Catholic mothers as a justification for their right to speak. Here, the position of Catholic motherhood becomes a platform for speech. In doing so, it sets the conditions of speech for people seeking to utilize it. In other words, Hasson's statement describes the subject position of Catholic motherhood within the Catholic Church.

Catholic motherhood is one role that exists within a community. The community itself assigns it status and forms the conditions by which it operates.

Catholic motherhood, as a role, is comprised by a set of practices that individuals occupying it do. It is also shaped by discursive and cultural norms regarding how these practices should be enacted. Thus, subject positions are made distinctive within a community through both rhetorical and structural processes.[2] Celeste Condit helpfully conceives of a subject position as a calcified public identity, created by communal expectations for how one should perform it. In other words, subject positions are created, sustained, and maintained by cultural evaluations of its ethos. Individuals operationalizing this subject position are constrained and enabled by the rhetorical and material resources that this position makes available. What is "sayable" and "doable" as a Catholic mother depends upon an individual's ability to perform within these expectations.[3]

And yet, individuals rarely belong to one community, nor are they limited to one role. They often maintain citizenships within several realms and play different roles within each of those communities. Even the term "Catholic Mothers" hints at the overlapping communities (and roles) women inhabit within the nuclear family, the religious community, and the nation-state. Hence, individuals live within multiple roles and communities, even as their ability to act within a given community is circumscribed by their subject positions. Scholars of citizenship and border rhetorics point to the ways citizenship and community as rhetorical forms delineate both the discursive and material roles that individuals occupy.[4] While most citizenship scholars write about an individual's relationship to the nation-state, their observations about the role of rhetoric in delineating subject positions and citizenship practices are helpful in considering communities more broadly.[5] They highlight how individuals can leverage the overlap that comes from living within multiple roles and communities to change structural norms of citizenship or how an individual is configured in relationship to communal authority and the co-constitutive civic imaginary.[6] That is to say, individuals can change not just the structural practices that inform their subject position but how the community imagines and evaluates this position. We are interested in how Catholic women have used the resources afforded to them by their overlapping citizenship within multiple communities to transform the structural norms and civic imaginary of the Catholic Church with regard to the subject position of Catholic mothers.

In this chapter, we demonstrate how Catholic women utilized the resources afforded through their secular citizenship, namely, the civil legal system, to seek redress in response to revelations of CPSA. By utilizing the resources of secular citizenship, Catholic women have been able to shift cultural expectations of its performance. While Hasson's summary illustrates the barriers to speaking that Catholic mothers continue to face in influencing the

Church's reaction to CPSA, her statement also illuminates the ways in which the subject position of Catholic motherhood has shifted over the past forty years. Catholic mothers have been a driving force within Catholic survivors' movements, have secured major legal victories for their children and, along with survivors and allies, have helped to usher in significant reforms within the national Catholic Church.[7] The statements that we survey and the accomplishments they represent make it clear that the subject position of Catholic motherhood has shifted to include and justify advocacy on behalf of children within the institutional Church. Good Catholic mothers do not simply involve their children in the life of the institutional Church; they also advocate for them and defend them within it.

We find evidence for these claims in the public statements of five women whose children were victims of CPSA, given as a part of interviews, legal testimony, and group advocacy.[8] Statements made by these women stretch through the three eras or "waves" of public revelation and litigation against the Catholic Church from the late 1980s to 2018.[9] We chose these women because they are representative of women whose children have been victims of CPSA and because they are unique in how they acted. By representative, we mean that their public statements reflect similar themes regarding the role of Catholic mothers prior to the experience of CPSA, similar conflicts with their identity as Catholic mothers after the revelation of CPSA, and similar justifications for taking civil legal action against the institutional Church. Their statements help us to understand the common narrative factors that have defined what being a good Catholic woman was and what a good Catholic mother is now.

These women have also impacted the fight for accountability and reform in unique ways. While noting some of the particulars of each woman's story, we highlight the experience of Jeanne Miller due to her outsized influence in shaping the narrative resources of the Catholic survivors' movement. Miller became a public figure through her experience advocating against CPSA during the late 1980s and was a pioneer in publicizing the problem.[10] In his ethnographic study of the early survivor's movement in Chicago, Brian Clites emphasizes how Miller's belief in the power of speech shaped the narrative forms and legal mechanisms utilized by subsequent survivors.[11] Like Barbara Blaine, the founder of the Survivors Network for those Abused by Priests whose efforts to achieve accountability within the Church are detailed by White-Farnham within this volume, Miller publicized her story in an attempt to create a community of survivors who could collectively seek redress from the Church. We emphasize the impact of Miller's rhetoric by beginning each section of the case study with her public statements.

The testimonies of the four subsequent women demonstrate the impact of Miller's advocacy and narrative force. Toni McMorrow and Sylvia Gameros are two women who filed cases on behalf of their children during the second wave of litigation against the Church or after the national scandal involving the Archdiocese of Boston.[12] Their cases, while filed in opposite ends of the country, illustrate the continued struggle for Catholic mothers to seek redress within the Church and the quickly evolving norm of utilizing the civil legal system as a means of justice seeking. Barbara Aponte and Letitia Peyton both filed claims on behalf of their sons in the wake of the third wave of litigation created by multiple Diocesan and statewide Grand Jury Investigations after 2010. All of the women surveyed demonstrate how Catholic women have utilized the legal system as a means of publicity and reform within the Church.[13]

Analyzing the statements made by women across time reveals the development of a shift in the subject position of Catholic motherhood. We stress similarities found in our cluster analysis of their statements, and we emphasize how the repetition of narrative themes and legal mechanisms utilized by survivors and advocates throughout the past thirty years played a causal role in creating new cultural expectations for Catholic mothers.[14] We find evidence for these claims by examining how women come to explain and understand their role as Catholic mothers after revelations of CPSA. This requires analyzing the themes that rhetors use to describe their past understanding of themselves as Catholic mothers, the effect of the revelation of CPSA on that understanding, and the mechanisms and beliefs by which they sought to transform the constraints of that previous position.

Women rhetors birthed these changes into being by claiming discursive resources from outside of their established subject position. Kendall Phillips refers to this movement as a rhetorical maneuver, a "trading in one's established—or positioned—ethos for one that is not already accepted within a particular space."[15] In response to the perceived constraints of their subject position, women "violated the proscriptive limits of [their] subject position and [spoke] differently by drawing upon the resources of another subject position" coterminously occupied.[16] As White-Farnham emphasizes in her analysis of women within the survivors' movement, failing to find an audience for their speech within the Catholic Church, mothers explored alternative forums and audiences for their complaints. Particularly, we illustrate how women utilized the avenue of law as a vehicle for publicity and as an alternative form of citizenship. In doing so, they repeated a series of themes to describe and justify their estrangement from former conceptualizations of Catholic motherhood and to invent a new constitution of the subject position.[17]

THE IMPACT OF CPSA ON THE SUBJECT POSITION OF CATHOLIC MOTHERHOOD

In this section, we utilize the public statements of the aforementioned women to understand how women understood the subject position of Catholic motherhood prior to revelations of CPSA, the impact of CPSA on this understanding, how women understood the role of the legal system in providing redress for CPSA, and the subsequent shift in women's conception of Catholic motherhood. To this end, we have highlighted four reoccurring themes found in these four movements.

Theme 1: Good Catholic Mothers Involve Themselves and Their Families in the life of the Church

What did Catholic motherhood mean to Miller, McMorrow, Gameros, Aponte, and Peyton prior to revelations of CPSA? And what did it look like to perform this position well? In the public statements offered by these five women, four themes or attributes arose. For all five women, being a Catholic mother meant being involved in their local parish, encouraging their children to be involved in their local parish, trusting priests, and trusting the institution of the Church.

In their public addresses, these women emphasized that prior to revelations of CPSA, deep ties existed between their own lives and their local parishes. For Jeanne Miller, being a good Catholic mother meant, first, being deeply involved in the local life of her parish. Church was the "heartbeat" of family life. She, herself, was involved in the religious education curriculum at her parish.[18] Barbara Aponte, writing twenty years and 500 miles away from Miller, reflected similar sensibilities. She was not only involved with her local parish, but worked for the Church.[19] Letitia Peyton, in her public testimony in 2018, described her parish as a small, safe family. She was involved at the Church, and her husband served as a Deacon.[20] In invoking their religious involvement in Church, all five women emphasized their own personal commitment to the Church in terms of belief and energy invested.

These women also stated that, prior to the revelation of CPSA, they had encouraged their children to be involved in the Church. Miller stated that she hoped her son would become a priest in the future and encouraged her son to be an altar boy.[21] Similarly, Peyton encouraged her son to spend time with their parish priest and become an altar boy.[22] Aponte sent her son to a Catholic high school.[23] All of these women stressed that their investment in the Church was such that they were willing to use their parental authority to involve their children as well. To be a good Catholic mother meant involving their children in the life of the Church.

Prior to revelations of CPSA, these women collectively stressed that they possessed a high degree of trust in their priests and the institution of the Church. McMorrow stated that she believed priests to be "safe" and "positive" influences in the lives of people.[24] Miller similarly reported that she was "thrilled" when her local parish priest started paying attention to her son, hoping it would encourage him in his aspirations to the priesthood.[25] Aponte's trust in priests was so absolute that she asked her son to rip out a page of a journal exercise in which he described trying to avoid Brother Stephen Baker's "weird" athletic treatments lest he get "Brother Steve" in trouble.[26] For each of these women, priests were positive, trustworthy, and safe. Being a good Catholic mother meant trusting priests, and, in turn, trusting their children with priests.

All of these statements point to expectations regarding citizenship for Catholic mothers within the Church. Individuals occupying the subject position of Catholic mothers would face the expectations that they involve themselves and their children in the life of the Church. To be a good Catholic mother was to trust religious leaders with their children and to trust the apparatus of the institutional Church. Performing this subject position well allowed one to live within community and to participate as a citizen. Citizenship within any community, Josue David Cisneros reminds us, is defined not simply through legal or written mechanisms but through a civic imaginary upheld by discursive and material practices and manifested through beliefs.[27] To be a good citizen was to uphold the civic imaginary regarding the role of Catholic mothers—involving themselves and their families, trusting priests and the institutional Church.

Theme 2: Revelations of CPSA Fracture Catholic Mothers' Relationship with the Institutional Church

All five women described the effect of revelations of CPSA in terms of loss and change in perception. For these women, revelations of CPSA fractured their relationship with the institutional Church, friends, family, and with their prior understandings of the world. Revelations of CPSA were depicted as a watershed moment in which the fracture within their experiences of Catholic citizenship ultimately required a renegotiation of their subject positions.

In their public testimonies and addresses, these women described a profound sense of loss in their Church and family lives at the revelation of CPSA. This loss affected their family life and their life within the Church. Miller described the fallout from revelations of CPSA as shattering her family life and her trust within the institutional Church.[28] McMorrow detailed in her court testimony how the fallout from CPSA destroyed her son's experience of normal age-appropriate experiences, such as finishing high school and attending senior prom.[29] Gameros and Peyton depicted an overwhelming sense of loss: loss of trust in their friendships and in their relationships with the Church community.[30] For example, Peyton emphasized her broken faith in priests themselves, going from being comfortable contacting any of them to trusting none of them.[31]

Revelations of CPSA caused fractures in their belief of the trustworthiness of the communal apparatus, affecting their relationships with fellow community members and institutional members alike. Community, Robert DeChaine reminds us, is imagined and, therefore complex and precarious—a constitutive fiction enacted by individuals who seek the common goal of communion.[32] Revelations of CPSA destroyed this constitutive fiction of community for these women, forcing them to reevaluate their own citizenship within it.

Theme 3: Good Catholic Mothers Seek Redress for CPSA

Though the women included in the case study had unique responses to the problem of CPSA, three themes emerged from their testimonies. First, women sought accountability and redress for CPSA initially through the Church. Second, in different ways, these women felt betrayed by the institutional Church and experienced alienation as a result. Lastly, as a result of this failure to find satisfactory redress through the Church, all five women sought redress through the civil legal system. The emergence of these three themes within the testimony of these women points to a concept of citizenship for good Catholic mothers. It was the failure of the Church to provide satisfactory resolution of their problem that prompted them to seek justice through the secular legal system.

A consistent theme among these women is that they first sought accountability through the institutional Church. In Miller's testimony, she confessed that, initially, it "never occurred to us to go to the police or take any legal action." Instead, she contacted the Diocesan religious director and learned that the abusive priest had already been reported to the Archdiocese for improper behavior. Armed with this knowledge, she strove to meet with members of the Diocesan hierarchy in an attempt to restrict access for her son's abuser and to find a means for her son to receive counseling.[33] Gameros, as a reaction to the revelation that her daughter had been abused, confronted members of the Church and Diocese about the rape.[34] Within days of her son coming to her with his allegations, McMorrow approached Church officials who assured her they would investigate—only to have it later revealed that the Church and legal investigations had found the allegation credible, yet the officials closed the case.[35] Aponte and Peyton reported meeting with their respective bishops to discuss allegations without finding satisfactory redress.[36]

Though different in the reasons for their dissatisfaction, all women reported experiencing alienation as a result of their treatment by the institutional Church. Miller described being ignored, then stonewalled, and, finally, "threatened with excommunication" after reporting her son's abuse.[37] Other women described their experience of silencing and disenfranchisement as a figurative excommunication. "From that point on," Gameros stated in relation to reporting the abuse, "[representatives from the Church] never called me or came near me. . . . It was like they wanted to lay all the blame on (my daughter). It was like they wished we would just go away." She felt further alienated by the news that the Diocese was helping the accused individual with legal assistance.[38] Peyton reported a similar experience. The reaction of the hierarchy demonstrated, for her, that the institutional Church was not taking the problem of CPSA seriously and that it was only the actions of faithful laity that kept the problem from being ignored. Aponte took similar umbrage stating, "I feel personally victimized by this church . . . devalued by this church, watching them demonstrate over and over that their primary goal is self-protection and self-promotion."[39]

Dissatisfied with the inaction of the institutionalized Church, women turned to the civil legal system for accountability and redress. Miller, as one of the first public figures in the fight against CPSA, argued that turning to the legal system violated what she thought was the correct posture of a good Catholic, characterizing it as "forgive and forget, and nod in the face of anything." But she also felt that she could not let the issue go while her son's abuser still had access to children. After discovering that the state attorney did not have sufficient evidence to convict her son's abuser, Miller and her family brought a lawsuit against the Diocese, arguing to get the Archdiocese to restrict the accused access to children and to get the Archdiocese to pay for counseling for the boys who were abused. The Archdiocese continued to refuse to acknowledge any wrongdoing on the part of the accused priest and would not pay for counseling.[40]

Though Miller was undeniably a pioneer in taking legal action against the Archdiocese, the other women testified to similar paths toward legal accountability. For Gameros, the Diocese's actions led her to file a suit seeking compensatory and punitive damages. Likewise, Aponte joined a suit against the Diocese of Altoona Johnstown and Bishop McCort High School as part of a survivor advocacy group.[41] Peyton filed criminal charges against her son's abuser and filed a civil action against the Diocese. She reported being dismayed that, despite finding out a history of CPSA within the Diocese, the Church had yet to take meaningful action to remedy the institutional problem of CPSA. McMorrow offered similar justifications for civil legal action against the institutional Church. The lawsuit proposed damages not simply for the event of CPSA but for the ensuing cover-up by the Church as well.[42] For each of these women, civil legal action provided an outside mechanism for seeking redress for CPSA in addition to accountability for the [in]actions of the institutional Church.

In Clites's analysis of the early survivors' movement in Chicago, he highlights the solidification of several of these themes, specifically the narrative that the institutional Church's action had forced victims to seek redress through the legal system. He quotes Tom Economus, Miller's successor in the advocacy organization VOCAL (Victims of Clergy Sex Abuse Linkup), as stating, "In the early days of VOCAL, we were vulnerable, fragmented people, who looked to their Church for help and have been turned away. . . . If the Church had *listened* to our pain, lawsuits would not have been filed."[43] Jennifer Balboni's analysis of survivors' motivations for seeking civil litigation revealed a similar trope. Civil lawsuits, this narrative suggests, were only required because of the inaction of the institutional Church.[44] As a result of the alienation and lack of satisfaction offered by the institutional Church, women turned to the civil legal system. In doing so, they used the resources available to them through their secular citizenship to demand accountability from their Catholic communities. Clites writes, "These victims were strategically leveraging one institutional identity in order to reform another," believing that by leveraging the microphones of alternative publics, they could ultimately reach and transform their Catholic community.[45] In the statements of these five women, we see this narrative in action: by seeking redress through the civil legal system, Catholic mothers believed they would be able to alter the response of the institutional Church and find accountability. In doing so, they withdrew the terms of their citizenship within the Church itself.

Theme 4: Good Catholic Mothers Advocate for Children within the Institutional Church

Though unique in how they reacted to revelations of CPSA, the statements of each woman illustrate three reoccurring themes regarding how women understood their own identities and responsibilities as Catholic mothers in the wake of CPSA allegations. First, each woman expressed feeling a responsibility to seek accountability from the institutionalized Church on behalf of their own children and others. Their duties as mothers, rather than Catholic mothers, became a justification for seeking accountability, even when it pitted them against the institutionalized Church. Second, the statements of each woman disclose an emphasis on the role of publicity as an aspect of accountability. Their lack of ability to find accountability within the institutionalized Church justified their public speech, even when it shed an unflattering light on the

Church. Finally, though different in how they reconceptualized faith, each woman expressed needing to redefine their faith in regard to the institutional Church. These three clusters illustrate a final shift in conceptualizations of what it means to be a good Catholic mother after CPSA.

In the wake of her lawsuit against the Archdiocese, Jeanne Miller found herself "morally, financially, and spiritually devastated." Her dissatisfaction with the resolution of the lawsuit (they settled due to financial constraints) led her to pursue the matter through other mechanisms such as writing and speaking on talk shows. This generated considerable publicity and Miller was inundated with stories of individuals who had similar accounts to her son. This knowledge led her to found one of the first survivor advocacy groups and push for reforms within the Church. "It's not over," she stated. "For me or for my son, or for any of the others that have suffered." For Miller, the fact that her son's experience was shared by so many others served as a justification for continuing to confront the institutionalized Church.[46]

The responsibility Miller felt toward her own children and others, even when confronted with the institutional Church, is mirrored in the statements and actions of the other mothers surveyed. For Aponte, the experience of the institutionalized Church's method for dealing with allegations led her to join a survivor' advocacy group, which advocated for settlements on behalf of victims and protested the Diocese and criminal proceedings of the Franciscan Friars that oversaw her son's abuser. McMorrow described the protection of her children and others as reason for bringing suit.[47] Peyton similarly justified a renewed sense of responsibility: "I want my children to say, our mom stood up and worked for change and justice in the church and made a difference. . . . My hope is that I can make a difference by becoming active in advocating for my son and other victims of clerical sexual abuse while helping to root out the evil and corruption that is in my church."[48] The perception of insufficient institutional remedies for CPSA justified, for all of these women, further advocacy on the behalf of children.

For these women, publicity was a key aspect of this advocacy. For Miller, the perceived intransigence of the institutionalized Church justified public action. Publicity was a way in which victim advocacy groups could keep public attention on the Church's actions and force meaningful reforms.[49] Aponte offered a similar account. From her perspective, the Church benefited from the silence of victims. "Speaking is healing," she urged in a message to victims. As she saw it, coming forth with public accounts helped embolden others to come forward and hold the Church accountable as well.[50] For Peyton, the failure of the institutional Church to make meaningful reforms meant that faithful laity had to speak out to "help to repair the damage done by the scandals that plague the church." Speaking before the summit of the

2018 Vatican Conference on CPSA, Peyton urged the Diocesan hierarchy to turn to the faithful laity to do what the Diocesan hierarchy had failed to do.[51] Additionally, McMorrow described the publicity as a way to hold priests and bishops accountable for following their own policies, emphasizing the importance of bringing her family's account forward to encourage other victims to speak out and protect other children.[52]

Clites's study emphasizes that the origin for the belief in the necessity of public speech lay in the early survivors' movement, and, in particular, the rhetoric of Jeanne Miller. Miller viewed publicity as integral to moral and legal accountability in the Church, as well as healing for survivors. Through her involvement in VOCAL, the first survivors' group, Miller solidified this belief within subsequent survivor narratives. In Clites's words, VOCAL "created an enduring model and identity of survivor hood of clergy abuse, providing the narrative elements, platforms, and meanings to voice. To be a survivor was to tell one's story, first to other survivors, and then to the public, to name one's accuser, and to demand moral and legal accountability."[53] We see within the public speech of these women a belief in the power of speech to not just hold the Church responsible within the secular realm but to use public pressure garnered by publicity to transform the Church itself. In doing so, women utilized the terms of publicity to redefine their own citizenship within the Church.

For each woman, the revelation of CPSA and the inaction of the institutionalized Church forced them to reimagine their spiritual identity. For Miller, "resurrecting" her belief system meant letting go of her faith in the institutionalized Church in favor of a more personal religion.[54] For Gameros, her faith in God remained intact, but her faith in the institutionalized Church was diminished.[55] For Aponte and McMorrow, revelations of CPSA left them unable to continue within the Catholic Church as a religious system.[56] Peyton kept her Catholic faith by disassociating the actions of members of the Diocese from the institutionalized Church. While experiencing a loss of faith in the institutional Church, she argued that the Church was comprised of "faithful laity" who could help the Church heal, if given the opportunity.[57] For each woman, the revelation of CPSA and experience of the inadequacy of the institutionalized response forced a reckoning with their own faith and relationship with the institution of the Catholic Church.

We can see in the statements of these women movements away from their prior understanding of what constituted a good Catholic mother toward a new understanding of the position. Prior to revelations of CPSA, good Catholic mothers trusted priests, involved their children in the life of the Church, and trusted the communal apparatus to provide means of redress for violations of communal norms. The inaction of the institutional Church led Catholic mothers to emphasize their responsibilities to their children and led them to utilize their secular legal standing to publicly hold the institutional Church accountable. Indeed, the failure of the institutional Church to meaningfully remedy childhood abuse became a form of a priori justification for stepping outside of established citizenship practices to seek redress. Though each woman configured her identity as a Catholic differently after revelations of CPSA, they are all similar in their belief that it is the responsibility of Catholic mothers to hold institutional actors accountable for child abuse. This belief is echoed in Hasson's statement.[58] Gone is the implicit trust in priests and the apparatus of the Church. In its place is the new subject position of Catholic mothers. Catholic mothers advocate for their children and other children within the life of the institutionalized Church.

CONCLUSION: CULTURE, POWER, AND THE (RE)MAKING OF A SUBJECT POSITION

The case study demonstrates how Catholic mothers, motivated by their perception of inadequate institutional redress, utilized the secular legal system as a means of seeking justice, accountability, and reform within the Church. These women came to see their duties as mothers to seek redress for their children and other children as incompatible with the mechanisms of redress offered by the Church. This perception became their justification for seeking reform in the secular realm. As a result, Catholic mothers, both individually and collectively, have successfully pushed for significant reforms within the Church and sought redress for victims. This process has shifted the subject position of Catholic motherhood itself. This is evidenced in the statements of these women and their newfound understanding of the position. It is also seen in the collective lobbying efforts of groups such as the Catholic Women's Forum. To be a Catholic mother, we have contended, is to safeguard and advocate for children within the Church.

We have argued that this shift in the subject position of Catholic motherhood is best understood through a concept of multiple citizenships. When significant violations of communal expectations occurred within their Catholic community, these women turned to the resources afforded to them through their secular communities for purposes of redress and reform. Publicity and the civil litigation system became the main modes of secular citizenship by which these women sought to transform their citizenship status within the institutionalized Church.

While the case study demonstrates how these women utilized the opportunities afforded them through multiple identities to transform their subject position, it also begs the question of why they were successful in their efforts. Here, we offer a broader observation regarding the relationship between overlapping areas of citizenship and power. Women were only able to leverage their secular legal identities and bring publicity to the issue of child sex abuse because of power differentials between the community of the institutional Church and the community of the nation-state. The nation-state offered a mechanism of redress that women could leverage against the community of the Church. However, child abuse within the institutional Church had to be recognized by a secular audience not just as a problem but as a legal problem. This was far from a historic inevitability.

Several causal factors can be identified that explain why women were able to effectively leverage the legal system to seek redress from the Church. First, the first wave of clergy sex abuse litigation was brought during an explosion of civil litigation, particularly against institutions. A series of federal reforms led to a proliferation of new statutes related to personal injury and employment claims.[59] Previous bans that kept lawyers from advertising their services directly to clients were overturned.[60] This had the effect of raising public awareness not just of lawyers' services but of different kinds of injuries that could be settled within a legal sphere. A language of rights, cultivated by the civil rights era within the 1960s, was circulated by this explosion of advertising. The status of civil litigation fundamentally changed in America during the late 1970s and 1980s, shifting the balance of power between individuals and institutions. This shift enabled secular communities to conceive of child abuse not just as a social problem but as a legal and institutional problem.[61]

A second causal factor that explains why women were able to successfully leverage one institutional identity against the other can be found in shifting cultural norms regarding child abuse itself.[62] During the 1970s, second-wave feminists seized upon the problem of child abuse, portraying it as a larger problem of patriarchal cultures and structures. This movement successfully mobilized two new vocabularies that were gaining traction within public parlance: the language of rights and the language of trauma, as utilized in therapeutic culture. Child abuse came to be seen as a durable problem that created lasting trauma for children. Women, particularly mothers within these movements, were authorized to speak on behalf of this trauma.[63] The first wave of litigation against the Church coincided with a rise in public concern over child abuse and the creation of new legislation surrounding child sex abuse. Women seeking to utilize law and publicity to confront the Church did so within a culture that was increasingly willing to treat child abuse as an issue of social and legal concern.[64] Women, such as Miller, seized upon these cultural changes, and in doing so, were able to translate them into repeatable strategies and themes for subsequent Catholic mothers. These causal factors help to illustrate the broader claim at stake here. Women were able to leverage their status as citizens and mothers of abused children to transform their subject positions within their community. But they were able to do so because of larger transformations in cultural evaluations of law and child abuse.

Women can and do utilize the rhetorical resources available to them to transform, advocate for, and disrupt their subject positions.[65] Our case study has demonstrated one such instance of transformation. Empowered by changes within cultural evaluations of child abuse and civil litigation, women leveraged their identities as mothers and secular citizens to transform Catholic motherhood.

NOTES

1. Patti Armstrong, "US Catholic Women Speak Out Before Vatican Summit," *National Catholic Register*, February 18, 2019. https://www.ncregister.com/news/us-catholic-women-speak-out-before-vatican-summit.

2. Robert DeChaine refers to this delineation as the process of rhetorical bordering or the demarcation of one community from another; Robert DeChaine, "Introduction: For Rhetorical Border Studies," in *Border Rhetorics: Citizenship and Identity on the US–Mexico Border*, ed. Robert DeChaine (Tuscaloosa: University of Alabama Press, 2012), 1–18.

3. Celeste Condit, "Public Health Experts, Expertise, and Ebola: A Relational Theory of Ethos," *Rhetoric & Public Affairs* 22, no. 2 (Summer 2019): 177–216.

4. Robert DeChaine, "Afterword: Tracking the 'Shifting Borders' of Identity and Otherness; Productive Complications and Ethico-Political Commitments," in *The Rhetorics of US Immigration: Identity, Community, Otherness*, ed. Johanna Hartelius (University Park: Penn State UP, 2015), 275–288.

5. Scholars have considered rhetoric's constitutive capacities as an integral part of citizenship—how it constructs the individual in relationship to the state and helps a community of individuals imagine themselves as a singular group. Vanessa B. Beasley, *You, the People: American Identity in Presidential Rhetoric* (College Station, TX: Texas A&M University Press, 2004); Jay P. Childers, "The Democratic Balance: President McKinley's Assassination as Domestic Trauma," *Quarterly Journal of Speech* 99, no. 2 (2013): 156–179.

6. We utilize the term multiple or overlapping citizenships to distinguish it from theories of hybridity, recognizing that citizenship within the nation-state imposes particular burdens that limit the analogy to citizenship within the Catholic church. Josue David Cisneros, *The Border Crossed Us: Rhetorics of Borders, Citizenship, and Latina/o Identity* (Tuscaloosa: University of Alabama Press, 2014), 89–92.

7. Brian Clites details the impact of Catholic mothers in early survivor movements, and the role of those movements in winning early lawsuits and moving the church toward the 2002 Dallas Charter. Timothy Lytton highlights the role of Catholic parents in early lawsuits. Brian Clites, "Breaking the Silence: The Catholic Sexual Abuse Survivor Movement in Chicago," (PhD Diss., Northwestern

University, 2015); Timothy Lytton, *Holding Bishops Accountable: How Lawsuits Helped the Catholic Church Confront Sexual Abuse* (Cambridge: Harvard UP, 2008).

8. We have pulled these public statements from statements made to the press, interviews, legal testimony quoted by newspaper statements, and testimony offered for advocacy purposes. A total list of those sources is listed here. Tim Evans, "Lawsuit: Church to Blame for Rape," *USA Today*, May 5, 2013, https://www.usatoday.com/story/news/nation/2013/05/05/lawsuit-church-to-blame-for-rape/2135933/; Ron Cassie, "Priest Sentenced to 10 Years Probation for Sex Offense," *Frederick News-Post*, March 11, 2016, https://www.fredericknewspost.com/archive/priest-sentenced-to-10-years-probation-for-sex-offense/article_9ff400bb-a476-573d-9510-801171ed9e0c.html; Cheryl Lavin, "An Unbroken Spirit: Conviction of Priest for Molestation Isn't Enough for a Mom Who Believes the Entire Church Shares the Guilt," *The Chicago Tribune*, January 6, 1993, https://www.bishop-accountability.org/news/1993_01_06_Lavin_AnUnbroken.htm; "Group Decries Baker Settlement," *The Altoona Mirror*, September 14, 2016, https://www.altoonamirror.com/news/local-news/2016/09/group-decries-baker-settlement/; Ben Myers, "Former Lafayette Diocese Priest Michael Guidry Sentenced to 7 Years for Abusing Altar Boy," *The Advocate*, April 30, 2019, https://www.theadvocate.com/acadiana/news/crime_police/article_16838f14-6acc-11e9-bc6d-ff46915e7314.html#:~:text=Ben%20Myers,-Author%20facebook&text=A%20former%20priest%20in%20the,altar%20boy%20four%20years%20ago.&text=The%20victim%20claimed%20he%20woke,after%20serving%20him%20pure%20gin.; Luke Ramseth, "'A Total Betrayal of Trust': St. Landry Parish Priest to Be Sentenced for Sex Abuse," *Lafayette Daily Advertiser*, April 26, 2019, https://amp.columbiadailyherald.com/story/news/2019/04/26/morrow-priest-sentenced-molesting-teen/3577703002/; Dave Sutor, "'I Paid for My Son to Be with a Pedophile': Ohio Mother Speaks Out about Son's Abuse, Suicide," *Tribune Democrat*, March 19, 2016, https://www.tribdem.com/news/i-paid-for-my-son-to-be-with-a-pedophile-ohio-mother-speaks-out-about/article_77775f30-ed6b-11e5-b7ab-d3eac084f551.html.; McMorrow as quoted in Melissa Block, "Sex Abuse Scandal Catches Up with Religious Orders," *NPR*, December 31, 2007, https://www.npr.org/templates/story/story.php?storyId=17728112#:~:text=Sex%20Abuse%20Scandal%20Catches%20Up%20with%20Religious%20Orders%20Father%20A.J.,in%20new%20assignments%20for%20years; Charles Radin, "Former Altar Boy Sues Priest in R.I.," *The Globe*, November 17, 2005. http://archive.boston.com/news/local/massachusetts/articles/2005/11/17/former_altar_boy_sues_priest_in_ri/; Vogrin, "Victims' Advocates Critical of Baker Sex-Abuse Settlement." *Tribune Chronicle*, September 4, 2016, https://www.tribtoday.com/news/local-news/2016/09/victims-advocates-critical-of-baker-sex-abuse-settlement/.; WJACTV, "Organization Seeking Answers to Alleged Abuse at Bishop McCort," *YouTube*, March 3, 2014, https://www.youtube.com/watch?v=Ofqty25P-Z0.; "Mom and lawyers unexpectedly confront predator priest on NYC sidewalk," Jeff Anderson & Associates, April 9, 2008, https://www.andersonadvocates.com/mom-lawyers-unexpectedly-confront-predator-priest-on-nyc-sidewalk/; Letitia Peyton, "Testimony from Mother of Victim of Clergy Sexual Abuse," *Catholic Women's Forum*, January 15, 2019, http://catholicwomensforum.org/wp-content/uploads/Testimony-Mother-of-Victim-of-Clergy-Sexual-Abuse

-January-2019-1.pdf; David Hurst, "Come Forward, Abuse Victims Urged," *The Tribune Democrat*, November 21, 2013, https://www.tribdem.com/news/local_news/come-forward-abuse-victims-urged/article_e7be2e6e-5028-5ba4-8ca8-71bc7f8453af.html; Carlyle Murphy, "Priest Removed From Job After Suit Alleging Abuse," *Washington Post*, November 17, 2005. https://www.snapnetwork.org/news/other-states/111705_cote_dominican_abuse_ri.html.

9. For more on characteristics of these waves, see Lytton, *Holding Bishops Accountable*.

10. While Miller has made many public statements, her own summary of her experience with CPSA and the survivors' movement can be found in Jeanne Miller, "The Moral Bankruptcy of Institutionalized Religion," in *Wolves Within the Fold: Religious Leadership and Abuses of Power*, ed. Anson D. Shupe (New Brunswick, NJ: Rutgers UP, 1998), 150–172.

11. Brian Clites, "Breaking the Silence," 193–233.

12. Tim Evans, "Lawsuit: Church to Blame for Rape," *USA Today*, May 5, 2013, https://www.usatoday.com/story/news/nation/2013/05/05/lawsuit-church-to-blame-for-rape/2135933/; Ron Cassie, "Priest Sentenced to 10 Years Probation for Sex Offense," *Frederick News Post*, March 11, 2016, https://www.fredericknewspost.com/archive/priest-sentenced-to-10-years-probation-for-sex-offense/article_9ff400bb-a476-573d-9510-801171ed9e0c.html.

13. Barbara Aponte has been an outspoken proponent and advocate within the Healing and Restoration movement. Letitia Peyton offered testimonial support for the Catholic Women's Forum submission to the 2018 Vatican Summit.

14. Sonja Foss, *Rhetorical Criticism: Exploration and Practice* (Prospect Heights, IL: Waveland Press, Inc., 1989), 367–370.

15. Kendall Phillips, "Rhetorical Maneuvers: Subjectivity, Power, and Resistance," *Philosophy and Rhetoric* 39, no. 4 (2006): 327.

16. Phillips, "Rhetorical Maneuvers," 312.

17. Medhurst points to this repetition as proof of cultural evaluations of the good, or in other words, cultural ethos. Martin Medhurst, "Religious Rhetoric and the *Ethos* of Democracy: A Case Study of the 2000 Presidential Campaign," in *The Ethos of Rhetoric*, ed. Michael Hyde (Columbia, SC: The University of South Carolina Press, 2004), 114–135.

18. Jeanne Miller as quoted in an interview with Cheryl Lavin, "An Unbroken Spirit: Conviction of Priest for Molestation Isn't Enough for a Mom Who Believes the Entire Church Shares the Guilt," *The Chicago Tribune*, January 6, 1993, https://www.bishop-accountability.org/news/1993_01_06_Lavin_AnUnbroken.htm.

19. "Group Decries Baker Settlement," *The Altoona Mirror*, September 14, 2016, https://www.altoonamirror.com/news/local-news/2016/09/group-decries-baker-settlement/.

20. Ben Myers, "Former Lafayette Diocese Priest Michael Guidry Sentenced to 7 years for Abusing Altar Boy," *The Advocate*, April 30, 2019, https://www.theadvocate.com/acadiana/news/crime_police/article_16838f14-6acc-11e9-bc6d-ff46915e7314.html#:~:text=Ben%20Myers,-Author%20facebook&text=A%20former%20priest

%20in%20the,altar%20boy%20four%20years%20ago.&text=The%20victim%20claimed%20he%20woke,after%20serving%20him%20pure%20gin.

21. Lavin, "Unbroken Spirit."

22. Luke Ramseth, "'A Total Betrayal of Trust': St. Landry Parish Priest to Be Sentenced for Sex Abuse," *Lafayette Daily Advertiser*, April 26, 2019, https://amp.columbiadailyherald.com/story/news/2019/04/26/morrow-priest-sentenced-molesting-teen/3577703002/.

23. Dave Sutor, "'I Paid for My Son to be with a Pedophile': Ohio Mother Speaks Out about Son's Abuse, Suicide," *Tribune Democrat*, March 19, 2016, https://www.tribdem.com/news/i-paid-for-my-son-to-be-with-a-pedophile-ohio-mother-speaks-out-about/article_77775f30-ed6b-11e5-b7ab-d3eac084f551.html.

24. Melissa Block, "Sex Abuse Scandal Catches Up with Religious Orders," *NPR*, December 31, 2007, https://www.npr.org/templates/story/story.php?storyId=17728112#:~:text=Sex%20Abuse%20Scandal%20Catches%20Up%20with%20Religious%20Orders%20Father%20A.J.,in%20new%20assignments%20for%20years.

25. Lavin, "Unbroken Spirit."

26. Sutor, "I Paid for My Son."

27. Cisneros, *The Border Crossed Us*.

28. Lavin, "Unbroken Spirit."

29. Cassie, "Priest Sentenced to 10 Years Probation for Sex Offense."

30. Evans, "Lawsuit: Church to Blame for Rape."

31. Myers, "Former Lafayette Diocese priest Michael Guidry Sentenced."

32. DeChaine, "Afterword," 277.

33. Miller as quoted in Lavin, "Unbroken Spirit."

34. Evans, "Lawsuit: Church to Blame for Rape."

35. Charles Radin, "Former Altar Boy Sues Priest in R.I.," *The Globe*, November 17, 2005. http://archive.boston.com/news/local/massachusetts/articles/2005/11/17/former_altar_boy_sues_priest_in_ri/.

36. Aponte as quoted in "Group Decries Baker Settlement"; Armstrong, "US Catholic Women Speak Out."

37. Lavin, "Unbroken Spirit."

38. Evans, "Lawsuit."

39. Barbara Aponte, as quoted in Vogrin, "Victims' Advocates Critical of Baker Sex-Abuse Settlement." *Tribune Chronicle*, September 4, 2016, https://www.tribtoday.com/news/local-news/2016/09/victims-advocates-critical-of-baker-sex-abuse-settlement/.

40. Miller has described this in multiple places, including Lavin, "Unbroken Spirit."

41. WJACTV, "Organization Seeking Answers to Alleged Abuse at Bishop McCort," *YouTube*, March 3, 2014, https://www.youtube.com/watch?v=Ofqty25P-Z0.

42. "Mom and Lawyers Unexpectedly Confront Predator Priest on NYC Sidewalk," Jeff Anderson & Associates, April 9, 2008, https://www.andersonadvocates.com/mom-lawyers-unexpectedly-confront-predator-priest-on-nyc-sidewalk/.

43. Economus, as quoted in Clites, "Breaking the Silence," 210.

44. Jennifer Balboni, *Clergy Sexual Abuse Litigation: Survivors Seeking Justice* (Boulder, CO: First Forum Press, 2011).

45. Clites, "Breaking the Silence," 220.

46. Miller as quoted in Lavin, "Unbroken Spirit."

47. Block, "Sex Abuse Scandal Catches Up," *NPR*.

48. Letitia Peyton, "Testimony from Mother of Victim of Clergy Sexual Abuse," *Catholic Women's Forum*, January 15, 2019, http://catholicwomensforum.org/wp-content/uploads/Testimony-Mother-of-Victim-of-Clergy-Sexual-Abuse-January-2019-1.pdf.

49. Miller, "Moral Bankruptcy."

50. Barbara Aponte as quoted in David Hurst, "Come Forward, Abuse Victims Urged," *The Tribune Democrat*, November 21, 2013, https://www.tribdem.com/news/local_news/come-forward-abuse-victims-urged/article_e7be2e6e-5028-5ba4-8ca8-71bc7f8453af.html.

51. Peyton, "Testimony from Mother of Victim."

52. McMorrow as quoted in Carlyle Murphy, "Priest Removed from Job After Suit Alleging Abuse," *Washington Post*, November 17, 2005. https://www.snapnetwork.org/news/otherstates/111705_cote_dominican_abuse_ri.html.

53. Clites, "Breaking the Silence," 201.

54. Lavin, "Unbroken Spirit"; Miller, "Moral Bankruptcy."

55. Evans, "Lawsuit."

56. Vogrin, "Victims' Advocates Critical"; Cassie, "Priest Sentenced to 10 Years Probation."

57. Peyton, "Testimony from Mother of Victim."

58. Hasson as quoted in Armstrong, "US Catholic Women Speak Out."

59. See also Walter K Olson, *The Litigation Explosion: What Happened When American Unleashed the Lawsuit* (New York: Truman Tally Books-Dutton, 1991); See Michael D. Johnston, "The Litigation Explosion, Proposed Reforms, and their Consequences," *Brigham Young University Journal of Public Law* 21, no. 1 (2007): 179–207.

60. For instance, a study conducted in the mid-1990s demonstrated that during this time, America spent five times as much as corresponding major industrial competitors on personal injury lawsuits. Similarly, the previous two decades witnessed the cost of injury litigation rise fourteenfold. Johnston, "The Litigation Explosion," 179, supra.

61. For more on the evolution of clergy sex abuse litigation, see James T. O'Reilly and Margaret S. P. Chalmers, *The Clergy Sex Abuse Crisis and the Legal Response* (Oxford: Oxford UP, 2014).

62. Joseph Davis offers a compelling look at the evolution of public conceptions of child abuse within the United States in *Accounts of Innocence* (Chicago: The University of Chicago, 2005).

63. Philip Jenkins, in particular, accounts for the changing discursive norms as they impact clergy sex abuse publicity and litigation. Philip Jenkins, *Pedophiles and Priests: Anatomy of a Contemporary Crisis* (New York: Oxford UP, 1996).

64. Jenkins, *Pedophiles and Priests.*

65. Kathleen J. Ryan, Nancy Myers, Rebecca Jones, *Rethinking Ethos: A Feminist Ecological Approach to Rhetoric* (Carbondale, IL: Southern Illinois UP, 2016).

BIBLIOGRAPHY

Armstrong, Patti. "US Catholic Women Speak Out before Vatican Summit." *National Catholic Register*, February 18, 2019. https://www.ncregister.com/news/us-catholic-women-speak-out-before-vatican-summit.

Balboni, Jennifer. *Clergy Sexual Abuse Litigation: Survivors Seeking Justice.* Boulder: First Forum Press, 2011.

Beasley, Vanessa B. *You, the People: American National Identity in Presidential Rhetoric.* College Station: Texas A&M UP, 2003.

Block, Melissa. "Sex Abuse Scandal Catches Up with Religious Orders." *NPR*, December 31, 2007. https://www.npr.org/templates/story/story.php?storyId=17728112#:~:text=Sex%20Abuse%20Scandal%20Catches%20Up%20with%20Religious%20Orders%20Father%20A.J.,in%20new%20assignments%20for%20years.

Cassie, Ron. "Priest Sentenced to 10 Years Probation for Sex Offense." *Frederick News-Post*, March 11, 2016. https://www.fredericknewspost.com/archive/priest-sentenced-to-10-years-probation-for-sex-offense/article_9ff400bb-a476-573d-9510-801171ed9e0c.html.

Childers, Jay P. "The Democratic Balance: President McKinley's Assassination as Domestic Trauma." *Quarterly Journal of Speech* 99, no. 2 (2013): 156–179.

Cisneros, Josue David. *The Border Crossed Us: Rhetorics of Borders, Citizenship, and Latina/o Identity.* Tuscaloosa: University of Alabama Press, 2014.

Clites, Brian. "Breaking the Silence: The Catholic Sexual Abuse Survivor Movement in Chicago." PhD diss., Northwestern University, 2015.

Condit, Celeste. "Public Health Experts, Expertise, and Ebola: A Relational Theory of Ethos." *Rhetoric and Public Affairs* 22, no. 2 (2019): 177–216.

Davis, Joseph. *Accounts of Innocence.* Chicago: The University of Chicago, 2005.

DeChaine, Robert. "Afterword: Tracking the 'Shifting Borders' of Identity and Otherness; Productive Complications and Ethico-Political Commitments." In *The Rhetorics of US Immigration: Identity, Community, Otherness*, edited by Johanna Hartelius, 275–288. University Park: Penn State UP, 2015.

———. "Introduction: For Rhetorical Border Studies." In *Border Rhetorics: Citizenship and Identity on the US–Mexico Border*, edited by DeChaine, 1–18. Tuscaloosa: University of Alabama Press, 2012.

Evans, Tim. "Lawsuit: Church to blame for rape." *USA Today*, May 5, 2013. https://www.usatoday.com/story/news/nation/2013/05/05/lawsuit-church-to-blame-for-rape/2135933/.

Foss, Sonja. *Rhetorical Criticism: Exploration and Practice.* Prospect Heights: Waveland Press, 1989.

"Group Decries Baker Settlement." *The Altoona Mirror*, September 14, 2016. https://www.altoonamirror.com/news/local-news/2016/09/group-decries-baker-settlement/.

Hurst, David. "Come Forward, Abuse Victims Urged." *The Tribune Democrat*, November 21, 2013. https://www.tribdem.com/news/local_news/come-forward-abuse-victims-urged/article_e7be2e6e-5028-5ba4-8ca8-71bc7f8453af.html.

Jenkins, Philip. *Pedophiles and Priests: Anatomy of a Contemporary Crisis*. New York: Oxford UP, 1996.

Johnston, Michael D. "The Litigation Explosion, Proposed Reforms, and their Consequences." *Brigham Young University Journal of Public Law* 21, no. 1 (2007): 179–207.

Lavin, Cheryl. "An Unbroken Spirit: Conviction of Priest for Molestation Isn't Enough for a Mom Who Believes the Entire Church Shares the Guilt." *BishopAccountability.org*, January 6, 1993. https://www.bishop-accountability.org/news/1993_01_06_Lavin_AnUnbroken.htm.

Lytton, Timothy. *Holding Bishops Accountable: How Lawsuits Helped the Catholic Church Confront Sexual Abuse*. Cambridge: Harvard UP, 2008.

Medhurst, Martin. "Religious Rhetoric and the *Ethos* of Democracy: A Case Study of the 2000 Presidential Campaign." In *The Ethos of Rhetoric*, edited by Michael Hyde, 114–135. Columbia: The University of South Carolina Press, 2004.

Miller, Jeanne. "The Moral Bankruptcy of Institutionalized Religion." In *Wolves within the Fold: Religious Leadership and Abuses of Power*, edited by Anson D. Shupe, 150–172. New Brunswick: Rutgers UP, 1998.

"Mom and Lawyers Unexpectedly Confront Predator Priest on NYC Sidewalk," Jeff Anderson & Associates, April 9, 2008. https://www.andersonadvocates.com/mom-lawyers-unexpectedly-confront-predator-priest-on-nyc-sidewalk/.

Murphy, Caryle. "Priest Removed From Job After Suit Alleging Abuse," *Washington Post*, November 17, 2005. Snap Network, Accessed April 21, 2021. https://www.snapnetwork.org/news/otherstates/111705_cote_dominican_abuse_ri.html.

Myers, Ben. "Former Lafayette Diocese Priest Michael Guidry Sentenced to 7 Years for Abusing Altar Boy." *The Advocate*, April 30, 2019. https://www.theadvocate.com/acadiana/news/crime_police/article_16838f14-6acc-11e9-bc6d-ff46915e7314.html#:~:text=Ben%20Myers,-Author%20facebook&text=A%20former%20priest%20in%20the,altar%20boy%20four%20years%20ago.&text=The%20victim%20claimed%20he%20woke,after%20serving%20him%20pure%20gin.

Olson, Walter K. *The Litigation Explosion: What Happened When America Unleashed the Lawsuit*. New York: Truman Tally Brooks-Dutton, 1991.

O'Reilly, James T. and Margaret S.P. Chalmers. *The Clergy Sex Abuse Crisis and the Legal Response*. Oxford: Oxford UP, 2014.

Peyton, Letitia. "Testimony from Mother of Victim of Clergy Sexual Abuse." *Catholic Women's Forum*, January 15, 2019. http://catholicwomensforum.org/wp-content/uploads/Testimony-Mother-of-Victim-of-Clergy-Sexual-Abuse-January-2019-1.pdf.

Phillips, Kendall. "Rhetorical Maneuvers: Subjectivity, Power, and Resistance." *Philosophy and Rhetoric* 39, no. 4 (2006): 310–332.

Radin, Charles. "Former Altar Boy Sues Priest in R.I." *The Globe*, November 17, 2005. http://archive.boston.com/news/local/massachusetts/articles/2005/11/17/former_altar_boy_sues_priest_in_ri/.

Ramseth, Luke. "'A Total Betrayal of Trust': St. Landry Parish Priest to Be Sentenced for Sex Abuse." *Lafayette Daily Advertiser*, April 26, 2019. https://amp.columbiadailyherald.com/story/news/2019/04/26/morrow-priest-sentenced-molesting-teen/3577703002/.

Ryan, Kathleen J., Nancy Myers, and Rebecca Jones. *Rethinking Ethos: A Feminist Ecological Approach to Rhetoric*. Carbondale: Southern Illinois UP, 2016.

Sutor, Dave. "'I Paid for My Son to Be with a Pedophile': Ohio Mother Speaks Out about Son's Abuse, Suicide." *Tribune Democrat*, March 19, 2016. https://www.tribdem.com/news/i-paid-for-my-son-to-be-with-a-pedophile-ohio-mother-speaks-out-about/article_77775f30-ed6b-11e5-b7ab-d3eac084f551.html.

Vogrin, G. "Victims' Advocates Critical of Baker Sex-Abuse Settlement." *Tribune Chronicle*, September 4, 2016. https://www.tribtoday.com/news/local-news/2016/09/victims-advocates-critical-of-baker-sex-abuse-settlement/.

WJACTV. "Organization Seeking Answers to Alleged Abuse at Bishop McCort." *YouTube*, March 3, 2014. https://www.youtube.com/watch?v=.

Chapter 7

Ethos as Presence in Lay Catholic Women's Rhetorics of Accountability

Jamie White-Farnham

I was twenty years old and a college student in my home state of Massachusetts when the *Boston Globe* Spotlight investigative team broke the story of the Boston Archdiocese covering up years of clergy perpetuated sexual abuse (CPSA). But, it was not really news. It had already been made clear, quietly, throughout my young Catholic life in my Irish-Italian American family of several generations that question marks about behavior or normalcy floated around some priests—in fact, two priests in my own family were persona non grata.

That fact is just one of the ways that the Catholic Church disenfranchised me, an obedient if sort of disagreeable daughter of a single mother—the type of kid who was willing to criticize, for instance, a homily castigating divorce. By the time I was fourteen or fifteen, I was making arguments about birth control at my parish's regularly scheduled children's religious classes, otherwise known as CCD, that I had learned from *Our Bodies, Ourselves*. No one ever engaged me on these points—rather, adults just told me I was being inappropriate. I was Confirmed, but within a few years the scandal broke, and I did not care about what the Church did, said, or thought again for a long time.

In 2017, on the occasion of the Church criticizing Girl Scouts USA's stance on reproductive justice, I found the Church's rebuke of Girl Scouts odd: since when has the Church cared about girls?[1] Dashing off a Facebook comment about the story, I was surprised to experience a moment of clarity: my formative Catholic experiences as a girl did more to sever my ties with the Church than the event I had been giving all the credit for twenty years. Perhaps I had chosen not to be Catholic; honestly, the choice predated me by eons. It did not matter if I was there—it was not for girls, my divorced mom, for people (women, anyway) who would discuss and argue, and it was not for me.

I share my origin story as a former Catholic to situate my interest in undertaking a feminist rhetorical study of public lay women who did not leave the Church despite both the acute sting of the scandal and the Church's chronic mistreatment and suppression of women and children. My own biases color my choice in topic and objects of study, and I offer an analysis of the rhetorics of accountability of lay Catholic women who did what I didn't feel called to do, namely, participate in projects of reform and recourse of the Catholic Church: Celia Viggo Wexler, journalist and Catholic activist, and Barbara Blaine, well-known activist and survivor of abuse.

My analysis of their rhetoric centers on their seeking of "accountability," a sort of rally cry of Catholic activists and those who sought justice for CPSA, a demand that can mean several things and that has resulted in victories on the side of change as well as unfulfilled promises. This analysis relies on new feminist interpretations and applications of the ancient concept of ethos drawn on the recent work of Christy I. Wenger as well as Beth Daniell and Letizia Guglielmo. While ethos is traditionally understood as a rhetorical appeal centering on a speaker's character, these feminist scholars construe ethos in material and bodily ways particular to women, and that apply to the cases I share here.

I draw on this inventive scholarship to frame my analysis of these women's rhetoric in circumstances in which the material factors of their rights and their bodily presence were held in about as low esteem as is possible within an institution in the United States. I suggest that their very presence and visibility in creating calls for accountability, in the particular twentieth and early twenty-first-century context of a Post-Vatican II Church and at the breaking of the Boston CPSA scandal, constitutes an ethos that stakes out a claim of their right to speak and to be heard as women in an institution which otherwise would—and did and does—ignore, counter, and actively suppress their bodies, voices, and contributions. I suggest that their rhetorics of accountability offer a feminist interpretation of the word "accountability" that complicates its traditional inward-focused purpose (accounting for one's actions) with the inclusion of acknowledging, listening, and adding the experiences of and voices of women (and children) into decision-making, justice seeking, and, ultimately, the structure of the Church. I posit this as a redefinition of a centuries-old word, and I argue that these women's diversion of the Church's attention to itself is an apt application of "accountability" and a way to rectify a long and problematic history: through outward action to listen and include others.

ETHOS AS PRESENCE

Daniell and Guglielmo as well as Wenger consider the ethos of women and their rhetorical action in very different contexts. In "Changing Audience,

Changing Ethos," Daniell and Guglielmo analyze the rhetoric of nineteenth-century women participating in the abolition and temperance movements, and Wenger considers how yogic theories and practices converge with rhetorical theory.[2] However, taken together, these two treatments suggest intriguingly that ethos is located within a person or must be claimed by a person—especially women—in rhetorical situations. Wenger, in particular, converts the idea of a "sponsoring institution" for rhetors as the speaker's own body.[3]

Of course, this articulation of ethos is quite distinct from a traditional definition of ethos, which is predicated on an assumption that one can or already is engaging in rhetorical planning or action. In that assumption, what is needed to "do ethos" is to draw from the catalog of rhetorical and artistic options in order to convey a certain character or create a certain relationship with the audience in the service of argument. The work of Daniell and Guglielmo and also of Wenger questions even the most basic assumptions of this conception of ethos: that one *has* an audience, that the traditional catalog is *available* to women, or a nonwhite person, or an otherwise ignored or actively oppressed speaker. In the modern conceptions under consideration here, ethos does not already exist to draw upon from the available means.

Instead, these feminist treatments more aptly define ethos as a claim about one's right to speak in the first place. This was necessary for nineteenth-century women, as Daniell and Guglielmo note: "As women in the nineteenth century attempted to speak for abolition and temperance, they realized that they had to argue first for the right to speak publicly."[4] In doing so, these women added an entirely new type of rhetor to the scene of politics, rhetoric, and argument in the nineteenth century, reflecting an ethotic claim: we can speak. Daniell and Guglielmo point out that, while twentieth-century women's rhetorical interruptions to the status quo were based on an argument about their civil rights *as women*, nineteenth-century women needed to argue first that they *were* women through religious arguments that speaking wouldn't decrease their femininity—and even if it did, they should be heard anyway. To unpack this ironic point, Daniell and Guglielmo's analysis reminds us that before the women would be heard, they first had to assure men that they existed in a form the men could find acceptable (i.e., feminine) while simultaneously changing the men's minds about listening to them *in* that acceptable form, when previously, the men hadn't.[5] The ethos here encumbers a dual shifting and stabilizing of identity, a classic double bind of womanhood.

In a quite distinct but complementary view of ethos, Wenger's "Creating Contemplative Spaces: Ethos as Presence and the Rhetorics of Yoga" suggests that ethos is located within a person or must be claimed by a person—especially women—in rhetorical situations. Wenger describes and compares a particular yogic theory and practice—extension and expansion—as a model for the actions and attitude necessary to make an ethotic claim. She writes that a yogic consideration of ethos would stem "from a body that by its very materiality is relational; this means that ethos both exists within bodies, guaranteed by their material presence, *and* between bodies, existing in the interactions between a speaker and an audience."[6] What is important about the fact that ethos exists within bodies/selves and between the bodies of the self and others is that both need attending to, not just one or the other, as traditional models have upheld, with ethos focusing on the speaker and pathos focusing on the audience. This perspective suggests a simultaneity and balance that a traditional conception of ethos as one's own character does not usually evoke.

To achieve a balance between the self and audience, Wenger brings the "spatial heuristics of yoga" into the conception of how women might stake an ethotic claim in a literal, bodily way. To foster that possibility, she introduces the dual actions of extension and expansion. Extension means attending to the rootedness of the self, and expansion encourages the person/rhetor to reach out to the community. To offer a fuller explanation of how these are both actions and attitudes, Wenger writes:

> Acts of extension [root] us in the personal body, helping us understand our immediate material-semiotic placement and provide a path toward self-determination, but they are not to be completed alone. Expansion complements extension because it reaches beyond the self's perceived center. The body unfolds and energy flows outward. Actions of expansion include the experience of creating spaces in new directions: opening the inner body and expanding to the experience of the external.[7]

Of course, in yoga, extension and expansion are meant to be taken quite literally as actions of the body. One can imagine extension as "self-rooting" by standing on the yoga mat, concentrating on their feet placement, the weight of gravity, their own balance. This prompts attention to one's own body, as well as one's own feelings, state of mind, well-being. At the same time, one can expand by filling their lungs with air, looking up, reaching with the arms—all actions that prompt one to think about what is around one's self, both in an immediate sense of the room as well as in a larger, relational, and community-oriented sense.

These "spatial heuristics" of extension and expansion link the physical actions with an attitudinal capacity and, in fact, a rhetoric theory that "translate into feminist rhetorical acts as they shift our experience of ourselves and others and lead to both personal and systemic change."[8] The dual nature of extension (attending to the self) and expansion (attending to the community) provides a natural foundation for my proposed feminist redefinition of accountability that will bear out presently in the rhetorics of accountability of Catholic lay women.

Finally, Wenger converts the idea of a "sponsoring institution" of Zan Meyer Gonçalves from a literal organization or forum for rhetors to "link private discourses and needs with public aims," to "the speaker's own body."[9] She writes that "within feminist theories of ethos as presence, the rhetor's own body becomes a 'sponsoring institution' if she only learns to dwell within it mindfully, to practice the self-reflexivity of extension and the other-directedness of expansion. In turn, activism becomes answerable to lived bodies in public spaces."[10] Wenger's refreshed understanding of women's positionality in the world, exemplified by Daniell and Guglielmo's study of women 200 years ago, is especially relevant to situations in which women have found themselves unwelcome, unable, and unexpected to speak—for instance, the Catholic Church in the United States in the late twentieth and early twenty-first centuries.

EXIGENCE FOR ACCOUNTABILITY

This volume contains many chapters that, together, present a centuries-long and multifaceted understanding of the many contexts in which women have participated, resisted, rejected, or changed the Catholic Church through rhetoric. In this section, I touch on recent history in order to situate women's calls for "accountability." Accountability itself is an unremarkable word; the *Oxford English Dictionary* notes its use in government and business without much variation since 1750: "The quality of being accountable; liability to account for and answer for one's conduct, performance of duties, etc. (in modern use often with regard to parliamentary, corporate, or financial liability to the public, shareholders, etc.); responsibility."[11]

Yet, as Daniell and Guglielmo suggest, Catholic women who seek accountability must first seek attention for their cause and gain the Church as an audience. This has been historically difficult for women to do, although many reform movements have gained momentum throughout the history of the Church. Angela Bonavoglia, writing in 2005, explains that the women's reform movement in the 1970s and 1980s was a "heyday" in terms of sheer numbers of women participating in conversations about how to diversify the Church's interests and afford women a role in decision-making in the organization.[12]

Cecelia Viggo Wexler explains that that period, known as the post-Vatican II period, constituted women's best chances for Church reform. Vatican II was a 1962 set of changes to Church doctrine and practices that excited both women religious and lay women and offered them hope for increased structural participation in church matters. Viggo Wexler characterizes Vatican II as the "Arab Spring" of Catholicism: "it ushered in a brief window of hope and transparency when it looked like democracy might prevail over rigid institutions, when collegiality—between pope and bishops, bishops and priests, and priests and laity—might become the norm."[13] Vatican II allowed women religious to dress in street clothes and have day jobs; for priests to face the congregation during Mass and say it in the vernacular; and women and lay men to study theology, among changes to other principles.

However, according to Viggo Wexler, the larger progressive promise of the measures did not materialize during the reigns of Popes Benedict and John Paul II, which together lasted from 1978 to 2013. She claims Catholics faced "a huge backlash" in "the increasing rigidity of the church, particularly as church leaders focused on sexual morality and the reproductive rights of women" and what she characterizes as an obsession with the unborn.[14]

Reactions to the popes' doubling down on misogyny over the years manifested as rhetorical calls to action and the formation of reform movements by women religious and lay people throughout the late twentieth century, as noted above. Interestingly, accountability was a watchword in the Catholic reform movement before the emergency of a CPSA scandal. According to Bonavoglia, even right-wing groups leveled critique at the lack of transparency and authoritarianism of the Church.[15] As such, Catholics began to demand that the Church be accountable to them in two main ways: by including them as stakeholders into the process of governance and—when articulating stances and decisions that did not bear out members' lived realities and expectations—answering for them.

These are natural and worthy goals for the reform of an organization, but the meaning and need for accountability would shift in 2002 with the international attention that the *Boston Globe* brought to the cover-up orchestrated by the Boston Archdiocese to protect priests who sexually abused children. This was not news to many victims and survivors, but what was new was the ability to speak of it, to connect with others who understood, and to seek redress. As is now well known, the *Boston Globe* uncovered years of paying off and keeping families quiet with nondisclosure agreements, shame, and intimidation: "Under an extraordinary cloak of secrecy, the Archdiocese of Boston in the last 10 years has quietly settled child molestation claims against at least 70 priests."[16]

In this context, accountability begins to take on additional forms apparent in the rhetoric of lay women engaging in this rally cry: Cecilia Viggo Wexler and Barbara Blaine. In the below analyses of their rhetorics of accountability, I draw on Wenger's definition of ethos as presence: "a deliberative rhetorical practice that positions ethos as presence."[17] The cases below evidence that the women's very presence—bodily, politically, materially—constitutes an ethos addressing the doctrinal suppression of women in the Catholic Church. Their calls for accountability are different; their goals are different. But, their very existence as women who would speak back to, at, about, or on behalf of the Catholic Church is significant in the particular context laid out above: the Catholic Church's specific attitude and actions toward sex, sexuality, sexual abuse, and history of repression of women.

CECELIA VIGGO WEXLER: ACCOUNTABILITY AS ACKNOWLEDGING WOMEN

Cecilia Viggo Wexler is a lay Catholic woman, feminist, and participant in the reform movement of the Church whose response to the topic of CPSA is ensconced in the larger problem of women and children's historical voicelessness in the Church. She is traditional in the sense that, despite her career-long critique of the Church, she remains a Catholic focused on the potential for change and accountability within the Church. Her rhetoric is accessible via her journalistic and critical writing and, in particular, her book entitled *Catholic Women Confront Their Church: Stories of Hurt and Hope* (2016). The book's main purpose is to ask, "was it possible to be a woman who was an independent thinker, a professional in the workplace, who firmly believed in women's equality, and still be a Catholic?"[18]

This is a provocative question that lays a foundation for my claim that the presence of Catholic lay women speaking critically of the church and working to further a progressive agenda as members constitutes a material and bodily ethos. In staking out Viggo Wexler's (and other women's) claims to speak, the nine women in this book, through their various projects of resistance and reform, are calling for an accountability from the Church that demands that they, as members, are treated as full participants—as people with strong faith, intelligence, and good ideas. The women profiled, like Viggo Wexler, came of age during or just after Vatican II, with its promises of a more egalitarian and laity-friendly—and perhaps woman-friendly—Church.

Therefore, their actions and rhetoric are aimed at two main areas of disenfranchisement: (1) the heavy focus on the control of women's bodies, rather than the spirit and love of social justice, which many women say remains their inspiration to be Catholic and which binds them to the fondness they hold for their hometown parish churches; and (2) the primacy of one's conscience as the seat of decision-making, rather than reliance on blind obedience to Church doctrine. Hand in hand with this perspective, the women tout their capacity and interest in their faith in God, rather than in their membership in the Church.[19]

Throughout her career, Viggo Wexler has critiqued the Church and particularly its obsession with sexual morality while there are projects of social justice that she and others argue plenty of Catholics believe are more important and that plenty of other Catholics, especially mothers in developing countries, would benefit from. She calls for the weight of the church to be thrown at the daily problems that everyday Catholics the world over face: "Our bishops continue to be obsessed with the unborn, gay marriage, and the contraception mandate in the Affordable Care Act . . . the American church has been an institution that shut its eyes to pedophilia among its ranks and when discovered, tried to cover it up and shush its victims. It is an institution that even today, condemns abortion more loudly than it ever did priestly abuse."[20]

In answer to her question, "is it possible to be a woman who is an independent thinker, a professional in the workplace, who firmly believed in women's equality, and still be a Catholic?" I posit that Viggo Wexler's question is a transitional call in the rhetoric of accountability to move from identifying and critiquing the fact that the Church has disenfranchised women's voices to asserting them anyway and documenting these voices as a project of visibility, of staking an ethotic claim to speak, on the part of resistant Catholic lay women.

BARBARA BLAINE: ACCOUNTABILITY AS LISTENING AND JUSTICE

Barbara Blaine is, perhaps, the best-known public figure and activist in the pursuit of justice for victims of CPSA in the Catholic Church. Her experience of being groomed and abused over her teenage years by her parish priest in Toledo, Ohio, in the 1970s was a painful secret until she became an adult when another survivor's story came to light. Her realization that the abuse she suffered—which she had disclosed to her parents and who were dismissed by their parish—and which had happened to others propelled Blaine into creating, in 1989, Survivors Network of those Abused by Priests (SNAP), an organization that "remains relentlessly vocal, bold and unself-conscious in its demands that offending priests and the hierarchy who covered for them be held accountable for their crimes—which they see as essential to the healing of victims and of the Church."[21]

Blaine's narrative provides an example of a former girl who survived sexual abuse by a priest, whereas boys' victimhood is often more in the spotlight. Bonavoglia explains the complications surrounding victimhood for girls whose abuse is often rationalized within the Church based on its retrograde attitude about the sinfulness and inevitability of women's sexuality when talking about minor children:

> Attorney Roderick MacLeish, Jr., who represented hundreds of victims of sexual abuse in the Boston archdiocese, told the *Boston Globe*: "It's almost a free pass when it comes to women and young girls." That follows, really in a Church where male clerics remain the godlike rulers and women—in the private lives and the public life of the Church—the most fiercely ruled. It also follows in a Church that sees women as second-class citizens, to be patronized and managed without voice, and that tends to see "womenandchildren" as a single entity, dismissible in a single swoop.[22]

In this context, the lack of accountability on the part of the Church centers around its unwillingness to listen to victims and to women victims in particular. In Blaine's specific case, the powers that be in her home parish gaslit her by suggesting that she had "misinterpreted" the actions of her rapist all those years. Bonavoglia characterizes the Church's refusal to listen and actions to dismiss or discredit survivors:

> The response of many clerics to survivors and their supporters [has] been woefully inadequate, too. Survivors and advocates told me about writing to bishops in an attempt to set up meetings and getting no response at all; trying to hand-deliver letters to bishops and being accused of trespassing on church property; being closed out of membership on local lay boards charged with reviewing sexual abuse allegations; and having priests to whom they and their families were very close to stop speaking to them when they become vocal advocates for survivors.[23]

As a rhetor, Blair faced a particular challenge: her condition of being a woman meant she would not be heard by an institution that, as has been established, does not value their voices or participation even in routine matters, let alone the highly charged matter of sexual assault. The rhetoric of SNAP may be best described by what Blaine's colleague and cofounder of SNAP, Peter Isley, said of her drive to seek justice for victims: "madness." Isley writes:

> And by "madness" I mean what the ancient Greek poet Aeschylus meant: "One must love to the point of seeming madness." Barbara's madness was the madness of a love for justice. What else, but a kind of mad love for the impossible would drive her to spend decades battling the Catholic Church to bring justice for survivors of childhood sexual assault, to bend the clerical upper regions and change what is arguably the single most unchangeable object on earth?
>
> There were no national or religious boundaries for Barbara when it came to survivors, no ocean or mountain range that formed impenetrable obstacles. Each survivor had a voice, a story, wherever they came from, whatever their

language, whatever their age, whatever their sexual orientation. She was determined that each be heard.[24]

With this understanding of Blaine's passion and drive, the rhetoric of SNAP is easily understood as twofold. The first is SNAP's direct, no-nonsense approach to accountability: legal justice. Blaine became a lawyer at age thirty-nine on her path to helping others. Her biggest and most visible effort to hold the Church accountable in a specific, legal way, was a 2011 effort appealing to the International Criminal Court at The Hague in the case "SNAP v. The Pope" to begin an investigation of the Vatican on the charge of crimes against humanity.[25] The specificity of legal justice as accountability is clear. For example, note the large blue button on SNAP's website in figure 7.1: "Report Abuse to Your AG [Attorney General]."[26] SNAP's direct approach to helping victims report to legal authorities corrects the many years that victims helplessly sought redress within the Church whom they trusted.

The second aspect of SNAP's rhetoric of accountability leans toward building an ethos of presence: outreach to victims. SNAP acknowledges and makes space for victims to come forward, to share their stores, to join a community that will understand and help them. The presence of victims and the accumulation of people with stories like Blaine's are important, both to helping others situate their own experiences and bring them comfort as well as to leading them to opportunities to seek legal justice. An ethos of presence is evident in SNAP's commitment to recording these stories through a partnership with StoryCorps to create a counternarrative to the monolithic history of the Church. According to SNAP, "In August 2014 SNAP entered

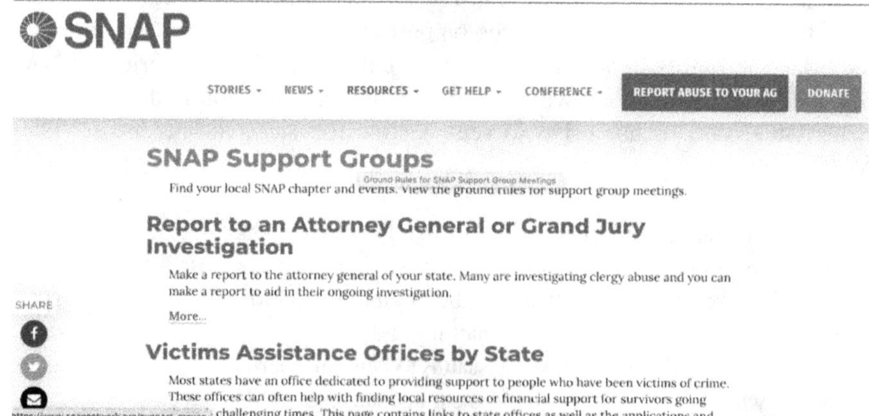

Figure 7.1 SNAP Balances a Rhetoric of Care and Outreach to Victims and Direct Legal Action as Accountability. *Source*: SNAPnetwork.org.

a community partnership with StoryCorps. Since 2003 StoryCorps has collected and archived more than 50,000 interviews with over 90,000 participants. With the storyteller's permission, each conversation is preserved at the American Folklife Center at the Library of Congress."[27] This partnership evidences the notion of an ethos qua presence; the pressure to make change has come from the accumulated presence of victims benefiting from Blaine's survivorship and direct call for legal accountability.

ETHOS AS PRESENCE AND A NEW FEMINIST ACCOUNTABILITY

My analysis of these women's rhetorical efforts offers a revised concept of accountability inspired by Wenger's extension/expansion heuristic of attending to the self and the community. As previously noted, the OED confirms the word's long-standing meaning of answering for one's actions in business or governing—an inward responsibility. However, as we have seen, for Blaine, accountability means to attend to the self, listening to the lived experiences and stories of others, as well as sharing with them the knowledge, tools, and resources to improve one's life in a terrible situation. For Viggo Wexler, it means something outward: to acknowledge those outside of the power structure and to consider their ideas and contributions worthy.

This multiply conceived definition of accountability suggests real actions that I believe are apt for feminist rhetorical thought and application. In a most hopeful and pluralistic feminist sense, an act of accountability can extend in the yogic sense, rooting to focus on the aggrieved by *revealing and countering* the problems and misdeeds of an institution and allowing those seeking redress to hold them to account for a specific instance. Furthermore, in the application of yogic expansion, an act of accountability should seek to *add* more and other valuable perspectives to the structure and processes of an institution so as to continue to address and improve the conditions for all. This set of actions is not only practical and inclusive, but it is also a philosophically generous response to ill treatment and crisis, an orientation of feminism and faith.

At the top of this chapter, I shared my backstory as a former Catholic and previewed my doubts that an institution like the Catholic Church is capable of including and respecting women. In their calls for accountability, these women have given me—and, I wish for them, the Catholic Church—needed ways to pursue recourse for and, eventually, to change an institution that perpetuates systematic violence against children and the oppression of women. They exemplify an ethos of presence by relentlessly extending their presence and expanding to reach out and speak on behalf of the interests of others—demanding a new accountability.

NOTES

1. Teresa Donnellan, "A History of the Friction between the Girl Scouts and the Catholic Church," *America Magazine*, May 12, 2017.

2. Beth Daniell and Letizia Guglielmo, "Changing Audience, Changing Ethos," in *Rethinking Ethos: A Feminist Ecological Approach to Rhetoric*, eds. Kate Ryan, Nancy Myers, and Rebecca Jones (Carbondale: Southern Illinois UP, 2016), 242–252; Christy Wenger, "Creating Contemplative Spaces: Ethos as Presence and the Rhetorics of Yoga," in *Rethinking Ethos: A Feminist Ecological Approach to Rhetoric*, eds. Kate Ryan, Nancy Myers, and Rebecca Jones (Carbondale: Southern Illinois UP, 2016), 80–93.

3. Wenger, "Creating Contemplative Spaces," 251.

4. Daniell and Guglielmo, "Changing Audience, Changing Ethos," 94.

5. Daniell and Guglielmo, "Changing Audience, Changing Ethos," 95.

6. Wenger, "Creating Contemplative Spaces," 244. Italics in original.

7. Wenger, "Creating Contemplative Spaces," 250.

8. Wenger, "Creating Contemplative Spaces," 251.

9. Wenger, "Creating Contemplative Spaces," 252.

10. Wenger, "Creating Contemplative Spaces," 252.

11. *Oxford English Dictionary Online* (2011) s.v. "Accountability," https://www-oed-com.

12. Angela Bonavoglia, *Good Catholic Girls: How Women Are Leading the Fight to Change the Church* (San Francisco: HarperOne, 2006), xi.

13. Cecilia Viggo Wexler, *Catholic Women Confront Their Church: Stories of Hurt and Hope* (Lanham, MD: Rowman & Littlefield, 2016).

14. Wexler, *Catholic Women Confront Their Church*, 7, 20.

15. Bonavoglia, *Good Catholic Girls*, 40.

16. Globe Spotlight Team, "Scores of Priests Involved in Sex Abuse Cases," *Boston Globe*, January 6, 2002.

17. Wenger, "Creating Contemplative Spaces," 251.

18. Wexler, *Catholic Women Confront Their Church*, 4.

19. Wexler, *Catholic Women Confront Their Church*, 9.

20. Wexler, *Catholic Women Confront Their Church*, 20.

21. Bonavoglia, *Good Catholic Girls*, 76.

22. Bonavoglia, *Good Catholic Girls*, 69.

23. Bonavoglia, *Good Catholic Girls*, 84.

24. Peter Isley, "The 'Madness' of Barbara Blaine: 'Flectere si nequeo superos, Acheronta movebo,'" *National Catholic Reporter*, October 12, 2017, https://www.ncronline.org/news/people/madness-barbara-blaine-flectere-si-nequeo-superos-acheronta-movebo.

25. "Survivor's Network of Those Abused by Priests v. the Pope, et al.," Childs Rights International Network Library, accessed 2019, https://archive.crin.org/en/library/legal-database/survivors-network-those-abused-priests-v-pope-et-al.html.

26. "Survivors Network of those Abused by Priests," SNAP, accessed February 15, 2021, https://www.snapnetwork.org.

27. "Audio Stories," SNAP, accessed February 15, 2021, https://www.snapnetwork.org/stories.

BIBLIOGRAPHY

"Archdiocese of Boston News and Press Archives." Archdiocese of Boston. Accessed February 11, 2021. https://www.bostoncatholic.org/news-and-press-archives.

"Audio Stories." SNAP. Accessed February 15, 2021. https://www.snapnetwork.org/stories.

Bonavoglia, Angela. *Good Catholic Girls: How Women Are Leading the Fight to Change the Church*. New York: HarperOne, 2006.

Boston Globe. "Spotlight Investigation: Abuse in the Catholic Church." Boston.com. Accessed February 10, 2021. http://archive.boston.com/globe/spotlight/abuse/archive/chronological.htm.

Daniell, Beth and Letizia Guglielmo. "Changing Audience, Changing Ethos." In *Rethinking Ethos: A Feminist Ecological Approach to Rhetoric*, edited by Kate Ryan, Nancy Myers, and Rebecca Jones, 80–93. Carbondale: Southern Illinois UP, 2016.

Donnellan, Teresa. "A History of the Friction between the Girl Scouts and the Catholic Church." *America Magazine*, May 12, 2017.

Globe Spotlight Team. "Scores of Priests Involved in Sex Abuse Cases." *Boston Globe*, January 6, 2002.

Henley, John. "How the Boston Globe Exposed the Abuse Scandal that Rocked the Catholic Church." *Guardian*, April 21, 2010.

Investigative Team of the Boston Globe. *Betrayal: The Crisis in the Catholic Church*. Boston: Back Bay Books, 2003.

Isley, Peter. "The 'Madness' of Barbara Blaine: 'Flectere si nequeo superos, Acheronta movebo.'" *National Catholic Reporter*, October 12, 2017. https://www.ncronline.org/news/people/madness-barbara-blaine-flectere-si-nequeo-superos-acheronta-movebo.

Lindsay, Jay. "Boston Archdiocesan Spokeswoman Leaves Post." *Associated Press* in Boston.com. May 7, 2003. https://www.bishop-accountability.org/news2003_01_06/2003_05_07_Lindsay_BostonArchdiocesan.htm.

Ryan, Kathleen J., Nancy Myers and Rebecca Jones. *Rethinking Ethos: A Feminist Ecological Approach to Rhetoric*. Carbondale: Southern Illinois UP, 2016.

"Survivors Network of those Abused by Priests." SNAP. Accessed February 15, 2021. https://www.snapnetwork.org.

"Survivor's Network of those Abused by Priests v. the Pope, et al." Child's Rights International Network Library. Accessed 2019. https://archive.crin.org/en/library/legal-database/survivors-network-those-abused-priests-v-pope-et-al.html.

Viggo Wexler, Cecelia. *Catholic Women Confront Their Church: Stories of Hurt and Hope*. Lanham, MD: Rowman & Littlefield, 2016.

Wenger, Christy. "Creating Contemplative Spaces: Ethos as Presence and the Rhetorics of Yoga." In *Rethinking Ethos: A Feminist Ecological Approach to Rhetoric*, edited by Kate Ryan, Nancy Myers, and Rebecca Jones, 242–252. Carbondale: Southern Illinois UP, 2016.

Part III

CATHOLIC LAY WOMEN'S ETHOS

Chapter 8

"A Leader and a Lady"

Catholic Women's Use of Business Writing to Create an Ethos of Professionalism and Catholic Lay Womanhood

Jennifer Crosby Burgess

In the 1950's handbook, *The Lady and the Law: Notes on Protocol and Parliamentary Procedure*, the National Council of Catholic Women (NCCW)[1] provides a detailed guide to Catholic lay organizational work. Using the character of Joan, the authors explain the "how-tos" of writing letters, organizing events, and interacting with clergy. Additionally, they present guidelines for following parliamentary procedure and suggestions for applying successful business practices in clubs and councils. In the process of imparting this guidance, they give to their readers an example of the ideal Catholic laywoman:

> The woman you admire the most is undoubtedly a lady. She has a rare and wonderful gift. Into all the everyday activities of her life this woman carries high the dignity of womanhood, combining affection with reserve. She commands respect and transmits it to her family, to her guests, and to her associates. She knows how to conduct herself, her household, and the functions which she sponsors. . . .
>
> Such a woman is Joan Beyer McCormick (Mrs. John Peter McCormick, to some). Wife of a businessman and mother of four, Joan is a truly charming woman. Or at least, Joan tries so hard to be a good wife, mother and lay leader that most people find her truly charming, too.
>
> But women like Joan aren't just born. They have learned to develop their poise and their personality. Reading and thinking and prayer and effort are required to play the role of womanhood to its fullest capacity.[2]

In the pages following this introduction, readers learn that Joan, or "the woman you admire the most," is both a lady and a leader. A "lady" is not merely a woman with desirable manners and good taste. She is also a woman devoted to her faith, her family, and her community. She, as depicted above, is knowledgeable and well read, and she is well versed on the intricacies of church hierarchy. In addition to her attention to decorum and etiquette, however, "the woman you admire the most" is also a good leader. Among her many skills, she can "conduct a meeting just as it should be conducted," and the reader can be just like Joan, as the authors explain:

> Perhaps now you're sure to send just the right invitation, conduct that meeting as it should be conducted, avoid that big, floppy hat when you're going to give a talk. Perhaps now, you'll see your husband, children, and fellow council members notice you with new respect. And perhaps you can transmit your new confidence to your friends, for Christian courtesy and charity must underlie even the smallest act.
>
> Perhaps you and Joan may even meet now, in your work for and with your organization and council. Do you think you will know each other? Do you think she may even think: "There is a leader and a lady."[3]

These closing remarks of the handbook illustrate that, in addition to being a faithful Catholic, Joan knows how to conduct business effectively and efficiently, how to communicate with audience members ranging from her fellow laywomen to high-ranking members of the clergy, as well as how to present herself properly and, in turn, her organization to those outside of the council/club.

This handbook was published in the late 1950s,[4] but its portrayal of the ideal Catholic laywoman and organized Catholic lay womanhood is vital to understanding the ethos-building work that American Catholic laywomen have engaged since the late nineteenth century. This ethos-building work has always been dually grounded in professionalism and Catholicity. In other words, in organizations from the parish level to the national level, Catholic laywomen have created, cultivated, and preserved a coexistent ethos that is, at all times, both highly professional and fundamentally Catholic.

DEFINING COEXISTENT ETHOS

In using the term "coexistent ethos," I draw on the work of several feminist rhetorical scholars who examine the ways that marginalized rhetors navigate situations in which their voices are silenced. As many scholars have demonstrated, marginalized rhetors find alternative ways to assert their ethos when the traditional "available means" of persuasion are unavailable to them. Recent discussions of ethos, specifically feminist theorizations of ethos, focus on the multiple ethē used by rhetors who do not have access to traditional means of persuasion. In *Women Physicians and Professional Ethos in Nineteenth-Century America*, Carolyn Skinner argues that marginalized rhetors—specifically women—may be able to leverage authoritative genres because "genre conventions can prompt them to display characteristics that are different from those typically associated with proper femininity."[5] Skinner draws on Risa Applegarth's argument that ethos can be understood as a "location among genres" in that "genres shape audience expectations, including expectations for *ethos*."[6] Adding to this conversation, the editors of *Rethinking Ethos: A Feminist Ecological Approach to Rhetoric* explain that "feminist ecological ethē open up new ways of envisioning ethos to acknowledge the multiple, nonlinear relations operating among rhetors, audiences, things, and contexts."[7]

Coexistent ethos draws from these theorizations of ethos, as it describes how individuals, groups, and organizations simultaneously embody more than one ethos in order to navigate successfully the multifarious, often conflicting, expectations and constraints that audiences place on them. To elucidate this concept of coexistent ethos, I look to a group of rhetors who worked diligently to construct, cultivate, and preserve a business ethos that would ensure a favorable response in their audience(s): American Catholic laywomen.

THE DEVELOPMENT OF CATHOLIC LAY WOMANHOOD

American Catholic laywomen's groups serve as a rich example of coexistent ethos, because the business ethos that they deployed, beginning with their earliest organizational work, could be interpreted as somewhat surprising. Unlike many of their Protestant counterparts who were already actively involved in social reform and community outreach efforts in the mid-nineteenth century, American Catholic laywomen did not engage actively with organizational efforts outside of the home until the end of the nineteenth century. According to scholars of American Catholicism, Katharine E. Harmon[8] and Deirdre Moloney,[9] the community outreach aspect of Catholic women's identity began to take root in the late nineteenth and early twentieth centuries due to rapid shifts in the roles of both the Catholic laity and Catholic women during that time period. One important socioeconomic influence was the slow yet significant development of the Catholic middle class in the United States during the late nineteenth century. While some Catholics had been involved in social reform and outreach efforts throughout the 1800s, the Catholic population did not begin joining these efforts in large numbers until the end of the century.[10]

Ruth Libbey O'Halloran and Mary Jo Weaver both argue that most Catholic women during much of the nineteenth century, many being recent immigrants, felt that charity work and social issues like suffrage were beyond their sphere. O'Halloran explains that "poor Catholic women . . . looked upon suffrage as the special province of well-to-do Protestant women."[11] Weaver expands on O'Halloran's point in positing that suffrage advocacy was "an upper-middle-class phenomenon, due in part to the relationship between voting rights and property ownership, [therefore] one would not expect to find many Catholic women active in the movement."[12] As Irish American and German American Catholics began to move into merchant and office-based positions, however, they left the working-class station for more middle-class stability. This shift in social situation, among other influential factors, led to opportunities for lay Catholic women to take on the work of community outreach.[13] With this change came a rise in American fraternal efforts[14] as well as the formation of what O'Halloran refers to as "Catholic lay womanhood."[15] As men's fraternal benefits societies and outreach organizations began—and excluded women from their organized work—women's fraternal benefits societies and parish-, diocesan-, and national-level outreach organizations took shape.

With these shifts in social status came the skepticism of the clergy toward newly minted middle-class Catholic women. As Moloney explains, American Catholics—specifically the American clergy—struggled with their understanding of the Catholic laywoman's role in the home, Church, and society as the Catholic middle class was established.[16] Some members of the American clergy deemed these women as "too Protestant," either in their recently acquired access to time for leisure or in their social outreach efforts. As a result, organized Catholic womanhood in America was a complex and heavily debated topic in the late nineteenth and early twentieth centuries, so members of lay Catholic women's organizations had to do a significant amount of work to convince their fellow Catholics and their clergy that they were, indeed, faithful to Catholic concerns. They also had to convince audiences that they were professional and capable of doing the work that their Protestant peers had been engaged in for decades. Ultimately, they had the task of portraying their organizations as both professional and Catholic in a sociocultural context that engendered doubt on both fronts. Conveying a coexistent ethos through their business writing allowed these groups to take on the challenge strategically.

DEVELOPING A BUSINESS ETHOS

Before examining the business writing of Catholic laywomen's organizations, it is important to show the connection between ethos and business writing. In the 1920 edition of their *Handbook of Business English*, George Burton Hotchkiss, head of the Department of Advertising and Marketing at New York University (NYU), and Edward Jones Kilduff, professor of Business English at NYU, explain the purpose and value of business English.[17] Successful business English leads to profit, but Hotchkiss and Kilduff contend that profit is gained as the result of "establishing good will" with the reader.[18] Thus, "the value of a business English message is, therefore, determined by its effectiveness in securing a favorable response from those to whom it is directed."[19] For Hotchkiss and Kilduff, and for many of their colleagues[20] in early twentieth-century America, the purpose and value of business writing was to secure the trust, or, as they say, "good will" of a potential client or customer. This good will was, in turn, linked to establishing the character of an organization—another point of much attention during this era, as the move from small, individually run companies gave rise to the modern American corporation and its contemporary office setting. Chairman of the United States Steel Corporation, Judge Elbert H. Gary, in his 1917 handbook titled *Character in Business*, displays this point, arguing that "the foundation of genuine success is character."[21] As such, in all genres of business writing, organizations create and communicate a business ethos to gain the trust of and instill confidence in audiences consisting of clients (potential or actual), customers, stakeholders, and the public.

By "business ethos," I mean the professional reputation and character that organizational writers[22] convey through a wide variety of business- and professional-writing documents. For some organizations, articulating a unified business ethos may be a simple task, as they may not need to navigate the complexities of attending to the expectations of diverse audiences. Cultivating a business ethos that "establishes good will" might be more challenging for other organizations due to the social constraints stemming from expectations based on any number of identifying factors that audiences place on the organization. Catholic laywomen's organizations fall into the latter group.

At any given time, the members of Catholic laywomen's organizations were composing messages for multiple audiences. As a result, Catholic laywomen's use of coexistent ethos is evident in the materials of groups ranging from national-, state-, diocesan-, and parish-levels. For the purpose of space, I limit my analysis to the business writing of one representative group—the Catholic Women's League of Columbus (CWL), a diocesan-level group organized in Columbus, Ohio, in January 1919. Despite differences in organizational structures and goals, Catholic laywomen's groups have always had to deploy a coexistent ethos of professionalism and Catholicity that consistently appealed to more than one audience—a coexistent ethos that is beautifully exhibited by the business writing of the CWL.

THE ANNUAL REPORT GENRE

Although members of the CWL produced a variety of business-writing genres, the annual report is a genre that fundamentally requires the "favorable response" from multiple audiences in order to be successful. As A. Charles Babenroth asserts in his *Modern Business English* (1931), the primary function of a report that includes recommendations (as an annual report does) is to "influence the reader's course of action."[23] These readers include the board of directors (and stockholders in a corporate situation), in addition to the public, "which consists of [multiple] interested parties."[24] The decisions or "courses of action" taken by the annual report readers could seriously impact the organization's future. The outward-facing nature of the annual report, therefore, makes it an ideal genre for examining the CWL's dexterous articulation of coexistent ethos.

In this analysis, I draw on Cynthia Haller's work in her 1997 article, "Revaluing Women's Work: Report Writing in the North Carolina Canning Clubs, 1912–1916." In this case study of women's clubs' report writing, Haller, expanding on Dorothy Winsor's examination[25] of how entry-level employees use documentation and recordkeeping to make their work visible and, therefore, more valuable, upholds the rhetorical importance of report writing and the rhetorical weight carried by reports.[26] She contends that "an examination of women's report work in a specific historical setting illustrates how the documentation of work can contribute to public acknowledgment and recognition of the value of women's work."[27] The clubs' work may have centered on food preservation, but Haller found that the importance of report writing was often emphasized as much as that of canning. Through documentation, the clubwomen accomplish four significant objectives: they redefine their work as valuable; they redefine their home kitchens as spaces of work and not just domesticity; they redefine themselves as professionals; and they maintain their professional identity.[28]

Like the canning clubs in Haller's study, members of the CWL use report writing to maintain an identity of professionalism and credibility in male-dominated spheres. Their reports also serve as distilled examples of Catholic women's use of audience-specific business-writing genres to uphold their coexistent ethos of professionalism and Catholicity. To best understand the importance of the CWL's reports, one must have a sense of the business-writing context in which members were producing their materials. Report-writing instruction delivers that situated insight.

Early twentieth-century America saw a surge in the publication of texts dedicated to report writing. The main audiences of these texts included engineers, scientists, junior executives, and business school students. Authors explain that, while the majority of their readers are professionals, their content is applicable to those outside of the corporations and industry. I frame the business-writing context in which the members of the CWL were writing with several examples of the annual report and report-writing resources that were widely available during that time. Examining these materials proves that resources regarding business-writing conventions were in wide circulation and easily accessible to members of Catholic laywomen organizations, and that members were conversant and skilled in producing documents following these conventions.

REPORT-WRITING MANUALS, GUIDES, HANDBOOKS, AND TEXTBOOKS

In *The Preparation of Reports: Engineering, Scientific, Administrative* (1923), Ray Palmer Baker walks his readers through the "Origins" of the report to "Elements," "Characteristics," and "Types" of reports then, finally, to numerous examples of reports.[29] Baker explains that, although the primary audience for his text is students, the book "contains a mass of material, never before brought together, which will make it valuable as a work of reference for those in active professional and business life."[30] This audience designation is important, as it confirms that texts such as Baker's could have seen a circulation beyond just those pursuing academic endeavors. In the early pages of the text, Baker's explanation of both the importance and characteristics of annual reports sounds strikingly similar to Babenroth's description of annual reports. Baker writes that "it is difficult to overemphasize the importance of yearly reports in private enterprises," ending the paragraph with the comment that "without such private reports, [the reports that pass from junior member to superior detailing the work of the year] no extensive organization can be maintained."[31] He then explains that the yearly report "is a kind of history" of the "condition, operation, and result" of the year's endeavors.[32]

Ralph U. Fitting also examines the purpose and importance of reports in *Report Writing* (1924). Like Baker, Fitting discusses various types of reports used in business and industry, splitting them into the three categories of "period report," "examination report," and "research report."[33] In discussing the period report, the subgenre under which the annual report would fall, Fitting notes that these reports provide insight into the regular activities of the organization in addition to "the exceptional events which project themselves above the regular contour of routine business."[34] In other words, the period report gives an organization the chance to outline its routine activities—the day in/day out business of keeping an organization running—and to highlight its accomplishments. Both of these elements lead to ethos building and cultivation, and both are seen in the annual report of the CWL.[35]

The same importance on report writing is echoed in various texts published throughout the 1920s and 1930s.[36] These texts define the importance of accurate and thorough reports as well as the need for well-written, audience-centered documents. A representative statement comes from the preface to Carl C. Gaum's and Harold F. Graves's *Report Writing* (1929). Gaum and Graves open their text stating that "the report-writer must meet several requirements. To borrow a term from public speaking, he must be 'audience-minded,' that is, he must write with an appreciation of the reader's point of view."[37] Gaum and Graves emphasize the importance of delivering content that is accurate and presented in a way that adheres to audience expectations. Each of these texts was written primarily for university students, yet available to readers beyond the university.[38]

This discussion of report-writing guides offers a mere glimpse into the abundance of instructional materials widely circulating in early twentieth-century America. The importance that these authors place on report writing is mirrored by the importance that the women in Haller's study of the North Carolina canning clubs place on their reporting and documentation. Similarly, the annual report of the CWL follows the conventions of report writing and the rhetorical weight of reporting that is detailed above. In addition to following business-writing conventions, however, the report authors incorporate elements of Catholicity consistently throughout their report. As a result, the group communicates a coexistent ethos of professionalism and Catholic fidelity in their report that was sure to "secure favorable response[s]" from all readers.

THE CWL: *1919–1921 YEAR BOOK*

The CWL was formed in January 1919 in response to the National Catholic War Council's request that Catholic women continue the work they had started as members of the Catholic Women's War Relief Council.[39] According to a history of the Catholic Women's League written by member Anna Sharon McAllister (1951), the Catholic Women's War Relief Council had just recently closed its Columbus, Ohio, office when this request was made. As a member of the National Catholic War Council, Bishop Hartley of the Diocese of Columbus asked that the Catholic women of his diocese continue their social service work because the adjustment to peacetime was "in no way less arduous than the demands of war time."[40] He asked for assistance with outreach efforts to newly arrived immigrants and to young girls who were entering the business world "in ever increasing numbers."[41] McAllister notes that "some 400 women responded promptly to the request of His Excellency with the immediate problem being the improvement of the civic and social conditions in the various diocesan foreign settlements."[42] The outreach work of these 400 women is documented in the CWL's first annual report.

The CWL's *1919–1921 Year Book* is a multipage report that follows the accepted conventions of annual report writing. The content of the report follows the chronology listed below:[43]

- Title Page
- Our Emblem
- "Woman"—a poem by Rev. Francis A. Gaffney dedicated to the Catholic Women's League of Columbus
- A Letter from our Bishop
- Outlook for the League by Miss James E. McNally
- The Catholic Women's League—Its Work by Miss Maud Flynn
- Officers for the Year
- Standing Committees
- Parish Chairmen
- List of Official Workers at the Community House (including job titles/descriptions)
- Announcements
- Statement of Receipts and Disbursements
- Copy of Letter from the 5th Avenue Savings Bank (verifying account balance)
- Report of the Auditing Committee
- Meetings (including dates and descriptions)
- Schedule of Activities by the Recreational Committee
- Constitution and By-Laws
- Miscellaneous
- List of Members
- Back Cover: In Memoriam

The scope of the document can be summed up in this list, as the authors present a history of the organization, a discussion of the organization's future plans, and an articulation of the group's values, goals, and mission as a Catholic community outreach group. This format follows basic reporting guidelines: yearly summary from the executive officer, current status of the organization, important data expressed in alphabetic and graphic form, and concluding comments from the secretary.[44] The formatting and the inclusion of these informative elements uphold the CWL's organizational ethos as one of professionalism and authority. When examining the bishop's letter and the remarks from CWL officers, we see the preserving of Catholic identity, also. Several elements of the report demonstrate the dexterous articulation of professional ethos and Catholic ethos as they coexist in the business ethos of the CWL.

The emblem of the CWL is the first content encountered on the report's title page. It consists of a cross enclosed by a circle. In the border circle around the cross, the text reads, "The Catholic Women's League of Columbus, Ohio." Under the circle are the words, "Faith and Service." This emblem does appear on the cover of the report, but with this appearance, the authors include an explanation—in alphabetic text—of the visual. The two components of the graphic are described in this manner:

> THE CROSS: The symbol of faith in right, in justice; the symbol of Him who died for truth and right and justice. The symbol of the faith that is the spring and the inspiration of doing for others according to justice and love.
>
> THE CIRCLE: The symbol of service; all embracing; equally dispensing its labor, its enfolding strength, to all without end; the symbol of enduring, complete service to all.[45]

The CWL's use of the cross and alphabetic text enclosed by a circle is reminiscent of the emblem of the National Catholic War Council (NCWC)—the organization from which the CWL originated. By invoking the visual representation of the NCWC, the CWL draws on the professional and Catholic ethos of a well-known, well-respected, and easily recognizable organization. The emblem acts as a visual symbol of the CWL's mission as well as a textual synopsis of its work, highlighting the group's Catholicity. This inclusion of the emblem and its related content as the first non-front-matter page of the document immediately grounds the CWL's report in the ethos of Catholic outreach and charity.

Following the emblem, the authors feature the voices of two clergymen: Rev. Francis A. Gaffney, who wrote and dedicated the poem "Woman" to the CWL, and Bishop Hartley, who penned a letter of support for the CWL's annual report. Opening the report with clergy voices is a wise ethos-building move. The CWL works directly with—and under the authority of—the Bishop of Columbus. His blessing is required for their continued work, but their early inclusion of his extolling comments that "the Bishop is very glad to learn that all our Catholic women are taking an active part in the Catholic Women's League—that your membership is growing—and much good is being accomplished" further builds their ethos as represented to their members, potential members, and other stakeholders interested in the work of the organization.[46] Bishop Hartley's enthusiastic support and Rev. Gaffney's affirmation would certainly endorse the CWL's work to parish priests who might promote the group to their parishioners.

In her "Outlook for the League," Mrs. James E. McNally outlines the work of the CWL as well as the motivation for carrying out that work:

> One of our principle duties is to extend a welcome hand to the stranger coming to our shores; to teach him to speak our language, to teach him to love our country, and to try to make him a happy and useful citizen. Another duty is to provide healthful and wholesome recreation for our girls in industrial occupations.[47]

She concludes with the following definition of the "Catholic spirit"—a Catholic spirit that is inextricably tied to community outreach:

> The Catholic spirit which governs the motives of the women of this League—that spirit of mutual sympathy, understanding, and personal help, cannot but be of benefit to the social life of all the people of Columbus. It will be a wholesome contribution to the community. I feel assured that our women will not fail in their duty.[48]

McNally grounds her remarks on the CWL's work in the identity of Catholic laywomen and their responsibility to extend assistance and outreach to their community. Within the framework of a formal business document, the CWL's mission of charity, benevolence, and civic duty is consistently articulated.

In the next section, "The Catholic Women's League—Its Work," Miss Maud Flynn clarifies the specific efforts, programs, and resources that the CWL offers to local eastern and southern European immigrants and young working women at its two community houses. For example, Flynn points to such community outreach work as "four classes in civics and English, three in dramatics, a choral society, an orchestra of little people, dressmaking and cooking classes, Boy Scouts, Girl Scouts, a flourishing mothers' club and a men's club, a poolroom, and showers are some of the attractions offered by the house."[49] Flynn highlights the organization's emphasis on community building and community outreach that specifically serves young women working in factories and newly arrived southern and eastern European immigrants. She also touches on the group's commitment to education, fine arts, and vocational training, and—ultimately—Americanization. As such, members of the CWL were fulfilling not only their Catholic duties but also their civic responsibilities.

This *Year Book* documents the work of the group, certainly in the record-keeping of events, accomplishments, and financial reporting. It also supplies the earliest history of the group. But the weight of rhetorical force lies in the ways that the members frame and, in effect, preserve their business ethos through the consistent illustration of the group's overlapping professional work and community outreach efforts. At every turn, the mission of the group and the responsibility of its members as the female Catholic lay apostolate are articulated. The ethos of the group as professional and fundamentally Catholic is explicated through the imagery and typeface on the front of the 1921 document, through the introductory material summarizing the purpose of the CWL, through the summary of the past two year's work, through the inclusion of the Constitution, and through the descriptions of each event that was on the calendar between June 1919 and June 1921. Through this detailed attention to alphabetic text, graphic elements, and page design, the authors successfully convey a business ethos simultaneously grounded in professionalism and Catholic identity. This use of coexistent ethos would certainly secure the "good will" of the various readers of the report.

CONCLUSION

There is no question that the members of the CWL were conversant in the report-writing practices of their contemporary context. Like the CWL, other American Catholic laywomen's groups established themselves as "professional" by engaging in the business-writing conventions and practices of their time. They also maintained their identity as Catholic laywomen by incorporating elements of Catholic doctrine and Catholic concepts of outreach and charity in the documents they composed to "do the work-a-day business" of their organizations. In doing so, they successfully navigated the male-dominated spheres of business, Church, and Catholic fraternal activity; effectively appealed to both their female peers and their male clergy; and skillfully constructed a coexistent ethos of professional authority and Catholic fidelity. In examining the business writing of American Catholic laywomen, this brief study asserts that coexistent ethos is a productive lens for analyzing and understanding the sophisticated rhetorical approaches that rhetors and organizations frequently engage. Here, the concept has supplied a frame to understand the ways that American Catholic laywomen like the CWL consistently labored to present themselves and their organizations.

At this point, it would be helpful to revisit the ideal image of Catholic lay womanhood seen in Joan, "the woman you admire the most." Joan embodies everything that members of Catholic laywomen's organizations strive to be: a professional, faithful, confident, and capable Catholic lady who is just as comfortable running a meeting or giving a speech as she is going to Mass or cooking for the homeless. She is well liked AND well respected by all who meet her, including her fellow laywomen, members of the clergy, and civic and community leaders. An image near the start of the handbook visually captures both the professionalism and Catholic fidelity that Joan symbolizes. She stands aloft a compass rose that is lined by icons symbolizing church, home, school, and community. With arms outstretched, Joan gracefully and confidently strides across the compass rose presumably tending to her church, in addition to familial and civic duties, with poise and care. This model Catholic laywoman embodies the same coexistent ethos of professionalism and

Catholic womanhood that we observe in the CWL annual report. Deploying a coexistent ethos of professionalism by following the conventions of the annual report genre and of Catholicity by incorporating Catholic imagery and principles, the CWL preserves a business ethos in its document that portrays its members as capable, competent women. The women of the CWL, along with members of other Catholic laywomen's groups, through their business writing, always present themselves as, just like Joan, "the woman you admire the most," prepared and qualified to stand aloft the compass rose of their communities and to take on their spiritual, familial, and civic duties with poise and care.

NOTES

1. Founded in March 1920, the National Council of Catholic Women is the national-level organization of Catholic women in the United States with state and diocesan affiliates around the country.

2. National Council of Catholic Women, *The Lady and the Law: Notes on Protocol and Parliamentary Procedure* (Washington: NCCW, 1950s), 3–4.

3. National Council of Catholic Women, *The Lady and the Law*, 36.

4. Although there is no date of publication on handbook, *The Catholic Mirror*, in Des Moines, IA, ran an article on January 29, 1960, referencing the handbook. The article, "Protocol and Parliamentary Law" notes that the handbook was "published a few years ago," so the date of publication was likely in the late 1950s.

5. Carolyn Skinner, *Women Physicians and Professional Ethos in Nineteenth-Century America* (Carbondale: Southern Illinois UP, 2014), 177.

6. Risa Applegarth, "Genre, Location, and Mary Austin's Ethos," *Rhetoric Society Quarterly* 41, no. 1 (2011): 52; Carolyn Skinner, *Women Physicians and Professional Ethos in Nineteenth-Century America* (Carbondale: Southern Illinois UP, 2014), 177.

7. Kathleen J. Ryan, Nancy Myers, and Rebecca Jones, eds., *Rethinking Ethos: A Feminist Ecological Approach to Rhetoric* (Carbondale: Southern Illinois UP, 2016), 3.

8. Katharine E. Harmon, *There Were Also Many Women There: Lay Women in the Liturgical Movement in the United States, 1926–1959* (Collegeville: Liturgical Press, 2013). In this study, Harmon explains that although Catholic women were involved in charitable work throughout the nineteenth century, they did not begin to join social outreach efforts in large numbers during the late 1800s.

9. Deirdre Moloney, *American Catholic Lay Groups and Transatlantic Social Reform in the Progressive Era* (Chapel Hill: University of North Carolina Press, 2002).

10. Harmon, *There Were Also Many Women There*, 54.

11. Ruth Libbey O'Halloran, *Organized Catholic Womanhood: The National Council of Catholic Women, 1920–1995* (PhD diss., Washington: Catholic University of America, 1996), 6.

12. Mary Jo Weaver, *New Catholic Women: A Contemporary Challenge to Traditional Religious Authority* (San Francisco: Harper and Row, 1985). Quoted in R.L. O'Halloran, *Organized Catholic Womanhood: The National Council of Catholic Women, 1920–1995* (PhD diss., Washington: Catholic University of America, 1996), 6.

13. Moloney, *American Catholic Lay Groups and Transatlantic Social Reform in the Progressive Era*, 6–7. Moloney explains that other significant influences include Pope Leo XIII's revised articulation of the role of the Catholic laity in *Rerum Novarum* in May 1891, a new wave of immigration consisting of many central and southern Europeans who did not organize into local groups as their Irish and German predecessors had (and who, therefore, needed organized assistance), and the post–World War I efforts of professionalization in the fields of social work and sociology.

14. See Christopher J. Kauffman, *Faith and Fraternalism: The History of the Knights of Columbus, 1882–1982* (New York: Harper & Row, 1982).

15. See Ruth Libbey O'Halloran, *Organized Catholic Womanhood: The National Council of Catholic Women, 1920–1995* (PhD diss., Washington: Catholic University of America, 1996).

16. Moloney, *American Catholic Lay Groups and Transatlantic Social Reform in the Progressive Era*, 178.

17. G.B. Hotchkiss and E.J. Kilduff, *Handbook of Business English* (New York: Harper & Brothers Publishers, 1920); Hotchkiss and Kilduff define "business English" as "all written messages that are used in transacting business."

18. Hotchkiss and Kilduff, *Handbook of Business English*, 1.

19. Hotchkiss and Kilduff, *Handbook of Business English*, 1.

20. Here is a small selection of some of the widely circulated business-writing handbooks during the early twentieth century: Frank M. Erkskine, *Modern Business Correspondence: A Practical Treatise on the Writing of Business Letters, Including Many Exercises in Word Study, Synonyms, Ad Writing, Punctuation, Etc.* (Indianapolis: The Bobbs-Merrill Company, 1907); Gustav S. Kimball, *Kimball's Business English with Lessons on Business Letter Writing, Capitalization, and Punctuation* (Indianapolis: The Bobbs-Merrill Company, 1908); G.B. Hotchkiss and E.J. Kilduff, *Handbook of Business English* (New York: Harper & Brothers Publishers, 1914, 1915, 1917, 1920); Benjamin J. Campbell and Bruce L. Vass, *Essentials of Business English and Business Letters: How To Write Them* (Jackson: Business English Publishing Company, 1915); James Melvin Lee, ed., *Language for Men of Affairs*: *Vol. II: Business Writing* (New York: The Ronald Press Company, 1920); Alta Gwinn Saunders and Herbert LeSourd Creek, eds. *The Literature of Business* (New York: Harper & Brothers Publishers, 1920); T.H. Bailey Whipple, *Principles of Business Writing* (East Pittsburgh: Westinghouse Technical Night School, 1924); James H. Picken, ed., *Business Correspondence Handbook* (Chicago: A.W. Shaw Company, 1927); A. Charles Babenroth, *Modern Business English* (New York: Prentice-Hall, 1931).

21. Elbert H. Gary, *Character in Business* (New York: Business Training Corporation, 1917), 5.

22. For a definition of "organizational writer," see Driskill, Linda, "Understanding the Writing Context in Organizations," in *Central Works in Technical Communication*, eds. Johndan Johnson-Eilola and Stuart Selber (New York: Oxford UP, 1994), 55–69.

23. A. Charles Babenroth, *Modern Business English* (New York: Prentice-Hall, Inc., 1931), 13.

24. Babenroth, *Modern Business English*, 426.

25. Dorothy Winsor "Genre and Activity Systems: The Role of Documentation in Maintaining and Changing Engineering Activity Systems," *Written Communication* 16, no. 2 (1999): 200–224; Dorothy Winsor, "Writing Engineering, Engineering Writing," *College Composition and Communication* 41, no. 1 (February 1990): 58–70.

26. Cynthia R. Haller, "Revaluing Women's Work: Report Writing in the North Carolina Canning Clubs, 1912–1916," *Technical Communication Quarterly* 6, no, 3 (1997): 281–292.

27. Haller, "Revaluing Women's Work," 282.

28. Haller, "Revaluing Women's Work," 282–283.

29. Ray Palmer Baker, *The Preparation of Reports: Engineering, Scientific, Administrative* (New York: The Ronald Press Company, 1923).

30. Baker, *The Preparation of Reports*, vi.

31. Baker, *The Preparation of Reports*, 78.

32. Baker, *The Preparation of Reports*, 78.

33. Ralph U. Fitting, *Report Writing* (New York: The Ronald Press, Co., 1924), 1.

34. Fitting, *Report Writing*, 6.

35. The importance and urgency of persuasive report writing was also articulated a few years prior to both Baker's and Fitting's texts by accountant, W. H. Bell in his *Accountant's Reports* (New York: The Ronald Press Company, 1921). Across 247 pages, Bell explains the need for more readability and audience-centered writing in accountants' reports, explaining that accountants' work goes largely unnoticed because readers either cannot interpret the facts and figures in the documents, or refuse to engage with the material as it is presented. As Bell argues, "the field work done by the accountant or his representative may be ever so good, but it will avail little if the report is not lucid or illuminating as well as accurate" (8). Through his book, Bell offers guidance and extensive illustrations regarding proper, audience-based report writing. In doing so, he upholds the report as one of the main tools for preserving business ethos.

A similar comment on the negative opinion toward a profession based on inadequate reporting is seen in Marjorie Bell's *Presenting Probation: A Study of Annual Reports* (1932). Marjorie Bell, writing eleven years later, is just as distraught as W. H. Bell when she refers to the negative public opinion that her profession receives. She introduces her forty-seven-page compilation of Annual Reports for the Probation Association with the following extended metaphor:

> Have you ever stood before a "trick" mirror which altered your outlines, made bulges where hollows should be, elongated you to string bean proportions, or reduced you to the size and symmetry of a croquet ball? You are not alone in this uncomfortable experience of

misrepresentation. Nor is it limited to human beings. In a not dissimilar way, social causes and movements have suffered just such distortion in the mirror of public opinion. (1)

The distorted public opinion that she bemoans is that of probation, "the social treatment of delinquents" (1). She attributes the skewed public perception of this work to the fact that probation is a relatively new field of work and to the fact that "its best friends have often failed to present it truly to the public" (1). As Marjorie Bell continues her discussion of the need for better representation, she finally asserts that "as a means of presenting to the public the methods and needs of probation work, there is no instrument which surpasses a well planned and well written annual report" (3). Although W. H. Bell is calling for better financial reporting and Marjorie Bell (no apparent relation) is calling for annual reporting, both are emphasizing the importance of report writing in presenting the value and authority of not just an organization, but an entire profession, to the public.

36. Alta Gwinn Saunders and Chester Reed Anderson, *Business Reports: Investigation and Presentation* (New York: McGraw-Hill, 1929); Carl C. Gaum and Harold F. Graves, *Report Writing* (New York: Prentice-Hall, 1929); Neil H. Borden and Edmund P. Learned, *Suggestions on Report Writing* (Cambridge: Harvard University, 1930); Amos Tuck School of Administration and Finance's Committee on Research, *Manual on Research and Reports: With Special Application to the Field of Business, Economics, and Public Affairs* (Hanover: Dartmouth College, 1931); Winward Prescott, *How to Write Reports: Business, Engineering, and Architectural* (Cambridge: Massachusetts Institute of Technology, 1932). Textbooks written by business professors and faculty committees such as these enjoyed extensive circulation with many of them seeing revised editions printed within five to ten years of the original publication.

37. Carl G. Gaum and Harold F. Graves, *Report Writing*, 2nd edition (New York: Prentice-Hall, 1942), vii.

38. As the Committee on Research at the Amos Tuck School of Administration and Finance notes in its *Manual on Research and Reports*, the text is "applied specifically to problems of business and finance, but most of the material is intended for general use."

Committee on Research, *Manual on Research and Reports with Special Application to the Field of Business, Economics, and Public Affairs* (Hanover: Amos Tuck School of Administration and Finance, 1931), 5.

39. The CWL continued to function within the Diocese of Columbus until the late 1990s.

40. Anna Shannon McAllister, "The Catholic Women's League" (Columbus: Catholic Women's League of Columbus, 1951), 1.

41. McAllister, "The Catholic Women's League," 1.

42. McAllister, "The Catholic Women's League," 1.

43. *Year Book of the Catholic Women's League of Columbus, Ohio, June 1919–June 1921* (Columbus: The Catholic Women's League of Columbus, 1921).

44. See texts such as Fitting, *Report Writing* ((New York: The Ronald Press, Co., 1924) for a discussion of the format of annual reports.

45. "Our Emblem," in *Year Book of the Catholic Women's League of Columbus, Ohio, June 1919–June 1921* (Columbus: The Catholic Women's League of Columbus, 1921), 2.

46. James J. Hartley, "A Letter from Our Bishop," in *Year Book of the Catholic Women's League of Columbus, Ohio, June 1919–June 1921* (Columbus: The Catholic Women's League of Columbus, 1921), 4.

47. Mrs. James E. McNally, "Outlook for the League," *Year Book of the Catholic Women's League of Columbus, Ohio, June 1919–June 1921* (Columbus: The Catholic Women's League of Columbus, 1921), 5.

48. McNally, "Outlook for the League," 5.

49. Maud Flynn, "The Catholic Women's League—Its Work." *Year Book of the Catholic Women's League of Columbus, Ohio, June 1919–June 1921* (Columbus: The Catholic Women's League of Columbus, 1921), 6–7.

BIBLIOGRAPHY

Amos Tuck School of Administration and Finance's Committee on Research. *Manual on Research and Reports: With Special Application to the Field of Business, Economics, and Public Affairs*. Hanover: Dartmouth College, 1931.

Applegarth, Risa. "Genre, Location, and Mary Austin's Ethos," *Rhetoric Society Quarterly* 41, no. 1 (2011): 41–63. https://doi.org/10.1080/02773945.2010.499861.

Babenroth, A. Charles. *Modern Business English*. New York: Prentice-Hall, Inc., 1931.

Baker, Ray Palmer. *The Preparation of Reports: Engineering, Scientific, Administrative*. New York: The Ronald Press Company, 1923.

Bell, Marjorie. *Presenting Probation: A Study of Annual Reports*. New York: National Probation Association, 1932.

Bell, W.H. *Accountants' Reports*. New York: The Ronald Press Company, 1921.

Borden, Neil H. and Edmund P. Learned. *Suggestions on Report Writing*. Cambridge: Harvard University, 1930.

Catholic Women's League of Columbus. *Year Book of the Catholic Women's League of Columbus, Ohio, June 1919–June 1921*. Columbus: CWL, 1921.

Culver, Dorothy Campbell. *Preparation of Public Reports and Documents: A Bibliography*. Berkeley: Bureau of Public Administration, University of California, 1936.

Fitting, Ralph U. *Report Writing*. New York: The Ronald Press Company, 1924.

Flynn, Maud. "The Catholic Women's League—Its Work." In *Year Book of the Catholic Women's League of Columbus, Ohio, June 1919–June 1921* by the Catholic Women's League of Columbus, 6–7. Columbus: The Catholic Women's League of Columbus, 1921.

Gary, Elbert H. *Character in Business*. New York: Business Training Corporation, 1917.

Gaum Carl C. and Harold F. Graves. *Report Writing*. 2nd ed. New York: Prentice-Hall, 1929.

Haller, Cynthia R. "Revaluing Women's Work: Report Writing in the North Carolina Canning Clubs, 1912–1916." *Technical Communication Quarterly* 6, no. 3 (1997): 281–292. https://doi.org/10.1207/s15427625tcq0603_4.

Harmon, Katharine E. *There Were Also Many Women There: Lay Women in the Liturgical Movement in the United States, 1926–1959*. Collegeville: Liturgical Press, 2013.

Hartley, James J. "A Letter from Our Bishop," In *Year Book of the Catholic Women's League of Columbus, Ohio, June 1919–June 1921*, 4. Columbus: The Catholic Women's League of Columbus, 1921.

Hotchkiss, G.B. and E.J. Kilduff. *Handbook of Business English*. New York: Harper & Brothers Publishers, 1920.

Kauffman, Christopher J. *Faith and Fraternalism: The History of the Knights of Columbus, 1882–1982*. New York: Harper & Row, 1982.

McAllister, Anna Shannon. "The Catholic Women's League." Columbus: Catholic Women's League of Columbus, 1951.

McNally, Mrs. James E. "Outlook for the League." In *Year Book of the Catholic Women's League of Columbus, Ohio, June 1919–June 1921* by the Catholic Women's League of Columbus, 5. Columbus: The Catholic Women's League of Columbus, 1921.

Moloney, Deirdre. *American Catholic Lay Groups and Transatlantic Social Reform in the Progressive Era*. Chapel Hill: University of North Carolina Press, 2002.

National Council of Catholic Women. *The Lady and The Law: Notes on Protocol and Parliamentary Procedure*. Washington: NCCW, 1950s.

O'Halloran, Ruth Libbey. *Organized Catholic Womanhood: The National Council of Catholic Women, 1920–1995*. PhD diss., Catholic University of America, 1996.

Prescott, Winward. *How to Write Reports: Business, Engineering, and Architectural*. Cambridge: Massachusetts Institute of Technology, 1932.

Ryan, Kathleen J., Nancy Myers, and Rebecca Jones, eds., *Rethinking Ethos: A Feminist Ecological Approach to Rhetoric*. Carbondale: Southern Illinois UP, 2016.

Saunders, Alta Gwinn and Chester Reed Anderson. *Business Reports: Investigation and Presentation*. New York: McGraw-Hill Publishers, 1929.

Skinner, Carolyn. *Women Physicians and Professional Ethos in Nineteenth-Century America*. Carbondale: Southern Illinois UP, 2014.

Smith, Dorothy. "The Social Construction of Documentary Reality." *Sociological Inquiry* 44, no 4 (October 1974): 257–268. https://doi.org/10.1111/j.1475-682X.1974.tb01159.x.

Weaver, Mary Jo. *New Catholic Women: A Contemporary Challenge to Traditional Religious Authority*. San Francisco: Harper and Row, 1985.

Winsor, Dorothy. "Genre and Activity Systems: The Role of Documentation in Maintaining and Changing Engineering Activity Systems." *Written Communication* 16, no. 2 (1999): 200–224. https://doi/pdf/10.1177/0741088399016002003.

Winsor, Dorothy. "Writing Engineering, Engineering Writing." *College Composition and Communication* 41, no. 1 (February 1990): 58–70.

Year Book of the Catholic Women's League of Columbus, Ohio, June 1919–June 1921. Columbus: The Catholic Women's League of Columbus, 1921.

Chapter 9

Mary Daly's Radical Ethos as Epistemic Voyage

Julianna Edmonds

Mary Daly's infamous persona as a radical feminist theologian, philosopher, and professor often overshadows her devotion to her role as professor of theology at Jesuit-run Boston College until she was asked to retire in 1999. What Daly is known for is her radical feminism that reached its pinnacle in her later, more radical texts when Daly self-identified no longer as a theologian, but as a philosopher, with published works such as *Gyn/Ecology: The Metaethics of Radical Feminism* (1978) and *Amazon Grace: Re-Calling the Courage to Sin Big* (2006), among others.

What remains to be discussed at length in conversations pertaining to Daly's radical feminist agenda is her initial attempt to reconcile with Catholicism in her first work, *The Church and the Second Sex*, as well as how this work differs so drastically from her subsequent works which blatantly contend that patriarchy uses Christianity to circulate cultural myths of female subordination. In fact, Daly apologizes for this first attempt at reconciliation with the Church in her later text, *Quintessence*. Mary Daly's first published work, *The Church and the Second Sex* (1968), offers a historical analysis of the Catholic Church's oppression of women throughout the centuries. However, her subsequently published text, *Beyond God the Father* (1973), expands the argument against Catholic patriarchy to encompass the misogyny of Western Christianity at large. In this text, Daly severs all ties with Catholic doctrine and begins her foray into "post-Christian" theology—a philosophical realm of thought she hoped would be more accommodating of her voice as a radical feminist and lesbian. What Daly's personal struggle with religion reveals is that even as she dismissed the ideologies of the Church, she did not initially break ties with Catholicism altogether, choosing, perhaps paradoxically, to remain affiliated through her profession with a religion that she thought "prolonged a traditional view of woman which at the same time idealizes and humiliates her."[1]

Through Daly's choice to continue working as a professor at a Catholic college, we can still see her desire to remain in adherence to Catholicism as a means of self-identification. As is evident in her historical analysis of the Church's systematic oppression, she accepts the past injustices committed toward women without dismissing the negative societal effects wrought from them. It is Daly's unanswered call for systematic reform for the future, then, that incites her rejection of a religion she feels has itself rejected her voice and her beliefs. Like other feminist religious rhetoricians before her, Daly ultimately suffers a displacement from religion on account of her personal worldview, but Daly rejects organized religion as both a public and private space, theorizing a new theology in her creation of the "Cosmic Covenant of Sisterhood" that is admittedly "Antichurch."[2]

A commonality among modern scholarly discussions of Daly's work is that they critique the nexus of Daly's rhetoric based solely upon her works subsequent to the publication of *The Church and the Second Sex*—works which notably reflect a more deeply rooted radical feminism than the rhetorical perspective Daly assumes in her inaugural publication. I argue that this scholarly analysis fails to incorporate the gradual progression of Daly's radicalism into its unitary view of her rhetorical authority. Furthermore, by viewing Daly's ethos as a critical process wrought from failed cohabitation with the discourse community of the Catholic Church, scholars can better understand Daly's rhetorical progression toward radicalism.

In this chapter, I illustrate that Daly's works have become progressively radical since the outset of her writing and that this continuum of radicalism is in direct response to Daly's first failed attempt at negotiating a listening stance toward the Church in her first work, *The Church and the Second Sex*. Her proceeding text, *Beyond God the Father*,[3] can be taken, then, as a response to this unsuccessful attempt at reconciliation between feminism, the Church, and patriarchy. More specifically, I address how Daly's two early theological works, *The Church and the Second Sex* and *Beyond God the Father*, most clearly delineate her contrasting rhetorical shifts from accommodation in the first work to polarization in the latter. Drawing on *The Church and the Second Sex* and *Beyond God the Father*, I will chart the shift in Daly's rhetorical perspectives from an initial position of reconciliation in the first text to a subsequent one of interruption in *Beyond God the Father*. Analyzing these first two theological works as a dichotomous conversation facilitates an understanding of the current scholarly response to Daly's work and reveals the development of her ethos as a rhetorician. I do not address radicalism as the defining characteristic of Daly's ethos. I suggest that the process of charting this rhetorical progression or Voyage to radical feminism, as Daly would term it, reveals that Daly adopted an ethos of interruption as a response to failed initial attempts at accommodation.

Conceptually, my discussion of interruption draws on Nedra Reynolds's theorization of interruptive agency articulated as a feminist appropriation which facilitates female agency and authority: "Agency is not simply about finding one's own voice but also about intervening in discourses of the everyday and cultivating rhetorical tactics that make interruption and resistance an important part of any conversation."[4] Likewise, my analysis of accommodation in Daly's texts aligns most closely with the definition of audience accommodation Wayne C. Booth provides in *The Rhetoric of Rhetoric: The Quest for Effective Communication:* "attention to the biases, beliefs, hopes and fears, emotional habits, and levels of comprehension about the subject."[5]

MARY DALY

Daly's life and work represent an intersection between religious feminism and education. This intersection, however, was often the source of tension for Daly. Daly's work pursues questions of theology and the patriarchal structures within religious spaces and texts. Her own educational background reflects this unceasing quest for knowledge of these patriarchal spaces. After earning a PhD in theology from Saint Mary's College, she completed two more doctorates in philosophy and theology from the University of Fribourg in Switzerland. She then sought to share this knowledge with others by joining the faculty of Boston College in 1966.

As Margalit Fox reports in the *New York Times*,

> A self-described "radical lesbian feminist," Professor Daly maintained a long, often uneasy relationship with Boston College, the Jesuit institution where she had taught theology since the 1960s. In 1999, Professor Daly left the college after a male student threatened suit when he was denied a place in her class on feminist ethics. She had long limited enrollment in some advanced women's studies classes to women only, maintaining that the presence of men there would inhibit frank discussion.[6]

Daly eventually retired in 1999, after allegedly facing pressure from Boston College. Through these clashes of feminism and theology, Daly's career demonstrates the struggle of occupying spaces that are exclusionary or even hostile to feminist ideologies. Her work reflects this exclusion in the gradual development of a post-Christian theology that has earned Daly regard as "her own kind of Wiccan-influenced radical feminist."[7]

DALY'S RHETORICAL PROGRESSION

In *Feminist Rhetorical Practices*, Royster and Kirsch identify two changes to the rhetorical landscape incited by "tectonic shifts" in feminist rhetorical practices: "One is breaking through the persistently elite, male-centered boundaries of our disciplinary habits, and the second is re-forming that terrain to create a much more open and expanded view of rhetorical performance, accomplishment, and rhetorical possibilities."[8] Daly's *Church and the Second Sex* can be viewed as fulfilling the first of these two changes: this text lays the foundation for a listening stance toward the Church by uncovering Catholicism's gendered biases, which are reflected and then reinforced through myth, language, and ideology. Daly's intent is one of reconciliation, and she includes men in this proposed journey of mitigating female degradation.

It is, perhaps, surprising that Mary Daly's work as a rhetorical theorist did not begin from an exclusionary stance but from an egalitarian perspective which envisioned both men and women as copartners in the process of overturning the Church's inherent advocacy of female suppression and erasure. Frances Gray claims that Daly's conception of the Church in *The Church and Second Sex* was an androgynous one: "For her, acceptance of women as equal partners in an androgynous church would lead to the transformation of the institution itself."[9] In an interview published three years after the publication of *The Church and Second Sex* (but prior to *Beyond God the Father*), traces of Daly's egalitarian mind-set are also present: "The women's revolution is challenging the patriarchal society—not to make a matriarchal society, but to bring about equality between women and men: a diarchy."[10]

Daly's equalist perspective during the publication of her first theological work can be interpreted as an effort to create her own ethos within the Church. Daly accomplishes this ethos of accommodation by means of audience awareness within *The Church and the Second Sex*. She does so by employing rhetorics of silence and listening which, as Wayne Booth articulates, are primary tools of successful argumentation: "All good rhetoric depends on the rhetor's *listening to and thinking about the character and the welfare of the audience*, and moderating what is said to meet what has been heard."[11] She strategically crafts her arguments within *The Church and the Second Sex* in such a way that facilitates and necessitates inclusion of men in the women's movement—a sharp contrast to *Beyond God the Father*, which promotes masculine erasure. Through her analysis of patriarchal myth, symbol systems, and language in *The Church and the Second Sex*, Daly offers a critique of Catholic doctrine without altogether alienating the audience or the Church.[12]

Throughout *The Church and the Second Sex*, Daly is careful to critique the belief systems of the Church without advocating a staunch rejection of religion, the Church, or men. She writes, for instance:

> Our, efforts, then, must be toward a level of confrontation, dialogue, and cooperation between the sexes undreamed of in the past, when the struggle for biological survival of the species and numerical multiplication had to take precedence over any thought of qualitative development of relation between the sexes.[13]

This rhetorical choice of maintaining neutrality between the sexes bolsters Daly's ethos within the Church and demonstrates an audience awareness that she lacks in her more radical texts. It is also interesting that, while modern scholarship has often criticized Daly's views of women for their homogenizing effects, she criticizes Catholicism for its symbol-oriented writing, which similarly fails to realize a pluralistic vision of femininity in the place of its prescribed universalization of women. Daly writes, "Symbols, which record human experience in shorthand, stress similarities—some of the frequently repeated elements of experience. What they leave out are the differences. It is especially the uniqueness and dynamism of the person which cannot be captured in the symbol."[14]

Discussing Daly's texts, Krista Ratcliffe has written that "at the intersections of myth, language, and ideology, we arrive at rhetoric."[15] Tracing these intersections is precisely at the heart of Mary Daly's early theological journey. *The Church and the Second Sex* chiefly argues that Catholicism's effort to relegate women to subordinate status is primarily maintained by a "defective symbol syndrome."[16] Ratcliffe observes the unique relation between symbol and metaphor within Daly's writing, and it is important to understand this difference in order to grasp Daly's conception of Catholicism's constricting "symbol syndrome": "Although symbols function as metaphors within Daly's theory of language, metaphors possess more possibilities than mere symbolic function."[17] Metaphors necessitate Be-ing, while symbols foster stasis. Complicit within this symbol system are elements of patriarchal myth, language, and ideology—all of which, Daly insists, work in unison to further the act of female denigration within the Church.

The Church and the Second Sex asserts that the myth of the "Eternal Feminine" serves as the primary deterrent for gender equality within the Church, since it links femininity to an unattainable ideal, which, in turn, results in stasis. Her critique of Marianism, the idolization of the Virgin Mary, is that it obscures the reality of the modern woman: "What it can spawn is that dream world which is precisely 'the metaphysical world of woman,' the ideal, static woman, who is so much less troublesome than the real article."[18] An ancillary effect of the "eternal feminine" myth is that it creates false binaries specific to women: "the 'good girl,' who is the Eternal Woman, is the only answer to the challenge of the 'bad girl,' who is The Girl of the world of James Bond, of *Playboy*, of advertising."[19] Central to

Daly's argumentative strategy here is that she differentiates between Mary as a historical figure versus a symbolic one. In a sense, Daly redefines Mary as a concept, and her argument hinges upon Mary's function within culture as a symbol or idea, rather than as a historical reality that should serve as a model to all women. She explains, "I am now talking about the symbols in people's imaginations as conveyed through the tradition of Jesus and Mary. These symbols can't really function as models for us in the twentieth century."[20] This argumentative strategy, in effect, provides Daly with a rhetorical buffer: she is not criticizing Mary in isolation, but what culture and society have projected onto her image and upon the image of females within the Church.

Daly also suggests that the symbol syndrome is perpetuated by the terminology of "the divine plan"—a static conception of being which is reinforced within culture by phrases like "God's ordinance" or "God's plan."[21] Daly identifies three specific rhetorical purposes for which Catholic doctrine employs this terminology, and she asserts that these purposes contribute to feminine subjection within the Church. All three of these uses facilitate the continuation of female silence more specifically. Cheryl Glenn has stated that silence has a presence and an importance: "Silence is rewarded only when signifying obedience or proper subordination: The sub-altern should not speak but feign rapt listening with their silence."[22] In analyzing these various rhetorics of "the divine plan" and "Mary as the model for all women," I argue that Daly is identifying the means by which the Church has prolonged female silence as well as female subjection, in general. Understanding the erasure of women as rhetorical silence also points to power differentials, as Glenn observes: "Like speech, the meaning of silence depends on a power differential that exists in every rhetorical situation: who can speak, who must remain silent, who listens, and what those listeners do."[23] Here Daly draws attention to the totality of the rhetorical situation which sustains female silence through patriarchal ideology and rhetoric.

Aside from prescribing a divinely sanctioned gender hierarchy, "the divine plan" terminology, according to Daly, is used as a rhetorical tool of manipulation to arouse certain desired emotional responses which are "unaccompanied by any critical understanding."[24] Daly notes, "First, as is generally recognized by those who study the uses of language, words and phrases are often used (consciously or unconsciously) for purposes other than that of communicating ideas."[25] Daly points out that by employing this specific rhetoric, clerical authors and Catholic doctrine have knowingly conditioned audiences, particularly women, to assent to patriarchy. They borrow God's authority for the purpose of inspiring reverence—and, ultimately, obedience—in the female audience; it is the use of God as justification for unsubstantiated claims of female inferiority. What such rhetoric results in is an eradication of free will and agency for females within the Church, as male leaders, aligning their ethos with God, rely upon ecclesiastical rhetoric to justify humanistic maltreatment. Daly asserts that the "divine plan" terminology promotes stasis among women, because it furthers false assumptions of changeless ideology. For Daly, and certainly for many modern women within the Church, the man-woman relationship is "evolving." But, as Daly observes, "The writers who are prone to invoke the 'the divine plan' hide this variety behind the monolithic mask of a supposedly changeless ideology."[26] Therefore, doctrine and ecclesiastical writing assume these divinely sanctioned terminologies as a means of silencing women who are not granted the agency to infuse masculine writings with female experience.

Although Daly's later works, indeed, gloss over gendered differences in favor of a homogenous conception of femininity, Daly, in *The Church and Second Sex*, seeks to broaden the scope of the effects wrought from the symbol system by including men in her argument. She counters the myth of the "Eternal Feminine" with the equally defective myth of the "Eternal Masculine": "the 'eternal masculine' itself is alienating, crippling the personalities of men and restricting their experience of life at every level. The male in our society is not supposed to express much feeling, sensitivity, aesthetic appreciation, imagination, consideration for others, intuition."[27] There are no traces in this early work of her later separatist ideology which keeps both men and the Church in opposition to feminism. Instead, the interdependence of the genders is envisioned as the means of eradicating the gender hierarchy. This is an argument for female inclusion *without* male erasure.

SHIFTING RHETORICAL STANCES

While *The Church and the Second Sex* demonstrates Daly's efforts to create her ethos within the Church, these rhetorical tactics are completely abandoned in *Beyond God the Father*, which, as the title suggests, advocates an erasure of masculinity in favor of female-identified language and ideology. *Beyond God the Father* establishes the second identified change within the landscape of feminist rhetorical terrain identified by Royster and Kirsch. Here, Daly, instead, advocates a feminist rejection of Christian doctrine, that is, a complete "exorcism" of God the Father, along with all of his sons. This shift in rhetorical stance marks the beginning of Daly's journey toward radical feminism and an exclusionary rhetorical performance[28] accomplished with an ethos of interruption.[29] Jablonski aptly articulates Daly's shift from a revision of the Church's doctrine to a blatant rejection of its mandates:

> Unless women denounced the entire conceptual apparatus of Christian theology, she argues, they would not be able to push beyond the boundary of religious

experience to where insight can grow. Daly's exodus from the ranks of the faithful carried with it the implication that once they "claimed the power of [their own] speech," Catholic women would no longer be bound by the language—or authority—of the orthodox Church.[30]

Beyond God the Father serves as an exorcism of the conceptual apparatus of the Church, and it reflects a strategic rhetorical choice on Daly's part, namely, to forego the language of the Church in order to critique it. James Chesebro, cited in "Rhetoric, Paradox, and the Movement for Women's Ordination in the Roman Catholic Church," suggests that in order for women to reconcile themselves to the Church, they must adopt a "pluralistic worldview": "the decision to embrace a paradoxical worldview is made possible through a reflexive rhetoric that combines a compensatory ideology of selfhood with a highly developed sense of rhetorical choice."[31] Daly's *The Church and Second Sex* employs this pluralistic worldview, while *Beyond God the Father*, in its rejectionist stance, does not incorporate such a conception.

In the opening of *Beyond God the Father*, Daly makes clear that proactive methodology must be paired with the revised theology proposed in *The Church and the Second Sex:*

> The method of liberation, then, involves a castrating of language and images that reflect and perpetuate the structures of a sexist world. It castrates precisely in the sense of cutting away the phallocentric value system imposed by patriarchy, in its subtle as well as in its more manifest expressions. . . . [W]omen are beginning to recognize that the value system that has been thrust upon us by the various cultural institutions of patriarchy has amounted to a kind of gang rape of minds as well as bodies.[32]

Liberation is only attainable once women have first dislodged themselves from the role of the "other"—a role which Daly claims is furthered by the myth of Eve. The power of this myth to project misogynistic images of the male-female relationship is "deeply embedded in the modern psyche,"[33] according to Daly. The greatest injustice, however, is that a failure to "exorcise evil from Eve" allows the patriarchal regard for women to be "metamorphosed into God's viewpoint."[34] This perspective marks a sharp change from Daly's inclusion of the male gender in *The Church and the Second Sex*. No longer are men and women equal helpmates in the challenge of female liberation, but there is, instead, a need for the exorcising of images and ideologies constructed solely by male thought. Daly advises not a revised version of the existent doctrine and its associated images but a replacement of them. While Daly, in *The Church and the Second Sex*, highlights the manner in which the myth of the eternal feminine causes damage to the image of the eternal masculine in modern culture, she does not employ this equalist tactic when addressing the myth of Eve. She discusses the myth of Eve as a means of redefining concepts of "original sin" and "the fall" from a radical feminist perspective: "Rather than a Fall *from* the sacred, the Fall now initiated by women becomes a Fall *into* the sacred and therefore into freedom."[35] What Daly does here is apply an alternate, feminist perspective with which to view the existent patriarchal myth, and, in doing so, she completely changes the use of myth within the context of religion. Her re-appropriation of the myth here bolsters her initial claim that ideologies are constantly in flux and are not subject to the rigidity that patriarchal religion has assigned them. This ideological paralysis is one which can only be overcome by women acting, without men, as a "sisterhood": "The positive refusal of cooptation means in effect the becoming of the sisterhood of women, which is necessary to overcome paralysis, self-hatred extended to women as a caste, self-depreciation, and emotional dependence upon men for a feeling of self-esteem."[36] Adopting an exclusionary stance, *Beyond God the Father* shows that, for Daly, the only effective type of change is radical change. Because the very language, symbol system, and ideology of the Church are all inherently patriarchal, Daly employs a form of interruption that thoroughly "exorcises" all residual misogyny from her conception of spirituality. Daly's proposed spirituality is termed a "Sisterhood."

Rather than molding her argument in such a way that facilitates a reconciliation between feminism and the Church, Daly blatantly creates rhetorical distance between the two conflicting entities by proposing that "Sisterhood" is strictly "Anti-church": "Even without conscious attention to the Church, sisterhood is in conflict with it. . . . This conflict arises directly from the fact that women are beginning to overcome the divided self and divisions from each other."[37] The traces of a radical rhetorical approach are readily apparent. In order to confront the existent divisions between the Church and women, Daly proposes a complete cessation from patriarchy, not an inclusion of its oppressive forces in her effort to overcome it. In order for women to find their way within the Church, they must reject it entirely in favor of Daly's "sisterhood." Daly draws on the concept of "sisterhood" not only to replace the concept of Church but also to illuminate how the Church exists as "a space set apart."[38] She asserts, "A church construed as space set apart, then—whether the term is intended to mean a building, an institution, or an ideological 'sacred canopy'—has certain propensities for serving as an escape from facing the abyss. It then becomes a place for spinning webs of counterfeit transcendence."[39] Daly's argument for sisterhood is an argument for departure from the Church[40] and a rejection of all its associated symbols and ideologies, that is, her argument for inclusion *necessitates* exclusion. While *The Church and the Second Sex* calls upon the Church and existent doctrine to include feminism within its vision, *Beyond God the Father* snips the ties that once bound the two systems in order to create a new, removed space for women.

This reconstruction of the Christian community, for Daly, is an opportunity for women's silence to be heard:

> The male religion entombs women in sepulchers of silence in order to chant its own eternal and dreary dirge to a past that never was. The silence *imposed* upon women echoes the structures of male hierarchies. It is important to listen to the structures of this imposed silence in order to hear the flow of the new sounds of free silence that are the voice of sisterhood as Antichurch.[41]

Daly demonstrates interruptive agency, as Reynolds theorizes it, by "intervening in discourses of the everyday" and by inventing not only new "rhetorical tactics"[42] but also new spaces for women's discourse to prevail over the patriarchal silencing characteristic of the Christian community that Daly observes. As Reynolds explains further, interruption is crucial for marginalized speakers who seek to disrupt discursive exclusion: "Through interruption and talking back, women rhetors can draw attention to their identities as marginalized speakers and writers as they also force more attention to the ideological workings of discursive exclusion."[43] In this way, Daly forces her audience to listen to women's silences.

SILENCE, LISTENING, AND ETHOS

Silence, ultimately, becomes the issue which links both of Daly's theological works. It is crucial to note that Daly, in her quest to combat the imposition of silence within *Beyond God the Father*, is not suggesting an open, listening stance akin to the one she adopts within *The Church and the Second Sex*.[44] She encourages women to "listen to the structures of this imposed silence"[45] in an effort to exorcise these structures from the female religious experience. "Listening," in *Beyond God the Father*, is a solely feminine experience, because, as Daly states, "men can and do avoid hearing women's new words while appearing to listen."[46] Furthermore, for Daly, language, if not purified through exorcism, becomes the mirror reflecting and reinforcing these limitations. She asserts that "women are starting to know now the defects of language because it is not ours."[47] Daly's theological works function as modern self-awareness projects exposing the constricting nature of words throughout history in order to highlight the magnitude of silence.[48]

Through Daly's use of interruption, it is clear that this rhetorical strategy is inextricably linked to identification in the rhetor's attempt to craft ethos. What Daly rejects (patriarchy, Christianity, oppressive ideology) directly defines her accepted philosophy and worldview. Tracing the evolution of Daly's rhetorical stances from accommodation to interruption demonstrates that ethos construction is never thoroughly stable but changes as the female rhetor finds herself caught between the struggle of personal self-identification and public alienation. By dislodging a rhetor's ethos from a single text, we might better understand it as an epistemic orientation enacted through the ongoing production of texts and shifting ideologies. Although modern scholarship scrutinizes in critical detail Daly's later radical feminist texts, this tendency merely uncovers what Daly has become but not what exactly has led her to this state of Be-coming.

These two texts, read as rhetorical conversation, suggest that merely "breaking through the boundaries" of a discourse community (in this case the Church's) is not always sufficient for achieving one's desired goal. Daly's progression toward a radical feminist philosophy indicates she believes that the act of rupturing the patriarchal belief system is only a potential catalyst for change; it must also be paired with the rhetorical art of creating a uniquely feminist perspective as a combatant against the traditional one. Daly's listening stance merely *reconciles* patriarchy to a neglected feminist reality, while her interruptive stance *transforms* these traditional ideologies by replacing them with new ones.

NOTES

1. Mary Daly, *The Church and the Second Sex* (New York: Harper & Row, 1968), 11.
2. Mary Daly, *Beyond God the Father* (Boston: Beacon Press, 1973), 155.
3. This work was written in 1973, five years after *The Church and the Second Sex*.
4. Nedra Reynolds, "Interrupting Our Way to Agency: Feminist Cultural Studies and Composition," in *Feminism and Composition Studies: In Other Words*, eds. Susan C. Jarratt and Lynn Worsham (New York: MLA Press, 1998), 58–73.
5. Wayne C. Booth, *The Rhetoric of Rhetoric: The Quest for Effective Communication* (Malden, MA: Wiley-Blackwell, 2004), 51.
6. Margalit Fox, "Mary Daly, a Leader in Feminist Theology, Dies at 81," *The New York Times*, January 6, 2010, http://www.nytimes.com/2010/01/07/education/07daly.html.
7. Elizabeth Hedrick, "The Early Career of Mary Daly: A Retrospective," *Feminist Studies* 39, no. 2 (2013): 557–572.
8. Jacqueline Jones Royster and Gesa Kirsch, *Feminist Rhetorical Practices: New Horizons for Rhetoric, Composition, and Literacy Studies* (Illinois: Southern Illinois UP, 2012), 29.
9. Frances Gray, "Elemental Philosophy: Language and Ontology in Mary Daly's Texts," in *Feminist Interpretations of Mary Daly*, eds. Sarah Lucia Hoagland and Marilyn Frye (University Park: Pennsylvania State UP, 2000), 228.

10. Mary Daly, "The Church and Women: An Interview with Mary Daly," *Theology Today* 28, no. 3 (1971): 349.

11. Booth, *The Rhetoric*, 54.

12. It is worth noting that Foss, Foss, and Griffin offer a different analysis of Daly's audience adaptation than I do, although their analysis glosses later works such as *Gyn/Ecology*, rather than the early theological works: "Audience adaptation, then, is not a means to make a message more acceptable but a foreground method of constraint that silences, denigrates, and manipulates women," 156. This was certainly the perception of Daly in the later works but is not fully applicable to her early theology in *Second Sex*.

13. Daly, *The Church*, 153.

14. Daly, *The Church*, 122.

15. Krista Ratcliffe, *Anglo-American Feminist Challenges to the Rhetorical Traditions: Virginia Woolf, Mary Daly, and Adrienne Rich* (Carbondale: Southern Illinois UP, 1996), 70.

16. Daly, *The Church*, 114.

17. Ratcliffe, *Anglo-American*, 72.

18. Daly, *The Church*, 119.

19. Daly, *The Church*, 128.

20. Mary Daly qtd. in "The Thin Thread of Conversation: An Interview with Mary Daly," Catherine Madsen, *Cross Currents* 50, no. 3 (Fall 2000).

21. Daly, *The Church*, 115.

22. Cheryl Glenn, *Unspoken: A Rhetoric of Silence* (Carbondale: Southern Illinois UP, 2004), 5.

23. Glenn, *Unspoken*, 9.

24. Daly, *The Church*, 116.

25. Daly, *The Church*, 116.

26. Daly, *The Church*, 117.

27. Daly, *The Church*, 152.

28. I do not term Daly's work "exclusionary" in the pejorative sense that many modern scholars do. I contend that this rhetorical shift from reconciliation with the Church to rejection of it is Daly's attempt at creating agency, after failed attempts to be "heard" in her prior text.

29. Laura Micciche conceives of rhetorical interruption as a displacement within the discourse, an idea which holds true for an analysis of Daly's rhetoric in *Beyond God:* "The intentional variety desires interruption as a political tool, the goal of which is to unstick normative conventions from fixed locations, making possible a questioning of what is in order to make claims for what might be." Laura Micciche, "Writing as Feminist Rhetorical Theory." In *Rhetorica in Motion: Feminist Rhetorical Methods*, eds. Eileen E. Schell and K.J. Rawson (Pittsburgh: University of Pittsburgh Press, 2010), 177.

30. Carol Jablonski. "Rhetoric, Paradox, and the Movement for Women's Ordination in the Roman Catholic Church," *Quarterly Journal of Speech* 74, no. 2 (1988): 168.

31. Carol Jablonski, "Rhetoric, Paradox, and the Movement for Women's Ordination in the Roman Catholic Church," *Quarterly Journal of Speech* 74, no. 2 (1988): 174.

32. Daly, *Beyond God*, 9.
33. Daly, *Beyond God*, 45.
34. Daly, *Beyond God*, 47.
35. Daly, *Beyond God*, 67.
36. Daly, *Beyond God*, 59.
37. Daly, *Beyond God*, 133.
38. Daly, *Beyond God*, 156.
39. Daly, *Beyond God*, 156.
40. Daly insisted that we have to "reconsider the world church" because "the church is wherever liberation exists." Daly, "Theology," 353.
41. Daly, *Beyond God*, 150.
42. Reynolds, "Interrupting Our Way to Agency," 59.
43. Reynolds, "Interrupting Our Way to Agency," 60.
44. Ratcliffe, for instance, defines rhetorical listening as "a stance of openness that a person may choose to assume in relation to any person, text, culture; its purpose is to cultivate conscious identification in ways that promote productive communication, especially but not solely cross-culturally." Ratliffe, "Interrupting Our Way to Agency," 25.
45. Daly, *Beyond God*, 169.
46. Daly, *Beyond God*, 169.
47. Daly, *Beyond God*, 152.
48. Cheryl Glenn has noted that speech and silence are not only related but also inseparable: "Given how our language works, then, speech and silence are not mutually exclusive; they are inextricably linked and often interchangeably, simultaneously meaningful. Speech and silence depend upon each other: behind all speech is silence, and silence surrounds all speech." Glenn, "Unspoken," 7.

BIBLIOGRAPHY

Booth, Wayne C. *The Rhetoric of Rhetoric: The Quest for Effective Communication.* Malden, MA: Wiley-Blackwell, 2004.

Daly, Mary. *Beyond God the Father: Toward a Philosophy of Women's Liberation.* Boston: Beacon Press, 1973.

Daly, Mary. *The Church and the Second Sex.* New York: Harper & Row, 1968.

Daly, Mary. "The Church and Women: An Interview with Mary Daly." *Theology Today* 28, no. 3 (1971): 349–354.

Daly, Mary. *Gyn/Ecology: The Metaethics of Radical Feminism.* Boston: Beacon Press, 1978.

Daly, Mary. *Quintessence . . . Realizing the Archaic Future: A Radical Elemental Feminist Manifesto.* Beacon Press, 1999.

Foss, Karen, Sonja Foss, and Cindy Griffin. *Feminist Rhetorical Theories.* Thousand Oaks, CA: SAGE, 1999.

Fox, Margalit. "Mary Daly, a Leader in Feminist Theology, Dies at 81." *The New York Times*, January 6, 2010. https://www.nytimes.com/2010/01/07/education/07daly.html.

Glenn, Cheryl. *Unspoken: A Rhetoric of Silence*. Carbondale: Southern Illinois UP, 2004.

Gray, Frances. "Elemental Philosophy: Language and Ontology in Mary Daly's Texts." In *Feminist Interpretations of Mary Daly*, edited by Sarah Lucia Hoagland and Marilyn Frye, 222–244. University Park: Pennsylvania State UP, 2000.

Hedrick, Elizabeth. "The Early Career of Mary Daly: A Retrospective." *Feminist Studies* 39, no. 2 (2013): 557–572.

Jablonski, Carol. "Rhetoric, Paradox, and the Movement for Women's Ordination in the Roman Catholic Church." *Quarterly Journal of Speech* 74, no. 2 (1988): 164–183.

Madsen, Catherine. "The Thin Thread of Conversation: An Interview with Mary Daly." *Cross Currents* 50, no. 3 (Fall 2000).

Micciche, Laura. "Writing as Feminist Rhetorical Theory." In *Rhetorica in Motion: Feminist Rhetorical Methods*, edited by Eileen E. Schell and K.J. Rawson, 173–190. Pittsburgh: University of Pittsburgh Press, 2010.

Ratcliffe Krista. *Anglo-American Feminist Challenges to the Rhetorical Traditions: Virginia Woolf, Mary Daly, and Adrienne Rich*. Carbondale: Southern Illinois UP, 1996.

Ratcliffe Krista. *Rhetorical Listening: Identification, Gender, Whiteness*. Carbondale: Southern Illinois UP, 2005.

Reynolds, Nedra. "Interrupting Our Way to Agency: Feminist Cultural Studies and Composition." In *Feminism and Composition Studies: In Other Words*, edited by Susan C. Jarratt and Lynn Worsham, 58–73. New York: MLA Press, 1998.

Royster, Jacqueline Jones and Gesa E. Kirsch. *Feminist Rhetorical Practices: New Horizons for Rhetoric, Composition, and Literacy Studies*. Carbondale: Southern Illinois UP, 2012.

Chapter 10

Metanoic Faith

Living Rhetorically in Dorothy Day's The Long Loneliness

Jimmy Hamill

As one of the most famous and revered Catholic women in American history, Dorothy Day lived her life at the intersection of Catholicism and social justice. Known for being one of the cofounders of the Catholic Worker Movement, a loosely organized system of urban and rural communities that shared in a vision of justice for the poor, Day had commitments to voluntary poverty, pacifism, and her Catholic faith challenged a nation as it evolved through the Great Depression, World War II, the McCarthy-Era, and the Vietnam War. Her legacy is undeniable, especially as the Catholic Church continues to evaluate her candidacy for sainthood. One of the defining characteristics of Day's legacy is her profound conversion to Catholicism in her early thirties, which became a hallmark of her fight for social justice. And while I marvel at the life and impact of Day, it strikes me how narrowly her ethos has been conceptualized. In other words, there is so much more to Day than being a Catholic activist. In "Not So Easily Dismissed: The Intellectual Influences and Rhetorical Voice of Dorothy Day—'Servant of God,'" Laurie A. Britt-Smith argues that mainstream and scholarly discourse on Day relegates her to an icon of the past and, more importantly, erases her credibility as a writer:

> The majority of what has been written about her focuses on the details of her life and her work as the co-founder of the Catholic Worker Movement and *The Catholic Worker*. This has a tendency to underplay her impact as an author, keeps her radicalism isolated to a particular time period, and significantly lessens, if not outright negates, the incubation of her ideas concerning social justice that occurred before her conversion to Catholicism at the age of thirty.[1]

I join Britt-Smith in wanting to complicate and expand the narratives created about Day, especially because of Day's prowess with the written word and the power of her own narratives.

In this chapter, I frame Day not only as a skilled author and writer but also as a talented *rhetorician*. Specifically, I argue that Day's autobiography, *The Long Loneliness*, demonstrates how Day lives rhetorically through an engagement with *metanoia*, or a "change of heart." Throughout the book, Day reflects on the ways that her class status, other people, and her faith moved her in pivotally different directions. What is significant about her employment of metanoia is not only how it transformed her as an individual but also how it transformed the spaces and structures in which she existed. This chapter expands existing scholarship on metanoia by highlighting how it can implicate institutions in questions of justice and equity. I will conclude by suggesting that Day's ethos should be reconsidered in light of Kathleen J. Ryan, Nancy Myers, and Rebecca Jones's conception of a feminist ecological ethos, which "is negotiated and renegotiated, embodied and communal, co-constructed and thoroughly implicated in shifting power dynamic."[2] Framing Day this way underscores the rhetorical sophistication of her embodied choices. It further shows how Catholic women more broadly have played dynamic roles in creating justice movements that continue to impact us today.

LIVING RHETORICALLY: DOROTHY DAY AND EMBODIED RHETORIC

In a prologue titled "Confession," Day begins her autobiography by locating the reader in a material and sensory space:

> When you go to confession on a Saturday night, you go into a warm, dimly lit vastness, with the smell of wax and incense in the air, the smell of burning candles, and if it is a hot summer night there is the sound of a great electric fan, and the noise of the streets coming in to emphasize the stillness.[3]

Demonstrating her narrative talent and journalistic specificity, Day makes a claim through this opening sentence: her autobiography, while a reflection on her spiritual journey and conversion, is ultimately a corporeal account of herself. In other words, she makes meaning of her life through the material circumstances and concrete experiences surrounding her day-to-day. Through the senses evoked here—sound, smell, touch, sight—she situates readers in the dark, hot confessional filled with "shutters of the little window between you and the priest," "ledges . . . narrow and worn," and "breviaries between confessions."[4] Understanding this helps us make sense of her writing style throughout the text, which pays explicit attention to the minute details of her relationships and surroundings. By anchoring us in the embodied experiences of her life, Day demonstrates how to *live rhetorically*, which I define as living with an awareness of the larger patterns and connections to make meaning and significance of one's experience. Thus, when Day provides us with intimate, in-depth details of her childhood home, the layout of her prison cell at Occoquan, or the various Catholic Worker homes around the country, she is both offering expository details and showing us a rhetorical awareness that enabled her to see her relationships and environments as interconnected.

Another way to put this is that Day highlights a kind of *embodied rhetoric* in her writing. Day was not a formal rhetorician and may not have used or known such a term; however, the intention with which she makes sense of her social location shows us a deep thoughtfulness and attention to power dynamics. Rhetoric scholar Abby A. Knoblauch defines embodied rhetoric as "a purposeful decision to include embodied knowledge and social positionalities as forms of meaning making within a text itself."[5] By paying attention to and writing through the ways her body inhabits and learns various spaces, Day better articulates the significance and stakes of the work she does. It enables her autobiography to be both an account of her life and a structural critique. Knoblauch asserts that when embodied rhetoric "draws attention to embodied knowledge—specific material conditions, lived experiences, positionalities, and/or standpoints—[it] can highlight difference instead of erasing it in favor of an assumed privileged discourse."[6]

In "Confession," Day uses her sensory opening to reflect more broadly on the difficulties of writing through her life story, which she sees as an act of Confession. She situates her difficulties in the disconnect between an emphasis on the self and the larger structural inequities of her world: "The sustained effort of writing, of putting pen to paper so many hours a day when there are human beings around who need me, when there is sickness, and hunger, and sorrow, is a harrowingly painful job."[7] She locates her own story within a much more complex system of injustice. This disconnect is specifically felt and articulated through the body: the writing process is "harrowingly painful" and requires a "sustained effort" of "putting pen to paper for so many hours a day." Day's body expresses its anger and discomfort with societal injustice through the sensation of pain, a pain occurring as she writes through her own account of enacting justice in the world. As readers, we hear and feel Day's exhaustion, thus making us more acutely aware of our own separation from the violence others experience.

We can also look at Day's pain as a bodily question to the world: how can we live while others barely survive? Janice Chernekoff argues that "[b]odily questions inspire rhetorical responses that inform and create intelligence."[8] In making meaning of her experiences through writing, she also creates meaning for her readers to answer their own bodily questions. While she asserts that the story is primarily speaking from her limited vantage point, I view her text as an attempt to answer or, at least, respond to the perplexities of suffering and injustice. Chernekoff elaborates on this body-rhetoric call-and-response: "To a significant degree, it is the body that experiences the question, endures the trials, and experiences the answers to the question. It makes sense, then, that the writing about such experiences will have a similar form; the experience influences the form of the reflection on it."[9] We can frame *The Long Loneliness* as one of many rhetorical responses Day offers to her body's question. Her autobiography recounts the ways she, as embodied rhetorician and as Catholic activist, tries to respond to insurmountable realities of the world. This embodied work enables Day not only to live her experiences with intention but also to be transformed by said experiences. Her ability to transform others while being transformed by others is one of Day's most noteworthy characteristics.

METANOIA AND TRANSFORMATION

To articulate more specifically Day's transformation, I turn to the rhetorical concept of *metanoia* (μετάνοια). Coming from the Greek prefix *meta* ("after") and noun *nous* ("mind"), metanoia is often defined as an "afterthought." When used in the context of Christian theology, metanoia usually means "repentance" for a moral failing of some kind. More recently, it has been seen as a "change of mind" or, more radically, a "change of heart." Given the looseness and multiplicity of metanoia's definitions, it can be difficult to parse out the distinctions between differing forms of metanoia. In *Metanoia: Rhetoric, Authenticity, and the Transformation of the Self,* Adam Ellwanger identifies three categories of metanoia: "rhetorical metanoia," which is a speaker's retraction and/or amendment of an earlier statement for a new idea; "spiritual metanoia," or a conversion to a life of Christ by changing one's habits and lifestyle in the spirit of repentance; and "modern metanoia" where one revises their ethos, which is seen not as a series of fixed traits or characteristics but, rather, as a result of differing discourses, which can be read as varying kinds of positionalities and identities.[10] Depending on our context, we can move quite literally among our different social locations to establish differing kinds of ethos, an essential component of metanoia. S. Michael Halloran etymologically frames ethos as place or "'a habitual gathering place'. . . . I suspect that it is upon this image of people gathering together in a public place, sharing experiences and ideas, that its meaning as character rests."[11] If we read ethos as a kind of place, then metanoia acts as a map or compass to highlight both where we are and where we want to go. Modern metanoia requires us to gather with ourselves and others to exchange and evaluate our priorities, investments, and limitations. In all of these categories, metanoia requires the ability to reflect on one's decisions, evaluate the meaning of past choices, and make revisions based on how one wishes to move forward differently. Metanoia is a rhetorical practice of metacognition, self-awareness, and revision.

Kelly A. Myers, one of the leading contemporary scholars on metanoia, frames it as an ongoing process:

> Rather than placing emphasis on isolated moments and available means, *metanoia* encourages broader consideration of the ways in which people move through experiences. More specifically, *metanoia* requires that a person look back on past decisions in order to move in a new direction. It calls for a larger process of re-vision in which a person is constantly revising and revitalizing understanding.[12]

Note the embodied language of Myers's analysis: there is an emphasis on *movement* through experiences that build over time in one's body. As these experiences grow, so, too, does the capability to move in different directions if we can honestly and authentically reflect on where our movements have taken us previously. To practice metanoia is to live in the spirit of the Roman god Janus, depicted as having two faces, one looking to the past as the other looks to the future. We must live in simultaneity, balancing the hard-learned lessons of the past with the ever-growing potential of the future. Living metanoically is to be always in movement and vulnerable to transformative circumstances.

One way of doing so is paying careful attention to ethos, particularly ethos as place or location. Nedra Reynolds builds off of Aristotle's *Nicomachean Ethics* to demonstrate the social and spatial components of ethos:

> Character is formed by habit, not engendered by nature, and those habits come from the community or culture. One identifies an individual's character, then, by looking to the community. An individual's *ethos* cannot be determined outside of the space in which it was created or without a sense of the cultural context. That cultural context, however, does not necessarily mean a conflict-free environment; a social group is not necessarily made up of like-minded individuals who gather in harmony.[13]

If we follow Reynolds here, our ethos is both a literal and figurative negotiation of values with our communities. We are formed by the cultures, peoples, and landscapes that surround us, whether by aligning with them or growing against them. To construct any sense of ethos or authority requires an intimate knowledge of the place that formed said ethos. We cannot view our ethos as a

God-given series of traits; rather, our ethos is more like a tapestry of experiences and insights that have been formed in a specific location by multiple hands. If we frame metanoia as a revision of one's own understanding of ethos, then metanoia, too, must engage with the practices and beliefs of a specific place and community to identify what transformation is possible. In other words, metanoia and transformation also require a complex understanding of the locations and values that make up our current ethos to then identify a different ethos that we want to become.

In order for this transformation to be possible, however, we must be open to feelings of loss or regret. What often spurs the possibility for transformation is the recognition that an opportunity was missed, a course of action was incorrect, or something dear was lost. Kelly A. Myers links regret and transformation through the process of metanoia: "Though the active state of metanoic transformation may seem incompatible with the seemingly passive state of regret, discussions of *metanoia* must begin by linking regret and transformation."[14] Note, again, the need for balance between "active" and "passive" states of being. If we think of our current state of being as a kind of ethos, and if we view ethos as place, then our present state is always an active engagement with our surroundings. Metanoia furthers this active state by questioning what we believe to be true about our ethos. Regret, on the other hand, locks us into a moment or location that has already been. We experience regret in circumstances where we can no longer negotiate the terms of a moment. Both states can teach us something. The passive experience of regret provides us with concrete examples of the kinds of values or practices we wish to change. The active state of metanoia allows us to consider what we currently have and what we will need to change in order to transform and live differently now and in the future. Being transformed by metanoia involves a holistic engagement with reflection, one that plays on our active and passive states, along with our bodies, minds, hearts, and spirits. The process of metanoia bridges the experience of regret with the possibility for transformation, and this process results in new awareness and openness to our lives. The key here is not to be overwhelmed by regret but, rather, to be fueled by it: "*Metanoia* involves reorientation, often spurred, but not consumed, by remorse."[15]

One way to do so is by considering metanoia as an opening of alternative, previously unconsidered doors. Zachary Beare writes about the experience of rejection from literature PhD programs and how that led him to his career in composition and rhetoric: "*metanoia* showcases the ways this missed opportunity afforded alternative paths that might (and indeed *did*) lead to discovery."[16] The benefit of viewing metanoia this way is twofold: it not only makes available new possibilities, but also it prepares us to be more critically aware and available to transformative possibilities in the future. It both opens new doors and makes us aware of those doors before we arrive at them. Building off *kairos*, which Richard Benjamin Crosby expands from the definition of "right timing" to "making the invisible visible . . . by positing revelation as the goal,"[17] metanoia changes our world by compelling us to new action through the unearthing and revealing of that which previously was not known to us.

What complicates metanoia is its interiority. Although metanoia is a rhetorical concept, which usually implies engagement with an audience or external agents, it is primarily experienced internally and individually. How do we make known and demonstrate metanoia if its primary experience occurs in our own minds and hearts? How can we prove we are experiencing it if we wish to? Adam Ellwanger writes:

> *Metanoia* always refers to some inward movement, some change of heart or mind. And if *metanoia* is an interior event, then it is always somewhat beyond the reach of rhetoric—immeasurable and unobservable. Much more accessible to rhetoricians are the discourses that describe and testify to the experience of that inward movement. Thus, inevitably, questions of authenticity arise.[18]

Couching his argument within the genre of the public apology, a genre he argues is inherently punitive, Ellwanger wrestles with the need to perform metanoia for an audience. When we experience transformation, the only ways we can make it known are through speech and actions. However, we can never fully articulate the *experience* of metanoia; while we can try to use rhetoric to convey it, there is a part of metanoia that lives beyond language. It is also crucial that metanoia does not exist to be proven or demonstrated in its own right. We, as actors of metanoia, can attempt to show what we have experienced, but metanoia does not ultimately exist for performance. As a result, any attempts to share metanoia are up to each of us to decide how we try to do so. This is what makes metanoia both so powerful and so unwieldy. It is why we need various kinds of texts to demonstrate the transformation. Even with these texts, we still have to lend our trust to the ethos of the speaker. We can never fully confirm the authenticity of one's transformation; instead, we continue to witness to a speaker's metanoia over time.

And witnessing is exactly what *The Long Loneliness* allows us to do. Through Day's writing, we witness the multiple metanoias of her life including the 1906 San Francisco earthquake; her imprisonment at Occoquan; the birth of her daughter, Tamar; her conversion to Catholicism; and her meeting with Peter Maurin, cofounder of the Catholic Worker Movement as well as Day's confidant and love. As Day guides us through each transformative moment, she builds the authenticity of her metanoia until it is seamlessly woven into the fabric of her movements. Without her autobiography, we would not have access to the significance of her transformation. In detailing some of the most striking metanoias in *The Long Loneliness*, I will show how Day uses embodied rhetoric to demonstrate a life steeped in metanoia.

DOROTHY DAY'S METANOIAS

One of Day's early formative experiences is the 1906 San Francisco earthquake. While briefly mentioned in her autobiography, its impact on Day's consciousness, both in terms of faith and social justice, is striking. Reflecting on her childhood, Day writes about nightmares related to death and the vastness of God. Having difficulty locating the exact timeline of these nightmares, Day ponders if they occurred before or after her experience of the earthquake. Describing a noise that continues to get louder in her dreams, Day connects these all-consuming nightmares to that time, "I remember these dreams only in connection with California and they were linked up with my idea of God as a tremendous force, a frightening impersonal God, a Voice, a Hand stretched out to seize me, His child, and not in love."[19] The trauma of the earthquake distorts Day's memory, especially because it is compounded by the sight of her mother fainting a few nights earlier, both of which she describes as "part of the world's tragedy."[20] This tragedy, combined with her burgeoning awareness of a divine presence in her life,[21] collides through the earthquake to create an image of God that is frightening, cold, and overwhelming. Her image of God transforms through the earthquake and becomes a symbol of terrifying awe, which contradicts the image of God she will hold later in her life. Although traumatic, this moment makes Day keenly aware of and concretizes an image of God, which will continue to transform throughout her life.

Despite the terror of the earthquake, Day also recounts a turning point in her desire to serve others in the world: "Another thing I remember about California was the joy of doing good, of sharing whatever we had with others after the earthquake, an event which threw us out of our complacent happiness into a world of catastrophe."[22] Here, Day anchors her childhood memories of California with the experience of serving others. This moment is so integral for her formation that she associates it with this portion of her upbringing. Day finds doing good to be not just pleasant but joyful. The radical emptying of their belongings to support others enables Day to see the world differently. Through the embodiment of a natural disaster and the relinquishing of material goods, Day sees a new world where complacency and ignorance are replaced by an awareness of and response to its suffering. While her work is more about charity and service than systemic reform, it offers Day a consciousness-raising that will continue to flourish as she moves through various activist spaces. She cannot unlearn this experience of suffering, and she will grow in her sensitivity to it in years to come.

In 1917, Day's radicalism is tested when she joins a growing number of suffragists, referred to as the "Silent Sentinels," in picketing the White House and President Woodrow Wilson to advocate for the federally recognized right of U.S. women to vote. She initially joins the movement because a friend of hers, Peggy Baird, decides to support it. Quickly, however, Day's investment in the cause grows. As the women silently approach the White House gates in purple and gold sashes, young boys begin to throw rocks at the women as sailors and soldiers rip banners out of their hands. These circumstances spur police wagons to arrive and take the suffragists to a police station where bail is posted for them before their sentencing trial the next morning. After repeating this process multiple times, suffragists who refuse to post bail are transferred to more harsh prison conditions.[23]

Sentenced to the Occoquan Workhouse in Lorton, Virginia, Day describes, in painful detail, the inhumane living conditions and torture she and thirty-two other women experience. As their spokeswoman announces a hunger strike until demands have been met, the superintendent, Mr. Whittaker, beckons guards to rush the holding room they are in and violently drag them to separate cells. Day is slammed multiple times into benches and on the floor as she tries to rejoin her friend Peggy. She recounts women being handcuffed to cell bars, overcrowding in single-occupancy cells, verbal harassment, rumors of whippings and bloodhounds, and the mental duress of being imprisoned for days.[24] In all of these descriptions, Day refuses to let us forget the physical and mental exhaustion this experience has on her and the other women. The corporeal description of suffering in her book is an intentional reminder of the stakes of injustice in the world: "Never would I be able to recover from this wound. . . . It was one thing to be writing about these things, to have theoretical knowledge of sweatshops and injustice and hunger, but it was quite another to experience it in one's own flesh."[25] Through the torturous experience in Occoquan, Day's radicalism is made flesh. Her abstract awareness of suffering becomes embodied and lived, which creates an unhealable wound. While painful, this wound offers Day a new awareness of the structural violences of her world. Liberation theologian Marcella Althaus-Reid notes that "*metanoia* needs to exceed the individual, transforming unjust structures of power and unequal relationships amongst people."[26] Day names a literal identity transformation as she begins to see herself implicated in the suffering of others, "I would never be free again, never free when I knew that behind bars all over the world there were women and men, young girls and boys, suffering constraint, punishment, isolation and hardship for crimes of which all of us were guilty."[27] Day shows us how her work to "do good" in the world has evolved since San Francisco: she now embraces radical vulnerability and suffering alongside marginalized communities. No longer will she simply try to help others by redistributing material resources or abstractly analyzing conditions of injustice. Instead, she will engage in a practice called "voluntary poverty," which Sean Barnette frames as *kenosis*, or an emptying of oneself.[28] Day's fight for justice is now embodied through her voluntary poverty and identification with the poor.

As Day grows in her political radicalism, she also experiences metanoia in her personal life. Through the birth of her daughter, Tamar, Day notices a merging of love and faith that changes the course of her life. At the time, Day is in a common-law marriage to Forster Batterham, who identifies as an anarchist with a deep suspicious of religion. Her prayer habits intensify as she feels immense gratitude and happiness about her pregnancy, but her deepened religious state, along with the pregnancy, strains her relationship with Forster. He believes the world is too broken to bring a child into it, and his antireligious position widens the chasm of their relationship. She writes, "Becoming a Catholic would mean facing life alone and I clung to family life. It was hard to contemplate giving up a mate in order that my child and I could become members of the Church."[29] She faces a choice: her daughter and her newfound faith or her partner, each of whom she loves fiercely.

This moment forces Day into a period of introspection and reflection, crucial processes for the development of metanoia. In her book, she details how her perspective on love evolves through Tamar, "Forster had made the physical world come alive for me and had awakened in my heart a flood of gratitude. The final object of this love and gratitude was God. No human creature could receive or contain so vast a flood of love and joy as I often felt after the birth of my child. With this came the need to worship, to adore."[30] She articulates an evolution in the layers of love she feels. Forster enables an awareness of and gratitude for her world, which ultimately brings her toward the ultimate goal of loving God. Yet, the only person who can come close to the vastness of her love for God is Tamar. Tamar's existence proves the deciding factor for Day whether to convert. The love for Tamar as love for God outweighs the initial love she feels for Forster, and this relationship with Tamar commits her to Catholicism. To be clear, it is not that Day suddenly relinquishes or sees her love with Forster as deficient. As Benjamin T. Peters writes: "Day tells the story of her conversion . . . as one of leaving behind her 'natural happiness'. . . . While Day regarded such natural happiness as good . . . she also recognized that ultimately it has to be given up in order to pursue a much greater happiness."[31] Day engages in a rigorous self-examination to determine what her greater purpose is in life. And this reflection leads to *action* motivated by love. Religious scholar Kevin J. O'Brien reminds us that, for Day, love is "the most powerful force in the universe, and she found resonance for this idea in the Catholic tradition, to which she then devoted herself."[32] While this choice dismantles her marriage to Forster, it opens the opportunity for a deepening relationship with God for both Tamar and Day, which is made concrete through Tamar's baptism and Day's own conversion to Catholicism.

Metanoia often brings with it feelings of pain, remorse, and uncertainty. While a powerful force for change, it is also a deeply unsettling one. Day's separation from Forster is a deeply painful one, and she makes clear in her book that her subsequent conversion is not a suddenly joyous occasion. In fact, she describes her participation in the Sacraments of Baptism, Confession, and Holy Communion as "grimly, coldly, making acts of faith . . . with no consolation whatsoever."[33] Day's ambivalence is understandable given her losing one of the major loves of her life because of this decision. Additionally, Day feels pulled between her desire to become a Catholic and her work with marginalized communities. Recognizing the ways that the Catholic Church is implicated in the economic violence of the world, she recounts, "I had become convinced that I would become a Catholic; yet I felt I was betraying the class to which I belonged, the workers, the poor of the world, with whom Christ spent His life."[34]

Perceiving the loss of both her partner and class communities, Day's book title, *The Long Loneliness*, takes on new meaning. David J. Leigh stresses the significance of loneliness in Day's early Catholic journey: "the dynamic of loneliness-seeking-communion . . . now drives her as a Catholic toward an image, of what she later calls the only answer to the long loneliness—'a community'—expressed in shared work and conversations around a supper table."[35] The community that Leigh refers to is the Catholic Worker Movement that she will create with Maurin. However, before she can sit at that table, she must first experience a new community with God. This community involves a new orientation and awareness to the presence and power of God in one's life. In "Dorothy Day's Christian Conversion," June O'Connor specifies that Day's conversion "was not simply a new recognition of God . . . it involved a *receptivity* to God as a personal and creative being *in her life and in relation to her other loves*."[36] Note O'Connor's emphasis on God as a "personal" and "creative" presence in her life. Day's conversion involves God meeting Day through her talents in her journalistic work. This is where she can be most attuned and open to a transformative force in her life.

When Day shares her experience covering the 1932 Hunger March in Washington, DC for a Catholic publication, she frames God as a metanoic presence in her work. Dissatisfied with the separation she feels while covering the march as a reporter and not an activist, Day falls into exasperation at Catholic University's national shrine after completing her story. She details a moment of "tears" and "anguish" as she prays to God to provide her an opportunity to become more open and committed to working with the poor.[37] She reckons with the lack of Catholic community in her life, and it appears that she will end this section of her book in despair. However, the final sentence offers a new kind of transformation on the horizon, possibly Day's greatest metanoia, "And when I returned to New York, I found Peter Maurin—Peter the French peasant, whose spirit and ideas will dominate the rest of this book as they will dominate the rest of my life."[38] In one sentence Day is able to link her plea to God with the delivery of a gift, a gift that meets her exactly where her need is. Through Maurin, Day will find the Catholic community for which she yearns as well as the opportunity to put her talents to practice in the form of the Catholic Worker Movement. While Day frames this moment as a gift from God, we can also see the rhetorical appeal Day uses, through desperate prayer, to name her needs and desires with boldness and earnestness. Her ability to move from ambivalence about her Catholic conversion to a desire to share in it with others demonstrates a change of mind and heart that bears more spiritual and social fruit in her life. In other words, Day is able to live through, reflect on, and communicate with the transformative potential of these moments in her life. Rather than viewing these events as isolated incidents, Day weaves a cohesive narrative that leads us to the greatest relationship of her life with Maurin.

The impact of Maurin on Day is undeniable. Together, they cofound the *Catholic Worker* publication and, subsequently, the Catholic Worker Movement, which currently has 204 communities globally. The Catholic Worker Movement's website states that its members "remain committed to nonviolence, voluntary poverty, prayer, and hospitality for the homeless, exiled, hungry, and forsaken. Catholic Workers continue to protest injustice, war, racism, and violence of all forms."[39] These values come directly from the values both Maurin and Day espouse. In fact, Day names Maurin as a guide and teacher who could motivate and champion the greatest causes: "Peter made you feel a sense of his mission as soon as you met him . . . he aroused in you a sense of your own capacities for work, for accomplishment."[40] Like Day, Maurin possesses a compelling rhetorical capacity to help people see a different vision of the world, a world where violence and greed are not at the center of social relationships. Maurin, unlike Day's former husband, emphasizes the inherent goodness of people and believes in its potential to enact justice in the world. He rejects any form of monetary payment for an exchange of necessities like food and housing, and he promotes almsgiving, regardless of his financial circumstance, with a responsibility for the well-being of his neighbor and community.[41] Together, Day and Maurin are able to live out the power of a metanoic life by reflecting on the structural sins of their world, imagine new possibilities for community formation, and commit their bodies and lives to enacting that vision for marginalized people. This ability to build hope and take action is at the center of Paul Farmer's remarks on metanoia: "Whatever it is you do, and you will do great things, try to *turn your road angst into hope and action*."[42] Hope and action permeate the communities Day and Maurin create, communities that are only possible because of the metanoic opportunities that Day utilizes.

Much of the remainder of *The Long Loneliness* is dedicated to the painstaking work Day and Maurin perform to begin their publication and larger justice movement. Maurin's presence and encouragement of Day helps to fuel her praxis and commitment to her vision. When writing about his death, Day describes Maurin as "another St. John."[43] Framing Maurin as one of Jesus's most beloved disciples, Day makes a claim about the transformative (and metanoic) impact Maurin has on her life. However, it is important to name that Day holds the same force and power in Maurin's life as well. While Day is often deferential in the way she credits others' influence on her, it is clear that their partnership is forged in a mutual love for God and desire to eradicate poverty and suffering in this world. It is also clear that Day is deeply aware of the transformative power of the experiences and relationships in her life. In *The Long Loneliness*, Day uses embodied rhetoric and metanoia to demonstrate a multitude of complex and interlocking identities that form the story of her life: child, radical, mother, Catholic, and cofounder. She is aware of the fluidity of these identities and never fails to locate herself within a more complex system of powers at hand.

RECONSIDERING DOROTHY DAY'S ETHOS

In the concluding section of this chapter, I will make the case for reconsidering Day's ethos in light of her work and demonstrate how Day is a prime example of a feminist ecological ethos. In the introduction to *Rethinking Ethos: A Feminist Ecological Approach to Rhetoric*, Kathleen J. Ryan, Nancy Myers, and Rebecca Jones trouble the Aristotelian conception of ethos as a rigid, fixed set of characteristics within the rhetor, a conception that focuses on patriarchal and exclusionary spaces. Instead, they opt for a "feminist ecological ethos" which recognizes the nuances and multiplicity of women's experiences within a broader system of patriarchal oppression. Additionally, a feminist ecological ethos "is a dynamic of multiple ethē among rhetors, audiences, and locations . . . paying attention to consequences, and taking responsibility for rhetorical acts, is crucial to ecological thinking."[44] In other words, a feminist ecological ethos is relational in nature, focused on both rhetor and audience and the larger social contexts in which they reside. To have a feminist ecological ethos is to recognize similarity and difference not simply in terms of identity but in terms of access to power and social location.

In many ways, a feminist ecological ethos requires a spirit of metanoia, which encourages constant reevaluation of one's circumstances and actions in the name of transformation. Feminist Catholic theologian Rosemary Radford Ruether links a "feminist metanoia" with the Christian concept of "soul-making," which she defines as "the journey of conversion and transformation toward self-realization, in relation to gender socialization."[45] Describing soul-making as a *journey*, Ruether recognizes the unending yet rewarding work of becoming more cognizant of one's location in the world. Reframing the conception of "conversion" as a consciousness-raising experience for women, Ruether further asserts: "We need to look at this process wholistically [*sic*]. Soul-making happens through transformative metanoia, which is both sudden insight and also slow maturation of a grounded self in relationship or community, able to be both self-affirming and other affirming in life-enhancing mutuality. It is both a gift and a task, grace and work."[46] In authentically reflecting on one's positionality, responding to new insights, and forming coalitions with others who are engaged in similar work, Ruether asserts that women can soul-make through the process of metanoia. A feminist metanoia is about establishing communities of women who refuse to be disenfranchised or ignored by violent patriarchal structures. Both "gift and a task, grace and work," I view a feminist metanoia as a demonstration of *love*, a love Day expressed through her words and actions.

Reflecting on Laurie A. Britt-Smith's concerns about Day's ethos, I believe more work needs to be done. In considering the rhetorical sophistication and prowess of Day and other Catholic women, we will be better equipped to engage in the kind of soul-making Ruether advocates. We will more "wholistically" identify and make meaning of the contributions and impacts Catholic women have had on the construction of Catholic communities. In Day's case, I have demonstrated how her rhetorical living strengthens the nuance and multiplicity with which we discuss her. Through analyzing her embodied rhetoric and metanoic practices, we can better understand how Day sees her life as a series of interconnected and deeply meaningful encounters and opportunities. Ultimately, highlighting Day's metanoic faith offers us the chance to revisit a beloved figure of Catholic history and transform our own understandings of her legacy.

NOTES

1. Laurie A. Britt-Smith, "Not So Easily Dismissed: The Intellectual Influences and Rhetorical Voice of Dorothy Day—'Servant of God,'" in *Remembering Women Differently: Refiguring Rhetorical Work*, eds. Lynee Lewis Gaillet and Helen Gaillet Bailey (Columbia: South Carolina University Press, 2019), 207.

2. Kathleen J. Ryan, Nancy Myers, and Rebecca Jones, "Introduction: Identifying Feminist Ecological Ethē," in *Rethinking Ethos: A Feminist Ecological Approach to Rhetoric*, eds. Ryan, Kathleen J., Nancy Myers, and Rebecca Jones (Carbondale: Southern Illinois UP, 2016), 11.

3. Dorothy Day, *The Long Loneliness: The Autobiography of the Legendary Catholic Social Activist* (New York: HarperOne, 1952), 9.

4. Day, *The Long Loneliness*, 9.

5. A. Abby Knoblauch, "Bodies of Knowledge: Definitions, Delineations, and Implications of Embodied Writing in the Academy," *Composition Studies* 40, no. 2 (Fall 2012): 52.

6. Knoblauch, "Bodies of Knowledge," 62.

7. Day, *The Long Loneliness*, 11.

8. Janice Chernekoff, "Embodied Rhetorics: Writing Rides from the Seat of a Bike," *KB Journal* 13, no. 2 (Summer 2018).

9. Chernekoff, "Embodied Rhetorics."

10. Adam Ellwanger, *Metanoia: Rhetoric, Authenticity, and the Transformation of the Self* (University Park: The Pennsylvania State UP, 2020), 5–6.

11. S. Michael Halloran, "Aristotle's Concept of *Ethos*, Or If Not His, Somebody Else's," *Rhetoric Review* 1, no. 1 (September 1982): 60.

12. Kelly A. Myers, "*Metanoia* and the Transformation of Opportunity," *Rhetoric Society Quarterly* 41, no. 1 (January 2011): 11.

13. Nedra Reynolds, "Ethos as Location: New Sites for Understanding Discursive Authority," *Rhetoric Review* 11, no. 2 (1993): 329.

14. Kelly A. Myers, "Metanoic Movement: The Transformative Power of Regret," *College Composition and Communication* 67, no. 3 (2016): 388.

15. Myers, "Metanoic Movement," 388.

16. Zachary Beare, "The Strange Practices of Serendipitous Failure: Considering Metanoia as an Alternative to Kairos," in *Serendipity in Rhetoric, Writing, and Literacy Research*, eds. by Maureen Daly Goggin and Peter N. Goggin (Louisville, CO: Utah State UP, 2018), 259.

17. Richard Benjamin Crosby, "Kairos as God's Time in Martin Luther King Jr.'s Last Sunday Sermon," *Rhetoric Society Quarterly* 39, no. 3 (Summer 2009): 265.

18. Adam Ellwanger, "Apology as Metanoia Performance: Punitive Rhetoric and Public Speech," *Rhetoric Society Quarterly* 42, no. 4 (September 2012): 312.

19. Day, *The Long Loneliness*, 21.

20. Day, *The Long Loneliness*, 21.

21. Day did not grow up in a religious household.

22. Day, *The Long Loneliness*, 21.

23. Day, *The Long Loneliness*, 72.

24. Day, *The Long Loneliness*, 75–79.

25. Day, *The Long Loneliness*, 79.

26. Marcella Althaus-Reid, "Education for Liberation," *Studies in World Christianity* 12, no. 1 (2006): 2.

27. Day, *The Long Loneliness*, 78.

28. Sean Barnette, "Hospitality as Kenosis: Dorothy Day's Voluntary Poverty," in *Rethinking Ethos: A Feminist Ecological Approach to Rhetoric*, eds. Kathleen J. Ryan, Nancy Myers, and Rebecca Jones (Carbondale: Southern Illinois UP, 2016), 137.

29. Day, *The Long Loneliness*, 137.

30. Day, *The Long Loneliness*, 139.

31. Benjamin T. Peters, "Ignatian Radicalism: The Influence of Jesuit Spirituality on Dorothy Day," *The Catholic Historical Review* 103, no. 2 (2017): 308.

32. Kevin J. O'Brien, *The Violence of Climate Change: Lessons of Resistance from Nonviolent Activists* (Washington, DC: Georgetown UP, 2017), 122.

33. Day, *The Long Loneliness*, 148.

34. Day, *The Long Loneliness*, 144.

35. David J. Leigh, *Circuitous Journeys: Modern Spiritual Autobiography* (New York: Fordham UP, 2000), 64.

36. June O'Connor, "Dorothy Day's Christian Conversion," *The Journal of Religious Ethics* 18, no. 1 (Spring 1990): 170.

37. Day, *The Long Loneliness*, 166.

38. Day, *The Long Loneliness*, 166.

39. "The Catholic Worker Movement," The Catholic Worker Movement, accessed October 20, 2020, https://catholicworker.org.

40. Day, *The Long Loneliness*, 171.

41. Day, *The Long Loneliness*, 170–171.

42. Paul Farmer, *To Repair the World: Paul Farmer Speaks to the Next Generation*, ed. by Jonathan Weigel (Berkeley, CA: University of California Press, 2019), 29.

43. Day, *The Long Loneliness*, 279.

44. Ryan, Myers, and Jones, "Introduction," 11.

45. Rosemary Radford Ruether, "Feminist Metanoia and Soul-Making," *Women & Therapy* 16, no. 2–3 (1995): 33.

46. Ruether, "Feminist Metanoia," 39.

BIBLIOGRAPHY

Althaus-Reid, Marcella. "Education for Liberation." *Studies in World Christianity* 12, no. 1 (2006): 1–4. Project MUSE.

Barnette, Sean. "Hospitality as Kenosis: Dorothy Day's Voluntary Poverty." In *Rethinking Ethos: A Feminist Ecological Approach to Rhetoric*, edited by Kathleen J. Ryan, Nancy Myers, and Rebecca Jones, 132–149. Southern Illinois UP, 2016.

Beare, Zachary. "The Strange Practices of Serendipitous Failure: Considering Metanoia as an Alternative to Kairos." In *Serendipity in Rhetoric, Writing, and Literacy Research*, edited by Maureen Daly Goggin and Peter N. Goggin, 257–266. Utah University State Press, 2018.

Britt-Smith, Laurie A. "Not So Easily Dismissed: The Intellectual Influences and Rhetorical Voice of Dorothy Day—'Servant of God.'" In *Remembering Women Differently: Refiguring Rhetorical Work*, edited by Lynee Lewis Gaillet and Helen Gaillet Bailey, 206–222. Columbia: South Carolina UP, 2019.

The Catholic Worker Movement, The Catholic Worker Movement. Accessed October 20, 2020. https://www.catholicworker.org.

Chernekoff, Janice. "Embodied Rhetorics: Writing Rides from the Seat of a Bike." *KB Journal* 13, no. 2 (Summer 2018).

Crosby, Richard Benjamin. "Kairos as God's Time in Martin Luther King Jr.'s Last Sunday Sermon." *Rhetoric Society Quarterly* 39, no. 3 (Summer 2009): 260–280, https://doi.org/10.1080/02773940902991411.

Day, Dorothy. *The Long Loneliness: The Autobiography of the Legendary Catholic Social Activist.* New York: HarperOne, 1952.

Ellwanger, Adam. *Metanoia: Rhetoric, Authenticity, and the Transformation of the Self.* State College: The Pennsylvania State UP, 2020.

Ellwanger, Adam. "Apology as Metanoic Performance: Punitive Rhetoric and Public Speech." *Rhetoric Society Quarterly* 42, no. 4 (September 2012), 307–329, https://doi.org/10.1080/02773945.2012.704118.

Farmer, Paul. *To Repair the World: Paul Farmer Speaks to the Next Generation.* Edited by Jonathan Weigel. Berkeley, CA: University of California Press, 2019.

Halloran, S. Michael. "Aristotle's Concept of *Ethos*, Or If Not His, Somebody Else's," *Rhetoric Review* 1, no. 1 (September 1982): 58–63, https://doi.org/10.1080/07350198209359037.

Knoblauch, A. Abby. "Bodies of Knowledge: Definitions, Delineations, and Implications of Embodied Writing in the Academy." *Composition Studies* 40, no. 2 (Fall 2012): 50–65.

Leigh, David J. *Circuitous Journeys: Modern Spiritual Autobiography.* New York: Fordham UP, 2000.

Myers, Kelly A. "*Metanoia* and the Transformation of Opportunity." *Rhetoric Society Quarterly* 41, no. 1 (January 2011): 1–18.

Myers, Kelly A. "Metanoic Movement: The Transformative Power of Regret." *College Composition and Communication* 67, no. 3 (2016): 385–411.

O'Brien, Kevin J. *The Violence of Climate Change: Lessons of Resistance from Nonviolent Activists.* Washington, DC: Georgetown UP, 2017.

O'Connor, June. "Dorothy Day's Christian Conversion." *The Journal of Religious Ethics* 18, no. 1 (Spring 1990): 159–180.

Peters, Benjamin T. "Ignatian Radicalism: The Influence of Jesuit Spirituality on Dorothy Day." *The Catholic Historical Review* 103, no. 2 (2017): 297–320, https://doi.org/10.1353/cat.2017.0064.

Reynolds, Nedra. "Ethos as Location: New Sites for Understanding Discursive Authority." *Rhetoric Review* 11, no. 2 (1993): 325–338, https://doi.org/10.1080/07350199309389009.

Ruether, Rosemary Radford. "Feminist Metanoia and Soul-Making." *Women & Therapy* 16, no. 2–3 (1995): 33–44, https://doi.org/10.1300/j015v16n02_06.

Ryan, Kathleen J., Nancy Myers, and Rebecca Jones. "Introduction: Identifying Feminist Ecological Ethē." In *Rethinking Ethos: A Feminist Ecological Approach to Rhetoric*, edited by Kathleen J. Ryan, Nancy Myers, and Rebecca Jones, 1–22. Carbondale: Southern Illinois UP, 2016.

Chapter 11

Word and Deed

Dolores Huerta, Chicana Feminism, and a Zurdo Ethos of Faith in Action

L Heidenreich

Many scholars and activists admire Dolores Huerta as the powerful cofounder of the United Farm Workers (UFW) Union. She negotiated the first farm-worker union contract with growers in California, successfully lobbied the California state legislature for bilingual drivers' license exams, and was at the forefront of those fighting for the Agricultural Labor Relations Act (1975) to establish California's labor relations board—necessary because decades earlier, Franklin Roosevelt's labor protections had failed to cover agricultural laborers in the United States. Huerta's success was, in part, due to the power of her words—in her negotiations but also in her speeches—moving workers and an ever-expanding community of allies to action.

Dolores Huerta, like her mother and like the many Mexicana and Chicana rhetors who came before her, constructed an ethos inextricably rooted in community where word and action fueled each other to build a dynamic ethos capable of expanding communities and calling those communities to action. The power of this community is most apparent when mapped as a weave in process: fabric on a loom. Huerta's community and, in relation, her ethos, were neither static nor homogenous but vibrant and active. Chicanismo, or pride in her Chicanx her community and heritage; family influences; and a particularly Chicana feminist Catholic faith formed Huerta's community and ethos—the space from which and with which she spoke. Dolores Huerta's ethos was/is ecological, enfleshed, *zurdo*, and expansive.

In the early twenty-first century, feminist rhetoricians such as Kathleen J. Ryan, Nancy Myers, and Rebecca Jones sought to claim and trouble ethos as a tool of women rhetors and rhetoricians, arguing that ethos, as a powerful tool and means of analysis, is most effective when rooted in "place, community, identity and social action."[1] Taking an approach they termed *ecological*, they noted ethos is best understood in the context of community and not in the isolated, abstracted universal individual of the Western, colonizing past. Similarly, Nedra Reynolds, writing just one decade earlier, mapped how ethos is best understood as a "mediation between the rhetor and the community."[2] She noted that "character is formed by habit, not engendered by nature, and those habits come from the community or culture. One identifies an individual's character, then, by looking to the community. An individual's ethos cannot be determined outside of the space in which it was created or without a sense of cultural context."[3]

In their call to recognize ethos as communal, Reynolds and Ryan et al. built upon the legacies of feminists of color who, throughout the 1980s, constructed and promulgated a philosophy of wholeness, community, and coalition, insisting that identity is rooted in history and community;[4] working from such rootedness, rhetors call their communities to action and, as well, expand the boundaries of their community. It is in the context of ethos as dynamic, Catholic, and communal, that the powerful work of Dolores Huerta becomes legible as a Chicana and Catholic feminist rhetoric of action: word and deed.

Chicanx activists of the late twentieth century, including Catholic Chicanas such as Dolores Huerta, spoke from a space shaped by their life experiences or what Chicana feminist Cherríe Moraga termed "theory in the flesh." Moraga and other twentieth-century feministas called attention to the ways in which our lived experiences and how we speak of and to those experiences—"the physical realities of our lives—our skin color, the land or concrete we grew up on, our sexual longings" ground our politics and our work.[5] This insistence on enfleshed politics and, I argue, an enfleshed rhetoric, shaped the words and actions of generations of Chicana activists grounding their/our words in our bodies, histories, and lived experiences.

Equally important to understanding the power of Huerta's words is another strain of Chicana feminism—one that insists on the power of building community through shared experiences and values in order to create an ever-expanding community. As discussed below, this expansive, community feminism allowed Huerta to call on the legacy of political activist and gay martyr Harvey Milk and to ask her audiences to pray for closeted gay men like the Rev. Tim Haggard. It is this broadening of community that Huerta embodied in her later work, where she pulled and pooled her audiences into *La Causa*, the cause of worker rights, and, in relation, the sacred human rights of all. This enfleshed, communal ethos, as a theory in the flesh, was also articulated by Chicana feminists in the 1980s, most notably by Gloria E. Anzaldúa in her vision of *El Mundo Zurdo*. People constructed as outsiders, "Third World women, lesbians, feminists, and feminist-oriented men of all colors," must come together in coalition—and in doing so to change the world.

> We are the queer groups, the people that don't belong anywhere. . . . Combined we cover so many oppressions. . . . Not all of us have the same oppressions, but we empathize and identify with each other's oppressions. We do not have the same ideology, nor do we derive similar solutions. Some of us are leftists, some of us practitioners of magic. Some of us are both. But these different affinities are not opposed to each other. In El Mundo Zurdo I with my own affinities and my people with theirs can live together and transform the planet.[6]

Speaking from a space of community and *herencia*—a heritage of Catholic justice teachings and of strong Mexicana and Chicana rhetors—Huerta became one of the most powerful women rhetors of the twentieth century, negotiating contracts, speaking before congress, and bringing ever-wider audiences into a community of justice.

Mapping the multiple roots of Huerta's Chicana feminist ethos makes visible the manner in which late twentieth-century Chicanas, with their words rooted in a communal ethos of social action, shaped the larger world around them. It also makes visible the less discussed reality that for some Chicana feminists, Catholicism stood in opposition neither to their activism nor to the ethos from which they spoke. Instead, a critical and feminist Catholicism was central to their words and deeds.

Thus, below I map the emergence of a Chicana feminist ethos in the late twentieth century, the multiple roots of Dolores Huerta's voice, including both the Catholic justice tradition in which she was raised, and the long tradition of powerful Mexicana and Chicana rhetors on whose shoulders she stood; critical and central to both of these traditions was her family. In closing, I analyze a speech delivered years after she had moved on from her formal position in the UFW—her keynote address to the Twenty-first National Conference on LGBT Equality. In this address, she boldly and visibly mobilized an ethos that is not individual but expansive and communal—rooted in her own Chicana and Catholic feminista community values, she brought her audience with her to a place of coalition and communion.

PRAYER, GIRL SCOUTS, SERVICE: CHILDHOOD MATTERS

Dolores Huerta was born into a working-class family in Dawson, New Mexico, in 1930, living the first five years of her life in the Southwest. Her father, Juan Fernández, was a second-generation immigrant who worked as a miner in the coal mines of Dawson. While she was raised by her mother, it is important to acknowledge that the strength of both of her parents would be visible in her later activism, for after they divorced, it was her father who went on to become active in the Congress of Industrial Organizations. He successfully ran for political office, serving as representative in the New Mexico State Legislature where he advocated for workers' rights.[7] Her mother's family had deep roots in the region, three generations in the U.S. national Southwest, a land that, to borrow the words of Gloria E. Anzaldúa, "was Mexican once, Indian always."[8]

Her mother raised her—her mother with the help of her grandfather, who prayed rosary with her and the family, and who encouraged her bold engagement with the world of words. Huerta's grandfather Herculano Chávez, who lived with the family for much of her formative years, encouraged her critical thinking and her bold speech. Christine Beagle notes how Chávez encouraged her to read periodicals and engaged her in discussions of current events, "instilling in her the passion for politics and the verbiage with which to express it."[9]

Following her divorce, Alicia Chávez moved her family to Stockton, California. The family settled in a multiracial, mixed-ethnic neighborhood—a new borderland—where Huerta grew and flourished. Huerta attended public schools, was active in the Girl Scouts and in Catholic youth organizations.[10] Her participation in the Girl Scouts was not a casual thread of her childhood, for she remained active in the organization for a full ten years. As an adult, she looked back and noted that "being a Girl Scout from the time I was eight to eighteen taught me many things. It built my self-confidence and taught me not to be shy about speaking in public."[11] As a woman committed to worker's rights, Huerta's mother, Alicia Fernández, set a strong example for her. Fernández worked two jobs as a cannery worker and as a waitress and saved enough money to buy her own restaurant. Later when, with her second husband, she was able to purchase a hotel, she sometimes allowed farm worker families to stay free of rent. Welcoming farm worker families to stay at her hotel could not have been a decision taken lightly; Fernández had worked two jobs raising the money to invest in the property.[12] While, as an adult, her father disapproved of Huerta's family structure, her mother modeled the value of healthy relationships over traditional or Church-approved relationships. Alicia Chávez divorced twice before meeting and marrying the man with whom she would share the rest of her life.[13]

A CATHOLIC ETHOS

It was this complex childhood that functioned to form and develop the critical Catholicism from which Huerta spoke. As her career progressed, from and within a national movement that constructed the community as family, Huerta insisted on constructing a feminist activist family while relying upon and mobilizing basic tenets of Roman Catholicism as central to her own ethos and that of the larger community.

Huerta made Catholicism her own, taking what was fruitful and incorporating it into her words and actions. She modeled a Chicana feminism that negotiated what Dolores Delgado Bernal termed "the contradictions of Catholicism," drawing strength and symbolic tools from an institution that spoke of justice and the dignity of the human person while it reproduced its own legacies of colonial and patriarchal violence.[14] It was her family that modeled this negotiation for her. The same grandfather who encouraged her to speak boldly also prayed rosary with her. Her mother left an unhealthy marriage, maintained her devotion to Our Lady and to El Santo Niño de Atocha, and raised her children in the faith.[15]

The centrality of Huerta's Catholic faith to her ethos is apparent in her words throughout her activist work, but, perhaps, most clearly in her interview with Vincent Harding where she spoke of the sacred labor of farmworkers: "If you had to be on a deserted island and you could only take one person with you, who would you take, an attorney or a farmworker? Right? I think that kind of gets it down. Because farm work is the most sacred work of all."[16] Her direct and powerful words echoed the official teaching of the institutional Church that "to defraud any one of wages that are his due is a great crime which cries to the avenging anger of Heaven. 'Behold, the hire of the laborers . . . which by fraud has been kept back by you, crieth; and the cry of them hath entered into the ears of the Lord of Sabaoth.'"[17] This insistence on respect for labor, while conveniently ignored by many in power, Roman Catholic growers and bishops alike, was part of Church teaching from the late nineteenth century into the present.[18] In the same encyclical where he wrote of the moral imperative of a just wage, Pope Leo XIII also wrote of the importance of unions.

> The most important of all are workingmen's unions, for these virtually include all the rest. . . . It is gratifying to know that there are actually in existence not a few associations of this nature, consisting either of workmen alone, or of workmen and employers together, but it were greatly to be desired that they should become more numerous and more efficient. We have spoken of them more than once, yet it will be well to explain here how notably they are needed, to show that they exist of their own right, and what should be their organization and their mode of action.[19]

The Church's long tradition of respect for workers shaped the family and faith context in which Dolores Huerta was raised and in which she grew. As discussed below, her upbringing shaped the ethos from and with which she spoke and worked, where faith in God, neighbor, and herself compelled her to take risks resulting in hope and labor rights for a generation of farmworkers in California and the nation. Where some Chicana feminists of her time rejected organized religion, specifically the Roman Catholic Church as hopelessly oppressive of women and aligned with the wealthy, Huerta learned from her mother. She constructed a faith and an ethos where the Church served as a source of justice and united people in an insistence of their own dignity and a demand for that same justice.

Huerta, like her mother, insisted on leaving unhealthy marriages; at the same time, she took from the Church that which was life-giving, sending her own children to Catholic schools, praying the rosary, and receiving Eucharist. In her later years, she commented on the importance of communion to the farmworkers, "The great thing was that [Chávez] always had the priest give absolution to people when we had these giant rallies and Masses with a thousand people. Then people could take communion."[20] She herself attended Mass weekly, and when she was at the home-base in Delano, she attended Masses with the UFW which, for several years, "had [their] own priest."[21]

LONG LINE OF RHETORS

Huerta's ethos was developed in the context of community, and Huerta's community shared a history of strong women rhetors. Here I mobilize the phrase "Long line of Rhetors," appropriating the words of Cherríe Moraga who reclaimed Doña Marina, also called Malintzín and Malinche, as a Chicana foremother, making the case that survival in a misogynist society is an act of resistance.[22] Born into a noble family but sold into slavery by them, Malintzín refused to be an object. This Indigenous rhetor survived among the Tabascans, until she was given as a prize of conquest to Cortés, ultimately becoming an indispensable translator for him and bearing their mestizo child.[23]

While male writers and activists often referred to Malinche as a race-traitor, during the late twentieth-century renaissance in Chicana feminism, Chicanas reclaimed this powerful icon. Malinche's family sold her into slavery yet she survived, they argued. Her survival was an act of resistance, both physical and rhetorical. Of importance to us here is that it was Malinche's speaking, her ability to translate from Maya to Nahuatl and, eventually, Spanish to Nahuatl, that made her indispensable to Cortés. Through her speech, she crafted a life of survival.[24] Cristina Devereaux Ramírez notes that from this act of translation emerges a theory of mestiza rhetoric, "the theory of mestiza rhetoric emerges in the moment Malintzín first spoke as translator, *not* when she gave birth to Cortés's child."[25] Thus, as Chicanas claiming the survival and resistance of the women who came before us from Malinche to our own mothers, we take part in a fraught yet powerful past. Mexicana and Chicana rhetors of the revolution built upon this legacy of resistance when they used their words to move a nation to action. Dolores Huerta built upon this same legacy when she called people to support the "revolution of the farm worker."[26] Dolores Huerta came from a long line of rhetors: the historico-mythic mother of mestiza women, and her daughters who spoke back from a place of community and social action to shape the world around them.

This heritage of strong women activists shaped and shapes the ethos of Chicana rhetors of Dolores Huerta's time and of our own. While some scholars write of Marianismo, or the expectation that Chicanas adopt the mythic submissiveness of the Virgin Mary, it is critical to acknowledge that we also share a rich heritage of rhetor-activists. The words and actions of mestiza women in Mexico and the United States are rich, deep, and complex. Following the bold survival of Malintzín, the Hieronymite nun Sor Juana Inés de la Cruz used her own words to challenge the double standard of seventeenth-century Mexico, going so far as to write feminist hymns. In a time when women were barred from formal education, Sor Juana became one of the leading poets of the Golden Age of Spanish literature.[27] Indigenous and mestiza women of her time took to the streets to demand food for their families.[28] Mexicana activism continued into the next century when, in 1778, women rose up in a strike against a work speedup at a factory in Mexico City.[29]

Chicana feminist rhetors trace their most direct lines to the women of the Mexican Revolution, a time of Mexicana activism in word and deed that supported the Revolution and demanded equality for women. It was at this time that Juana Gutiérrez de Mendoza, later praised as wielding her pen with the strength and acumen of Sor Juana Inés de la Cruz, published the paper *Vésper*, calling workers to organize and all Mexicans to revolution;[30] Elisa Acuña y Rossetti founded *La Guillotina*, a pro-Zapata newspaper; and Dolores Jiménez y Muro served as a brigadier general in Zapata's army. Like Huerta, Jiménez y Muro worked with her pen and her words to bring justice to exploited laborers. It was she who "wrote the preface to Zapata's program for agrarian reform in Mexico."[31] She also served as the president of Las Hijas de Cuauhtémoc, a revolutionary women's group that fought for women's political rights after the war.[32]

As noted by Gabriela Cano, the women of the Mexican Revolution fought for revolution *and* for women's rights "with their pens."[33] Their words and deeds demonstrate how rhetoric that moves people to action has a long and rich history among feministas. The power of such rhetoric was/is in community—in an ethos that functioned/s as a mediation—"a shared experience among members of a community, and the community decides, in turn, what constitutes justice, temperance, bravery, or ethics."[34]

The long line of women rhetors was not restricted to the Mexican side of the border. As Blackwell and Pérez note, our feminisms are not contained by the colonial border that scars our homelands.[35] At the turn of the century, while supporting Mexicana/o revolutionary efforts, Andrea and Teresa Villarreal published a feminist newspaper on this side of the border, *La Mujer Moderna*. They, like Sara Estela Ramírez, fought for justice in the United States and in Mexico.[36]

In writing of the words and deeds of Dolores Huerta, it is important to note that one of the most famous Chicana rhetor-activists of the early twentieth century was born in the United States—Emma Tenayuca. Tenayuca, like Huerta, was raised by a family that actively worked for justice and that valued the power of words. The grandparents who raised Tenayuca were readers of the Anarcho-Syndicalist paper *Regeneración*, and her grandfather took her to the *Plaza del Zacate* (a public square) on Sunday outings to listen to Magonistas, revolutionaries who spoke and organized on both sides of the border.

Tenayuca is best known as the leader of the 1939 pecan sheller's strike where over 6,000 workers participated, making it the largest labor strike in San Antonio up until that time.[37] By the age of seventeen, she was engaged in community activism, joined the picket line against the Finck Cigar factory, and was arrested.[38] Her niece would later reflect:

> She was compelled to do something about the human suffering she witnessed. She was aware of human injustice–even as a child. . . . Because of her deep compassion, she couldn't ignore it. It happened that she was a gifted speaker and organizer, and could mobilize workers. She was able to communicate to people that by working together, they could change their condition.[39]

Tenayuca was known as La Pasionaria (the passionate one), a name that would later be awarded to Dolores Huerta, calling to mind the ethos of justice and love of community possessed by both. Gabriela González notes that "[Tenayuca] organized men and women, formed coalition across ethnic lines, stormed the mayor's office, lead a historic strike, banged on the door of politicians, and stirred up large crowds with inspirational speeches that earned her the nickname La Pasionaria."[40] At her funeral, Carmen Tafolla dedicated a powerful poem speaking to her legacy,

La Pasionaria we called her,
bloom of passion,
because she was our passion
because she was our corazón-
defendiendo a los pobres,

speaking out at a time when neither Mexicans nor women
were expected to speak out at all.[41]

THEORY FROM OUR FLESH

While Chicanas and Mexicanas share a rich history of feminist rhetor-activists, Huerta's early life experiences beyond her family played an equally significant role in shaping her ethos. In this she was not unique from other Chicanas of her time. In speaking of Huerta's ethos, then, we must speak of the community ethos of her time, a time when, for Chicanas, personal and community ethē wove together in a dynamic and empowering demand for justice.

Huerta was at the forefront of a new era in Chicana feminism. Like the women of the Revolution and the labor activists of the 1930s (Emma Tenayuca, Josefina Fierro de Bright, and Luisa Moreno), Huerta took a leading role in labor and justice organizing in a time when few men recognized women as leaders. Her words and actions became part of a larger renaissance in Chicana feminism where women insisted on the sovereignty of their bodies, access to health care, education, and political voice. They challenged the gender roles that dominated not just Chicanx homes but homes of the dominant culture as well.[42]

The collective Chicana feminist ethos from which Huerta spoke and to which she contributed with her words and deeds was markedly different from the masculinist ethnonationalist ethos that came to dominate so many Chicanx organizations of the 1970s, especially those on college campuses.[43] The Chicano Movement of the late twentieth century was revolutionary: it critiqued U.S. imperialism and the U.S. war in Vietnam, it insisted on the dignity of workers, and it rejected rugged individualism. Yet the men of the movement, and some women as well, did not reject the patriarchal structures of the colonizers.

Chicana feminists, building on the words and deeds of generations of strong women, critiqued this flaw. Feminists such as Mirta Vidal mapped how the sexism against which they struggled was a product of colonial violence:

> The submission of women, along with institutions such as the church and the patriarchy, was imported by the European colonizers, and remains to this day part of Anglo society. Machismo—which as it is commonly used, translates in English into male chauvinism—is the one thing, if any, which should be labeled an "Anglo thing."[44]

Feminista organizations such as Las Hijas de Cuauhtémoc at California State University Long Beach, an organization that took its name from the revolutionary Mexicana organization of the same name, called attention to the structural roots of sexist violence, noting, "We recognize that we are oppressed as Raza and as women. We believe that the struggle is not with the male but the existing system of oppression. But the Chicano must also be educated to the problems and oppression of La Chicana so that he may not be used as a tool to divide by keeping man against women."[45] Throughout the movement, Chicanas built upon the work of their foremothers to create spaces of voice and power. Like the identity and discourse of Chicano nationalism, Chicana feminism engaged a discourse of family; however, the family it constructed was necessarily disruptive, allowing for women's leadership and building on the strong women rhetor-activists of the past. Eventually, as in the work of Anzaldúa, Moraga, Urquijo-Ruiz, and Galarte, it would queer the family and the very politics of Chicanismo.

WALKING THE PATH TO EL MUNDO ZURDO

The herencia that nourished the soil in which the young Huerta grew was rich. From rhetor nuns to labor encyclicals to a mother who took the Catholic faith and made it her own, Huerta's early years taught her the power and value of community and of the role of faith in creating a better world. Huerta took this rich heritage with her as she entered a life of activism. Not surprisingly, she entered onto this new path with her family.

Several biographers note her involvement in the Community Service Organization (CSO) as marking her shift from service work to activism and into lobbying and bold leadership. Fred Ross, its founder, recruited Huerta as a leader because of her leadership and rhetorical skills. Margaret Rose, one of her earliest biographers, documented that the move to the CSO was a family move. In the 1950s when Dolores Huerta became active in the CSO it was with her mother and her aunt.[46] Until this time, Huerta had been active in service organizations such as the Teresitas and Club Azul y Oro but not justice organizations.[47] The Community Service Organization, while it had "service" in its name, was very much a justice organization. The ethos with which Huerta would speak as vice president of the UFW, and later as the founder of the Dolores Huerta Foundation, was familial and communal.

Huerta worked for the CSO from 1955 to 1962, registering voters, fighting against police harassment, and working for health care for the poor. By the time she left the CSO, she had also successfully lobbied legislators at the state capital for, among other things, an old-age pension, the right to register voters door-to-door, and bilingual drivers' license exams. Her lobbying experience was an asset when, with César Chávez, she went on to cofound the UFW.[48] By the 1970s, her words and deeds were indispensable to the success of the UFW. Margaret Rose wrote of Huerta's daily, fierce activism:

> A four-day trip to Michigan in 1974 [typified] her total immersion and dedication to *la causa*:
>
> In addition to boycott day, Dolores participated in a rally on the University of Michigan [Ann Arbor] campus, an Ecumenical Service in Detroit, a reception of trade union women, sponsored by the Coalition of Labor Union Women (CLUW) and a Mexican Independence Day Celebration in Pontiac Michigan. Dolores appeared on two television programs, radio programs and did taped interviews. On the boycott day rally we got news coverage on 2 Detroit T.V. stations, a newspaper story, several radio stations and three feature articles were written on Dolores.[49]

While Huerta was quickly becoming the consummate feminista rhetor-activist, the faith and the family that so strongly influenced her values—her mother, her aunt, and her grandfather continued to shape her words and deeds well into the next century. It shaped her leaving the CSO to help found the UFW, raising her own children in the Catholic faith, and speaking out for LGBTQ rights.

EXPANSIVE QUEER FAITH—EXPANSIVE QUEER ETHOS

In January 2009, Huerta was invited to deliver the keynote address at the Twenty-first National Conference on LGBT Equality. Held in Denver, Colorado, a local newspaper wrote of her upcoming address, including a brief biography of her life with excerpts from an interview where she spoke of her approach to organizing: "We have a lot of groups, like silos, but not a lot of cross-fertilization between the organizations, I think we need to hook up joint forces of people who are working on different progressive issues, like gay rights, immigrants' rights, pro-choice, the peace and anti-war movements. People need to come together."[50]

The interview foreshadowed the speech to come, where she would pull the audience into her communal ethos and call them together,

> But we're all together now. We're going to reach out to each other, we're going to come together, we're going to walk the union picket lines, we're going to write letters for legislation, for the [Employee] Free Choice Act, to stop incarcerations of our Latino and African-American youth. Okay? More money for education. We're going to come together, to work together, and we're going to

> say, in Spanish, working together we can make it happen. Bring on human rights for everyone. Sí se puede.[51]

Huerta's call for and to action flowed from a larger context of faith, where a critical people's faith, passed down from her mother and grandfather, shaped the ethos from which she spoke and helped to make her work possible. She left a salaried job, helped found an agricultural union when earlier unions had failed, and raised her family in voluntary poverty. Equally important, it anchored her, as from an enfleshed ethos, she insisted on women's rights and LGBTQ rights as central to working for justice; she rejected "silos," making visible Anzaldúa's Mundo Zurdo. Her ethos functioned to pull her audiences into a world of word and deed, reminding them that they were part of a larger human family that needed to work and pray for each other.

As argued by Sowards, faith was not an additive to Huerta's work; it was central.[52] This intersection of faith and action was present in even the most basic watersheds of her children's lives. Raising her eleven children in voluntary poverty while working to change the world was an act of faith in action. Huerta chose to raise her children in the Church, which meant public rituals of faith celebrated as specific coming-of-age markers in their lives: first communion and, for many as well, confirmation. Huerta later recalled how her daughter did not have decent shoes for her Confirmation, yet that poverty was both a product of her faith and constitutive of it. She reflected,

> I didn't have money to buy my daughter Celeste shoes for her confirmation and so she had these white shoes [that] were all torn with holes on them . . . and I see Celeste coming down the aisle with her torn tennis shoes and I'm kind of flinching, and just behind her, there's several farm worker children that are down the aisle with torn tennis shoes and to me that was a sign.[53]

A faith that witnessed grace in the everyday where words and deeds are rooted in and committed to the well-being of the community allowed Huerta to build community and to move people to action. So it was that in Denver she called LGBTQ communities to action: words and deeds. She spoke from a space of expansive community—where ethos is "a mediation."[54] She consistently used the first person plural, stressing the unity of herself with the audience: "we need to educate each other about each other's movements," "another way our movements here can come together [is] to put the pressure on congress people and our senators, [and] say vote for legalization for all of our undocumented people that we have in our country right now." By the end of her keynote, speaking from an ethos of expansive Catholic Chicanisma, she had called her audience to join together, to lobby, and to pray.

Throughout her 2009 address, justice was treated as a seamless garment. The influence of her mother as well as Benito Juárez and the papal encyclicals were present in her opening call to justice, which was not about LGBTQ equality as an isolated issue but of the growing income gap in America, "If we look back, say, forty years ago, you know, what a chief executive officer of a corporation got compared to a worker was maybe forty times more than a worker. Well today, it's almost close to five hundred more than a worker."[55] Having provided that economic context Huerta called on the community to lobby. As the preeminent Chicana lobbyist, her credentials, her years of Chicana feminist words and deeds, allowed her to use her ethos to normalize such action on the part of all. And so she called on the conference participants to "put pressure on our congress people and our senators, say vote for legislation for all of our undocumented people."[56] From a zurdo ethos, Huerta spoke of science and she spoke of historical coalitions, such as that between the farmworker movement and the effort to get Harvey Milk elected to the board of supervisors in San Francisco.

Perhaps the clearest example of this expansive ethos was her call for conference participants to pray for the former evangelical preacher Tim Haggard. Three years earlier, Haggard, who had preached that marriage equality was contrary to Christian values, was exposed as sexually active outside his marriage, that is, sexually active with a male prostitute with whom he sometimes consumed illegal drugs. Haggard resigned his position as pastor of the megachurch New Life and tried his hand at the insurance business. But just as the negative publicity and scandal surrounding his life's contradictions seemed to have calmed, news broke out of other same-sex encounters and relationships. News also broke of New Life offering a settlement to another young man with whom he had an affair.[57] While some might have been inclined to lash out at the hypocrisy of Haggard, indeed, some in the press did, Huerta's response was compassion—public compassion. In her address, she asked the queer audience to pray:

> Here we have that movie about Harvey Milk that's being nominated, and also in the newspaper we have this other movie that's about the Preacher Haggard, right? And they were saying, the Larry King show was saying, that he was a disgraced preacher. And I was just watching the interview that Larry King was having before I came over here, and he's trying to say, "Yes, I still have sexual thoughts," and I thought to myself. This poor guy. Why is he disgraced? Is he disgraced because he had sex with a prostitute, or are they saying he's disgraced because the man has gay, sexual thoughts? I think it's very, very sad for Mr. Haggard. I think we should all pray for him to get the courage to come out, okay?[58]

And so Huerta asked the crowd to pray for Haggard and then she reminded them of their shared humanity:

> So, we have only one human race, and where did our human race begin? Africa. We have a very educated group here, yes. Africa, yes. As our human race went across the planet they went to the Orient, Asia, got lighter in skin, came down the Bering Strait to the Americas. One of our tribes got lost. They went way up north where it's really cold and they got really really white. . . . So if we can remember this, that we're all one human family. We're all related—we're all brothers and sisters.[59]

By her words, she brought the audience into her reality, a world without borders, shaped by her faith, her struggle, and the strong women who came before her.

Then she brought the people to church. For Huerta, for whom labor was/is sacred, and for whom it was critical that the whole community be able to participate in communion, the power of unity and community had to be brought into the space. Bringing the audience into communion with each other for the cause of justice she concluded:

> So now, let's do a couple of "vivas." Vivas means "long live," okay. I want to say one for Harvey Milk. I'll say, "Long live Harvey Milk" and we'll all shout "Viva!" at the top of our lungs and we'll say one for César Chávez, also whose spirit is still with us, the spirit of non-violence and of serving others. All right? Okay. I'll go first and you just shout "viva!" at the top of your lungs.

Huerta's call to the audience to come together to chant and shout "viva" and "Sí se puede" was not incidental but part of the Catholic and feminist ethos from which she spoke. Over two decades earlier, at the close of her keynote address at the Annual Convention of the American Public Health Association, she told the participants "This is very important. This is like kind of praying together in unison."[60] The ability to see people together shouting for justice as prayer was not an aberration but a product of a lifetime of faith in action:

Viva Harvey Milk!
Viva César Chávez!
Viva Dr. Martin Luther King!

Milk, Chávez, King—by the 1990s, Huerta's ethos was queer, indeed, queer and Catholic. For any who did not follow the development and deployment of that ethos over time, this might be surprising; however, given the strong role of a pragmatic and expansive faith in her life and the life of her mother, such expansiveness can be seen as the consequence of a life well lived, a matured response to life's ongoing contradictions. In calling on LGBTQ communities to advocate for all humankind, Huerta claimed LGBTQ communities as part of her constituency, her zurdo world, her world beyond silos.

The expansive ethos from which Dolores Huerta addressed the Twenty-first National Conference on LGBT Equality grew from the deep soil of New Mexico and Stockton, California. It was nurtured by a mother and aunt and grandfather who saw young Chicanas as fully human. It was nourished by a faith that questioned. Her mother modeled how a woman could reject the hierarchy's letter of the law and choose healthy relationships, even while raising her children in the faith—a faith built not on traditions such as Mass and rosaries alone, but also on justice and a commitment to the poor: "El respeto al derecho ajeno es la paz." In her work as a rhetor-activist, Huerta did not stand alone. While she stood as a beacon to other Chicana rhetor-activists of her generation and the generation that followed, she came from a long line of rhetors. Her words and deeds, planted in community and nourished by her family, fueled an expansive, dynamic, and zurdo ethos calling communities across generations to action.

NOTES

1. Kathleen J. Ryan, Nancy Myers, and Rebecca Jones, "Introduction: Identifying Feminist Ecological Ethē," in *Rethinking Ethos: A Feminist Ecological Approach to Rhetoric*, eds. Kathleen J. Ryan, Nancy Myers, and Rebecca Jones (Carbondale: Southern Illinois University Press 2016), 6.

2. Nedra Reynolds, "Ethos as Location: New Sites for Understanding Discursive Authority," *Rhetoric Review* 11 no. 2 (Spring 1993): 328.

3. Reynolds, "Ethos as Location," 329.

4. Cherríe Moraga and Gloria E. Anzaldúa, *This Bridge Called My Back : Writings by Radical Women of Color* (Watertown, MA: Persephone Press, 1981); Ada Isasi-Díaz and Yolanda Tarango, *Hispanic Women: Prophetic Voice in the Church* (Minneapolis: Fortress Press, 1992); Audre Lorde, *Sister Outsider: Essays and Speeches* (Trumansburg, NY: Crossing Press, 1984).

5. Moraga and Anzaldúa, *This Bridge*. See also Dolores Delgado Bernal, "Using a Chicana Feminist Epistemology in Educational Research," *Harvard Educational Review* 68, no. 4 (Winter 1998): 555–581, https://doi:10.17763/haer.68.4.5wv1034973g22q48; Candace Zepeda, "Chicana Feminism," in *Decolonizing Rhetoric and Composition Studies: New Latinx Keywords for Theory and Pedagogy*, eds. Iris D. Ruiz and Raúl Sánchez (New York: Palgrave Macmillan US, 2016), 137–151. doi:10.1057/978-1-137-52724-0-10.

6. Gloria E. Anzaldúa, "La Prieta," in *This Bridge Called My Back: Writings by Radical Women of Color*, eds. Cherríe Moraga and Gloria Anzaldúa, 3rd edition (Berkeley: Third Woman Press, 2002), 233.

7. Margaret Rose, "Dolores Huerta: The United Farm Worker's Union," in *A Dolores Huerta Reader*, ed. Mario T. García (Albuquerque: University of New

Mexico Press, 2008), 44: Christine Beagle, "Siete Lenguas: The Rhetorical History of Dolores Huerta and The Rise of Chicana Rhetoric" (PhD diss., University of New Mexico, 2015), 44.

8. Gloria E. Anzaldúa, *Borderlands/La Frontera: The New Mestiza*, 4th edition (San Francisco: Aunt Lute, 2012), 25.

9. Beagle, *Siete Lenguas*, 45.

10. Beagle, *Siete Lenguas*, 41–44; Richard Griswold del Castillo and Richard A. Garcia, *César Chávez: A Triumph of Spirit* (Norman: University of Oklahoma Press, 1995), 62–64.

11. California Museum Activity Guide, "Dolores Huerta Girl Scout Patch," 3, https://www.californiamuseum.org/sites/main/files/file-attachments/camuseum_girlscouts_doloreshuertapatch_activitysheet_0.pdf.

12. Stacey K. Sowards, *¡Sí, Ella Puede!: The Rhetorical Legacy of Dolores Huerta and the United Farm Workers* (Austin: University of Texas Press, 2019), 35–36; Beagle, *Siete Lenguas*, 41–42; Alicia Chávez, "Dolores Huerta and the United Farm Workers," in *Latina Legacies: Identity, Biography, and Community*, eds. Vicki L. Ruiz and Virginia Sánchez Korral (Oxford: Oxford University Press, 2005), 242.

13. Margaret Rose, "Dolores Huerta: The United Farm Worker's Union," in *A Dolores Huerta Reader*, ed. Mario T. García (Albuquerque: University of New Mexico Press, 2008), 9.

14. Dolores Delgado Bernal, "Using a Chicana Feminist Epistemology in Educational Research." *Harvard Educational Review* 68, no. 4 (Winter 1998): 561, 570, https://doi:10.17763/haer.68.4.5wv1034973g22q48.

15. Dolores Huerta, "Dolores Huerta on Spirituality: Interview with Mario T. García, June 1, 2007," in *A Dolores Huerta Reader*, ed. Mario García (Albuquerque: University of New Mexico, 2008), 333.

16. Vincent Harding, "Interview with Dolores Huerta," in *A Dolores Huerta Reader*, ed. Mario T. García (Albuquerque: New Mexico UP, 2008), 185.

17. Leo XIII, "Rerum Novarum," The Holy See (May 15, 1891), Par. 20. http://www.vatican.va/content/leo-xiii/en/encyclicals/documents/hf_l-xiii_enc_15051891_rerum-novarum.html.

18. Marco G. Prouty, *César Chávez, the Catholic Bishops, and the Farmworkers' Struggle for Social Justice* (Tucson: University of Arizona Press, 2006), 4, 29–50.

19. Leo XIII, "Rerum Novarum," par. 49.

20. Mario T. García, "Dolores Huerta on Spirituality: Interview with Mario T. García, June 1, 2007," in *A Dolores Huerta Reader*, ed. Mario T. García (Albuquerque: University of New Mexico Press, 2008), 337.

21. Griswold del Castillo and Richard García, *César Chávez*, 334, 342.

22. Cherríe Moraga, *Loving in the War Years: Lo Que Nunca Pasó Por Sus Labios* (Cambridge, MA South End Press, 1983).

23. Pilar Godayol, "Malintzin/La Malinche/Doña Marina: Re-Reading the Myth of the Treacherous Translator," *Journal of Iberian and Latin-American Studies* 18, no. 1 (2012): 63–65. See also Adelaida R. Del Castillo, "Malintzín Tenepal: A Preliminary Look into a New Perspective," in *Essays on La Mujer*, eds. Rosaura Sánchez and Rosa Martínez Cruz, 1973 (Los Angeles: Chicano Studies Center Publication, 1977), 62–64.

24. Del Castillo, "Malintzín Tenepal," 124–129; Cordelia Candelaria, "La Malinche, Feminist Prototype," *Frontiers: A Journal of Women Studies* 5, no. 2 (Summer 1980): 1–6; Norma Alarcón, "Chicana's Feminist Literature: A Re-vision through Malintzín/or Malintzín: Putting Flesh Back on the Object," in *This Bridge Called My Back*, 202–211; Caroline Tracey, "La Malinche Chicana," *Nexos (México)* 41, no. 497 (2019), https://www.nexos.com.mx/?p=42178.

25. Cristina Devereaux Ramírez, *Occupying Our Space: The Mestiza Rhetorics of Mexican Women Journalists and Activists, 1875–1942* (Tucson: University of Arizona Press, 2015), 39.

26. Dolores Huerta, "1966 March and Rally in Sacramento." Farmworker Movement Documentation Project, https://libraries.ucsd.edu/farmworkermovement/media/oral_history/ParadigmArchive/arc%2029.pdf.

27. Electa Arenal and Amanda Powell, *The Answer/La Respuesta : Including a Selection of Poems* (New York: Feminist Press, 1994), 31–36, 148–149.

28. Rita E. Urquijo Ruiz, "Researching Chicana Role Models: Indigenous Women's Participation in the Corn Riots of 1692" (paper presented at the National Association for Chicana/Chicano Studies *(NACCS)*, Chicago, IL, March 2002).

29. Adelina Zendejas, "Ellas y La Vida: Lucha y Conquista De Los Derechos Femeninos," *Debate Feminista* 8 (1993): 401, www.jstor.org/stable/42624164.

30. Devereaux Ramírez, *Occupying Our Space*, 138.

31. Yolanda Alaniz and Megan Cornish, *Viva la Raza: A History of Chicano Identity and Resistance* (Seattle: Red Letter Press, 2008), 96.

32. Alaniz and Cornish, *Viva la Raza*, 95–96; Maylei Blackwell, *¡Chicana Power!* (Austin: University of Texas Press, 2011), 104–109.

33. Gabriela Cano, "Más de un Siglo de Feminism en México," *Debate Feminista* 14 (October 1996): 347.

34. Reynolds, "New Sites for Understanding," 328.

35. Blackwell, *¡Chicana Power!*, 18, 103–109; Emma Pérez, *The Decolonial Imaginary: Writing Chicanas into History* (Bloomington: Indiana University Press, 1999), 55–74.

36. Blackwell, *¡Chicana Power!* 107–109; Alaniz and Cornish, *Viva la Raza*, 96; Pérez, 68–69.

37. Blackwell, *¡Chicana Power!* 48–49; Beagle, *Siete Lenguas*, 89–90; Vicki L. Ruiz, *From Out of the Shadows*, 78–80.

38. Gabriela González, "Carolina Munguía and Emma Tenayuca: The Politics of Benevolence and Radical Reform," *Frontiers: A Journal of Women Studies* 24, no. 2/3 (2003): 200–229. http://www.jstor.org/stable/3347357; Arlene Sánchez-Walsh, "Emma Tenayuca, Religious Elites, and the 1938 Pecan-Shellers' Strike," in *The Pew and the Picket Line: Christianity and the American Working Class*, eds. Christopher D. Cantwell et al. (Champaign: University of Illinois Press, 2016), 145–162.

39. González, "Carolina Munguía and Emma Tenayuca," 211.

40. González, "Carolina Munguía and Emma Tenayuca," 221–222.

41. González, "Carolina Munguía and Emma Tenayuca," 233.

42. Blackwell, *¡Chicana Power!*, 168–171.

43. Francisco J. Galarte, "Transgender Chican@ Poetics: Contesting, Interrogating, and Transforming Chicana/o Studies," *Chicana/Latina Studies* 13, no. 2 (Spring 2014): 127. Galarte, in addressing the emergence of a trans Chican@ ethos, argues that trans Chican@ activism and, in relation, a trans Chican@ ethos, are possible because of the work of Chicana feminists who emerged from and worked within the Chicano movement of the late twentieth century while rejecting the masculinist ethos which dominated many organizations.

44. Mirta Vidal, *Chicanas Speak Out*—Women*: The New Voice of La Raza* (Atlanta: Pathfinder Press, 1971), 6, Duke University Libraries, Repository Collections and Archives, https://repository.duke.edu/dc/wlmpc/wlmms01005.

45. Blackwell, *¡Chicana Power!*, 87.

46. Rose "Dolores Huerta," 11.

47. Rose "Dolores Huerta," 10; K.K. Ottesen, "Heeding the Call of Activism," *Washington Post*, July 10, 2017. *Gale In Context: Opposing Viewpoints*, https://ntserver1.wsulibs.wsu.edu:2482/apps/doc/A498249114/OVIC?u=pull21986&sid=OVIC&xid=a0bc7769.

48. Richard Griswold del Castillo and Richard Garcia, *César Chávez*, 67–68; Julie Felner, "Woman of the Year," in *A Dolores Huerta Reader*, ed. Mario T. García (Albuquerque: University of New Mexico Press, 2008), 127.

49. Margaret Rose, "Traditional and Nontraditional Patterns of Female Activism in the United Farm Workers of America," in *A Dolores Huerta Reader*, ed. Mario T. García (University of New Mexico Press, 2008), 61.

50. Huerta, quoted in Coleen O'Connor, "Gay-Rights Activists Seek Change," *Denver Post*, January 27, 2009, https://www.denverpost.com/2009/01/27/gay-rights-activitists-seek-change-at-conference-in-denver/.

51. Dolores Huerta, "Keynote Speech at 21st National Conference on LGBT Equality," Denver Colorado, January 29, 2009, Iowa State University Archives of Women's Political Communication, https://awpc.cattcenter.iastate.edu/2017/03/09/keynote-speech-at-21st-national-conference-on-lgbt-equality-jan-29-2009/.

52. Sowards, *¡Sí, Ella Puede!*, 113–127.

53. Sowards, *¡Sí, Ella Puede!*, 109.

54. Reynolds, "New Sites for Understanding," 328.

55. Huerta, "Keynote."

56. Huerta, "Keynote."

57. "New Allegations Surface against Haggard," *Christian Century*, February 2009, 17; 53–54, *EBSCOhost*, search.ebscohost.com/login.aspx?direct=true&db=a9h&AN=36634857&site=ehost-live.

58. Huerta "Keynote"

59. Huerta "Keynote"

60. Sowards, *¡Sí, Ella Puede!*, 116.

BIBLIOGRAPHY

Alaniz, Yolanda and Megan Cornish. *Viva la Raza: A History of Chicano Identity and Resistance*. Seattle: Red Letter Press, 2008.

Alarcón, Norma. "Chicana's Feminist Literature: A Re-Vision through Malintzín/ or Malintzín: Putting Flesh Back on the Object." In *This Bridge Called My Back: Writings by Radical Women of Color*, edited by Cherríe Moraga and Gloria Anzaldúa, 3rd edition, 202–211 Berkeley: Third Woman Press, 2002.

Anzaldúa, Gloria. "La Prieta." In *This Bridge Called My Back: Writings by Radical Women of Color*, edited by Cherríe Moraga and Gloria Anzaldúa, 3rd edition, 220–233. Berkeley: Third Woman Press, 2002.

Anzaldúa, Gloria. *Borderlands/La Frontera: The New Mestiza*, 4th edition. San Francisco: Aunt Lute, 2012.

Arenal, Electa and Amanda Powell. *The Answer/La Respuesta : Including a Selection of Poems*. New York: Feminist Press, 1994.

Beagle, Christine. "Siete Lenguas: The Rhetorical History of Dolores Huerta and the Rise of Chicana Rhetoric." PhD diss., University of New Mexico, 2015.

Bernal, Dolores Delgado. "Using a Chicana Feminist Epistemology in Educational Research." *Harvard Educational Review* 68, no. 4 (Winter 1998): 555–81. https://doi:10.17763/haer.68.4.5wv1034973g22q48.

Bernal, Dolores Delgado. "Learning and Living Pedagogies of the Home: The Mestiza Consciousness of Chicana Students." *International Journal of Qualitative Studies in Education* 14, no. 5 (2001): 623–639. https://doi:10.1080/09518390110059838.

Blackwell, Maylei. *¡Chicana Power!* Austin: University of Texas Press, 2011.

California Museum Activity Guide. "Dolores Huerta Girl Scout Patch." Accessed July 28, 2020. https://www.californiamuseum.org/sites/main/files/file-attachments/camuseum_girlscouts_doloreshuertapatch_activitysheet_0.pdf.

Candelaria, Cordelia. "La Malinche, Feminist Prototype." *Frontiers: A Journal of Women Studies* 5, no. 2 (Summer 1980): 1–6.

Cano, Gabriela. "Más de un Siglo de Feminism en México." *Debate Feminista* 14 (October 1996): 345–360.

Chávez, Alicia. "Dolores Huerta and the United Farm Workers." In *Latina Legacies: Identity, Biography, and Community*, edited by Vicki L. Ruiz and Virginia Sánchez Korral, 240–254. Oxford: Oxford University Press, 2005.

Cypess, Sandra Messinger. *La Malinche in Mexican Literature from History to Myth*. Albuquerque: University of Texas Press, 1991.

Del Castillo, Adelaida R. "Malintzín Tenepal: A Preliminary Look into a New Perspective." In *Essays on La Mujer*, edited by Rosaura Sánchez and Rosa Martínez Cruz, 124–129. Los Angeles: Chicano Studies Center Publication, 1977.

Devereaux Ramírez, Cristina. *Occupying Our Space: The Mestiza Rhetorics of Mexican Women Journalists and Activists, 1875–1942*. Tucson: University of Arizona, 2015.

Dokoupil, Tony. "The Lost Shepherd." *Newsweek*, January 19, 2009, pp. 53–54. Academic Search Complete.

Felner, Julie. "Woman of the Year." In *A Dolores Huerta Reader*, edited by Mario T. García, 133–139. Albuquerque: University of New Mexico Press, 2008.

Fremantle, Anne, and Weigel, Gustave. *The Papal Encyclicals in their Historical Context*. New York: Putnam, 1956.

Galarte, Francisco J. "Transgender Chican@ Poetics: Contesting, Interrogating, and Transforming Chicana/o Studies." *Chicana/Latina Studies* 13, no. 2 (Spring 2014): 118–139.

García, Mario T. "Dolores Huerta on Spirituality: Interview with Mario T. García, June 1, 2007." In *A Dolores Huerta Reader*, edited by Mario T. García, 331–345. Albuquerque: University of New Mexico Press, 2008.

Godayol, Pilar. "Malintzin/La Malinche/Doña Marina: Re-Reading the Myth of the Treacherous Translator." *Journal of Iberian and Latin-American Studies* 18, no. 1 (2012):61–76. http://doi:10.1080/14701847.2012.716645.

González, Gabriela. "Carolina Munguía and Emma Tenayuca: The Politics of Benevolence and Radical Reform." *Frontiers: A Journal of Women Studies* 24, no. 2/3 (2003): 200–229. http://www.jstor.org/stable/3347357.

Griswold del Castillo, Richard, and Garcia, Richard A. *César Chávez: A Triumph of Spirit.* Norman: University of Oklahoma Press, 1995.

Harding, Vincent. "Interview with Dolores Huerta." In *A Dolores Huerta Reader*, edited by Mario T. García, 177–185. Albuquerque: New Mexico University Press, 2008.

Hrynkow, Christopher W. "'If You Want Peace, Work for Justice:' Assessing Pope Paul VI as a Peacebuilder on the Levels of Insight and Action." *Peace and Conflict Studies*. 24, no. 2 (2017): Article 2. https://nsuworks.nova.edu/pcs/vol24/iss2/2.

Huerta, Dolores. "Keynote Speech at 21st National Conference on LGBT Equality." Denver Colorado, January 29, 2009. Iowa State University Archives of Women's Political Communication. https://awpc.cattcenter.iastate.edu/2017/03/09/keynote-speech-at-21st-national-conference-on-lgbt-equality-jan-29-2009/.

Huerta, Dolores. "Dolores Huerta on Spirituality: Interview with Mario T. García, June 1, 2007." In *A Dolores Huerta Reader*, edited by Mario García, 331–345. Albuquerque: University of New Mexico, 2008.

Huerta, Dolores. "1966 March and Rally in Sacramento." Farmworker Movement Documentation Project. https://libraries.ucsd.edu/farmworkermovement/media/oral_history/ParadigmArchive/arc%2029.pdf.

Isasi-Díaz, Ada and Yolanda Tarango. *Hispanic Women: Prophetic Voice in the Church*. 1988. Minneapolis: Fortress Press, 1992.

Leo XIII. "Rerum Novarum." The Holy See. May 15, 1891. http://www.vatican.va/content/leo-xiii/en/encyclicals/documents/hf_l-xiii_enc_15051891_rerum-novarum.html.

Lorde, Audre. *Sister Outside: Essays and Speeches*. Trumansburg, NY: Crossing Press, 1984.

Moraga, Cherríe, *Loving in the War Years: Lo Que Nunca Pasó Por Sus Labios*. Cambridge, MA: South End Press, 1983.

Moraga, Cherríe and Gloria E. Anzaldúa. *This Bridge Called My Back: Writings by Radical Women of Color*. Watertown, MA: Persephone Press, 1981.

"New Allegations Surface against Haggard." *Christian Century*, February 2009. *EBSCOhost*, search.ebscohost.com/login.aspx?direct=true&db=a9h&AN=36634857&site=ehost-live.

O'Connor, Coleen. "Gay-Rights Activists Seek Change." *Denver Post*, January 27, 2009. https://www.denverpost.com/2009/01/27/gay-rights-activitists-seek-change-at-conference-in-denver/.

Ottesen, KK. "Heeding the Call of Activism." *Washington Post*, July 10, 2017. *Gale In Context: Opposing Viewpoints*, https://ntserver1.wsulibs.wsu.edu:2482/apps/doc/A498249114/OVIC?u=pull21986&sid=OVIC&xid=a0bc7769.

Pérez. Emma. *The Decolonial Imaginary: Writing Chicanas into History.* Bloomington: Indiana University Press, 1999.

Prouty, Marco G. *César Chávez, the Catholic Bishops, and the Farmworkers' Struggle for Social Justice.* Tucson: University of Arizona Press, 2006.

Reynolds, Nedra. "Ethos as Location: New Sites for Understanding Discursive Authority." *Rhetoric Review* 11 no. 2 (Spring 1993): 325–338.

Rose, Margaret. "Dolores Huerta: The United Farm Worker's Union." In *A Dolores Huerta Reader*, edited by Mario T. García, 3–22. Albuquerque: University of New Mexico Press, 2008.

Rose, Margaret. "Traditional and Nontraditional Patterns of Female Activism in the United Farm Workers of America." In *A Dolores Huerta Reader*, edited by Mario T. García, 53–73. University of New Mexico Press, 2008.

Ruiz, Vicki L. *From Out of the Shadows: Mexican Women in Twentieth-century America.* New York: Oxford University Press, 2008. *ProQuest Ebook Central.* https://ntserver1.wsulibs.wsu.edu:2171/lib/wsu/detail.action?docID=472363.

Ryan, Kathleen J., Nancy Myers, and Rebecca Jones. "Introduction: Identifying Feminist Ecological Ethē." In *Rethinking Ethos: A Feminist Ecological Approach to Rhetoric*, edited by Kathleen J. Ryan, Nancy Myers, and Rebecca Jones, 1–22. Carbondale: Southern Illinois UP, 2016.

Sánchez-Walsh, Arlene. "Emma Tenayuca, Religious Elites, and the 1938 Pecan-Shellers' Strike." In *The Pew and the Picket Line: Christianity and the American Working Class*, edited by Christopher D. Cantwell et al., 145–166. Champaign: University of Illinois Press, 2016.

Sowards, Stacey K. *¡Sí, Ella Puede!: The Rhetorical Legacy of Dolores Huerta and the United Farm Workers.* Austin: University of Texas Press, 2019.

Tafolla, Carmen. "La Pasionaria." *Frontiers: A Journal of Women Studies* 24, no. 2/3 (2003): 233–236. www.jstor.org/stable/3347359.

Tracey, Caroline. "La Malinche Chicana." *Nexos (México)* 41, no. 497 (2019). https://www.nexos.com.mx/?p=42178.

Urquijo-Ruiz, Rita E. "Researching Chicana Role Models: Indigenous Women's Participation in the Corn Riots of 1692." *National Association for Chicana/Chicano Studies (NACCS)*, Chicago, IL, March 2002.

Vargas, Zaragoza, "Tejana Radical: Emma Tenayuca and the San Antonio Lavor Movement during the Great Depression." *Pacific Historical Review* 66, no. 4 (1997): 553–580.

Vidal, Mirta. *Chicanas Speak Out—Women: The New Voice of La Raza.* Pathfinder Press, 1971. Duke University Libraries, Repository Collections and Archives. https://repository.duke.edu/dc/wlmpc/wlmms01005.

Zendejas, Adelina. "Ellas y La Vida: Lucha y Conquista De Los Derechos Femeninos." *Debate Feminista* 8 (1993): 401–413. www.jstor.org/stable/42624164. Accessed August 10, 2020.

Zepeda, Candace. "Chicana Feminism." In *Decolonizing Rhetoric and Composition Studies: New Latinx Keywords for Theory and Pedagogy*, edited by Iris D. Ruiz and Raúl Sánchez, 137–151. New York: Palgrave Macmillan US, 2016. doi:10.1057/978-1-137-52724-0-10.

Part IV

WOMEN RELIGIOUS' NEGOTIATIONS OF ETHOS

Chapter 12

Sister Miriam Joseph's Rhetorical Advocacy

The Trivium and Renaissance Rhetoric at St. Mary's College, 1931–1960

Joseph Burzynski

In "Dreams and Play: Historical Method and Methodology," Robert Connors offers one of the more evocative metaphors for historical work: "All of historical work, then, is provisional, partial—fragments we shore against our ruin. We are trying to make sense of things. It is always a construction. It is always tottering."[1] If we extend the metaphor, we can consider histories as more or less stable structures and evaluate how they figuratively adhere to disciplinary codes and zoning. The problem—indeed, feature—of historiography is that it is, as Connors suggests, provisional, partial, fragmentary, and incomplete. We are always making our case.

In Cinthia Gannett and John Brereton's collection *Traditions of Eloquence: The Jesuits and Modern Rhetorical Studies*, Jesuits engage rhetoric to be, depending on the period in Jesuit educational history, in/visible, survive, flourish, thrive, or revived. Narratively, this telling of rhetorical history presents the Jesuits as prime agents and catalysts for rhetorical education and, particularly, rhetoric in higher education in the United States. The collection certainly makes a convincing case for the importance and conspicuity of rhetoric in Jesuit educational tradition, and it makes the case that among all communities religious, the Jesuits, as individual scholars, teachers, and as a collective with an educational mission, have, perhaps, the most responsibility for the mid-twentieth-century rhetorical revival. As Gannett and Brereton note in their chapter of their collection, the early twentieth-century split between English and communications saw rhetoric *survive* in speech classes and only be *revived* midcentury by Jesuits like Walter Ong and Daniel Fogarty as well as those trained by Jesuits, most significantly, Edward

Corbett.[2] This Jesuit-centered narrative is dominant for a very good reason: the figures who were in the Jesuit ecosystem have shaped our modern sense of the discipline for nearly seventy-five years.

How, then, does the idea of a Jesuit-inspired midcentury rhetoric survival shift when we come across Sister Miriam Joseph's 1937 *The Trivium in College Composition and Reading*? She was not Jesuit educated, nor did she have a Marshall McLuhan type figure like Walter Ong. Further, what does it mean to rhetoric's revival in the 1950s when her *Shakespeare's Use of the Arts of Language* appeared in 1947, three years before the first edition of *College Composition and Communication*? Each of these texts contains a rhetorical spark that shines faintly in what a Jesuit-centered rhetorical history might label an early twentieth-century rhetorical dark age. Joseph's rhetorical teaching, scholarship, leadership, and advocacy serve as an important reminder that all histories, indeed, are tottering.

In this chapter, I will outline Joseph's advocacy and contributions to early twentieth-century composition and rhetoric studies, compare ways that she, as a member of a Catholic women's religious community, argued for and shaped a pedagogy that both followed and departed from the Jesuits, as well as discuss how her advocate/advocacy ethos may have limited her influence in mid-twentieth-century rhetoric and composition disciplinary conversations that oriented toward classical rhetoric and an Aristotelian sense of ethos.

THE TRIVIUM AT ST. MARY'S

When the first issue of *College Composition and Communication* was published in 1950, the twenty-eight executive committee members were listed by institution, as is still customary today, and further organized by institutional categories. Listed as representing Liberal Arts Colleges and St. Mary's College is Sister Miriam Joseph, C.S.C.[3] Sister Miriam Lenore Joseph Rauh, a member of the Sisters of the Holy Cross, earned her bachelor's degree from St. Mary's and her PhD from Columbia University. She began teaching at St. Mary's College in 1931, and she served as department chair in 1947–1969.[4] In the early years of *College Composition and Communication* and the Conference (CCCC), Joseph's name stands out as a member of a Catholic congregation and can be found scattered throughout Secretary's Reports documenting her participation and reelection to the Executive Committee and presence on a variety of workshops with titles like "Organization and Administration of the Freshman Composition Course" and "Composition Career After Freshmen Year."[5,6] The early front matter and committee reports of composition and rhetoric's then nascent flagship conference and journal remind the contemporary scholar that some of the topics we churn over have a timeless quality and, to echo the George Orwell phrase, require a constant struggle.[7]

What further makes Joseph's early CCCC leadership and rhetorical expertise noteworthy, however, are the solid rhetorical-pedagogical foundations upon which she built her career and advocated for rhetoric in first-year writing curricula in the 1930s, 1940s, and 1950s, a time when composition in higher education curricula was often, at best, the province of an introductory class or two, and rhetoric had yet to (re)gain the curricular status and relevance that would propel the field's growth from the 1960s. Moreover, Joseph did not advocate for rhetoric alone. Her 1937 *The Trivium in College Composition and Reading*, the textbook that she, in part, created for St. Mary's, is concerned with ways that logic, grammar, and rhetoric can come together to improve the composition student. Undeniably, it is more important to consider Joseph's ethos and subject position because she is a figure with a significant early twentieth-century rhetorical presence whose work was sparsely cited by the folks (mostly men) who would lead the rhetorical (mostly classical) charge in the 1950s and 1960s. In fact, it is slightly misleading to suggest that Joseph's curricular worldview was based on composition. Rather, the rhetoric and composition courses she advocated for, designed, and wrote about seem to have been an avenue through which to educate college students in the trivium's intellectual possibilities. Joseph used logic, grammar, and rhetoric to advocate for, among other things, her students, the liberal arts, faith, and a particular intellectual worldview.

In the 1940s, Joseph articulated her advocacy for a two-semester writing course sequence organized around grammar, logic, and rhetoric in the pages of the *CEA Critic* and its forerunner, *The Newsletter of the College English Association*. While I will discuss her advocacy in more detail later in this piece, I want to first provide an overview of her pedagogy and the ways that a Sister of St. Mary both echoed and departed from the Jesuit rhetorical tradition. Joseph's two-course composition sequence both fulfilled the mission of her congregation and work at St. Mary's *and* attempted to recover the trivium (and by extension, rhetoric) for the twentieth-century American female college student, as St. Mary's College was (and remains) a Catholic women's liberal arts college in Notre Dame, Indiana. Joseph's application and adaptation of classical education from the late 1930s firmly presents her as one of those early figures in the newly coalescing composition and rhetoric field who connected the modern teaching of writing, reading, thinking, speaking, and listening to rhetorical curricula of previous historical periods. In this line of thinking, Joseph's scholarship is based on service to her students, institutional community, religious congregation, and God, and her work embodies the trope of the female rhetor simultaneously theorizing and applying her rhetorical and theoretical lenses.[8] An additional layer to her scholarly and curricular work is her mission and labor as a Catholic sister to educate students toward an active and contemplative Christian life. The platform upon which she carried out that mission was the trivium; it extended to both her classroom and her scholarship. In many ways, Joseph's trivium is rooted in a particular time and place—the Renaissance trivium of 1500's England and continental Europe—that Joseph presents as the ideal version of the trivium from which mid-1900's college students can participate and learn.

To best understand Joseph's scholarly and pedagogical worldview, we can look to her book-length projects: *The Trivium in College Composition and Reading*[9] and 1947's *Shakespeare's Use of the Arts of Language. The Trivium in College Composition and Reading*, a textbook that shaped the two-semester freshmen writing sequence at St. Mary's for well over thirty years, simultaneously argued for the trivium in first-year writing classes and played the role of textbook for the classes themselves.[10] *Shakespeare's Use of the Arts of Language* both served as a rhetorical analysis of the Bard of Avon's works and argued that the type of rhetorical education available to young men during the English Renaissance could be beneficial to the modern student. The connection between these two scholarly lines of inquiry brings Joseph's trivium-based worldview into focus.

Joseph's writing suggests that she genuinely idealized English Renaissance schooling. Joseph's scholarship focused on Shakespeare's rhetorical style and provided analysis down to phrasing and diction. The early sections of *Shakespeare's Use of the Arts of Language* serve as both a recap of the Western Rhetorical Tradition from Aristotle and an argument for the robust nature of English Renaissance rhetorical scholarship and teaching. A popular, almost cliché topic in Shakespeare circles is speculation around how someone for whom there is no evidence of formal grammar school education produced such a collection of layered, allusion-filled plays and sonnets. In *Shakespeare's Use of the Arts of Language*, Joseph presents the thread from which she places so much intellectual hope for the contemporary student and their application of Renaissance education. After all, if it worked in Tudor England, it could work in Notre Dame, Indiana:

> The extraordinary power, vitality, and richness of Shakespeare's language are due in part to his genius, in part to the fact that the unsettled linguistic forms of his age promoted to an unusual degree the spirit of free creativeness, and in part to the theory of composition then prevailing. It is this last which accounts for those characteristics of Shakespeare's language which differentiate it most from the language of today, not so much in the words themselves as in their collocation. The difference in habits of thought and in methods of developing a thought results in a corresponding difference in expression principally because

> the Renaissance theory of composition, derived from an ancient tradition, was permeated with formal logic and rhetoric, while ours is not.[11]

Joseph is not suggesting that modern students will become Shakespeare if they take up a composition education comprised of grammar, logic, and rhetoric, but she does present the idea that a rhetoric-centered composition curriculum affords students with the greatest potential, as composition should cover the effective structuring, organizing, and preparing of ideas. Here, Shakespeare is the figure upon which Joseph builds credibility for a trivium-based composition classroom. A contemporary scholar can only imagine the pedagogical politics of English departments in the 1930s and 1940s. Using Shakespeare's education as an argument upon which to bring logic, grammar, and rhetoric into the composition classroom might have held some sway.

In addition to a pedagogical argument for the trivium, Joseph highlights ways of thinking; she mentions "difference in habits and thought" as a focus of her curriculum. Joseph's formulation of and advocacy for the trivium seems to be chasing a more rounded, three-dimensional composition curriculum. The close connection between habits of mind and moral development that forms the core of Joseph's scholarship and pedagogy parallels the Jesuit pedagogical-rhetorical history compiled by Gannett and Brereton. In the Foreword to *Traditions of Eloquence*, John O'Malley, S.J., writes about the connection between rhetoric and a life of meaning and purpose:

> Such talk of virtue leads to an altogether radical question: Is it too much to speak of a "rhetorical philosophy of life"? I am inclined to think that it is not. Rhetoric in the humanistic tradition was not simply a discipline, not simply the culminating discipline, but the discipline that imbued the whole system with its finality and gave it a life-shaping force. I repeat: The rhetor was a certain kind of person. . . . Almost from its inception, the rhetorical tradition had a moral center.[12]

Joseph's suggestion that the trivium can lead to "difference in habits and thought" is, perhaps, the most significant feature for Joseph and the mission of her Catholic college. O'Malley echoes this curricular philosophy as something similarly central to Jesuit rhetorical education. Again, in a parallel to O'Malley's Jesuit rhetorical formulation, Joseph argues that if composition scholarship is based on a close study of the liberal arts, then the curriculum can serve both pedagogical and faith-based ends:

> The utilitarian or servile arts enable a man to be a servant—of another man, of the state, of a corporation, or of a business enterprise of his own—and so to earn a living. The liberal arts, in contrast, teach him how to live; they train his faculties and bring them to perfection; they enable him to rise above his material

> environment to live an intellectual, a rational, and therefore a free life in gaining truth. The Word Himself said, "You shall know the truth; and the truth shall make you free."[13]

Joseph's pedagogy flows from the idea that the trivium could serve students' learning and bring them closer to God. Of course, rhetoric is only one component of the trivium, but Joseph's trivium and Jesuit rhetorical education maintain a moral imperative. Morality is not presented as a primary outcome in the telling of most twentieth-century composition and rhetoric histories, but it is the implied beginning and end for both Joseph and the Jesuits. Just as rhetoric played a role in the Jesuit educational mission, so, too, does Joseph's pedagogical and scholarly arguments for the trivium befit the mission of the Sisters of the Holy Cross: to discern the needs of their community and respond.[14]

A closer look at *The Trivium in College Composition and Reading* suggests that there are further parallels between Joseph's trivium-based worldview and the Jesuit's rhetorical history. Joseph lays out the two-semester course sequence in great detail. Each semester is divided into three areas: composition, reading, and thinking. In the first semester, composition is divided into narration, description, verse-writing, and composition based on literature, including analysis, interpretation, comparison, and criticism. In the second semester, composition moves to exposition—including the familiar essay, definition paper, preliminary research paper, and longer research paper—argumentation for brief debate, and composition based on literature, again including the same modes as the first semester.[15] In the first semester, reading covers epic, satire, drama, romance, short story, and lyric poetry; in the second semester, reading examines literary essay, essays on education and culture, autobiography and biography, satire, criticism, narrative, and philosophical exposition.[16] The thinking section encompasses Joseph's own original prose and research. The first semester covers the liberal arts, the nature and function of language, general grammar, terms and their grammatical equivalents, propositions and their grammatical expression, and relations of simple propositions. The second semester covers the simple syllogism, relations of hypothetical and disjunctive propositions, fallacies, and a brief summary of induction.[17] Discipline of mind is important to Joseph, and it is clear through the way that she presents this textbook:

> The trivium is the organon, or instrument, of all education at all levels, because the arts of logic, grammar, and rhetoric are the arts of communication itself in that they govern the means of communicating—namely, reading, writing, speaking, and listening. . . . The trivium is used vitally when it is exercised in reading and composition. It was systematically and intensively exercised in the

> reading of the Latin classics and in the composition of Latin prose and verse by boys in the grammar schools of England and the continent during the sixteenth century. This was the training that formed the intellectual habits of Shakespeare and other Renaissance writers.[18]

The trivium's *instrumentality* and *vitality* that form intellectual habits again dominate Joseph's curricular rationale. While her course descriptions can be read narrowly as a barely more than a modes-of-discourse model, the coming together of logic, grammar, and rhetoric is always striving to alter students' habitus. Relatedly, in *Traditions of Eloquence*, David Leigh, S.J., offers the following as being among essential traits of Jesuit education:

> An integrated curriculum with the best of the old and the best of the new of each era.
>
> The use of teaching/learning methods that incorporate the active self-education of the students.
>
> A foundation of liberal education with four student goals: preparation for significant work; leadership for a more just society; integration of intelligence, feeling, and eloquence; and maturity in spiritual and social responsibilities.[19]

Moreover, John O'Malley, S.J.'s Foreword to *Traditions of Eloquence* reminds us of the connection between living a complete life and a greater, more common good.

Comparing Joseph's philosophy against the Jesuits suggests not much difference between the two, or, rather, that any differences between the two come down to, in a sense, scope: At her institution, Joseph instigates a revival of a centuries-old curricular organization; the use of rhetoric by the Jesuits and those influenced by the Jesuits was more malleable and adapted for the times. Indeed, one might go so far as to say that these *essential traits* of Jesuit education are traits of most well-intentioned education. Joseph, then, presents an interesting figure, one who was simultaneously ahead of the rhetoric-in-English-departments trend line while also apart from it because her insistence on applying all three of logic, grammar, and rhetoric to composing, reading, and thinking in first-year composition classes flowed from Renaissance English education.

JOSEPH'S ETHOS: THE ADVOCATE/ADVOCACY

In many ways, *The Trivium in College Composition and Reading* is as much advocacy project and argument as it is a first-year writing textbook. The difference between Joseph's pedagogy and, for instance, the Jesuits is that she needed to make her case at all. Joseph consistently and repeatedly needed to argue for the trivium, as her position never allowed for her the same authority that, for example, the Jesuits held. In part, there are obvious material reasons for her position: the Jesuits are centuries older and have a longer, more institutionalized educational mission, while the Sisters of the Holy Cross are younger and have far fewer institutions. Additionally, Joseph was a woman; the Jesuits, men.

But in the marketplace of ideas within which disciplinary conversations are purported to exist, how were Joseph's work and ideas received and treated? Recovering the historical cadence of Joseph's reception by the greater disciplinary community requires a rethinking of ethos that differs from the Aristotelian ethos that so easily affords the Jesuits centrality.

In their Introduction to *Rethinking Ethos: A Feminist Ecological Approach to Rhetoric*, Kathleen Ryan, Nancy Myers, and Rebecca Jones remind us of the still-dominant sense of Aristotelian ethos

> where a rhetor's constructed ethos is comprised of his intelligence, good will, and good character . . . created and used, primarily, in a homogenous community among male orators in positions of power, whether in the context of law, politics, or public events and then taken up again by men over time in ways that continued to hinder if not halt women's abilities to speak and be heard.[20]

Joseph's contemporaries heard her; however, the discipline's faint recollection of this hearing is telling. Joseph's ethos does not come from the Aristotelian position that holds, for example, individual Jesuits, institutions, and Jesuit-educated figures as our rhetorical forefathers. Ryan, Myers, and Jones's theorizing of ecological ethē helps the contemporary rhetorical historian reimagine Joseph's place and importance to prewar rhetorical advocacy. Here, Joseph represents the counter history, a decentering of classically centered rhetorical history and the *revival* mythos. Again, as Ryan, Myers, and Jones suggest,

> Feminist ecological ethē open up new ways of envisioning ethos to acknowledge the multiple, nonlinear relations operating among rhetors, audiences, things, and contexts (i.e., ideological, metaphorical, geographical). This theorizing recognizes all elements of any rhetorical situation as shifting and morphing in response to others (persons, places, things), generating a variety and plurality of ethos, or ethē.[21]

Indeed, approaching Joseph requires sensitivity to such nonlinear, ecological relations. If we look at Joseph's Aristotelian credibility markers, if you will, we have every right to expect a larger presence in the transition to rhetoric's post-1950's revival. During a period of relatively little rhetorical work within the English discipline, she produced two books: a rhetorical study of the most widely studied figure in English programs and a textbook outlining and arguing for a ready-made curriculum for a two-semester composition sequence. She was a founding member of the *College Composition and Communication* executive board. For at least a decade, she was active across several committees at the annual conference, and, as I will introduce below, a figure of no less ethos-in-the-Aristotelian-sense than I. A. Richards took to the pages of *The Kenyon Review* to review her *Shakespeare's Use of the Arts of Language*. What, then, causes the gap? Why does Sister Miriam Joseph of the Sisters of the Holy Cross rate often, at best, representation-by-footnote in the telling of rhetoric and composition in the twentieth century?

The following sections illustrate that Joseph, like many other religious women, did not promote herself, but, instead, promoted her ideas as well as how these ideas could allow students to have closer relationships with God. With this selfless advocacy, however, Joseph made herself more capable of being marginalized. In other words, her intellectual energy and capital were spent advocating for the discipline and rhetoric's link to living a Christian life at the expense of burnishing her own reputation and status.

INCOMPATIBLE ADVOCACY

Clearly, academia's tendency to privilege an Aristotelian ethos means that (male) figures like Corbett and Ong are prized and widely anthologized. Joseph's advocacy work, however, does not lend itself to anthologizing. Rather, Joseph's writing is inextricably bound to her time and place, and it is difficult—if not unproductive—to read her work without approaching her ethos differently. It is difficult, for instance, to understand her incessant desire to bring together grammar, logic, and rhetoric without also having a sense of the changing relationship between and among English departments, literary studies, composition requirements, and needs of the various communities and constituencies to which she had an obligation. As I outline below, Joseph's pre-mid-twentieth-century scholarly and curricular advocacy can be seen productively as disciplinary spadework that provided space and momentum for rhetoric's 1960's revival.

In 1941, shortly after the publication of *The Trivium in College Composition and Reading* and ten years into her time at St. Mary's, Joseph took her trivium advocacy to the pages of the *Newsletter of the College English Association*, a forerunner to the *CEA Critic*. Joseph notes criticisms of first-year writing that have been leveled at the course and its various iterations across institutions, states, and regions. She writes of the confusion of objectives in the freshman class, and she notes that a healthy sign in the first-year writing class is the then current "tendency to get at the roots of the problem in composition and reading by attention to thinking."[22] Further, she squarely, and in rather clear-eyed terms, states her position on where deficiencies in first-year writing courses can be found:

> What are or should be the aims of freshman English? At Saint Mary's College, Notre Dame, Indiana, the aim is to increase the student's skill in reading, writing, and thinking. Content is subordinated to developing three essential skills: correct thinking, intelligent reading, effective writing. This clarifies objectives.[23]

"Correct," "intelligent," and "effective" are conspicuous adjectives here, and they indicate where she broadly departs from Jesuits and classicists (or, rather, where classicists like Ong, Murphy, and Corbett will eventually depart from her). Whereas Jesuits and classicists find value in rhetoric's ability to aid the order and planning of argument, Joseph finds value in the coming together of logic, grammar, and rhetoric to cultivate higher habits of mind, including a student's connection to the divine. Never far from her overall approach is the idea that her curriculum is primarily designed for Catholic students as an aid in their continued connection to God. Surely, Joseph's insistence on connecting intellectual skills and moral teaching is not afield of a Jesuit education, but it does represent a connection that secular classicists do not make.[24]

Joseph's curricula had a distinct moral component, but the learning objectives that were to be had from freshman English for Catholic college students always came back to the relationship between reading, writing, and thinking. For Joseph, rhetoric alone was not sufficient. The whole of the trivium was the most effective curricular organization to achieve her desired intellectual and moral ends:

> Education is the highest of arts in the sense that it imposes forms (ideas and ideals) not on matter, as do other arts, for instance, carpentry or sculpture, but on mind; and these forms are received by the pupil not passively but through active cooperation. In true liberal education, as Newman explained, the essential activity of the student is to relate the facts he learns into a unified organic whole, to assimilate them as the body assimilates food, or as the rose assimilates matter from the soil and thereby increases in size, vitality and beauty.[25]

In these selections you can clearly see the simple thread that brings her teaching philosophy together and articulates it for a wider disciplinary audience. Great works are the closest humanity can get to the divine on Earth. If we teachers can come together with students to follow a similar path, we might, if we are rigorous and true, ourselves approach the divine. The composition classroom's high moral and intellectual possibilities lead to a fulfilling, contemplative, spiritual life.

In *The Trivium in College Composition and Reading*, Joseph further grounds this teaching philosophy in what she describes as the "intransitive character of the liberal arts":

> The active and the contemplative Christian life compared. The primary purpose of both is the glory of God, but they differ in means and in secondary purpose. The purpose of the active life is transitive: to do good to others by preaching the word of God, by teaching, or by relieving the distress of the sick or needy. The purpose of the contemplative life is intransitive: to perfect the agent, the soul that contemplates. Since the perfecting of the soul by increasing its participation in the life of God, who dwells in it by grace, is in itself the higher work, contemplation is in itself superior to action.[26]

Joseph's composition advocacy cannot be separated from a life of service and Christian faith and, by extension, the mission of her congregation. To be sure, her argument, in part, speaks directly to teachers. "To teach," after all, is a transitive verb, one whose action is meant to transfer, in this case, the highest good for the soul. Indeed, Joseph's composition classroom's ambition for students' souls is a course outcome the Jesuits only hint. Here, Joseph seems to bring together, in the composition classroom, faith and intellectual skill in ways above and beyond the scope of most composition and rhetoric theorists.

In 1949, Joseph, again, took to the pages of a College English Association publication to argue and advocate for her trivium-based course and discuss student assessment measures as her St. Mary's course was approaching its fifteenth year. Joseph offered a litany of assessment figures to support the success of the trivium curriculum. For instance, she noted that after her trivium-based classes, one class rose from the thirty-first to the sixtieth percentile on the Thurstone Psychological Examination of the American Council of Education.[27] In "The Trivium in College," Joseph continued to advocate for her ambitions for a trivium-based first-year writing sequence. In the sequence of Joseph's writings, it had been over a decade since she first wrote to the College English Association audience to argue for a composition course that was more than the merely instrumental, mechanistic courses that dominate the early part of the twentieth century. She consistently argued for freshman composition's higher order objectives. Joseph reiterated that a trivium-guided freshman English class would be the ideal starting point for students to "exercise . . . their ability at the highest level" and that the course deserved its place in any curriculum "provided that the student is increasing in skill to the measure of his ability."[28]

For Joseph, the liberal arts serve a higher purpose:

> In the exercise of the liberal arts, however, the action begins in the agent and ends in the agent, who is perfected by the action; consequently, the liberal artist, far from being paid for his hard work, of which he receives the sole and full benefit, usually pays a teacher to give him needed instruction and guidance in the practice of the liberal arts. A student who realizes that he is working for his own good and not for his teachers (who, in fact, are working for him) has a true conception of his work and will do it gladly, with alacrity and a sense of freedom.[29]

AN ECOLOGICAL PERSPECTIVE

Clearly, Joseph's advocacy language is idealized. That is, after all, what advocates do: they extoll the virtues of an as-yet-to-be-experienced future. Here, we can read in this argument the hope for a composition class that is more than a class in editing or rote recitation. Her application may have been prescriptive, but her teaching philosophy was anything but paint-by-numbers. For her time, her contributions were extraordinary—but today forgotten. Ryan, Myers, and Jones's ecological rethinking of ethos and formulation of the advocate/advocacy ethos helps the contemporary scholar refigure Joseph's work as important elements of composition and rhetoric's disciplinary past. Their discussion of such an advocate/advocacy ethos can sensitize the modern scholar to the ecological and deeply communal nature of Joseph's pedagogical and scholarly work as well as to how this ethos allowed her to succeed with her efforts while also being marginalized by our field. After all, if one is to agree with or acknowledge rhetoric's popularity and connection to composition curricula in the 1960s, then these trends were not likely to have come from nowhere. Surely rhetoric's *revival* came from many figures, including those whose work revolved more around advocating than theorizing.

In the lens that Ryan, Myers, and Jones formulate in *Rethinking Ethos*, Joseph can productively be re-seen as the entelechial advocate, and her work is perpetually a repetition of either pedagogical or critical discussion side by side advocating for both her argument and her right to articulate her argument to a wider audience. We can see this in the first words of the Preface to *The Trivium in College Composition and Reading*:

> This book, together with a collection of Western World literature, provides matter for a coordinated course in introductory English reestablishing the trivium in the study of composition and literature, somewhat as it was exercised in the grammar schools of sixteenth century England and continental Europe.[30]

While Joseph's work thrived in one corner of Indiana, her scholarship and curricular advocacy never took off with a very wide audience. Perhaps

Joseph's work retained too much of the pastoral for an increasingly secular academic culture. Indeed, as I argued earlier, Joseph's work retained a pointedly spiritual focus that even the Jesuit's rhetorical work did not overly emphasize. However, another reason may well be her failure to promote herself as she advocated for her theories.

To consider the question of Joseph's overall position in the field, I first turn to I. A. Richards's 1949 review of *Shakespeare's Use of the Arts of Language*. Richards begins his review by acknowledging the size and scope of Joseph's undertaking to organize and identify rhetorical devices throughout Shakespeare's works.[31] To be sure, Joseph's *Shakespeare's Use of the Arts of Language* (and *The Trivium*) is meticulous. Where Richards finds fault, however, is Joseph's drawing a thread from Shakespeare's (probable) education to his success, to the idea that the modern student—if presented with the same rhetorical training—can accomplish, if not the same heights, something corresponding to their respective potential. Perhaps Richards is also revealing something about his own view on the possibilities of education:

> Educators have been patiently trying for some 50 years—with only slight success so far, it is true—to discover something reliable about the causal connections between teaching procedures and outcomes. This sort of confident blindness to the complexities is among the chief obstacles. In this instance common sense can detect the absurdity; not so in all cases. And I do not think the logical and rhetorical tools presented in this volume are a sufficient supplement to common sense in the undertaking. We must conclude, I believe, that even were it established that Shakespeare had received the most thorough school grounding through precept and practice, nothing would be proved either as to his debt to it or as to any general desirability of such modes of teaching.[32]

Richards does have a point. Joseph's clear intellectual affection for Shakespeare and the possibilities of a trivium-based education are evident throughout her books and articles. Perhaps it is the mixture of faith, of educating students in a way that is intended to help them be closer to God, that undermines her cause to a more popular (and almost certainly more secular) disciplinary world. Richards closes by articulating his skepticism: "And now it is not easy to see in these by-products of scholastic drudgery the issue of an original concern with the salvation of man."[33]

Conspicuously, in the 1960s as her own career was winding down, prominent male rhetorical scholars cited Joseph as an English Renaissance rhetorical authority. Joseph's scholarly work did capture attention and serve as a reference for several prominent male scholars, including Edward Corbett, James J. Murphy, and Walter Ong, S.J. However, Joseph's (and, to be fair, that of other rhetorical scholars who specialized in periods other than classical) marginalization by citation can also be seen in articles by Walter Ong, S.J., and James J. Murphy. In his 1968 "Tudor Writings on Rhetoric," Ong cites Joseph's *Shakespeare's Use of the Arts of Language* within a half-page long footnote that lists the book as "other useful works," an interesting description of a book devoted to the rhetorical devices found in arguably *the* writer of the Tudor period, if not the entire Modern English period.[34] By the 1960s, Joseph's work from 1947 could have seemed dated, to be sure, but one cannot help but read an overly broad note into his acknowledgment.

In some ways, James Murphy's citational treatment of Joseph (and, again, previous generations of rhetorical scholars) is more conspicuous. Murphy is not dismissive or malicious to these earlier scholars, but it is easy for contemporary readers to lose track of the political-academic climate in the 1960s. Rhetoric of any period was still searching for a foothold in English departments against the conventional, historical practice of literary criticism, but momentum and novelty were on rhetoric's side. In his 1965 address to the MLA, Wayne Booth warned against "a shoddy revival of rhetoric . . . unless we take thought of what we are doing."[35] In his retelling of an effort to avoid such shoddiness, Murphy's 1966 "The Four Faces of Rhetoric" presents a narrative of a meeting held at the 1964 MLA in New York (chaired by Murphy himself) titled the "Conference on Rhetoric and Literature."[36] He begins his essay with, again, an idea that can be seen repeating itself down through the succeeding generations:

> Many a teacher these days seems to be making the discovery—like the character in the French play discovering prose—that he has been teaching rhetoric all his life and didn't know it. At least, the current rash of books, articles and speeches on the subject would indicate a tide of interest that might even earn itself the title of a trend.[37]

Murphy lists the four faces of rhetoric as "Rhetoric as a Subject with a History," "Rhetoric as Theory without Relation to Time," "Rhetoric as a Set of Formulated Precepts," and "Rhetoric as Recognizable Structure in Literary Works." Further, he lists Joseph as an exemplar of the first face: "For example, the rhetoric of Cicero or Quintilian; a typical modern study is *Rhetoric at Rome* or *Rhetoric in Shakespeare's Time*."[38] Casting "many a teacher" (or, indeed, many a scholar) as *discovering* they have been teaching rhetoric works rhetorically to champion a field-wide shift. At best, this framing minimizes previous contributions; at worst, it erases them entirely.

One might imagine some bemusement among previous generations of rhetorical scholars at their treatment during rhetoric's upward trend. Joseph's *Trivium* and its attempt to make rhetoric relevant for the modern student predated Corbett's *Classical Rhetoric* by twenty-eight years; her book on

Shakespeare's rhetoric predated Ong by twenty-one years. Today, scholars of this period in composition and rhetoric studies know that a light switch was not flipped in 1960 that ushered in classical rhetoric. The uncomfortable idea is that this new generation of scholars knew that they were building upon generations of scholarship, but the perceived novelty and trendiness—not to mention the baseline turbulence of the 1960s—seemed to draw a line beyond which Joseph and other earlier rhetorical scholars were not recognized.

Joseph's citational marginalization is easy to see. Her scholarship and pedagogy do not lend themselves easily to classical, Aristotelian-based ethos that, for sake of ease, drives the "according to" style of academic writing and culture. She positioned her scholarship and pedagogy as an advocate, as a service to her communities, and not as some rhetorical groundbreaker looking to revolutionize the field. No, if she had any hopes to advocate for her rhetorical worldview to a wider audience, it was to be embodied in those students who followed the intellectual path that she set before them. In fact, her pedagogical call to update and enhance a Renaissance ideal is itself an almost hyper-conservative move. For thirty years, Joseph's curriculum that was, in part, based on a high regard for Shakespeare and the idea that the educational conventions of Renaissance England that likely produced him held sway in one corner of Indiana. The trivium-based first-year writing sequence at St. Mary's ended with her retirement. No, Joseph's trivium-based course was not perfect. What curriculum is?

But this tottering telling of Sister Miriam Joseph's story keeps the question alive, both for Joseph and a host of early twentieth-century scholars and teachers (and no few who were in members of non-Jesuit communities religious): What have our histories of pre-1960's composition and rhetoric missed? In a time when rhetorical scholars were repurposing rhetoric for the composition classroom, why do our predominating histories suggest an early century vacuum? In the case of this writing, why has a figure who served in the founding leadership of the Conference on College Composition and Communication and who had multiple book-length projects during a time of scant rhetorical scholarship been largely overlooked?

CONCLUSION

Joseph's trivium advocacy (and her emphasis on rhetoric's utility in the composition classroom) had come thirty years before the classical rhetoric "revival" of the 1960s and 1970s. Further, Joseph's rhetorical history and curriculum for the modern classroom is rhetorically based on the English Renaissance, whereas the rhetorical classicists led by works like Corbett's 1965 *Classical Rhetoric for the Modern Student* firmly embrace historical figures like Aristotle and Cicero, rhetorical canons, and topoi. Clearly, Joseph's rhetorical history was valued as evidence of a rhetorical revival that could inform the composition classroom. Corbett's 1963 "The Usefulness of Classical Rhetoric" lists Joseph as an authority of English Renaissance Rhetoric[39] and his 1968 "What is Being Revived" includes her among others who have "in recent years . . . so ably chronicled" the history of rhetoric.[40]

The rhetoric revival of the 1960s needed to, in part, make its case to the broader English field. This intellectual territorial claiming is the way of all such trends and swings. After all, the rhetorical thread that we can follow down to today—the rhetorical period that "won" the 1950s and 1960s and dominated to the exclusion of other periods for a generation—connects back to classical rhetoric. However, a contemporary scholar might suggest that Corbett's citation of Joseph and others from the preceding decades was as much an effort to acknowledge as it was to set aside. Corbett's citation politics minimize nonclassical rhetoric and, arguably, rhetoric as just-another-means through which to analyze literature, both of which marginalized Joseph's English Renaissance expertise and application of rhetoric to Shakespeare.

There is still (thankfully and rightfully) much work to do in this early twentieth-century period. One point, however, is certain: that Renaissance rhetoric, grammar, logic, and rhetoric-as-just-another-way-to-talk-about-great-literature were all out of favor yet also the grounds upon which Sister Miriam Joseph carefully curated the curricular world of St. Mary's is certainly a testament to her faith and service to her community. Additionally, approaching her ethos through an ecological framework provides a more accurate sense of her contributions to rhetoric and composition. Exploring Joseph through the lens of an ecological ethos tells us that we have much more work to do.

NOTES

1. Robert Connors, "Dreams and Play: Historical Method and Methodology," in *Methods and Methodology in Composition Research*, eds. Gesa Kirsch and Patricia Sullivan (Carbondale: Southern Illinois UP, 1992), 20.

2. Cinthia Gannett and John C. Brereton, *Traditions of Eloquence: The Jesuits and Modern Rhetorical Studies* (New York: Fordham, 2016), 153–155.

3. "Front Matter," *College Composition and Communication* 1, no. 1 (1950): 1–2. https://www.jstor.org/stable/355659.

4. "Celebrating 175 Years: Sister Miriam Lenore Joseph Rauh," accessed March 1, 2021. https://www.saintmarys.edu/175th-anniversary/portraits/sister-miriam-lenore-joseph-rauh-csc.

5. "Organization and Administration of the Freshman Communications Course: The Report of Workshop No. 4, Section A." *College Composition and Communication* 3, no. 4 (1952): 9–11. https://doi:10.2307/354937.

6. Other early workshop and committee reports are populated by women of various religious congregations. The "Organization" committee alone lists Sisters Mary Aquin (Nazareth College), Mary Camille (Felician Academy), Mary Chrysostom (Mt. Mary College), Mary Edwardine (Mercy College), Mary Justine (Ursuline College), Mary Lenore (St. Joseph High School), and Mary Tullin (Madonna College); "Organization and Administration of the Freshman Communications Course," 14.

7. George Orwell, "In Front of Your Nose," accessed, March 1, 2021. https://www.orwellfoundation.com/the-orwell-foundation/orwell/essays-and-other-works/in-front-of-your-nose/.

8. Katharine Ronald and Joy Ritchie. *Available Means* (Pittsburgh: University of Pittsburgh, 2001), xvii; in *Available Means*, Kate Ronald and Joy Ritchie assert that women rhetors rarely have had the luxury to spend time with theory alone; rather, women often simultaneously have to argue for speaking space while making their argument itself.

9. Miriam Joseph, *The Trivium in College Composition and Reading* (Mansfield Centre: Martino, 2014). This article uses the 1948 edition of *The Trivium*, which Martino Publishing reprinted for contemporary distribution in 2014. Earlier editions were published in 1937 and 1940.

10. *The Trivium* was used at a women's college, but the pronouns used throughout are variations on he/him. This is an historical curiosity now, but certainly conventional at the time.

11. Miriam Joseph, *Shakespeare's Use of the Arts of Language* (Mansfield Centre: Martino, 2013), 3.

12. John O'Malley, "Foreword," in *Traditions of Eloquence: The Jesuits and Modern Rhetorical Studies*, eds. Cinthia Gannett and John C. Brereton (New York: Fordham, 2016), xi.

13. Joseph, *The Trivium in College Composition and Reading*, 3.

14. "Our Mission," Sisters of the Holy Cross, accessed March 1, 2021. https://www.cscsisters.org/our-mission/.

15. Joseph, *The Trivium in College Composition and Reading*, x.

16. Joseph, *The Trivium in College Composition and Reading*, x.

17. Joseph, *The Trivium in College Composition and Reading*, x.

18. Joseph, *The Trivium in College Composition and Reading*, 4.

19. David Leigh, "The Changing Practice of Liberal Education and Rhetoric in Jesuit Education," in Gannett and Brereton, in *Traditions of Eloquence: The Jesuits and Modern Rhetorical Studies*, eds. Cinthia Gannett and John C. Brereton (New York: Fordham, 2016), 133.

20. Kathleen Ryan, Nancy Myers, and Rebecca Jones, *Rethinking Ethos: A Feminist Ecological Approach to Rhetoric* (Carbondale: Southern Illinois University Press, 2017), 5.

21. Ryan, Myers, and Jones, *Rethinking Ethos*, 3.

22. Miriam Joseph, “Freshmen English,” *The Newsletter of the College English Association* 3, no. 5 (1941): 4.

23. Joseph, “Freshmen English,” 4.

24. If anything, classicists frame rhetoric as a civic tool, one whose use is for the health and well-being of civic discourse and good governance.

25. Joseph, “Freshmen English,” 5.

26. Joseph, *The Trivium in College Composition and Reading*, 2–3.

27. Miriam Joseph, “The Trivium in College,” *CEA Critic* 11, no. 5 (1949): 8.

28. Joseph, “Freshmen English,” 4.

29. Joseph, *The Trivium in College Composition and Reading*, 2.

30. Joseph, *The Trivium in College Composition and Reading*, 1.

31. I.A. Richards, “The Places and the Figures,” *The Kenyon Review* 11, no. 1 (1949): 18, http://www.jstor.org/stable/4333005.

32. Richards, “The Places and the Figures,” 24.

33. Richards, “The Places and the Figures, 30.

34. Walter Ong, “Tudor Writings on Rhetoric,” *Studies in the Renaissance* 15 (1968): 41, https://doi.org/10.2307/2857004.

35. James J. Murphy, “The Four Faces of Rhetoric: A Progress Report,” *College Composition and Communication* 17, no. 2 (1966): 55, http://doi:10.2307/354669.

36. Murphy, “The Four Faces of Rhetoric,” 55.

37. Murphy, “The Four Faces of Rhetoric,” 55.

38. Murphy, “The Four Faces of Rhetoric,” 57.

39. Edward P.J. Corbett, “Usefulness of Classical Rhetoric,” *College Composition and Communication* 14, no. 3 (1963): 163, http://doi:10.2307/355052.

40. Edward P.J. Corbett, “What is Being Revived?” *College Composition and Communication* 18, no. 3 (1967): 168, http://doi:10.2307/355690.

BIBLIOGRAPHY

“Celebrating 175 Years: Sister Miriam Lenore Joseph Rauh.” Accessed March 1, 2021. https://www.saintmarys.edu/175th-anniversary/portraits/sister-miriam-lenore-joseph-rauh-csc.

Connors, Robert. “Dreams and Play: Historical Method and Methodology.” In *Methods and Methodology in Composition Research*, edited by Gesa Kirsch and Patricia Sullivan, 15–36. Carbondale: Southern Illinois UP, 1992.

Corbett, Edward P.J. “Usefulness of Classical Rhetoric.” *College Composition and Communication* 14, no. 3 (1963): 162–164. http://doi:10.2307/355052.

Corbett, Edward P.J. “What is Being Revived?” *College Composition and Communication* 18, no. 3 (1967): 166–172. http://doi:10.2307/355690.

“Front Matter.” *College Composition and Communication* 1, no. 1 (1950): 1–2. https://www.jstor.org/stable/355659.

Gannett, Cinthia and John C. Brereton. “Introduction: The Jesuits and Rhetorical Studies—Looking Backward, Moving Forward.” In *Traditions of Eloquence: The*

Jesuits and Modern Rhetorical Studies, edited by Gannett and Brereton, 1–35. New York: Fordham, 2016.

Gannett, Cinthia and John C. Brereton. *Traditions of Eloquence: The Jesuits and Modern Rhetorical Studies*. New York: Fordham, 2016.

Joseph, Miriam. *Shakespeare's Use of the Arts of Language*. Mansfield Centre: Martino, 2013.

Joseph, Miriam. *The Trivium in College Composition and Reading*. Mansfield Centre: Martino, 2014.

Leigh, David. "The Changing Practice of Liberal Education and Rhetoric in Jesuit Education" In *Traditions of Eloquence: The Jesuits and Modern Rhetorical Studies*, edited by Cinthia Gannett and John C. Brereton, 125–137. New York: Fordham, 2016.

Murphy, James J. "The Four Faces of Rhetoric: A Progress Report." *College Composition and Communication* 17, no. 2 (1966): 55–59. http://doi:10.2307/354669.

O'Malley, John. "Foreword." In *Traditions of Eloquence: The Jesuits and Modern Rhetorical Studies*, edited by Cinthia Gannett and John C. Brereton, ix–xiii (New York: Fordham, 2016).

Ong, Walter. "Tudor Writings on Rhetoric." *Studies in the Renaissance* 15 (1968): 39–69. https://doi.org/10.2307/2857004.

"Organization and Administration of the Freshman Communications Course: The Report of Workshop No. 4, Section A." *College Composition and Communication* 3, no. 4 (1952): 9–11. https://doi.org/10.2307/354937.

Orwell, George. "In Front of Your Nose." Accessed March 1, 2021. https://www.orwellfoundation.com/the-orwell-foundation/orwell/essays-and-other-works/in-front-of-your-nose/.

"Our Mission." Sisters of the Holy Cross. Accessed, March 1, 2021. https://www.cscsisters.org/our-mission/.

Richards, I.A. "The Places and the Figures." *The Kenyon Review* 11, no. 1 (1949): 17–30. http://www.jstor.org/stable/4333005.

Ronald, Katharine and Joy Ritchie. *Available Means*. Pittsburgh: University of Pittsburgh, 2001.

Ryan, Kathleen, Nancy Myers, and Rebecca Jones. *Rethinking Ethos: A Feminist Ecological Approach to Rhetoric*. Carbondale: Southern Illinois UP, 2017.

Chapter 13

"Holiness Is Not for Wimps"

The Rhetoric of Mother Angelica

Jennifer L. Bay

This chapter examines the rhetorical tactics of Mother Mary Angelica (1923–2016), foundress of the Eternal Word Television Network (EWTN) and arguably one of the strongest popular media influences on Catholicism in the twentieth century. In a world where faith-based arguments are ascendant, our scholarship needs to better understand how faith-based, affective, and nontraditional forms of rhetorical persuasion operate, especially via contemporary media. Mother Angelica showcased how her own rhetorical prowess, based on an everyday sensibility, both espoused and challenged the Church's powerful, tradition-based patriarchy.

Founded in a garage in Alabama in 1981, EWTN is the world's largest religious media network, reaching over 350 million homes in 145 countries. Until 2001, Mother Angelica hosted several weekly shows on EWTN in which she provided scriptural interpretation, answered questions from telephone callers, and hosted guests. She also published over twenty books. Through her expansive media influence, Mother Angelica developed a rhetorical presence certainly unmatched by any contemporary religious woman and, perhaps, even beyond just religious circles. More impressive is that she did all of this with a high school education, one in which her grades were so poor that she had trouble finding a religious order that would accept her.[1]

In this chapter, I analyze the rhetorical moves Mother Angelica makes in different rhetorical situations: her long-running exchange with Cardinal Mahony and other Church officials on whether she should be subject to Church authority for her teachings on EWTN (and whether the network should be Church controlled); her teachings on her television programs, which often challenged Church hierarchy and functioned as its own grassroots, populist theology; and her arguments to solicit funds to support her ministry. Taken together, these examples demonstrate the success of a woman rhetorician who did not rely on silence[2] to achieve her aims and whose rhetorical listening[3] was less than perfect. It is the embrace of the nontraditional role of a Catholic-cloistered nun espousing traditional Catholic values—and then some—that allowed Mother Angelica to cultivate a worldwide audience.

In what follows, I provide some historical background on Mother Angelica's rhetorical education, then I proceed to discuss how she engaged with various audiences to achieve her goals. Most of her rhetoric emerges via her television shows, since her primary engagement with the world was via the EWTN network. A cloistered nun engaging with audiences on camera offers a unique perspective on Catholic women's rhetoric as most religious sisters, in this collection and elsewhere, engaged with audiences primarily through print media. The fact that a cloistered nun could harness the power of visual and digital media to evangelize attests to the rhetorical power she wielded through a complex embodiment of ethos.

Much of the scholarship on women rhetoricians has been on explicitly feminist rhetoricians, or women who advanced what we might see as liberal or progressive agendas. In contrast, Mother Angelica's agenda was decidedly not feminist nor liberal. What she did was make space for Catholic women to speak out publicly on their authentic, everyday connections to God. In short, everyday people like Mother Angelica could form their own theological understandings of the Bible and the Church without being completely beholden to the Papal hierarchy. This sort of ethos could be termed "ecological." As Kathleen J. Ryan, Nancy Myers, and Rebecca Jones detail, "women's ethos construction can be read as ecological thinking" because it relies on a dynamic of many nonlinear interactions with audiences, rhetors, and contexts.[4] Mother Angelica's ethos developed from a variety of grassroots rhetorical contexts, endeavors, interactions, and relationships, all of which allowed her to challenge patriarchal structures of the Church and adopt a voice that resonated with ordinary publics.

BACKGROUND AND HISTORY OF MOTHER ANGELICA

Born Rita Rizzo in Canton, Ohio, in 1923 to John and Mae Rizzo, Mother Angelica faced a difficult childhood. According to biographer Raymond Arroyo, her mother, Mae Rizzo, had only a fifth grade education and her father, John, abandoned the family when Rita was two or three years old. She and her mother moved in with her Italian maternal grandparents in the "Italian ghetto" of southeast Canton. Her grandparents operated a saloon next door where Rita interacted with diverse groups of people: "she would converse with prostitutes, members of the mob, men returning from the mills, Mamooch—an Italian woman who roamed the streets, praying—and the black people who shared her neighborhood," Arroyo writes.[5] Arroyo hypothesized that these interactions instilled within Rizzo an ability to empathize and to "relate easily with individuals with diverse backgrounds."[6] Indeed, Rita Rizzo would live through the divorce of her parents, the emotional instability of her mother, the Great Depression, and poverty. As a child of divorce, Rita was so ostracized at St. Anthony's Catholic School that her mother withdrew her. Later, as a preteen, Rita helped her mother's dry cleaning business by driving around collecting dry cleaning payments and delivering clothes to customers on Saturdays.

These early years paint a picture of a young woman who was forced to grow up quickly, interact with diverse individuals in a crime-ridden and impoverished area, and work in many different business environments. While Rita Rizzo was not a performer per se, we do know that she was one of the first female drum majorettes in the McKinley High School band. However, simultaneously, classmates report that Rita had no close friendships and kept to herself. Arroyo reports her missing two months of school her junior year and failing three subjects.[7] If Rita Rizzo was destined for rhetorical distinction, it would not show up in her formal educational experiences.

Rita Rizzo did not attend college and, instead, took on a wartime job at Timken Roller Bearing Company in 1942. Surprisingly, she served as a secretary for the vice president of advertising in which she "wrote and edited copy, organized layouts for ad campaigns, and even learned to operate some machinery."[8] According to a coworker, she was a "hit" with her boss. Considering her failing grades, Rita Rizzo's ability to empathize with and reach diverse audiences, as cultivated in her grandfather's saloon and neighborhood, was an asset to her work for Timken. This audience awareness would become an asset in her ability to reach average people through her television programs.

As readers can see, Mother Angelica's early history is not entirely clear. While Arroyo relied on his own interviews with Mother Angelica over many years, her history is cobbled together through the sort of "critical imagination," as outlined by Jacqueline Jones Royster and Gesa E. Kirsch in *Feminist Rhetorical Practices* which entails to "think between, above, around, and beyond this evidence to speculate methodologically about probabilities, that is, what might likely be true."[9] The two biographies of Mother Angelica, both written by men, emphasize one major influence in the early life of Rita Rizzo: the Canton mystic Rhoda Wise. In 1939, Rita Rizzo began to be afflicted with searing stomach pains, which only increasingly worsened over time. On January 8, 1943, a friend suggested to Mae

Rizzo that she take her daughter to the home of Rhoda Wise, a local mystic who was purported to have been miraculously healed of inoperable cancer, to have been visited by Jesus Christ and St. Thérèse of Lisieux, and to have experienced the stigmata. That night, Rita and her mother went to the Wise home, a shotgun house located next to the county dump. Mrs. Wise received Rita and her mother. At the end of the visit, she gave Rita a copy of a novena to St. Thérèse of Lisieux. "Wise did not touch Rita or pray over here," Arroyo notes.[10] Rita and her mother faithfully prayed that short novena; immediately following the ninth day, Rita experienced the worst stomach pain of her life before it suddenly disappeared, never to return again.

What kind of ethos was young Rita Rizzo developing? As rhetorician Michael J. Hyde tells us, ethos can point to an essential relationship between the self, community, and God.[11] What we see in these early affective experiences is an emerging ecology of ethos consisting of prayer, humility, sacrifice, diversity of experience, and more—all influencing how Rizzo moved through the world. As a result of her healing by Rhoda Wise, Rita Rizzo started to discern a vocation. Rhoda Wise provided a list of possible religious communities. However, as previously mentioned, her grades were so poor that none of the teaching orders would accept her.[12] While she visited more active orders like the Josephites who were engaged with lay missions, Rizzo was told she was more suited for a contemplative order, which required separation or cloister from the outside world. She would not be permitted to go outside of her convent, unless with explicit permission, or see others except through a grill or screen—an irony considering what her future held.

In 1945, Rita Rizzo was vested as a cloistered, contemplative Poor Clare Nun of Perpetual Adoration, taking the name Sister Mary Angelica of the Annunciation. Once she became Sister Angelica, we do not have evidence that she underwent a strict theological education in the convent. Neither of her biographers talks about coursework or other education she took as a novice. In fact, contemplative orders such as the one to which Angelica belonged were devoted to prayer, not works. As cloistered, Angelica was completely separated from the outside world, with only time for adoration, prayer, and reading. While there is no clear evidence of the texts she would have read, we can speculate using critical imagination to enact Ignatian spirituality, which is the foundation for spiritual discernment in most holy orders. Part of Ignatian spiritual direction involves attempting to imagine the Biblical narrative that is being contemplated, even placing oneself in that story as a way to understand it more deeply. The evidence of this influence comes out in her focus on imaginative discourse in her Bible studies and talk shows.

RHETORICAL BEGINNINGS IN BIRMINGHAM

Mother Angelica's rhetorical beginnings started in a surprising twist. While she was using an electric floor waxer, she had an accident that put her in the hospital. She promised God that if she was healed, she would establish a monastery in the Southern United States to minister to African Americans. She survived her ordeal, and, in 1961, Mother Angelica moved to Birmingham, Alabama, to institute a new foundation for her Order. The Poor Clare Nuns of Perpetual Adoration are cloistered, contemplative nuns at Our Lady of the Angels Monastery in Irondale, Alabama.[13] Despite its cloistered status, Angelica's monastery would serve as a burgeoning rhetorical opportunity.

Almost as soon as she arrived in Alabama, Mother Angelica started speaking publicly, and, ironically, to raise money for the cloistered monastery, a groundbreaking event, as this was the first time she had ever spoken in public. Arroyo cites Angelica's speaking technique as she detailed on March 22, 1961: "I think the best preparation is to have no preparation. Jesus will tell me what to say when the time comes."[14] She made the rounds of Birmingham to garner support for her project, all the while supervising the workers building the monastery. She also wrote a monthly letter soliciting funds for the project. In 1962, at the urging of one of her Sisters, she recorded her first talk, entitled "God's Love for You," which would sell many copies. A few years later, she was asked to write essays for the *Review for Religious* magazine. These early experiences of speaking for audiences, then writing for them, would lead her to compose longer works, including over twenty books and, later, establishing her television network.

Mother Angelica led a Bible study in the early 1970s that served as a foundation for many of the small books that she published. She explained that she always wrote out the "talks" she would give to her Sisters on a yellow legal pad while in adoration of the Blessed Sacrament, implying that sitting with Jesus inspired her words. She started audio recording these talks, then videotaped them, to be aired on the Christian Broadcasting Network and local affiliates. The story of the founding of EWTN started when Mother Angelica noticed a movie being shown on a local television station that had been airing her programs. Called *The Word*, the movie espoused what Angelica thought were blasphemous values. When she confronted the station manager, he rebuffed her and told her to start her own television station. She responded that she would. And she did, building a studio in a garage and naming it "The Eternal Word Television Network" in response. EWTN started out with her own programming, produced by the Sisters, and the network quickly progressed to satellite.

On her television programs, she adopted a talk show format and led viewers through more of the close Bible readings she had first enacted with her

Sisters, reading a passage from the Gospel and asking viewers commonsense questions like: Did you ever wonder what those shepherds were doing out in the field? Or what do you think Peter was thinking about when he cut off the ear of that soldier? She asked viewers to place themselves in the positions of various figures in the Bible, not as imitation but, in the vein of Royster and Kirsch, as a sort of critical imagination[15] to better understand the personal meaning to viewers' lives. In short, Mother Angelica brought everyday people into a shared imaginative space, which is, in itself, a growth of ethical living. Arroyo calls her approach a "theology of the street—an approach to Scripture that was immediately relatable to daily living."[16] No longer would ordinary people need to understand the Bible from a priest's point of view, but they could enter that space themselves and experience God in their own personal way.

After her Biblical interpretations, Mother Angelica took telephone callers who sought out her individual guidance. Often, she would be less likely to provide exhortations or direct advice and more likely to pray with and for the caller, right then and there. Recalling her encounter with Rhoda Wise as a young girl, we might surmise that Mother Angelica might have imitated the same approaches that personally affected and healed her.

If Mother Angelica operated from rhetorical imitation, what can we say about the ethos she developed? In Ryan, Myers, and Jones's term, it was ecological, connected, "negotiated and renegotiated, embodied and communal, co-constructed and thoroughly implicated in shifting power dynamics."[17] She would continue to adapt her rhetorical style according to context, moving from an early ethos grounded in mystical approaches to a more popular evangelical style in the local Birmingham area, and then to a public broadcast context with millions worldwide. In each of these rhetorical opportunities, she would refine and continue to develop a rhetorical style based on her background as an average, uneducated woman living in the world.

MOTHER ANGELICA'S RHETORICAL STYLE

We might describe Mother Angelica's style as a form of populist rhetoric that conveyed everyday sensibility. She questioned people's actions and words when they defied common sense, and yet she also sympathized with each and every caller who was struggling because she herself had struggled in many ways. She was passionate, had a temper, spoke in haste, and sometimes judged unfairly, but in these moments, she allowed her humanity to shine forth, connecting with her audience on a deeply personal level.

In what follows, I highlight three different examples of Angelica's rhetorical style: her arguments to solicit funds to support her ministry, her approach to her live television programs, and her long-running exchange with Cardinal Mahony and other Church officials on whether she should be subject to Church authority for her teachings on EWTN (and whether the network should be Church controlled). This last example is particularly important since women—and especially most notably religious women—have no formal ability to speak to or challenge Church hierarchy. Mother Angelica's teachings on EWTN soon came to function as their own grassroots, populist theology that reflected what many everyday people felt and thought. In a Church governed by a hierarchy in faraway Rome, the voice of an elderly common-sensed nun speaking to common human experiences held sway. In each of these examples, we see a woman who transgressed the traditional confines of her cloister to deploy rhetorical tactics that shifted perceptions of religious women's agency.

"KEEP US BETWEEN YOUR GAS AND ELECTRIC BILLS"

Before she came to Alabama, Mother Angelica embodied an entrepreneurial spirit. In her cloistered community in Ohio, she engaged the Sisters in making and selling fishing lures to support the dream of her monastery. She came to Alabama with funds from those continued sales but had no other money to build her monastery and fund her community. Time and again, what we see with Mother Angelica is her complete and total trust that God will provide the monetary support necessary for her mission. Mother Angelica bought first and paid later. For example, when she ordered her first satellite dish for the network, she had no money to pay for it. She was completely sure that God would put someone or something in her life to financially support her projects. Arroyo quotes her as calling this approach a theology of risk, or doing anything that God asks you at all costs: "He expects me to operate on a faith level, not a knowledge level. . . . He expects me to operate—if I don't have the money, if I don't have the brains, if I don't have the talent—in faith."[18] This complete and total faith would spur her speaking, writing, and media engagements—in short, her rhetorical opportunities. This faith is what allowed her to raise money for her ministry. Deploying a sort of dry humor, Mother Angelica was able to see how her every encounter was an opportunity to further her mission. While lacking the credit to complete her FCC license, at Mass one day, Mother Angelica ran into a "chubby" guy who had just sold his company to a local businessman. "The Lord said to me, 'There's your letter of credit,'" Mother Angelica conveyed.[19] And she was able to secure the credit needed to get EWTN on the air.

Unlike other rhetoricians who may have depended on their intellectual abilities, Mother Angelica constantly called on her faith ability. Her ethos was not her own but was God's. She was able to build her ethos on the everyday experiences of her youth, infused with a trust and faith in God's will for her life. To trust that God will provide the money, provide the words, and provide the opportunities is a different sort of rhetorical act. It acknowledges a humanity supported by divinity.

This trust in God for financial support also demonstrated her ability to turn a phrase with her audiences. At the end of each of her broadcasts, Mother Angelica would ask viewers to send donations. "Remember to keep us between your gas and electric bills," she would remind viewers. The mailing address was always "Mother Angelica, Irondale, Alabama 35210." No street or road name or EWTN. The use of her name rather than the network was a powerful rhetorical choice as viewers would think they were donating to the nun on television, not to a network. Similarly, the lack of a mailing address indicated how well known she was in the local community. No one needed an address to know where Mother Angelica lived, which supported the powerful ethos she was developing along with her network.

She never passed up an opportunity to fundraise and make jokes and side comments during her "Mother Angelica Live" shows, which conveyed her need for funding. In one instance, she noted that "the Lord doesn't want your pocketbook. Angelica wants your pocketbook."[20] This kind of separation between faith in God and her ministry is significant because it demonstrates, unlike other popular, faith-based television figures, she was clear that God did not call viewers to give to the speaker. In fact, Mother Angelica never requested money directly from viewers, but asked for their prayers and acts of faith. In the same episode, she asked viewers for their repentance during the Advent season. Mother Angelica invited her callers to thank God for something and to repent from something. Each caller added their Thanksgiving to God—often thanks for Mother Angelica's programming—and told her from what they wanted to repent. Angelica would then offer advice and prayers for the caller's intentions. Interspersed with phone calls would come Angelica's exhortations and questions openly to the studio audience, comprising an interesting rhetorical ecology that directly involved God, Mother Angelica, and local and remote audiences, all building a shared sense of faith in the everyday.

Mother Angelica's rhetorical prowess derived from her ability to interact directly with people, a hard-fought battle throughout her life due to her status as a cloistered nun. As she was developing the idea for the network, she gave talks throughout the country, which delivered an early form of funding for the project. But she ran into opposition when the Vatican discovered she had been leaving her cloister and wanted her to cease her talks immediately. Time after time, she was able to pray her way out of it, finding advocates for her causes in the Church who would mitigate her problems. These advocates were always impressed by what she was doing for God as a seemingly insignificant cloistered nun.

GOD NEEDS DODOES

The insignificance and everydayness of Mother Angelica is what endeared her to her audience, but it is also what allowed her to build her ministry in a patriarchal and hierarchical religious institution. One of her most famous phrases was that God needs dodoes. She used the dodo bird as an analogy to herself and to other religious figures. In a visit to Jim Bakker's PTL show in the 1970s, Mother Angelica explained, "I am convinced God is looking for dodoes. He found one: me! There are a lot of smart people out there who know it can't be done, so they don't do it. But a dodo doesn't know it can't be done. God uses dodoes: people who are willing to look ridiculous to do the miraculous."[21] Likening herself to an awkward bird with little fear that it could not fly, Mother Angelica was able to demonstrate her humility to her audience and to show them that anything was possible. If God called her with all of her faults and problems, He could call anyone. She likened the Apostles to dodoes as well explaining, in an early "Mother Angelica Presents" episode, that they did not know any better than to follow Jesus. If we use our reason and our logic, what would we think of apostles who left everything to follow Jesus? Reading from the Gospel of Matthew, she asks viewers to look at what happens when Peter encounters the risen Jesus while they were fishing. She asks, "Why are you so afraid of a God who makes breakfast?"[22] This ability to relate events in the Bible to our everyday world was a refreshing change from traditional theology, which comes down through Church dogma, tradition, and male representatives. We might call her rhetoric "populist" because it touched the lives of so many people across the world for its down to earth and everyday qualities.

What distinguishes Mother Angelica as a populist rhetorician is her use of the vernacular to articulate Catholic dogma, especially in contrast with and as a challenge to the more formal rhetoric of Church hierarchy. She had many unique expressions that relied on inspirational everyday language, including clever lines such as:

> Holiness is not for wimps, and the Cross isn't negotiable, sweetheart. It's a requirement.
>
> If you're breathing and you've got two legs, you're called to holiness.
>
> God wants you to be in the world, but so different from the world that you will change it. Get cracking.

These phrases stand in stark contrast with much of the more formal rhetoric of the Church espoused by well-educated priests and other elite theologians who covered more ethereal subject matter. Before Mother Angelica, there had been a few populist Catholic preachers, such as Venerable Fulton Sheen,[23] but they followed a more traditional rhetorical approach. Sheen, for instance, whose media prowess has been compared with Mother Angelica, offered more lecture-style teaching approaches in his television programs of the 1950s. In contrast, Mother Angelica deployed a folksy humor and self-deprecation that endeared her to audiences who wanted to see a Catholic leader who was human like them.

Moreover, her personal Biblical explications, which ran through her television shows, were refreshing because they did not come from a priest or theologian. With the possible exception of Dorothy Day, there were few—if any—popular female Catholic writers or speakers before the 1990–2000s. Much of her explication did not come from theologians or Church figures but from her own Biblical interpretations. In "The Road to Emmaus" episode of *Mother Angelica Live*, she explains to her audience: "This is not in the scriptures so don't look for it. I have my own rendition."[24] Armed with her copy of the Bible with its cross-stitched cover, Mother Angelica would move through a passage of scripture pausing to provide interpretations, ponder questions, and connect to the contemporary worlds. She was able to relate scripture to the lives of real people, making connections to the working world, to parenting, and to dealing with family issues. Viewers could imagine figures in the Bible as everyday people with problems just like them. Moreover, she was able to immediately address such everyday issues with prayer. After her Biblical exegesis, she would take callers, and more often than not, the solutions she posed to them were not theological or doctrinal but grounded in prayer. This ability to interpret scripture for everyday consumption and respond with prayer delighted her audiences but would get her in hot water with the hierarchy of the Church. Mother Angelica was showing her flock that they did not need the Church to form their own understandings about faith and religion.

FEUD WITH CARDINAL MAHONY

As Mother Angelica gained worldwide popularity, greater scrutiny by the Church ensued. One of her most famous exchanges would come with Cardinal Mahony, who later became archbishop of Los Angeles. On November 12, 1997, Mother Angelica spent an hour on her show criticizing Mahony's pastoral letter on the Eucharist, called "Gather Faithfully Together: A Guide for the Sunday Mass,"[25] for what she thought was an insufficient emphasis on the doctrine of transubstantiation. She said, "I'm afraid my obedience in that diocese would be absolutely zero. And I hope everybody else's in that diocese is zero."[26] It was scandalous for a Catholic to speak publicly to millions of people to advocate for disobedience to such a high Church leader, but it was not uncommon for Mother Angelica. As Wetzel notes, Mother Angelica had a pattern of confrontation with Church authorities that was part of her feisty, popularist style.[27] "As a woman with power in the church," he explains, "she was both a product of and reaction to" the Vatican II Church reforms of the 1960s.[28] Vatican II provided more opportunities for women and lay leaders to engage in liturgy and other activities of the Church. Haberski comments that Angelica was responding to Vatican II's call to engage with the world, and she chose to do this through contemporary media.[29] These reforms would seemingly allow Angelica a more entrepreneurial and active role in the Church. Yet, ironically, Angelica pushed back on some of the more progressive measures in favor of traditional aspects of the Mass. Vatican II, then, gave her the voice to speak out against some of its reforms.

In a letter on November 14, 2020, Mahony immediately demanded an apology writing, "For you to call into question my own belief in the Real Presence is without precedence. To compound the matter, your call for my people to offer zero obedience to their Shepherd is unheard of and shocking."[30] He argued that she was accusing him of heresy. A few days later on her live broadcast, Angelica read parts of Mahony's letter to the audience saying, "I do want to apologize to the cardinal for my remarks, which I'm sure seemed excessive" before continuing to offer further six critiques of his position. She argued that "it is very confusing to people when leaders seem to ignore the real problems in the church that need to be addressed, seem to tolerate and encourage liturgical fuzziness and practices that don't, to me, show or manifest the holiness of the sacrifice of the Mass, that awesome gift where you and I can be really present at Calvary."[31] These point-by-point critiques were not issued in the written form of a letter, as Mahony had done, but given live and on the air to millions of viewers. Whereas the Church hierarchy could present ideas in printed forms that took time to distribute and share, Mother Angelica could go directly to the people. In an era before social media sharing, she sought an immediate response. She shared it on the air, I would hypothesize, so that she could control the response better. A private written exchange would not have an audience but sharing it on the air immediately would.

Beyond controlling the response, reading to a live audience would be a common rhetorical strategy for Mother Angelica to gain support. She frequently read letters she received to her Sisters, whether those were problems related to EWTN or other important news and information. By reading a letter aloud, she could add commentary and respond immediately in a kind of back-and-forth manner. Sharing with her Sisters demonstrated her commitment to the community as well as that she needed an audience to work through her ideas. Her rhetoric was dependent on the responses of a live audience, one that helped her to think through and externalize her thoughts. This sense of rhetorical immediacy was another aspect of her ethos as it reflected how everyday people might respond to a disagreeable statement and illuminated her as a woman of action.

Mother Angelica sent a copy of her live show with a written apology to Mahony, but it was not enough. Mahony continued to demand a formal apology from Angelica in multiple letters to her, her bishop, and, finally, to Rome where he called for a canonical investigation into her statements. He claimed that her on-air apology was not really an apology because of her additional commentary, invoking canon law that only the pope could correct a bishop. Of interest here was the conflict between two different rhetorical ecologies: Angelica's was firmly entrenched in modern, on-air media with an audience while Cardinal Mahony's was still back in an official letter format appropriate to a formal, Church hierarchy.

He continued to seek an apology but never got one. Angelica stayed firm and true to her faith in what she saw as true: Jesus's presence in the Eucharist. She was bolstered by certain bishops and cardinals who secretly supported her. Arroyo quotes an older cardinal in the Curia as saying, "Mother Angelica has the guts to tell him [Mahony] what we do not."[32]

Mahony eventually succeeded in having the Holy See investigate EWTN, asking various questions of the network: Under what authority was EWTN? Who owns EWTN? These questions were intended to provoke a discussion about who controlled the network and what theological authority approved EWTN's programming. Questions had always swirled about the relationship between the network and the Church. Of course, Mother Angelica was the driving force behind the network—the content of its programming and structure. As Neuhaus reports, Angelica had "a record of not being intimidated by clericalist threats. At a conference a couple of years ago, she is said to have refused to interview several bishops on EWTN and they questioned her authority to turn them down. 'I own the network,' she explained."[33] What is significant about these questions are that they publicly challenged Church hierarchy and the Church's stature as the only source for theological doctrine. Surely an elderly nun could not espouse official Church theology on air without Vatican approval.

As the inquiries proceeded, Mother Angelica hosted an official visitation by Archbishop Gonzalez in early 2000 at the new Our Lady of the Angels Monastery she had built 1 hour from Irondale and the EWTN studios. Gonzalez asked her, "This monastery? Who gave you permission to build this?" Mother Angelica replied, "The Lord, He asked me to build him a temple. And after that, I didn't think I needed anyone else's permission."[34] Gonzalez proceeded to investigate EWTN's and the monastery's finances, looking for irregularities. Arroyo reports that the Sisters and Mother Angelica believed that Rome wanted to take over in order to destroy the network. Gonzalez did not want Angelica to surrender control of the network to the laity. He advised that "to surrender the network to lay hands as far too risky, and the veto power too precious to forfeit."[35] Mother Angelica, though, knew that in order to save the network, she needed to do exactly that. On March 17, 2000, Mother Angelica officially retired, and the EWTN board amended the bylaws to disconnect the order and monastery from the network.

Throughout this extended conflict with Mahony and the Church hierarchy, Mother Angelica stayed true to her own ethos, which was driven by her faith, commitment to God, and everyday common sense over hierarchical authority. In order to save what she had built for God, she had to protect it from the patriarchy of the Church. These public and contentious challenges to Church hierarchy by a religious sister are almost unheard of, but Mother Angelica's rhetorical prowess was bolstered by an ethos grounded in personal faith and commonsense belief. She had the strength of a believing audience behind her as well as her own trust in understanding the tenets of the faith. An elderly, uneducated, but media-savvy nun was able to advance her vision within an institution that historically did not value her as authoritative. Ironically, Cardinal Mahony was removed from public ministry in 2013 because of his role in the Church's sex abuse scandal.

CONCLUSION

Mother Angelica's approach mirrors many Catholic women's rhetorical approaches and answers a significant question that guides most of the chapters in this book: in a male-dominated Church hierarchy, how does a woman gain rhetorical power? By occupying an everyday, nonthreatening, humorous disposition. While Mother Angelica gained a great deal of power in the later part of her life, that power came from the viewers and supporters of her programming.

Over and over again, Mother Angelica challenged the Church hierarchy in word and action, whether that was in building a non-Church sanctioned media empire or defending what she thought was core values of Catholicism on air. The defense of these values was, in many ways, what some people thought but did not have the guts to say, and they helped to build a more popular conservatism in the Church. Mother Angelica's appeals to eternal values and traditional approaches reached many Catholics who were dismayed by Vatican II and some of the more liberal changes in the Church.

Moreover, Mother Angelica was able to make these challenges to the Church because of an ethos that shifts and develops over time, drawing in her audiences and making them feel at home. As Michael Hyde observes in his introduction to *The Ethos of Rhetoric*, "the *ethos* of rhetoric directs one's attention to the 'architectural' function of the art: how, for example, its practice grants such *living room* to our lives that we might feel more *at home* with others and our surroundings."[36] Angelica's ethos, of course is almost a literal embodiment of this understanding. Through her broadcasts, she occupied the living rooms of her audience members' homes, introducing the Catholic faith with a folksy humor and nonthreatening demeanor. For the everyday viewer, she was a gentle and kind nun who, nevertheless, told it like it was.

An ecological rhetoric swirls and circulates in particular environs. Ecology has its etymological roots in oikos, or home in Greek. Bringing theology and faith out of a hierarchical Church and into the home allowed viewers to tap into their own feelings and everyday understandings of faith. Her nun's habit was, in a sense, a visual embodiment of the Church that allowed viewers to realize she had some authority as a religious figure but not in the hierarchical sense. For better or for worse, Angelica's ethos provided an opportunity for everyday people to determine their own beliefs about God, while still grounding them in Catholic dogma. In sum, she extended what could be called "church" out of official buildings and into the homes of the faithful.

Rhetorical theory can learn a lot by examples such as Mother Angelica. In an extremely institutionalized and gendered setting like the Church, Mother Angelica's embrace of a nontraditional role—a cloistered nun leading a media empire who engaged in a populist rhetoric—seemed ridiculous at the time, but it was the way that she cultivated a worldwide audience. As one of her most famous quotes attests: "Unless you are willing to do the ridiculous, God will not do the miraculous." We have other examples of rhetoricians today who gain attention and popular support by speaking in simple terms, relating to everyday people, and understanding their experiences, hopes, and dreams. What I think we must do as rhetorical theorists is investigate, classify, and recognize the more affective approaches to interacting with audiences, not as critiques but as true apprehensions of why those approaches work. This is not just about grasping pathos in a robust way but appreciating more mystical, embodied, and affective relations to the world and one another, which themselves can function as powerful forms of persuasion. If the power of Mother Angelica's ethos emerged through an awareness of the everydayness of faith, more attention needs to be paid to how both God and the everyday function rhetorically in audiences.

We live in a polarized world where rhetoric has become ascendant, despite its demonization. Audiences are persuaded by rhetoric that makes them feel a particular way, whether that is belonging, angry, or peaceful. Looking at popular female rhetorical figures in the Church such as Mother Angelica can help us learn how rhetoric can be used to draw in audiences with an everyday rhetoric. Rather than alienating audiences with a formal or official Church message, Angelica conveyed a message of truth and acceptance, all the while challenging the Church hierarchy with her own form of conservatism and tradition. What we learn here is that Catholic women like Angelica relied on a rhetoric of faith based on a larger hierarchy of obedience to God. Using arguments that transcended human hierarchies and authority, Mother Angelica was able to build an unparalleled media empire, one that still exerts a great deal of power in Catholic popular rhetoric today. Understanding how she built that empire through traditional and nontraditional rhetorical tactics might help us to forge new paths for women and laity in the Church.

NOTES

1. Raymond Arroyo, *Mother Angelica: The Remarkable Story of a Nun, Her Nerve, and a Network of Miracles* (New York: Doubleday, 2005), 36.
2. Cheryl Glenn, *Unspoken: A Rhetoric of Silence* (Carbondale: Southern Illinois UP, 2004).
3. Krista Ratcliffe. *Rhetorical Listening: Identification, Gender, Whiteness* (Carbondale: Southern Illinois UP, 2005).
4. Kathleen J Ryan, Nancy Myers, and Rebecca Jones, "Introduction: Identifying Feminist Ecological Ethē," in *Rethinking Ethos: A Feminist Ecological Approach to Rhetoric*, eds. Kathleen J. Ryan, Nancy Myers, and Rebecca Jones (Carbondale: Southern Illinois UP, 2016), 2–3.
5. Arroyo, *Mother Angelica: The Remarkable Story of a Nun*, 11.
6. Arroyo, *Mother Angelica: The Remarkable Story of a Nun*, 11.
7. Arroyo, *Mother Angelica: The Remarkable Story of a Nun*, 23.
8. Arroyo, *Mother Angelica: The Remarkable Story of a Nun*, 26.
9. Jacqueline Jones Royster and Gesa E. Kirsch, *Feminist Rhetorical Practices: New Horizons for Rhetoric, Composition, and Literacy Studies* (Carbondale: Southern Illinois UP, 2012), 71.
10. Arroyo, *Mother Angelica: The Remarkable Story of a Nun*, 33.
11. Michael J. Hyde, "Introduction: Rhetorically, We Dwell," in *The Ethos of Rhetoric*, ed. Michael Hyde (Columbia: University of South Carolina Press, 2004), xiv.
12. Arroyo, *Mother Angelica: The Remarkable Story of a Nun*, 36.
13. "Poor Clares of Perpetual Adoration at Our Lady of the Angels Monastery in Hanceville, Alabama," Poor Clares of Perpetual Adoration, December 31, 2020, https://olamnuns.com/.
14. Arroyo, *Mother Angelica: The Remarkable Story of a Nun*, 95.
15. Royster and Kirsch, *Feminist Rhetorical Practices.*
16. Raymond Arroyo, ed., *Mother Angelica's Private and Pithy Lessons from the Scriptures* (New York: Doubleday, 2008), xiii.
17. Ryan, Myers, and Jones, "Introduction," 11.

18. Arroyo, *Mother Angelica: The Remarkable Story of a Nun, Her Nerve, and a Network of Miracles*, 153.

19. Arroyo, *Mother Angelica: The Remarkable Story of a Nun*, 152.

20. Mother Angelica Live, aired on December 3, 1991, on EWTN.

21. Arroyo, *Mother Angelica: The Remarkable Story of a Nun*, 149.

22. Mother Angelica Presents, aired in 1980 on EWTN.

23. Sheen was an American bishop known for his preaching on television.

24. "The Road to Emmaus," *Mother Angelica Live*, aired May 16, 2000, on EWTN.

25. Roger Mahony, "Gather Faithfully Together: A Guide for the Sunday Mass, Pastoral Letter on the Liturgy," September 4, 1997, http://old.la-archdiocese.org/cardinal/Documents/1997-0904_Pastoral_Letter_GatherFaithfully.pdf.

26. Paul Vitello, "Mother Mary Angelica who founded Catholic TV network dies at 92," *The New York Times*, March 27, 2016, https://www.nytimes.com/2016/03/29/us/mother-mary-angelica-who-founded-catholic-tv-network-dies-at-92.html.

27. Dominic Wetzel, "The Rise of the Catholic Alt-Right," *Journal of Labor and Society* 23, no. 1 (2020): 34.

28. Wetzel, "The Rise of the Catholic Alt-Right," 34.

29. Heidi Schlumpf, "How Mother Angelica's Miracle of God became a Global Media Empire," *National Catholic Reporter*, June 19, 2019.

30. John Allen, "Mahony Appeals to Rome about Angelica," *National Catholic Reporter*, January 13, 1998.

31. Allen, "Mahony."

32. Arroyo, *Mother Angelica: The Remarkable Story of a Nun*, 264.

33. Richard Neuhaus, "The Case of the Uppity Nun." *First Things: A Monthly Journal of Religion and Public Life*, no. 83 (1998): 66+. *Gale Academic OneFile*, accessed May 1, 2021, 66.

34. Arroyo, *Mother Angelica: The Remarkable Story of a Nun*, 301.

35. Arroyo, *Mother Angelica: The Remarkable Story of a Nun*, 302.

36. Hyde, "Introduction," xiii.

BIBLIOGRAPHY

Allen, John. "Mahony Appeals to Rome about Angelica." *National Catholic Reporter*, January 30, 1998. http://natcath.org/NCR_Online/archives2/1998a/013098/mahony.htm.

Arroyo, Raymond, ed. *Mother Angelica's Private and Pithy Lessons from the Scriptures*. New York: Doubleday, 2008.

Arroyo, Raymond. *Mother Angelica: The Remarkable Story of a Nun, Her Nerve, and a Network of Miracles*. New York: Doubleday, 2005.

Glenn, Cheryl. *Unspoken: A Rhetoric of Silence*. Carbondale: Southern Illinois UP, 2004.

Hyde, Michael J. "Introduction: Rhetorically, We Dwell." In *The Ethos of Rhetoric*, edited by Michael J. Hyde, xiii–xxviii. Columbia: University of South Carolina Press, 2004.

Mahony, Roger. "Gather Faithfully Together: A Guide for the Sunday Mass, Pastoral Letter on the Litergy." September 4, 1997. http://old.la-archdiocese.org/cardinal/Documents/1997-0904_Pastoral_Letter_GatherFaithfully.pdf.

Mother Angelica Live. Aired on December 3, 1991. EWTN.

Mother Angelica Presents. Aired on 1980. EWTN.

Neuhaus, Richard. "The Case of the Uppity Nun." *First Things: A Monthly Journal of Religion and Public Life*, no. 83 (1998): 66+. *Gale Academic OneFile.*

"Poor Clares of Perpetual Adoration at Our Lady of the Angels Monastery in Hanceville, Alabama." Poor Clares of Perpetual Adoration. December 31, 2020. https://olamnuns.com/.

Ratcliffe, Krista. *Rhetorical Listening: Identification, Gender, Whiteness.* Carbondale: Southern Illinois UP, 2005.

Royster, Jacqueline Jones and Gesa E. Kirsch. *Feminist Rhetorical Practices: New Horizons for Rhetoric, Composition, and Literacy Studies.* Carbondale: Southern Illinois UP, 2012.

Ryan, Kathleen J, Nancy Myers, and Rebecca Jones. "Introduction: Identifying Feminist Ecological Ethē." In *Rethinking Ethos: A Feminist Ecological Approach to Rhetoric*, edited by Kathleen J. Ryan, Nancy Myers, and Rebecca Jones, 1–22. Carbondale: Southern Illinois UP, 2016.

Schlumpf, Heidi. "How Mother Angelica's 'Miracle of God' Became a Global Media Empire." *National Catholic Reporter*, June 19, 2019. https://www.ncronline.org/news/media/how-mother-angelicas-miracle-god-became-global-media-empire.

"The Road to Emmaus." *Mother Angelica Live.* Aired May 16, 2000. EWTN.

Vitello, Paul. "Mother Mary Angelica Who Founded Catholic TV Network Dies at 92." *The New York Times*, March 27, 2016. https://www.nytimes.com/2016/03/29/us/mother-mary-angelica-who-founded-catholic-tv-network-dies-at-92.html.

Wetzel, Dominic. "The Rise of the Catholic Alt-Right." *Journal of Labor and Society* 23, no. 1 (2020): 31–55. https://onlinelibrary.wiley.com/doi/full/10.1111/wusa.12466.

Chapter 14

A Time to Be Queer

Challenging the Rhetoric of Acceptance through the Works of Sister Joan Chittister

Beth Buyserie

In aspiring to honor the dignity of the human person, religions often advocate for love and acceptance of all people. However, various religious rhetorical practices often use the term "religious freedom" to justify discrimination and hatred against LGBTQ people. The disturbing undercurrent of this religious rhetoric calls the faithful to "love" and "accept" queer folks, while carefully denouncing their sexuality. These qualified messages of love and acceptance should make audiences of these messages question religious-based definitions of these terms. For example, in "Always Our Children," a statement on marriage and family, the U.S. Catholic bishops foreground queer sexuality as "painful" and "wrong," while encouraging parents of queer individuals to be "accepting and loving [of] your child as a gift of God."[1]

Given the ethos traditionally granted to such teachings, I argue the rhetoric behind these contradictory statements is perhaps even more dangerous than outright condemnation, for it claims full recognition of the dignity of all persons while, simultaneously, qualifying that dignity. When the language of love and acceptance, of dignity and respect, is used to infer anything other than radical embrace of a person's inherent self-worth and identity, we should examine how this language also harms—and how it is antithetical to the social justice values of the Catholic Church. And when the Catholic Church and others who equate religious freedom with discrimination implicitly or explicitly promote such views, we should also consider how the Catholic rhetorical tradition contributes to our current moment.

Yet within Catholicism, there *are* activists and rhetoricians who expose how these exclusionary teachings affect the Church's ethos. One such religious leader is Sister Joan Chittister, a Sister of the Order of Benedict, who has advocated for peace and justice in both the Church and society for over forty years.[2] As a Benedictine Sister, Chittister advocates for women,[3] people of color, prisoners, the poor, the environment, and all other groups marginalized by society and the Church. In her multiple writings, including books such as *The Time is Now: A Call to Uncommon Courage*, Chittister calls for sustained change to address and reconcile the interconnected structural sins of racism, sexism, neglect of the poor and marginalized, as well as destruction of the environment in which we all live. Though not Chittister's sole focus, she regularly examines discrimination faced by LGBTQ communities as part of her broader message of social justice.[4] Her unapologetic calls for radical change illustrate how religious leaders outside the Catholic hierarchy can help both the faithful and broader society discern what it means to accept and love all of God's people. As Chittister asserts, "anything that degrades or demeans or destroys a person in any way is not love, no matter how loudly proclaimed."[5] Chittister is clear: acceptance of others does not come with qualifiers.

In this chapter, I analyze several of Chittister's key texts on love and social justice, writings which collectively challenge the ethos of exclusionary Church teachings. In this analysis, I bring a queer lens to Chittister's message, arguing that her liberatory rhetoric brings an unrealized queer potential to the Catholic Church. This reference to queer refers not only to sexuality but also to a queer ethos that interrogates harmful norms. As activist Cathy Cohen stresses, our understanding of the term queer should go beyond simple identity categories. Instead, Cohen urges us to seek coalitional approaches to challenge the institutional practices that oppress, silence, and dismiss multiple groups of people.[6] Chittister embraces this coalitional approach, consistently foregrounding the perspectives of women and people of color, as well as people from a variety of religious faiths, in order to honor the combined, authentic ethos of those most marginalized in Church and society. Though Chittister herself does not overtly draw on queer theory, she continually models a questioning and queer ethos in her writings when she complicates our traditional notions of love and acceptance.

Rather than seeking only to critique, Chittister's assertions are rooted in the conviction that the Church she loves has yet to fulfill its promise to its people. In drawing on feminist and queer rhetorics, she interrogates why a Church that proclaims universal love would deny people full participation—and, hence, co-creation—in its ministry.[7] Instead, Chittister wants the Church to "talk to all of us so that all persons are dignified and included in the church's understanding of itself."[8] As she discusses in *On Women*, "I am a feminist precisely because I am a Catholic—not as a reaction to what is wrong about the Church but as a response to what is right about the Church."[9] As she clarifies, her "commitment to the equality, dignity, and humanity of all persons and my determination to change structures to enable equality" stems from "the energizing good that is inherent for women [and all other marginalized people] in the Church . . . even when I cannot see it yet being brought to fullness."[10] In this, Chittister's task is a challenging one: critiquing the patriarchal oversight and ethos of the Catholic Church that, in her perspective, fails to live up to God's call for creation while, simultaneously, promoting deeper devotion to the essential life-giving teachings of that same institution.

As Chittister confronts institutional norms, she foregrounds the ethos of one's lived experience and sense of self. Therefore, in this chapter, I suggest that Chittister redefines ethos beyond traditional notions of credibility. I begin by discussing ethos through a queer and questioning lens. In analyzing several of her key texts, I then illustrate how Chittister reconstructs traditional ethos: by challenging the presumed authority and credibility of institutions whose implicit denial of the fullness of humanity for all persons exposes the cracks in their teachings. Throughout this chapter, I underscore Chittister's redefinition of ethos as being authentic, an ethos that comes from one's deepest self. In presenting this self-actualized ethos, Chittister calls for both Church and society to examine their own authority, as well as to listen and respond to the lived experiences—the embodied credibility and renewed ethos—of those who are most disregarded by these same institutions. For Chittister, this probing ethos is necessary to bring the Church into its full calling—and for the Catholic Church to contribute actively to a life-giving rhetorical tradition. In following her expansively queer approach to questioning authority, I also incorporate the works of various religious and spiritual leaders who join with Chittister in challenging the ethos of religious messages that seek to qualify the dignity of creation—and who advocate for a self-actualized ethos that embraces one's authentic self.

As I discuss concepts of ethos and authenticity, I know some may be confused by me connecting the concept of queer to Catholic rhetoric—though, as a dear friend once reminded me, queer and Catholic can indeed sustain each other, even in supposed contradiction. I also recognize that many queer theorists might object to me connecting queer—a concept that seeks to challenge binaries and restrictive definitions—with a religious institution partly responsible for maintaining those norms. I bring these two perspectives together because I live daily with this contradiction. As a queer Catholic—a white woman who has been Catholic my whole life but who only began identifying as queer in my late thirties—I turn to Chittister to discern my own voice in a Church that somehow seems to think differently of me now that I, as Chittister would defend, am coming into wholeness for God's plan for my life. The Church's rhetoric of conditional love and acceptance for LGBTQ people—a qualified love, at best—never resonated with me, even when I identified as straight. Now that I identify as queer, I examine still more deeply the teaching that would deny the belief that all sexualities are a testament to God's love and creation. Like Chittister, I hold a questioning ethos. Such examining also makes possible a queer and Catholic ethos, which Chittister draws from as a Catholic activist and rhetorician. Engaging Sister Joan's rhetoric through queer theory underlines the power of her ethos: exposing the harm of institutional practices and accentuating the humanity and lived experiences of those who have been stripped of traditional forms of ethos. Through her words, Chittister's queer, Catholic, inquisitive ethos also reaffirms her love for a Church whose faith sustains the core of her being.

REFRAMING ETHOS

In their edited collection *Rethinking Ethos: A Feminist Ecological Approach to Rhetoric*, Kathleen J. Ryan, Nancy Myers, and Rebecca Jones remind us that the "classical concept of ethos was created and used, primarily, in a homogenous community among male orators in positions of power."[11] Because of ethos' ties to patriarchy, power, and whiteness, the editors use their collection "to disrupt everyday definitions of *ethos* as 'credibility' or 'character.'"[12] The problem with connecting ethos solely to credibility, they note, is that credibility and authority are often structurally denied to groups who fall outside the norm. As such, classical concepts of ethos are markedly unqueer.

In this vein, Stacey Waite begins their chapter in *Rethinking Ethos* by utilizing queer theory to disrupt this commonplace understanding of a normative ethos. Waite explores how a "queer ethos can interrupt normative ways of looking."[13] Because ethos is so often used against marginalized groups, Waite is suspicious of traditional framings of ethos. Waite explains this contentious relationship with ethos, noting, "Because 'ethos' as a term has some historical and linguistic ties to ethics and morality, a queer writer like myself can feel repelled by them; after all, 'morality' and 'ethics' and 'good character' are, in many ways, dangerous terms for queers, terms constantly used against us in public debate and in material circumstances."[14] As Waite stresses, the "presumption that ethos has something to do with 'good' character, with an essential self that can be inherently good and then expressed"[15] is highly problematic. In keeping with Waite's premise, Chittister's writings create an alternative to this limited and unhelpful understanding of ethos.

Like Waite, Chittister constructs an alternative ethos as she advocates for all those who fall outside a normative and patriarchal framework of credibility. This alternative ethos also honors the role of pathos in establishing credibility. For example, in *Dear Joan Chittister: Conversations with Women in the Church*, Chittister admits she is angry with the continued forms of injustice, an emotional response often used to dismiss the credibility and lived experiences of people who rise up to resist their own oppression. In challenging this harmful norm, Chittister's work intersects with Audre Lorde, who writes of the "uses of anger."[16] Chittister's Catholic feminist ethos embraces Lorde's queer insight on anger through a Catholic lens. Chittister writes, "I began to realize . . . that anger was a gift of the Holy Spirit too. Anger, I began to understand, wasn't something to get rid of. Anger was a fuel that fired the engine of change. It was a signal that people . . . were beginning to reject whatever the racism, sexism, and institutionalized violence that held them captive."[17] In discussing holy anger as a legitimate response to systemic and normative oppressions, Chittister fashions an ethos that disrupts detached and "rational" definitions of authority. Her constructed ethos interrupts any authority that uses its power to maintain inequity.

Chittister insists all people form an authority that stems from their inherent worth and humanity. As such, she clearly frames ethos and ethics in terms of justice. As Chittister writes in *The Time Is Now*, those who seek to enact their faith more fully must be a people committed to truth and equity, people who "refuse to be pawns in the destruction of a global world."[18] In this call, a call that extends to everyone on the planet, not simply those who are Catholic, Chittister clarifies that in order to enact credibility in our faith and religious commitments, we must be:

the person who says no to everything that is not of God.
No to the abuse of women.
No to the rejection of the stranger.
No to crimes against immigrants.
No to the rape of the trees.
No to the pollution of the skies.
No to the poisoning of the oceans.
No to the despicable destruction of humankind for the sake of more wealth, more power,
more control for a few.
No to death.[19]

In connecting the Catholic rhetorical tradition with justice, Chittister also believes:

while saying no, the prophet also says yes.
Yes to equal rights for all.
Yes to alleviating suffering.
Yes to embracing the different.
Yes to the God who made you.
Yes to life.[20]

These commitments to justice and life, to equity and seeking meaningful difference, Chittister would advocate, are key for an ethos truly reflective of the Catholic rhetorical tradition.

Chittister's justice-based ethos is not rigid or static but flexible. Chittister might follow Waite's definition of ethos, which "embraces the self as a shifting and contradictory formation, one that cannot be reduced to 'good' or 'bad.'"[21] Chittister's use of rhetoric, which predicates the possibility of change in both the Catholic Church and society, relies on this continual negotiation of ethos. As Ryan et al. discuss, ethos is not stable.[22] Rather, ethos must be able to shift and change in order for it to be effective, particularly when defying systems of oppression that are also constantly shifting. In connecting this continuous negotiation of ethos with queer, Waite contends that "'Queer' works like a sheet of ice—whatever we put there slips and slides, impossible to pin down."[23] As such, Chittister's concept of shifting ethos applies not only to herself as speaker but also to the Catholic Church itself: we are called to disrupt the supposedly stable ethos of the institution, not to reject the core of our faith but to insist that it grow. In destabilizing the ethos of absolute authority, Chittister makes space for the very queries that can transition a people from merely existing in a faith tradition to participating actively in its creation.

QUESTIONING AUTHORITY

Throughout her collected writings, Chittister asks us to create an authentic ethos by questioning any authority that would deny our deepest self. Interrogating authority, however, can be a dangerous calling, particularly when questions are perceived as inherently threatening to our audience's ethos. As Chittister points out, "We like our religions served calm. We call quiet 'unity.'"[24] Resisting how we are treated by holders of traditional ethos is also dangerous, for as Chittister observes, "To be what you are, to say what you think, to do what you need to do to be your most developed self means to risk rejection."[25] Yet Chittister encourages us to create a self-actualized ethos and to redefine our understanding of obedience and goodness. She declares, "Nothing can be off limits to discussion, to exploration, to possibility. Questions are not an indication of chaos, they are an indication of concern."[26]

While questioning authority is not part of the Catholic Catechism, Chittister affirms that we must contest any harmful structures upheld by the institutional Church's ethos. To do so, she joins with queer rhetors outside of the Catholic faith tradition, who expose how the ethos of religious texts and materials can be used to harm. In this section, I feature several authors indirectly in conversation with Chittister because, collectively, they illustrate the power of both their own and Chittister's rhetoric: the message that confronting traditional ethos demands others acknowledge our full spirituality and humanity. For example, in *Fashioning Lives: Black Queers and the Politics of Literacy*, Eric Darnell Pritchard explores how Black queers use spiritual literacy practices to challenge the normative harm caused when religious texts are misused to justify hatred and rejection of Black queers.[27] Scripture passages, Pritchard notes, are often used to "validate" a homophobic and racist response to a person's lived experience. In response, Pritchard presents stories of Black queer folks who use these same scriptures to celebrate their own existence by "challenging the harmful use of [religious] texts and ideologies"[28] as a survival strategy. As both Chittister and Pritchard insist, this inquisitive posture creates a self-actualized ethos that rejects religious harm and allows people to exist as (in the case of Pritchard's participants) Black, queer, *and* religious: authentically whole and holy.

In seeking space for a self-actualized ethos, Chittister pointedly resists any institutional ethos that endorses what Pritchard might describe as "spiritual violence,"[29] which Pritchard clarifies is "any 'assault upon the integrity or dignity of a person when that person is told that, because of who she or he is, she or he is not loved and accepted by God, and is in fact rejected and condemned by God.'"[30] In naming this practice of spiritual violence, both Chittister and Pritchard challenge normative and harmful interpretations of religious texts and traditions. In a letter to Chittister, a woman named Meghan also questions the Church's ability to exclude and harm, asking, "Where could I turn when the place that was the foundation of my life was the place causing the pain?"[31] Meghan eventually affirms her own ethos by claiming, "I am a Catholic woman, a member of the body of Christ. . . . I am not a burden or a nuisance. I am intelligent, capable, and lovable. My God dwells in me and with me just as much as God is in and with them."[32] Pritchard reiterates this reclaiming of spiritual ethos. Pritchard interviews Ella Mosley, a Black transgender woman who believes since Jesus died to save everyone, she must "challenge any interpretations of religious texts that exclude and condemn others."[33] In contrast, Mosley foregrounds "her own definition of what *true* Christians believe."[34] In this, Mosley creates "a Black transgender Christian identity on her own terms,"[35] an identity that also allows her to construct her own ethos. As Chittister and Pritchard illustrate, such an explorative and self-actualized ethos both help to combat spiritual violence and deepen one's spiritual practices.

In describing possibilities for life-affirming choices, Chittister maintains that a refusal to challenge religious authority and traditional forms of ethos can be potentially harmful to one's internal ethos. Questioning and resisting, she writes, "takes patience, takes commitment, takes the strength to claim who I am and insist on remaining who I am."[36] Pritchard provides another example of these life-sustaining practices, highlighting interviews with Black queers who critique their family's choice "for being part of a church community where they could not and would not critically question the church's teachings" on sexuality.[37] Such a lack of inquiry can cause parents to denounce their children: a form of supposed religious freedom and reliance on traditional ethos steeped in spiritual violence and which requires constant resistance.[38] Yet despite the importance of examining one's beliefs, Chittister acknowledges that such resistance to institutional norms can be wearying on the soul.[39] Nevertheless, Chittister, like Pritchard, insists that regardless of the person's faith or non-faith background, these questions must be asked. Such enquiries not only allow a person to grow in their self-defined faith journey but also are necessary for survival and the continual development of a self-actualized ethos.

In addition to promoting individual ethos, Chittister suggests that the institutional Church, if it is to repair the harm done by its focus on normative and traditional ethos, should take seriously the concerns raised by marginalized and oppressed Catholics. For example, in speaking from his position as an openly gay Black Catholic theologian, Fr. Bryan N. Massingale decries the structural sin of racism and its connections to the Church.[40] Although Massingale is committed to the Church he loves, he is critical of the white supremacy that, in addition to enacting spiritual violence, makes him and his Black religious colleagues "invisible in Catholic theological discourse"[41] due to "the deeply entrenched racism that is an endemic part of the American ethos."[42] Like Chittister, Massingale asks poignantly, "Why do I keep doing what I am doing for a church that would be more comforted by my absence and silence? A church that would be happier if I just walked away?"[43] While the U.S. bishops are teaching against the structural sin of racism, writing that we need "a genuine conversion of heart, a conversion that will compel change, and the reform of our institutions and society,"[44] Massingale stresses that the Catholic Church will need to make significant changes to its theological practices before it can "become a proactive force for racial justice."[45] Such a proactive force, both Chittister and Massingale would profess, comes in recognizing the credibility of a critical analysis and the inherent self-worth and ethos of those who must ask the questions to survive.

Chittister herself, in critiquing a Church that would deny women full inclusion in its ministry and theology, asks, "Can a Woman Be Catholic?"[46] This critical inquiry redefines the ethos of a group structurally outside the hierarchy and authority of the institutional Church. Chittister observes, "It is the question that will not go away, for it makes every other dimension of the faith either true or false. . . . Either we are all receptacles of grace or we are not."[47] Similarly, Fr. James Martin, who ministers to LGBTQ Catholics, describes another ethos-driven challenge that he often hears from queer Catholics: "How can I stay in a church that treats me like this?"[48] While Martin believes there is growing support for LGBTQ communities in the Catholic Church,[49] the fact that queer Catholics must consider leaving indicates that their ethos and inherent worth are not fully recognized. As I believe Chittister, Massingale, Martin, and others would maintain, the fact that many Catholic leaders believe they are supportive of Catholics who are women, people of color, and queer does not necessarily translate into action—nor to an answer to these critical questions.

That said, Chittister emphasizes that those who are posing questions still have a responsibility to do more than simply ask. Her ethos, an expression of her authentic and affirming self, calls others to action. In examining hierarchical authority, she challenges her readers to consider how a reframing of credibility and ethos requires work on our part. As Chittister observes, "The question, 'What will you do?' is at the core of spiritual maturity, of spiritual commitment. To follow Jesus means that we, too, must each do something to redeem our battered, beaten world from the greed that smothers it."[50] Chittister reminds us that society often praises those who toil for the poor—provided that no one wonders why the poor are poor to begin with and they remain poor.[51] Others, she observes, advocate for change but unintentionally neglect the individual's humanity. Chittister rejects these "empty questions"[52] where we engage in false binaries of which is better: love of the person or a structural change to improve their conditions. She instead models the ethos of Dorothy Day, whom she says, "did both" and "refused to choose one over the other."[53] As such, Chittister exposes the ethos of theological practices that would highlight the false contradiction between being a loving Church and, for example, "ministering . . . to the LGBTQ community."[54] We need both social change (prophecy) and love (charity), she proclaims, in order to fulfill our mission as a Church whose theology demands "uncommon generosity" and "uncommon courage."[55] Otherwise, she says, "charity [love] without prophecy [change] can serve only to make the world safe for exploitation."[56]

As Chittister promotes the inquisitive posture that would have us reflect on our responsibility and commitment to structural change, she simultaneously invites us to consider the risks of silence and inaction: practices that so often uphold the ethos of institutions at the expense of the marginalized and oppressed. Here, again, her rhetoric clearly and queerly intersects with that of Audre Lorde, whose rallying cry "Your Silence Will Not Protect You" is still widely proclaimed.[57] As Chittister explains, "Suffering in silence when the suffering is patently unjust may only serve to increase pain for everyone else as well. On the other hand, to continue to name the evil, to continue to call for justice, to refuse to be silent, can only encourage others to do the same."[58]

In rejecting silence, Chittister and Lorde declare that a self-actualized ethos must also reject the words and actions that seek to harm.

Chittister is aware that refusing to be silent is not always welcomed. In discussing such public servants as St. Óscar Romero, Chittister reminds us that "[p]eople call him a saint now"[59] for his work serving the poor and marginalized. However, she teaches, as archbishop of San Salvador, Romero was not always so praised—and his opponents went to great lengths to silence him and discredit his ethos. Chittister notes that "once the troublemaker is silenced, the public can afford to revere their now tamed selves."[60] In illuminating the notion of taming, Chittister professes that we must reflect on institutions that, rather than seeking change, merely seek to make the unwanted ethos and perspective more acceptable. In claiming to love the oppressed, including those in LGBTQ communities, the Catholic rhetorical tradition is highly implicated, unfortunately, in these "acceptable" practices. As Sister Jeannine Gramick discusses in the documentary *In Good Conscience*, which promotes her work advocating for the rights of LGBTQ Catholics, "It seems lesbian and gay people are accepted by the Vatican as long as they are silent."[61] In this documentary, Gramick affirms, "Lesbian and gay people have a rightful place in the Church just like everyone else"—an assertion that might only be fulfilled if we reframe ethos in terms of authenticity and refuse to be silent.

REFRAMING LOVE, RESPECT, AND ACCEPTANCE

Although concepts of love and acceptance can be used to degrade a person's self-worth and ethos, Chittister stresses the importance of deep love, respect, and acceptance as central to a life-affirming ethos. Throughout her writings, Chittister exemplifies what she means by radical love and justice. In *Dear Joan Chittister: Conversations with Women in the Church*, Chittister and ten Catholic women write letters to each other in which they examine the role of women in the Church, seeking a space where their identities as women who both love and question the Church can come into wholeness with each other. Their scrutiny, rather than a sign of hopelessness or outright rejection of faith, enacts a self-actualizing ethos, connecting these women to the Church they love while demanding better of it. In one letter to Allison, a gay Catholic woman, Chittister affirms that Allison has written about a "beautiful subject: the power of acceptance to release us from dejection by those who claim to love us unconditionally, as Jesus does. Unconditionally—whoever and whatever we are."[62] In her own letter to Chittister, Allison describes a group of Catholic religious women in the St. Joseph Worker program who, after she came out to them, unconditionally loved and accepted her. Allison writes,

> I received only welcome, support, and enthusiasm from my community. I basked in ways they celebrated me as I began to share myself more authentically with the world. These friends asked enthusiastically for details of my understanding of my sexuality, responding to my coming out with eager questions and excitement as they would to any of our friends beginning a new relationship.[63]

This type of active and unconditional love is crucial. As Allison emphasizes, "Without sisterhoods like the one I experienced in the St. Joseph Worker program we cannot sustain our own participation in an environment as conditionally supportive as the institutional Catholic Church."[64]

The phrase "conditionally supportive" haunts me as a bitter truth. Sadly, queer and other marginalized Catholics are not always certain of the unconditional love that these women religious poured forth on Allison. Allison herself writes of a response to her coming out that certainly should not come from those who profess a faith in an all-loving God:

> Coming out as a Catholic woman, while beautiful and important, was also painful. I experienced rejection from old friends, previous sisterhoods, who used to count as community. When I shared with them my heart, my present truth, the ways I saw God in the fullness of my sexuality, my wonderings and my thanks, I expected to be held in trust by the group. . . . Instead, my trust was betrayed, my truth was discounted, my understanding of God was denied. . . . And my rejection came, not only from people I had loved, but from a church I had loved, with whom I had also shared my heart.[65]

Chittister's response to Allison is stunningly beautiful. Chittister replies with words that are fully life affirming:

> Being gay is a very personal thing, an internal thing. It is a core component of sense of self. The recognition of gayness, straightness, transgenderism is part of coming to the fullness of life. It is the glorious, life-giving act of self-awareness. At this point, a person begins to embrace the wholeness of the identity they know to be part and parcel of who they are as a person and what they have been created to be.[66]

Chittister's embrace of Allison's whole self illustrates how love, respect, and acceptance require nothing less than complete love. Anything less than radical and fully encompassing love, Chittister believes, goes against a faith that honors God's plan for creation. In *On Women*, Chittister names the absence of this radical love as an evil and absence of God. She writes, "the greatest evil starts with the suppression of any peoples. When any group feels that they have the right to destroy, enslave, suppress, or ignore any other part of the human race, God is not there."[67] Chittister continues: "once you refuse to allow other human beings to develop to the fullness of themselves, that's the epitome of evil. . . . And if you and I sit back and say nothing about it, we're part of it."[68] These unwavering commitments to active and unconditional love wedded to justice and equity demonstrate the depth of Chittister's definition of love.

At the end of her letter, Chittister encourages Allison—and all of us—to "*let authenticity be the sermon your life speaks*. Then, and only then, can the rest of us become authentic ourselves."[69] In this, queer Catholics and all people who do not fit within institutional norms of credibility can take comfort in the fact that ethos, rather than being conferred by others and recognized only when it mirrors institutional norms, is, in fact, self-actualized. Not only is this form of ethos based on our own authenticity, Chittister stresses, but without our own authentic selves, creation is not complete. Authenticity is multifaceted, she continues, demanding that we bring all of our complex selves—and the complex selves of others—into relation with each other. In other words, authenticity, in addition to being who we are, requires that we grow, that we rhetorically listen to that which is outside of our immediate spheres. This is a challenging and ongoing task. As Chittister upholds, "Authenticity is one of the most demanding things in life to achieve. Being what we look like, becoming what we seem to be, is the task of a lifetime."[70] That said, Waite would caution us not to associate authenticity with static and fixed identities, suggesting, "A queer ethos uncovers and unleashes possibilities—the potentials for ideas that say: *you can do your life differently* or *you don't have to live that way*"[71]—possibilities that are truly life affirming.

However, these same concepts of love and acceptance, while often used positively, can be steeped in qualifiers that deny an inherent ethos. As such, Chittister believes those marginalized in the Church must not accept anything less than radical love as a sign of respect, and she emphatically challenges the ethos of those who, for example, "argue for the right to discriminate against those who are gay . . . on religious grounds."[72] In this line of inquiry, Chittister is joined by Fr. Massingale, who, as an openly gay Black theologian, advocates for both racial and sexuality justice within the Catholic Church. In a 2020 video during Pride Month, Massingale attests that LGBTQ people "are beloved children of God. . . . [W]e are loved, we are loving, we are lovable. God made us that way,"[73] demonstrating how an expansively queer ethos rejects any qualifiers to our inherent self-worth. But, he continues, predominantly white members of the LGBTQ community should not become too comfortable with any self-actualized ethos that does not also reject the structural sin of racism; the goal, Massingale proclaims, is to "make this world one where *all* of God's children are truly valued."[74] As Chittister and Massingale elucidate, the language of respect must always correspond with loving actions. Whenever the language of love and acceptance serves only to mask judgment and condemnation, we must scrutinize that definition of ethos.

Both Chittister and Massingale explicitly examine false notions of love and respect for marginalized communities, challenging the ethos of a Church that claims to love all persons, but whose treatment of marginalized groups signals otherwise. For example, in *Racial Justice and the Catholic Church*, Massingale exposes the history of racism in the Catholic Church, and, at one point, analyzes a social justice statement put forth by a group of Black Catholics in 1924. Their statement includes the resolution that "we do not wish to be treated as 'a problem,' but as a multitude of human beings, sharing a common destiny and the common privilege of the Redemption with all humankind,"[75] a desire that continues to resonate with all marginalized Catholics. In response to that document, a group of white Catholics later resolved "to be kind and courteous"[76] to people of color—a condescending definition of love and respect that, as both Massingale and Chittister would contend, continued to justify social inequities.

In using these two documents to critique contemporary rhetorical practices, Massingale observes, "The contrast could not be more glaring: one approach advocates social transformation; the other calls for good manners. One presses for justice; the other counsels kindness."[77] He adds, "The white resolutions have no call for systemic change. Rather they focus on treating Black individuals with courtesy, decency, and respect,"[78] a harmful ethos that Massingale argues still continues today. Here, Massingale joins Chittister in critiquing any ethos that promotes kindness and tolerance at the expense of structural change. In both their approaches, Chittister and Massingale underline the stark contrast between words that claim to promote the dignity of a group and actions that actually do so. Simple respect and courtesy, they contend, do not equate to the deep commitments to justice and love that are the core of the faith—and they encourage us to engage in a line of critical reflection that will promote such structural change.

In her writings, Chittister repeatedly confronts such structural inequities and watered-down definitions of love and respect. She models the types of questions we all might pose, asking, "As long as the poor are being fed, why raise the wages it would take to enable them to feed themselves? It enables employers to go on underpaying and overworking the very people who have made them their wealth."[79] In a similar vein, I ask therefore, what is the use of saying that the world should respect the dignity of queer individuals if that same Church continues to qualify its definition of love? To assert that love and respect can be couched in terms that still separate queer people from the fullness of creation? To mirror Chittister's line of inquiry, as long as queer folks are "respected" and "accepted," why change societal and Church norms that would fully recognize our humanity?

As children of God, queer Catholics, Chittister declares, are not simply meant to be respected at a distance. Instead, all queer people should be valued for their inherent gifts to the Church and authentic ethos. Like Chittister, Jesuit priest Fr. James Martin also urges that we redefine respect. In his book *Building a Bridge: How the Catholic Church and the LGBT Community Can Enter into a Relationship of Respect, Compassion, and Sensitivity*, Martin reframes the language of respect to signify something more positive and active. Martin posits that "*Respect* . . . means acknowledging that LGBT Catholics bring unique gifts to the church—both as individuals and as a community."[80] Like Chittister, Martin encourages the Church "to meditate on how LGBT Catholics build up the church with their presence."[81] This definition of respect, Martin emphasizes, must include "accepting [queer people] as beloved children of God and *letting them know* that they are beloved children of God,"[82] an approach that Chittister would agree combines both word and action to communicate an ethos of love.

Throughout her writings, Chittister insists that true respect is active and potentially disruptive, capable of creating an ethos that enacts structural change. Chittister reiterates that for respect and acceptance to enhance a life-giving ethos, it must be paired with "the call to co-creation" and affirming love in all our words and actions.[83] Affirmation, Chittister professes, requires a love that is not demoted. Her fellow Benedictine, Anglican lay woman Esther de Waal, echoes Chittister in claiming, "It is only when I am loved . . . for who I *am* that I can become myself, unique and irreplaceable."[84] There is power in active, co-creative love and respect. This, Chittister would have us know, is very different from the dangerous rhetoric of tolerance and acceptance—which she advocates must be replaced with radical love and justice.

CONTINUING TO QUESTION

As Chittister clarifies in *On Women*, "church is not a place; it is a process."[85] As a Catholic who has only relatively recently identified as queer, I am still in the process of finding my revised place and ethos in the faith that I love. Chittister, Massingale, and others marginalized by the Church continually ask: Why stay in a Church that rejects you? The answers to this question are personal and often painful. "I stay in it," Chittister reveals, "even when staying in it, for a woman, is full of pain, frustration, disillusionment and, far too often, even humiliation."[86] Nevertheless, she continues, "I stay in the church because there is nowhere else I know that satisfies in me what the church itself teaches us to seek—a sacramental life that makes all life sacred."[87] Massingale relates his own decision to continue believing in a Church that has not yet fully repented of the structural sins of racism and homophobia:

"The will to persevere stems from a core conviction that I am called to the Catholic community because that community needs me and my voice if it is to be 'catholic' in reality and not simply in rhetoric."[88] While each Catholic will have to decide their own reasons for remaining in—or leaving—the Church, I also stay because I believe in a deep sustaining love that equates faith with justice. Yet Chittister proclaims that "until the church answers the . . . question [of equity and justice] in a way that makes the Gospel real and all of humanity human, the integrity of its sacraments, its theology and its structures are at stake."[89] Until the Church answers this petition, we must continue to question the stable and contradictory ethos of the Church.

Establishing an authentic ethos within a Church that uses the concept of religious freedom to qualify concepts of love is admittedly exhausting. Chittister has been a key figure whose connection of justice and equity with the Catholic rhetorical tradition continues to sustain me. In *The Time Is Now*, Chittister emphasizes that we can choose to "quit a road that is going somewhere we do not want to go" or "surrender to the forces of resistance that obstruct our every step toward wholeness."[90] At times, I admit, I feel as though the Church itself would wish me to choose this path of surrender simply because I am now embracing the gift of my sexuality. Alternatively, Chittister hopes and insists on a better version of the Church, encouraging us "to refuse to accept . . . the present and insist on celebrating the coming of an unknown, but surely holier, future."[91] Until this promise of a holier future manifests, Chittister's constant themes of deep and affirming love provide space for daily action, continued questioning, and authentic ethos in our discipline, society, and the Catholic Church.

NOTES

1. United States Conference of Catholic Bishops, "Always Our Children: A Pastoral Message to Parents of Homosexual Children and Suggestions for Pastoral Ministers," 1997, accessed November 15, 2020, www.bishop-accountability.org/resources/resource-files/churchdocs/AlwaysOurChildren.htm.

2. "Joan Chittister," Benetvision, accessed November 28, 2020, https://joanchittister.org.

3. In the spirit of life-giving practices, I clarify that when I write about women, I am referring to all people who identify as women. While Chittister does not overtly or repeatedly make this distinction, she acknowledges thinking along the gender binary at the expense of the whole person is dangerous.

4. Joan Chittister, *Dear Joan Chittister: Conversations with Women in the Church*, ed. Jessie Bazan (New London: Twenty-Third Publications, 2019), 28–33; Joan Chittister, *The Time Is Now: A Call to Uncommon Courage* (New York: Convergent, 2019), 34.

5. Joan Chittister, *For Everything a Season*, 2nd edition (Maryknoll: Orbis Books, 2013), 35.

6. Cathy Cohen, "The Radical Potential of Queer? Twenty Years Later," *GLQ: A Journal of Lesbian and Gay Studies* 25, no. 1 (2019): 140–144.

7. Joan Chittister, *From the Writings of Joan Chittister: On Women*, eds. Jacqueline Sanchez-Small, Colleen Leathley, and Mary Lou Kownacki (Erie: Benetvision, 2020).

8. Chittister, *On Women*, 56.

9. Chittister, *On Women*, 8.

10. Chittister, *Dear Joan*, 8.

11. Kathleen J. Ryan, Nancy Myers, and Rebecca Jones, "Introduction: Identifying Feminist Ecological Ethē," in *Rethinking Ethos: A Feminist Ecological Approach to Rhetoric*, eds. Kathleen J. Ryan, Nancy Myers, and Rebecca Jones (Carbondale: Southern Illinois University Press, 2016), 5.

12. Kathleen J. Ryan, Nancy Myers, and Rebecca Jones, "Preface," in *Rethinking Ethos: A Feminist Ecological Approach to Rhetoric*, eds. Kathleen J. Ryan, Nancy Myers, and Rebecca Jones (Carbondale: Southern Illinois University Press, 2016), vii.

13. Stacey Waite, "The Unavailable Means of Persuasion: A Queer Ethos for Feminist Writers and Teachers," in *Rethinking Ethos: A Feminist Ecological Approach to Rhetoric*, eds. Kathleen J. Ryan, Nancy Myers, and Rebecca Jones (Carbondale: Southern Illinois UP, 2016), 72.

14. Waite, "Queer Ethos," 71–72.

15. Waite, "Queer Ethos," 72.

16. Audre Lorde, *Sister Outsider: Essays and Speeches* (Berkeley: Crossing Press, 2017, first published 1984), 124.

17. Chittister, *Dear Joan*, 116.

18. Chittister, *The Time Is Now*, 15.

19. Chittister, *The Time Is Now*, 15–16.

20. Chittister, *The Time Is Now*, 16.

21. Waite, "Queer Ethos," 72.

22. Ryan, Myers, and Jones, *Rethinking Ethos*, 2–6.

23. Waite, "Queer Ethos," 71.

24. Chittister, *The Time Is Now*, 33.

25. Chittister, *On Women*, 35.

26. Chittister, *On Women*, 37.

27. Eric Darnell Pritchard, *Fashioning Lives: Black Queers and the Politics of Literacy* (Carbondale: Southern Illinois University Press, 2017), 153–191.

28. Pritchard, *Fashioning Lives*, 176.

29. Pritchard, *Fashioning Lives*, 166.

30. Pritchard, *Fashioning Lives*, 154; Pritchard credits the term "spiritual violence" to "United Methodist minister and spiritual activist Reverend Jimmy Creech."

31. Chittister, *Dear Joan*, 71.

32. Chittister, *Dear Joan*, 72–73.

33. Pritchard, *Fashioning Lives*, 176.

34. Pritchard, *Fashioning Lives*, 176, italics in the original.

35. Pritchard, *Fashioning Lives*, 176.
36. Chittister, *Dear Joan*, 75.
37. Pritchard, *Fashioning Lives*, 178–179.
38. Pritchard, *Fashioning Lives*, 178.
39. Chittister, *The Time Is Now*, 62.
40. Bryan N. Massingale, *Racial Justice and the Catholic Church* (Maryknoll: Orbis Books, 2010).
41. Massingale, *Racial Justice*, 166.
42. Massingale, *Racial Justice*, 85.
43. Massingale, *Racial Justice*, 167.
44. United States Conference of Catholic Bishops, "Open Wide Our Hearts: The Enduring Call to Love—A Pastoral Letter Against Racism," 2018, 7, accessed November 29, 2020, www.usccb.org/issues-and-action/human-life-and-dignity/racism/upload/open-wide-our-hearts.pdf.
45. Massingale, *Racial Justice*, 179.
46. Chittister, *On Women*, 19.
47. Chittister, *On Women*, 19.
48. James Martin, *Building a Bridge: How the Catholic Church and the LGBT Community Can Enter into a Relationship of Respect, Compassion, and Sensitivity* (New York: Harper One, 2017), 63.
49. Martin, *Building a Bridge*, 64.
50. Chittister, *The Time Is Now*, 15.
51. Chittister, *The Time Is Now*, 32.
52. Chittister, *The Time Is Now*, 33.
53. Chittister, *The Time Is Now*, 34.
54. Chittister, *The Time Is Now*, 34.
55. Chittister, *The Time Is Now*, 35.
56. Chittister, *The Time Is Now*, 35.
57. Audre Lorde, *Your Silence Will Not Protect You: Essays and Poems* (London: Silver Press, 2017).
58. Chittister, *Dear Joan*, 76.
59. Chittister, *The Time Is Now*, 33.
60. Chittister, *The Time Is Now*, 33.
61. *In Good Conscience: Sister Jeannie Gramick's Journey of Faith*, dir. Barbara Rick (New York: Out of the Blue Films, 2004).
62. Chittister, *Dear Joan*, 31.
63. Chittister, *Dear Joan*, 29.
64. Chittister, *Dear Joan*, 30.
65. Chittister, *Dear Joan*, 29–30.
66. Chittister, *Dear Joan*, 32.
67. Chittister, *On Women*, 63.
68. Chittister, *On Women*, 63.
69. Chittister, *Dear Joan*, 33, my emphasis.
70. Chittister, *Dear Joan*, 49.
71. Waite, "Queer Ethos," 74, original emphasis.

72. Chittister, *The Time Is Now*, 39.
73. Bryan Massingale, "Father Bryan Massingale's Message for LGBTQ Catholics," posted June 17, 2020, video, 4:02, https://www.youtube.com/watch?v=qXlI8NumSAA.
74. Massingale, "Message for LGBTQ Catholics."
75. Massingale, *Racial Justice*, 48.
76. Massingale, *Racial Justice*, 49.
77. Massingale, *Racial Justice*, 50.
78. Massingale, *Racial Justice*, 50.
79. Chittister, *The Time Is Now*, 35.
80. Martin, *Building a Bridge*, 24, original emphasis.
81. Martin, *Building a Bridge*, 25.
82. Martin, *Building a Bridge*, 27, original emphasis.
83. Chittister, *The Time Is Now*, 16.
84. Esther de Waal, *Living with Contradictions: An Introduction to Benedictine Spirituality* (Harrisburg: Morehouse Publishing, 1997), 46, original emphasis.
85. Chittister, *On Women*, 84.
86. Chittister, *On Women*, 84.
87. Chittister, *On Women*, 85–86.
88. Massingale, *Racial Justice*, 167.
89. Chittister, *On Women*, 19.
90. Chittister, *The Time Is Now*, 13–14.
91. Chittister, *The Time Is Now*, 14.

BIBLIOGRAPHY

Benetvision. "Joan Chittister." Accessed November 28, 2020. https://joanchittister.org.

Chittister, Joan. *Dear Joan Chittister: Conversations with Women in the Church*, edited by Jessie Bazan. New London, CT: Twenty-Third Publications, 2019.

Chittister, Joan. *For Everything a Season*, 2nd edition. Maryknoll, New York: Orbis Books, 2013.

Chittister, Joan. *From the Writings of Joan Chittister: On Women*, edited by Jacqueline Sanchez-Small, Colleen Leathley, and Mary Lou Kownacki. Erie, Pennsylvania: Benetvision, 2020.

Chittister, Joan. *The Time Is Now: A Call to Uncommon Courage*. New York: Convergent, 2019.

Cohen, Cathy. "The Radical Potential of Queer? Twenty Years Later." *GLQ: A Journal of Lesbian and Gay Studies* 25, no. 1 (2019): 140–144.

de Waal, Esther. *Living with Contradictions: An Introduction to Benedictine Spirituality*. Harrisburg: Morehouse Publishing, 1997.

Lorde, Audre. *Sister Outsider: Essays and Speeches*. Berkeley: Crossing Press, 2017.

Lorde, Audre. *Your Silence Will Not Protect You: Essays and Poems*. London: Silver Press, 2017.

Martin, James. *Building a Bridge: How the Catholic Church and the LGBT Community Can Enter into a Relationship of Respect, Compassion, and Sensitivity*. New York: Harper One, 2017.

Massingale, Bryan N. *Racial Justice and the Catholic Church*. Maryknoll, New York: Orbis Books, 2010.

Massingale, Bryan N. "Father Bryan Massingale's Message for LGBTQ Catholics." Posted June 17, 2020. https://www.youtube.com/watch?v=qXlI8NumSAA.

Pritchard, Eric Darnell. *Fashioning Lives: Black Queers and the Politics of Literacy*. Carbondale: Southern Illinois University Press, 2017.

Rick, Barbara, dir. *In Good Conscience: Sister Jeannine Gramick's Journey of Faith*. New York: Out of the Blue Films, 2004.

Ryan, Kathleen J., Nancy Myers, and Rebecca Jones. "Introduction: Identifying Feminist Ecological Ethē." In *Rethinking Ethos: A Feminist Ecological Approach to Rhetoric*, edited by Kathleen J. Ryan, Nancy Myers, and Rebecca Jones, 1–22. Carbondale: Southern Illinois UP, 2016.

Ryan, Kathleen J., Nancy Myers, and Rebecca Jones. "Preface." In *Rethinking Ethos: A Feminist Ecological Approach to Rhetoric*, edited by Kathleen J. Ryan, Nancy Myers, and Rebecca Jones, vii–xii. Carbondale: Southern Illinois UP, 2016.

United States Conference of Catholic Bishops. "Always Our Children: A Pastoral Message to Parents of Homosexual Children and Suggestions for Pastoral Ministers." A Statement of the Bishops' Committee on Marriage and Family. Accessed November 15, 2020. www.bishop-accountability.org/resources/resource-files/churchdocs/AlwaysOurChildren.htm, 1997.

United States Conference of Catholic Bishops. "Open Wide Our Hearts: The Enduring Call to Love—A Pastoral Letter Against Racism." A Statement of the Ad Hoc Committee Against Racism. Accessed November 29, 2020. www.usccb.org/issues-and-action/human-life-and-dignity/racism/upload/open-wide-our-hearts.pdf, 2018.

Waite, Stacey. "The Unavailable Means of Persuasion: A Queer Ethos for Feminist Writers and Teachers." In *Rethinking Ethos: A Feminist Ecological Approach to Rhetoric*, edited by Kathleen J. Ryan, Nancy Myers, and Rebecca Jones, 71–88. Carbondale: Southern Illinois UP, 2016.

Chapter 15

Standing in the Eye of the Storm

The Eternal Habits of U.S. Women Religious

Jamie L. Downing

When, in 2009, news emerged that the Catholic Church planned to investigate the work and lifestyle of U.S. American women religious which had, in the words of Cardinal Franc Rodé, led some of the sisters to "ways that take them outside communion with Christ in the Catholic Church,"[1] the sisters, under scrutiny, recognized the stakes of the moment. The inquiry's primary target was the Leadership Conference of Women Religious (LCWR), an organization comprised of sisters who are leaders within their congregations and who, in turn, represent almost 80 percent of the nearly 49,000 U.S. American women religious.[2] Taken by surprise, the LCWR Executive Board did what came most naturally—gathered their membership, shared what they knew, listened to concerns—and then, got back to work rededicating themselves to the service of the communities in which they lived.

As the inquest wore on, LCWR leaders worked doggedly to challenge public assumptions about Catholicism and assert authorship over the sisters' identity,[3] plotting a defense of the organization rooted in the Catholic sisters' carefully cultivated ethos. At each turn, LCWR leaders framed organizational choices as rooted firmly in Catholic tradition and theology. Internally, this response manifested in a stalwart adherence to principles of discernment and dialogue as nonnegotiable processes of organizational decision-making. Externally, the sisters took advantage of their media spotlight to shed light on the often underacknowledged or invisible work long performed by women religious across the nation. In each instance, the LCWR refused the roles prescribed by the Church's contemporary disciplinary bodies, instead presenting itself as performing the most meaningful theologically sanctioned (if not often-celebrated) service of the Church.

The LCWR did not engage confrontationally with the Vatican hierarchy, opting instead to place the sisters' service—public manifestations of private faith—squarely within public view. The sisters' enactments of their long-practiced character emulate what S. Michael Halloran suggests is an older, more concrete understanding of ethos: "a habitual gathering place" predicated on "sharing experiences and ideas."[4] In so doing, the sisters enacted rhetorical practices rooted deeply within the history of women religious: reflection, discernment, and listening. Such practices are the same as those explored by Kathleen Ryan, Nancy Myers, and Rebecca Jones in their discussion of ethos practices often embraced by women and other marginalized groups who construct ethē beyond the modes of communication deemed valuable by those who hold power but are, nevertheless, modes rooted in "rich traditions."[5] As this chapter illustrates, LCWR members constructed an ethos of vowed women religious by emphasizing how deeply the practices, or habits, that guide their vowed communities are rooted in strong adherence to Gospel teachings. The members also publicly highlighted the networks of communities fostered through long-term, habitual service. That is, rather than adjusting their modes of communication to meet the expectations of their masculine interlocutors, LCWR members leaned into their callings, filling up and exceeding the expectations outsiders had held for the role.

In this chapter, I explicate LCWR responses to the investigations by situating the sisters' ministries as demanded by their vows as women religious. The LCWR tied contemporary doctrine to histories of dedicated service to leverage its members' ethos as moral agents beyond the sanction of the Church hierarchy. In doing so, they situated the sisters' ministries as within the boundaries of Church teaching and demanded by their vows as women religious. I argue the LCWR engaged in the enactment of an ethos that demonstrated that the sisters' habitual positions, values, and actions are also enactments of the Church's highest moral ideals. To this end, I first contextualize the Vatican inquiries and historicize the LCWR's positionality before exploring the ethos LCWR cultivated in response to processes that saw "women religious, and especially their leaders, stand in the eye of an ecclesiastical storm."[6]

Throughout this chapter, I address the LCWR response to tensions brought to the fore through the announcement of two formal investigations into the organization in 2008. The first emerged when the Vatican's Congregation for the Doctrine of the Faith (CDF) announced its intention to assess LCWR doctrine. As the organization responsible for defending Church doctrine, in part by ensuring fidelity in its enactment by vowed representatives, the CDF identified three concerns motivating the doctrinal assessment: LCWR's advocacy on issues involving pastoral care for LBGTQ+ community members, the addresses at "annual Assemblies manifest[ing] problematic statements and serious theological, even doctrinal errors," and "a prevalence of certain radical feminist themes incompatible with the Catholic faith" in LCWR programming.[7]

The second probe was instigated by the Congregation for Institutes of Consecrated Life and Societies of Apostolic Life (CICSAL), the Vatican body charged with overseeing matters related to consecrated religious life, most prominently orders of monks and other religious orders. Referring to its intention to conduct a "respectful 'sister-to-sister' dialogue,"[8] CICSAL ordered an apostolic visitation of U.S. women religious on matters regarding their quality of life, ministry, and financial status. In spite of CICSAL formally framing the apostolic visitation as an "experience of prayerful reflection, self-evaluation, and dialogue,"[9] comments from other Vatican officials belied this tenor.

Though the doctrinal assessment and the apostolic visitation were officially separate, overlapping timeframes and shared motivating issues, along with agreements between the LCWR and relevant Vatican bodies to avoid public comment, often resulted in media coverage and public conversation that blurred the two investigations into one.[10] In many ways, the LCWR took advantage of this conflation to ensure what coverage did occur was focused on the sisters' missions, roles, and community impacts. I take a similar tack: acknowledging the differences between the assessment and visitation but treating the LCWR response within a unified public frame, an approach that allows for more careful attention to the sisters' communication of their ethos as vowed women religious.

THE SEEDS OF DISPUTE

Founded in 1956 as the Conference of Major Superiors of Women at the behest of the Vatican, the LCWR was created to uphold three primary aims: supporting the spiritual welfare of U.S. American women religious, facilitating their religious ministry, and promoting collaboration between Catholic associations, clergy, and religious. Membership in the conference has always been restricted to women who are leaders within their congregations, and the conference currently consists of approximately 1,350 women religious.[11]

The seeds of the 2008 controversy had germinated for years. Perhaps the most noteworthy flashpoint occurred in 1979 when Sister Theresa Kane used her address welcoming Pope John Paul II to the United States to plead that all areas of ministry be opened to women. Kane's bold speech embodied concerns of conservative Catholics who, even in 1979, worried the LCWR had strayed from Church teachings.[12] While most women religious do not take such active stances on women's ordination, the LCWR has established a reputation of actively supporting socially liberal positions.

To many, it seemed that CICSAL valued the visitation's formal procedure over the insights the women could offer into the quality of their lives as vowed religious, thus rendering the visitation's findings unrepresentative of their lived realities. Sister Fran Ferder wrote in *Catholic Culture* that the Visitation's "topics of the 'conversation' are less about a desire to know the heart of the other, and more about getting information," lamenting "visitations worthy of the name are supposed to generate spontaneous leaping of life within—not a report—especially a report that will not be previewed by those whose lives it describes." Similarly, CICSAL's own actions belied its professed intent.[13] For instance, speaking on Catholic television station EWTN, Cardinal Raymond Burke, prefect of the Vatican's highest judiciary body, stated that "if [the LCWR] can't be reformed, it doesn't have a right to continue."[14]

As LCWR statements publicly communicated its members' surprise and frustration, the organization also set a clear tone of stalwart dedication to dialogue and the right for sisters to understand their own charisms. Leaders framed the dual probes as carried out at the behest of a structure run amok with power, positioning the LCWR as holding tightly to the most important tenets of Christian life. Yet, throughout their responses, LCWR leadership reiterates sisters' commitments to their vows and to the Catholic Church through two, intertwined, tactics. First, congregations combed their histories, reacquainting themselves with foundresses' charisms and using this knowledge to justify and articulate current organizational positions. These histories rooted sisters in Catholic doctrine, allowing them to refuse prescribed definitions proffered by Church hierarchies, in control of their own religious narratives. Second, the LCWR used media coverage of the sisters' activism to keep the ongoing investigations in current discourse, swaying opinion against the Vatican. Combined, the sisters' responses demonstrate an ethos of deep commitments to contemporary communities motivated by devotion not to the Vatican but to the Catholic Church as intended and enacted by Jesus. The sisters' responses made clear their ethē were not reactionary or temporal; they were habitual, at the core of their vowed identity.

SUBVERSION AND INCARNATION

The LCWR's initial public response was measured and conciliatory; however, the organization made clear its members would not simply submit to the culture-changing directions implicit in the investigations' announcements. Feminist theologian Sister Sandra Schneiders spoke to these tensions in an email to colleagues unintentionally made public and, with permission, published by the *National Catholic Reporter*. She called the assessment "a hostile move" whose conclusions "are already in," advising sisters to "receive [Vatican officials] politely and kindly . . . as uninvited guests who should be received in the parlor, not given run of the whole house."[15] LCWR statements firmly rooted the organization's current positions as the direct result of prayerful responses to past Vatican directives, rejecting outright the Church's assertions that their ministries had strayed from Catholic teachings and that their quality of life had been in any way compromised.

While many, both within and outside the Church, identify the Vatican II Council as the primary catalyst for the evolution of the role of women religious, transformative impulses had defined the group for decades prior. For instance, a 1950 letter from Pope Pius XII called for a meeting of religious Superiors General lest "the holy laws of each Institute degenerate into an assemblage of exterior regulations uselessly imposed, whose letter, in the absence of the spirit, kills."[16] Between 1962 and 1965, the Second Vatican Council further animated this spirit of renewal by approving a directive instructing religious orders to seek guidance within the original sources of Christianity, return to the spirit of orders' founders, and adapt to the conditions of contemporary times. Though Vatican II did not alter doctrine, Carol Jablonski states the Council "catapulted the Church from the medieval to the modern era."[17] In decreeing the Church to be "truly and intimately linked with humankind and its history," called to "the perfection of charity," Vatican II recentered the focus of vowed religious toward growth, that is, "spiritual, human, intellectual and professional—within the context of their common charisms."[18]

The prayerful contemplation prompted by these reforms revised foundational assumptions concerning the role of women religious in the church. Schneiders argues that "[women] religious—probably without consciously intending such a thing—were subverting the domination system of the patriarchal church by incarnating in their community life an alternative not only to patriarchy but to all forms of coercion-based exercise of power."[19] The changes "undermined the operational authority of the Church's hierarchy," reconfiguring the ways both vowed religious and laity understand their relationships to the Church. During the investigations, LCWR leadership encouraged congregations to revisit their institutes' founding documents and records of decisions made following Vatican II. As they poured over historical records seeking to understand their predecessors' choices, the sisters reengaged practiced habits. Sister Anne Marie Mongoven wrote that these documents, authored by congregational founders and subsequent leaders, served to stabilize and focus LCWR responses: "We asked what our founders wanted of us. How did they foresee us preaching the Gospel and serving the Church?"[20]

THE HABIT OF CONTEMPLATIVE DIALOGUE

From the outset, the LCWR emphasized processes of dialogue and prayer. The LCWR Board encouraged "leaders to reflect on the stories of heroic service and creative fidelity of their own members" before entering into the visitation. They also thanked international "women religious who have offered their prayer and fasting for our work," calling the actions a sign of "support [which] has only strengthened the great solidarity that exists among us as we together carry out the mission of LCWR."[21] These statements underscored the importance of prayer and community in the face of uncertainty, as well as the seriousness with which members entered into the investigations.

Public statements implicitly and explicitly made clear that LCWR practices did not warrant scrutiny but were, in fact, evidence of the highest callings of Christian life. Habitual processes reinforced dedication to these missions. As Arthur B. Miller reminds us that the most familiar translation of ethos—as character—is an impoverished choice. Better, he states, to understand the concept as "habit," describing ethos as "an accustomed place," a dwelling place that comes about through practiced communal negotiation and interaction.[22] Through study, prayer, and dialogue, sisters continually renewed and internalized the ethos practiced by those who came before. These practices also made explicit the structures of power in which their orders operated. In their discussions of feminist ethos, Ryan et al. point out that such meditation confers an authority to speak and act with full commitments to the politics of their locations—and ethical responsibility to critique the structures in which they are embedded.[23] And so the LCWR did.

In a press release following the announcement of the visitation in February 2009, the LCWR expressed thinly veiled betrayal, stating the group lacked sufficient information to "determine how their participation in the visitation can be beneficial to US religious life, the church, and the world," particularly given the "significant discernment and study processes already inherent in religious life . . . [that] have long served to make women religious keenly aware of their individual, communal and ecclesial strengths and challenges."[24] Similarly, in April, LCWR expressed disappointment in learning about the assessment from a *National Catholic Reporter* article, rather than official communication of some sort, particularly because the sisters had "always been clear that we are open to dialogue with our US bishops."[25] LCWR statements framed the conference's intention to cooperate with and engage in the inquests, despite being blindsided by the assessment's announcement, thereby positioning the LCWR as a victim of the whims of the larger, patriarchal Church. At LCWR's annual assembly in August, leaders again affirmed "their orders have always been fully accountable to the Church and plan to collaborate with the Vatican in these studies," asserting that the women "have remained faithful to the reform and renewal of their communities called for by the Second Vatican Council that . . . includes serving at and speaking from the margins of the Catholic Church."[26]

The LCWR not only called for dialogue in public press statements but also modeled the practice. For example, following the release of the doctrinal assessment, board members developed sessions at the annual assembly to address members' concerns. Leaders shared experiences and thoughts about their interactions with Vatican officials. Archbishop J. Peter Sartain, tasked with guiding the proscribed five-year oversight period, spoke to the assembly. LCWR members had space to ask questions and give suggestions concerning the organization's next steps.[27] The sessions, "conducted in a process of contemplative discernment where time was provided for prayer, silence, and respectful listening,"[28] modeled the dialogic style the LCWR had sought throughout their interactions with the Vatican. There was space for all perspectives, time for individual reflection, and a forum to share reactions with fellow stakeholders.

When, during an August 2012 press conference, then-president Sister Pat Farrell was pressed to explain what LCWR sought, she told reporters the organization hoped to be "recognized and understood as equals in the church, that our form of religious life can be and *is* respected and affirmed . . . for the ability to openly and honestly search for truth together."[29] Schneiders expressed a "desire to de-escalate the conflict," but she asserted that "there are non-negotiables," including the understanding that the bishops are not uniquely privy to the voice of God.[30] The investigations' opaque processes violated the discernment U.S. American women religious understood as vital to the enactment of their relationship to the Church.

RESISTANCE TO A HIERARCHICAL MINDSET

The bishops conducting the reviews, however, approached the investigations from an altogether different perspective, relying on their position as guardians of established doctrine to justify the probes. Certain bishops even accused the LCWR of using the dialogue to undermine Church authority "when sisters disagree about basic matters of Catholic faith or moral practice."[31] Bishop Leonard Blair, a Vatican delegate, noted that if "by dialogue they mean that the doctrines of the church are negotiable and . . . somehow, we find a middle ground about basic church teaching on faith and morals, then no. I don't think that is the kind of dialogue that the Holy See would envision."[32] Cardinal William Levada who, until June 2012, headed the CDF, granted a rare interview to the *National Catholic Reporter* in which he expressed frustration at the LCWR's insistence on ongoing dialogue, calling interactions with the group "a dialogue with the deaf."[33] The Church's investments rest in its status as "the medium for transmitting and conveying the truth of tradition already established," rather than "developing or revising the truth of the living tradition of the Catholic faith."[34] Engaging within what Roderick Hart called the doctrinal genre, bishops presented arguments on behalf of "the doctrine, not themselves," linking the investigations' ethos to long-settled truth beyond the influence of individual bishops.[35]

Such a hierarchical mind-set was anathema to the women religious who remained committed to open dialogue. Sisters revisiting their foundresses' charisms found commitments to the poor at the center of early organizational missions. As waves of European immigration had added to the number of vowed religious in the States throughout the nineteenth century, tensions and cultural rivalries that permeated secular society did not simply disappear behind convent walls. Rather, these institutions fostered a uniquely American religious culture as people worked across ethnic lines in pursuit of common goals in schools, hospitals, and other institutions, resulting in a particular Americanized religious culture.[36]

This spirit of egalitarianism informed the ways sisters understood themselves, their relationships to each other, and their role within the Church. For example, in the 1950s, women religious founded the Sister Formation Conference (SFC) to address frustrations with the lack of training afforded to sisters assigned to teach in parochial schools.[37] Under the leadership of Sisters Mary Emil Penet and Annette Walters, the SFC operated through nonhierarchical, egalitarian principles uncommon within the larger Church. Carol Coburn relates that as Sisters Annette and another sister argued with an Italian representative from the Sacred Congregation for the organization's continued independence. He silenced them with a wave of the hand, shouting, "Oh you Americans and your democracy!"[38] Although amusing in itself, the anecdote illustrates an entrenched mind-set that set U.S. American women religious apart from their international counterparts.

While John XXIII is often credited with opening the Church's doors to the secular world, Coburn maintains that U.S. American women religious had passed through them long before.[39] Decades of visible, community-focused service helped institutions to navigate tides of anti-Catholic bigotry and facilitate the formation of identity at home in both U.S. American and Catholic traditions. The Vatican's call to live out the Gospel outside church walls directed many congregations' ministerial paths. In addressing the needs of vulnerable populations with whom they found themselves in community, sisters lived an enacted Gospel carving out what Melissa Browning and Emily Reimer-Barry deemed "pulpitized spaces" beyond church walls.[40] Sifting through congregational archives reintroduced twenty-first-century women religious to the values of their foundresses and the ways their predecessors had lived out these values during previous times of uncertainty. The LCWR encouraged its members through a habit of re-membering, that is, seeking to understand how the places, events, and people entwined within the archives come to impose themselves on present material circumstances.[41] Though Vatican II is remembered as the turning point in communal history, sisters' calls to serve were embedded in their congregations' prayerfully considered foundations.

IMMUTABLE LAWS, IMMUTABLE HABITS

Far from the result of waning dedication to the Catholic Church, the LCWR framed its commitments in the social world as linked directly to reforms instigated by the Vatican. The LCWR confidently spoke from what James Darsey calls a prophetic voice, which embraces a "meaningful incivility" using logic drawn from "immutable law, beyond the reach of humankind."[42] By refusing to adapt to its audience, prophetic rhetoric operates outside of the expectations of Western rhetoric. Instead, those who take up a prophetic voice purposefully violate expectations to highlight powerful institutions' culpability for injustices perpetuated from their positions comfortably within current structures. Sister Joan Chittister reminded *National Catholic Reporter* readers that sisters have long been accused of operating in spaces beyond the limits of their callings, bearing scorn and judgment for work that is now lauded as brave and just.

Their courage, she contends, has been "too easily domesticated," shrugged off as "just what sisters are supposed to be doing."[43] The sisters' righteous incivility reflected Nedra Reynolds's argument that people "inscribe *who* they are by showing *where* they are."[44] Citing women religious who educated women when such efforts were considered frivolous, who served as Civil War battlefield nurses, who dedicated themselves to the civil rights, Chittister illustrates that

> for hundreds of years, over and over again, women religious have found themselves at the junction between past and future. . . . They did not succeed because their numbers were large or their influence was great or their social support was either broad-based or obvious. They succeeded because they refused to allow the ideas of the past to become the cement of the future. They succeeded because of the courage of women who went where they were told not to go.[45]

LCWR leaders framed the most recent inquest in light of this usable past. Accused of being unfaithful to their vows and unfit to serve the Church, those women religious "[dealt] head-on with the social justice questions of their time and so saved the church in the process."[46] Now, it was incumbent upon contemporary women religious to do the same.

Similarly, Schneiders positioned the sisters as protecting its core ethos from the corruption embraced by its current hierarchy. She wrote, "It is precisely because the prophet is addressing the actual situation, publicly lamenting current oppression as contrary to God's will, and energizing real people to imagine and strive for an alternate future, that the prophet is often perceived as dangerous to the status quo."[47] In many ways, the LCWR embraced the CDF's labels, framing themselves as intimately familiar with the needs of those they served in ways inaccessible to those higher in the Church hierarchy. Accepting this, the LCWR left the public to enthymatically consider the path truly reflective of God's path.

To the LCWR, feminism does not represent a disavowal of Catholicism but, rather, a mandate to live out Christ's radical inclusivity by standing in community with those on the margins. Even if this means standing up to those who purport to represent the will of God itself. When then LCWR president Florence Deacon was asked if she accepted the label of radical feminism, Deacon enthusiastically agreed noting that, by feminism, the Vatican seemed to refer to "the radical idea that women are people,"[48] quipping in another interview that she "could show them some real radical feminists."[49] Any appearance of radicalism on the part of LCWR stemmed from the distorting influence of an increasingly distant hierarchy.

The sisters knew they were, according to most understandings of the Catholic Church's structure, at a disadvantage in terms of power. However, by using the rhetoric within their founding charisms, LCWR representatives anchored their positions as prayerfully informed by Church guidance, as well as by their own organizational and congregational histories. The spirits of service, prayer, and nonhierarchical structure long served as the bedrock of communal life. By demanding meaningful dialogue, the LCWR refused to reach stasis with the bishops regarding the sisters' roles in the Church. They chose to remain in their customary place—dwelling with those in the margins to whom they ministered over those at the center whom they ought purportedly to obey. In spite of the bishops' promise to listen to the sisters, the dialogic frame of discourse was simply beyond the hierarchy's practiced ability to hear.

LIVING OUT A PUBLIC FAITH

Both the investigators and the sisters under scrutiny attempted to tie themselves to tradition and the faithful commitments of Christ's call. Whereas the CDF's efforts to bring the LCWR back to its "fundamental Christological center and focus of religious consecration,"[50] the LCWR framed this effort as subject to the shifting tides of hierarchical politics. It was inevitable that the LCWR would come into conflict with the Church hierarchy due to the sisters' focus on the needs of the poor. Schneiders states sisters "are not called as part of the hierarchy to act as agents of the institutions but as prophets among the People of God."[51] Farrell furthered that this difference in calling set the obligations of women religious as distinct from those of ordained clergy, stating "a bishop, for instance, can't be on the street working with the homeless. He has other tasks. But we can be."[52] As prophets of the localized Church, women religious do not understand themselves as servants of the Vatican, but rather, as servants of God.

While the LCWR and CDF agreed not to communicate with the media about ongoing negotiations, the sisters took advantage of their newfound spotlight to bolster their public authority, becoming even more outspoken in their advocacy efforts. Sister Simone Campbell explained: "we thought, 'how can we use this attention to be of service to the people that we care about?' Having this much attention—we're not used to that as Catholic sisters. It seemed like a great convergence to have this notoriety used for the sake of our mission."[53] The LCWR embraced its counter-public position as outsiders within the Catholic Church, challenging public perceptions of Catholic theology by presenting a Gospel open to all, despite seemingly exclusionary doctrinal rhetoric associated with the traditional church. The LCWR used media interest in their plight to mold their public ethos as harbingers of an open, just, and loving church, both through increasing the visibility of their activism and the creation of a public narrative representing this legacy.

Meaningful work within the public eye was nothing new to the LCWR. Bernadette McCauley suggests that, with far greater numbers than their male counterparts, women religious serve as "the face of American Catholicism," presenting a "benevolent and non-threatening church to non-Catholics."[54] Sisters' outward focus responds to a gap between the Church's tradition. Kristin Heyer clarifies that "rather than holistically attending to relational patterns and social contexts," issues are often "isolated" by the Church's formal procedures. The LCWR, she contends, addresses them directly, "in light of the reach of its communitarian personalism."[55]

NUNS ON THE BUS

It was here that the LCWR embarked on their most visible response to the Vatican investigations in the form of their Nuns on the Bus initiative. The project was sponsored by NETWORK, a Catholic lobbying organization. Though they are not officially affiliated, the CDF's report had explicitly mentioned the LCWR's intertwined relationship with NETWORK in its reasoning for its assessment.[56] Ignoring this explicitly stated concern, the LCWR joined with NETWORK on this tour featuring a rotating group of women religious who piled into a brightly painted bus with a podium, signs, and other equipment. Aptly dubbing themselves "Nuns on the Bus," the sisters crisscrossed the country to "prophetically speak for justice and advocate for adequate federal policies."[57]

The first trip, called "Nuns Drive for Faith, Family, and Fairness," focused on highlighting organizations that serve the nation's neediest and protesting the proposed national budget, which NETWORK head Sister Simone Campbell deemed an "amoral document" because of its severe cuts to social service organizations.[58] The sisters provided both an affective moral presence and an alternative to the budget, which had been proposed by Wisconsin representative Paul Ryan who had justified the cuts by appealing to his Catholic faith.[59] Campbell told the Cedar Rapids *Gazette* that her "astute political analysis was 'liar, liar pants on fire.'"[60] Speaking directly to those responsible for the bill, the tour stopped at the offices of congressional officials who voted in favor of Ryan's budget plan. Of the representatives, Campbell explained the sisters "just think they didn't have enough information. They didn't know the fullness of Catholic social teaching. They're not bad people. It's just that they made a vote that will hurt people."[61]

In addition to attempting to visit congressional representatives, the tour featured stops at dozens of social service organizations supported primarily by Catholic sisters. The tour led the sisters to a soup kitchen and picket line in Milwaukee,[62] low-income housing developments in Chicago, an adult literacy center in Detroit, and a childcare ministry in Philadelphia.[63] The Nuns on the Bus countered accusations that their materials and work were out of step with Church stances on abortion and gay rights by showcasing countless ministries dedicated to the preservation of life. In addition to drawing much-needed attention to the organizations, the sisters' visits demonstrated the depth and breadth of support that women religious—including those outside of leadership positions—provided communities as a core element in the fulfillment of their religious vows.

The tour was so successful that NETWORK sponsored tours in subsequent years with themes drawn from the year's most salient issues:

- 2013's "Raise Your Hands, Raise Your Voice" spanned 6,500 miles across fifteen (primarily southern) states was dedicated to immigration reform. The tour advocated shifting focus from securing the border to family unity and humane policy, including clearing bureaucratic backlogs and creating a path to citizenship for undocumented residents.[64]

- The 2015 tour, "Bridge the Divides, Transform Politics," coincided with Pope Francis's first visit to the United States and responded to the pontiff's "radical call [to] change our politics, not just our policies."[65] The route took the sisters to "places where there are differences of opinion, to nourish conversations about the serious work of governance," filming video clips of the people they met along the way so Pope Francis could hear the narratives of "folks that he otherwise wouldn't be able to see or hear from."[66]
- In 2016, "Mend the Gaps: Reweaving the Fabric of Society" sought "to bring a politics of inclusion to divided places, change the conversation to mending the vast economic and social divides in our country, and counter political incivility."[67] Calling themselves "Pope Francis voters" who make themselves "equal opportunity annoyers" of both political parties, the sisters stopped at both the Democratic and Republican National Political Conventions.[68]

Campbell, who had not planned on touring in 2016, said the vitriolic lead-up to the 2016 presidential elections made the choice to hit the road again easy.[69] Similarly simple was the decision to remain in Washington, DC, in 2017 to lobby against congressional attempts to repeal the Affordable Care Act.[70]

The tours modeled the role of listening and dialogue that the sisters had insisted upon in their conversations with Vatican officials. The LCWR did not emphasize dialogue to gain undue voice. Rather, the practice represented a crosscutting value, foundational to the ways in which sisters understood themselves as vowed religious.

On tour, the nuns were "compared to rock stars," often climbing off their bus to screaming fans holding signs and wearing commemorative T-shirts.[71] At times, support came from high-profile advocates. At the kickoff of 2014's tour in Iowa, then-vice president Joe Biden, who was just beginning his 2016 presidential run, told an assembled crowd that "the Nuns on the Bus fought like the devil for health care," adding, "I know no group of people who bring a greater sense of justice and passion to what they do."[72] Support from Biden—a self-professed "Catholic school kid" who, at a meeting with Pope Benedict, suggested the Pontiff "lighten up" because he was "being entirely too hard on the American nuns"[73]—was unsurprising.

The tours' intentional model of ecumenical inclusion fostered relationships across religious boundaries. Stops often featured listening sessions or workshops cohosted with Protestant and non-Christian partners and spotlighted services sponsored by non-Catholic organizations. At the inaugural tour's concluding rally, Sayyid Sayeed, national director of the Islamic Society of North America's Office of Interfaith and Community Alliances, pointed to sisters' universal ethic of care, saying, "Nuns on the Bus speak for not just Catholics, not for Christians only, not for Jews. They speak for all of us."[74]

Through their intentionally inclusive designs, tours lived out the Vatican II's call for an outward-facing, ecumenical Church, garnering support and attention from all manner of political allies.

Formally justified as a way to draw attention to the causes supported by the supposed "radical feminists," tours were, in no small part, invaluable PR campaigns for the LCWR. Resulting media coverage almost uniformly framed the initial 2012 tour against the backdrop of the Vatican investigations and accentuated the enthusiasm with which the public welcomed the nuns. At the end of the 2012 tour, one man who had been finishing a "We Love You Sisters" sign explained that he saw "the sisters [as] everything that is good with the church, so it's amazing that the hierarchy is choosing to attack them. . . . The bishops are in a bad state of affairs right now."[75] The LCWR entered the public sphere enthusiastically, reinvigorating the "public face of Catholicism"[76] for the twenty-first century. In doing so, the sisters highlighted their habitual work as inextricable from America's social safety net. The LCWR positioned the sisters, who labored among the nation's neediest, as under attack from a Church hierarchy out of touch with the reality of those needs.

Never explicitly stated, Nuns on the Bus provided a study in contrasts between the sisters and the male clergy involved in the inquiries. High-ranking clergy were given respect due to their positions within the hierarchy; women religious lived out a faith through visible praxis which placed themselves in direct community with those whom they served. In Kansas City, Campbell told the assembled crowd that only community could be counted on to provide solutions to society's problems claiming, "We the people can do it. Not we the politicians, not we the really, really rich people, not even we the economy."[77] As a part of this "we," sisters typically joined the tour for only a few stops before returning to their home cities to continue their work. So situated, women religious responded to the most pressing needs in the communities they served.

REVISING THE PUBLIC IMAGINARY

Though without formal power, the LCWR used the investigations to reinscribe a particular understanding of women religious in the public imaginary. By taking control of their own stories, via tours, social media, and, most notably, a documentary dedicated to LCWR's mission and history, sisters bridged the space between political issues and personal experience. By embracing their identities as women religious, sisters blurred boundaries between private and public, sacred and profane, muddying understandings concerning the limits of appropriate civil discourse. As vowed religious, the sisters spoke from positions of moral authority, using their platforms to introduce the voices of marginalized community members. By centering these narratives, women religious grant humanity to issues the norms of rational critical discourse would prefer left in the abstract. Centering these conversations in the public square, women religious rewrite and reform the roles prescribed by the Catholic hierarchy, relying instead on experiential knowledge rooted in their own prophetic discernment.

Once the LCWR encountered Vatican representatives who truly invested in building relationships, progress could—slowly and deliberately—be made. One such sympathetic ear belonged to Archbishop J. Peter Sartain who was tapped to manage oversight of the organization after the submission of the assessment. Sartain entered into the process by issuing a statement that mirrored LCWR language, affirming he "remain[ed] committed to working to address the issues of doctrinal assessment in an atmosphere of prayer and respectful dialogue." Sartain added that the groups must "work toward clearing up any misunderstandings, and I remain truly hopeful that we will work together without compromising church teaching or the important role of the LCWR."[78] The archbishop openly listened to the sisters as they expressed betrayal at the CDF's accusations, even requesting the nuns provide him with documents about the Vatican's post-conciliar instructions so he could understand the organization's history and mission. By rooting interactions with the LCWR in a spirit of dialogue, Sartain demonstrated that the LCWR's priorities, values, and position within the Church were acknowledged and understood.

Despite Sartain's gesture toward community with the women religious, as evidenced through his consistent use of first person plural pronouns when discussing his work with the LCWR, power imbalances could not be leveled. While the terms of the discussions followed the desires of the LCWR, the terms of the relationship were set entirely by the Vatican. Dialogic possibilities were limited by the boundaries of accepted doctrine.

THE HOPE OF RE-MEMBERED HABITS

The conclusion of the dual investigations, then, was, at best, unsatisfying. At worst, it reified the position of the LCWR as fully subject to the whims of the Vatican hierarchy, leaving sisters feeling betrayed by the Church to which they had vowed their lives. The experiences, however, also pointed to the possibility of alternative futures. By holding tightly to the legacies of still-present pasts, LCWR leaders steadfastly embraced the ethos so painstakingly practiced and refined by sisters who came before. Supported by media curiosity, public letter writing campaigns, and local rallies, the LCWR reinscribed public understanding of the role of vowed women religious. Refusing to deviate from the processes at the core of their organizational ethos, LCWR leaders shepherded membership through the ecclesiastical storm. As the clouds cleared, the LCWR emerged with a refined understanding of the necessity of their roles in the contemporary moment—assured of the fact that their prophetic work might someday bear out the fruit of a more just world.

NOTES

1. Franc Rodé, "From Past to Present: Religious Life Before and After Vatican II," transcript of speech delivered at Stonehill College, September 27, 2008, https://www.ewtn.com/catholicism/library/from-past-to-present-religious-life-before-and-after-vatican-ii-9851.
2. LCWR, "About LCWR," accessed June 1, 2021, https://lcwr.org/about.
3. Erin Brigham, "Women Religious and the Public Voice of Catholicism," *The Journal of Feminist Studies in Religion* 21, no. 2 (Fall 2015): 109, https://doi.org/10.2979/jfemistudreli.31.2.109.
4. S. Michael Halloran, "Aristotle's Concept of Ethos, or If Not His Somebody Else's." *Rhetoric Review* 1, no. 1 (1982): 60, http://www.jstor.org/stable/465559.
5. Kathleen J. Ryan, Nancy Myers, and Rebecca Jones, "Introduction: Identifying Feminist Ecological Ethē," in *Rethinking Ethos: A Feminist Ecological Approach to Rhetoric*, eds. Kathleen J. Ryan, Nancy Myers, and Rebecca Jones (Carbondale, IL: Southern Illinois UP, 2016), 2.
6. Fabrizio Mastrofini, "'Rebel' Nuns Receive Religious Freedom Award," *Vatican Insider*, November 19, 2012, http://vaticaninsider.lastampa.it/en/world-news/detail/articolo/usa-stati-uniti-estados-unidos-suore-nuns-monjas-19867/.
7. Congregation for the Doctrine of the Faith (CDF), "Doctrinal Assessment of the Leadership Conference of Women Religious," The Holy See, April 18, 2012, https://www.vatican.va/roman_curia/congregations/cfaith/documents/rc_con_cfaith_doc_20120418_assessment-lcwr_en.html.
8. João Braz de Aviz, "Apostolic Visitation Final Report," US Council of Catholic Bishops, September 8, 2014, https://www.usccb.org/beliefs-and-teachings/vocations/consecrated-life/apostolic-visitation-final-report.
9. de Aviz, "Apostolic Visitation."
10. Margaret Susan Thompson, "Circles of Sisterhood: Formal and Informal Collaboration Among American Nuns in Response to Conflict with Vatican Kyriarchy," *Journal of Feminist Studies in Religion* 32, no. 2 (2016): 64, https://doi.org/10.2979/jfemistudreli.32.2.06.
11. LCWR, "About LCWR," accessed June 1, 2021, https://lcwr.org/about.
12. Christine Schenk, *To Speak the Truth in Love: A Biography of Theresa Kane, R.S.M.* (Maryknoll, NY: Orbis Books, 2019), 1–8.
13. de Aviz, "Apostolic Visitation."

14. Michelle Boorstein, "U.S. Nuns Seek 'Open Dialogue' with Rome Over Disputes," *The Washington Post*, August 10, 2012, https://www.washingtonpost.com/local/us-nuns-seek-open-dialogue-with-rome-over-disputes/2012/08/10/64ab2534-e31b-11e1-98e7-89d659f9c106_story.html.

15. Sandra Schneiders, "We've Given Birth to a New Form of Religious Life," *National Catholic Reporter*, February 27, 2009, https://www.ncronline.org/news/global-sisters-report/weve-given-birth-new-form-religious-life.

16. Anne Marie Mongoven, "We Did What the Church Asked Us to Do." *National Catholic Reporter*, August 7, 2009. https://www.ncronline.org/news/global-sisters-report/we-did-what-church-asked-us-do.

17. Carol J. Jablonski, "Aggiornamento and The American Catholic Bishops: A Rhetoric of Institutional Continuity and Change," *Quarterly Journal of Speech* 75, no. 4 (1989): 416, https://doi.org/10.1080/00335638909383888.

18. Phyllis Zagano, "Ministry by Women Religious and the U.S. Apostolic Vistation," *New Blackfriars* 92, no. 1041 (September 2011): 594, https://www.jstor.org/stable/43251556.

19. Sandra Schneiders, *Prophets in Their Own Country: Women Religious Bearing Witness to the Gospel in a Troubled Church* (Maryknoll, NY: Orbis Press, 2011), 116.

20. Anne Marie Mongoven, "We Did What the Church Asked Us to Do."

21. J. Lora Dambroski et al., "Public Statement from the LCWR Officers," LCWR, April 23, 2009, https://lcwr.org/media/april-23-2009-lcwr-officers-statement-doctrinal-assessment-lcwr.

22. Arthur B. Miller, "Aristotle on Habit (εθō) and Character (ηθō): Implications for the *Rhetoric*," Speech Monographs 41, no. 4 (1974): 310–311, https://doi.org/10.1080/03637757409375855.

23. Ryan, Myers, and Jones, "Introduction," 8–9.

24. Jean Wincek and Nancy Reynolds, "Tracing the Apostolic Visitation through a Chronology of Primary Sources," in *Power of Sisterhood: Women Religious Tell the Story of Apostolic Visitation*, eds. Margaret Cain McCarthy and Mary Ann Zollman (Lanham, MD: University Press, 2014), 50.

25. LCWR, "April 23, 2009—LCWR Officers Statement on Doctrinal Assessment of LCWR," April 23, 2009, https://lcwr.org/media/april-23-2009-lcwr-officers-statement-doctrinal-assessment-lcwr.

26. Wincek and Reynolds, "Tracing," 50.

27. LCWR, "Leadership Conference of Women Religious Assembly Explores Concerns of the Global Community," August 19, 2013, https://lcwr.org/sites/default/files/calendar/attachments/lcwr_2013_assembly_press_release_-_8-19-13.pdf.

28. LCWR, "Leadership Conference of Women Religious Assembly Explores Concerns of the Global Community," August 19, 2013, https://lcwr.org/media/2013-lcwr-assembly-and-board-meeting.

29. Jamie Manson, "LCWR's Annual Meeting: Some Reflections and A Little Backstory," *National Catholic Reporter*, August 15, 2012, https://www.ncronline.org/blogs/grace-margins/lcwrs-annual-meeting-some-reflections-and-little-back-story.

30. Laurie Goodstein, "National Nuns' Group Dodges Showdown with Vatican," *The New York Times*, August 10, 2012, https://www.nytimes.com/2012/08/11/us/national-nuns-group-seeks-dialogue-with-vatican.html.

31. CDF, "Doctrinal Assessment."

32. Leonard Blair, interview by Terry Gross, "Bishop Explains Vatican's Criticisms of U.S. Nuns," *Fresh Air on NPR*, July 25, 2012, https://www.npr.org/transcripts/157356092.

33. John L. Allen, "Exclusive Interview: Levada Talks LCWR, Criticism in the States," *National Catholic Reporter*, June 15, 2012, https://www.ncronline.org/blogs/all-things-catholic/exclusive-interview-levada-talks-lcwr-criticism-states.

34. Bradford Hinze, *Practices of Dialogue in the Roman Catholic Church: Aims and Obstacles, Lessons and Laments* (New York: Continuum International Publishing, 2006), 260–261.

35. Roderick P. Hart, "The Rhetoric of the True Believer," *Speech Monographs* 38, no. 4 (1971): 258, https://doi.org/10.1080/03637757109375718.

36. Carol K. Coburn, "An Overview of the Historiography of Women Religious: A Twenty-Five-Year Retrospective," *U.S. Catholic Historian* 22, no. 1 (2004): 6, http://www.jstor.org/stable/25154889.

37. Coburn, "An Overview," 14.

38. Carol K. Coburn, "Uneasy Alliance: A Look Back at American Sisters and Clerical Authority," *Global Sisters Report*, July 13, 2015. https://www.globalsistersreport.org/column/trends/uneasy-alliance-look-back-american-sisters-and-clerical-authority-27881.

39. Sandra Schneiders, *Prophets in Their Own Country: Women Religious Bearing Witness to the Gospel in a Troubled Church* (Maryknoll, NY: Orbis Press, 2011), 116.

40. Melissa Browning and Emily Reimer-Barry, "Preaching, Sexuality, and Women Religious: Listening to Prophetic Voices at the Margins of Religious Life," *Theology & Sexuality* 19, no. 1 (2013): 83, https://doi.org/10.1179/1355835814Z.00000000020.

41. Anne-Marie Fortier, "Re-Membering Places and the Performance of Belonging(s)," *Theory, Culture & Society* 16, no. 2 (April 1999): 42, https://doi.org/10.1177/02632769922050548.

42. James Darsey, *The Prophetic Tradition and Radical Rhetoric in America* (New York: NYU Press, 1997), x.

43. Joan Chittister, "Wanted: Women of Spirit in Our Own Time," *National Catholic Reporter*, August 11, 2010, https://www.ncronline.org/news/global-sisters-report/wanted-women-spirit-our-own-time.

44. Nedra Reynolds, "Ethos as Location: New Sites for Understanding Discursive Authority." *Rhetoric Review* 11, no. 2 (1993): 325, http://www.jstor.org/stable/465805. (emphasis original)

45. Chittister, "Wanted."

46. Chittister, "Wanted."

47. Schneiders, "We've Given Birth."

48. Florence Deacon, interview by Gayle King and Anthony Mason, *CBS This Morning*, March 11, 2013. www.cbs.com/shows/cbs_this_morning/ video/2342231215/rebel-nuns-talks-female-priestswomen-in-church/.

49. Ada Calhoun, "Radical Habits," *The New York Times*, October 26, 2013, https://www.nytimes.com/2012/10/28/magazine/sister-florence-deacon-the-rebel-nun.html.

50. CDF, "Doctrinal Assessment of the Leadership Conference of Women Religious."

51. Schneiders, "*Prophets*," 116.

52. Pat Farrell, interview by Terry Gross, "An American Nun Responds to Vatican Criticism," *Fresh Air* on National *Public Radio from WHYY*, July 17, 2012, https://www.npr.org/2012/07/17/156858223/an-american-nun-responds-to-vatican-condemnation.

53. Andrew Fredericks, "Sister Simone Campbell on What Drives 'Nuns on the Bus,'" *Moyers on Democracy*, June 27, 2012, https://billmoyers.com/2012/06/27/sister-simone-campbell-on-what-drives-nuns-on-the-bus/.

54. Bernadette McCauley, "Nuns' Stories: Writing the History of Women Religious in the United States," *American Catholic Studies* 125, no. 4 (2014): 51–68, https://doi.org/10.1353/acs.2014.0067.

55. Kristin Heyer, "A Feminist Appraisal of Catholic Social Thought," speech delivered as part of Fall Lecture Series, Lane Center for Catholic Studies and Catholic Social Thought, University of San Francisco, November 9, 2007, https://www.academia.edu/4433442/A_FEMINIST_APPRAISAL_OF_CATHOLIC_SOCIAL_THOUGHT.

56. Network, "Network History," accessed June 1, 2021, https://networklobby.org/about/history/.

57. Network, "Nuns on the Bus," accessed June 1, 2021, https://networklobby.org/nunsonthebus/.

58. Manya A. Brachear, "Nuns on the Bus Protest Campaign Rolls into Chicago," *The Chicago Tribune*, June 20, 2012, https://www.chicagotribune.com/news/ct-xpm-2012-06-20-ct-met-nuns-on-the-bus-20120620-story.html.

59. Michael O'Loughlin, "Paul Ryan Defends Poverty Reform Efforts to a Catholic Nun," *America: The Jesuit Review*, August 22, 2017, https://www.america-magazine.org/politics-society/2017/08/22/paul-ryan-defends-poverty-reform-efforts-catholic-nun.

60. The Gazette Editorial Board, "Nuns' Shared-Sacrifice Pitch Rings True," *The Gazette*, June 22, 2012, https://www.thegazette.com/2012/06/22/nuns-shared-sacri-fice-pitch-rings-true.

61. Brachear, "Nuns on the Bus."

62. Barbara Miner, "The Nuns are Here! The Nuns are Here!," *Milwaukee Journal Sentinel*, June 20, 2012, http://archive.jsonline.com/blogs/purple-wisconsin/159706575.html.

63. Sally Steenland, Hannah Moser, and Elana Leopold, "An Overview of the Nuns on the Bus Tour," *Center for American Progress*, July 17, 2012, americanprogress.org/issues/religion/news/2012/07/17/11924/an-overview-of-the-nuns-on-the-bus-tour/.

64. "Nuns Hit the Road Again for Real Immigration Reform," *Angelus*, June 18, 2013. https://angelusnews.com/local/california/nuns-hit-the-road-again-for-real-immigration-reform/.

65. "Nuns on the Bus 2015: Bridge the Divides, Transform Politics," *Network Nuns on the Bus*, accessed July 2, 2021. https://bus.networklobby.org/bus2015/?fbclid=IwAR1dJKzq6ksmV3z1qm6k30aPw3_Btesee_xG19kRsqd0qx-QM9WaHsxRBYM.

66. David Gibson, "New 'Nuns on the Bus' Tour to Highlight Pope Francis' US Visit and Agenda," *Washington Post*, August 26, 2015, https://www.washingtonpost.com/national/religion/new-nuns-on-the-bus-tour-to-highlight-pope-francis-us-visit-and-agenda/2015/08/26/116628de-4c0d-11e5-80c2-106ea7fb80d4_story.html.

67. Network "Networks' Nuns on the Bus is Coming to Madison!" accessed July 2, 2021, https://networklobby.org/wp-content/uploads/2016/06/madison-flyer.pdf.

68. Judith Valente, "A Ride with The Nuns on the Bus," WGLT, July 14, 2016, https://www.wglt.org/post/ride-nuns-bus.

69. Katharine Rhodes Henderson, "The Content of our Character," *The Hill*, August 4, 2016, https://thehill.com/blogs/ballot-box/290406-the-content-of-our-character.

70. Sarah Jaffe, "Nuns of the Bus Take Capitol Hill by Storm," *Bill Moyers*, July 25, 2015, https://billmoyers.com/story/nuns-bus-take-capitol-hill-storm/.

71. Chris Lisee, "Catholic Nuns' Bus Tour Concludes in Nation's Capital," *Religious News Service*, July 2, 2012, https://religionnews.com/2012/07/02/catholic-nuns-end-bus-tour-in-washington/.

72. Jason Horowitz, "Biden, a Catholic School 'Kid,' Praises Nuns Under Fire from the Vatican," *The New York Times*, September 14, 2014, https://www.nytimes.com/2014/09/18/us/politics/biden-drawing-on-his-past-expresses-common-cause-with-activist-nuns.html.

73. Horowitz, "Biden, a Catholic School Kid."

74. Lisee, "Catholic Nuns' Bus Tour."

75. Marin Cogan, "Sister Act: The Nuns on the Bus Come Home to D.C." *GQ* July 3, 2012, https://www.gq.com/story/sister-act-the-nuns-on-the-bus-come-home-to-dc.

76. Sandra M. Schneiders, "'That was Then, This is Now': The Past, Present, and Future of Women Religious in the United States," Woman & Spirit Lecture, Saint Mary's College and the University of Notre Dame, September 24, 2011. https://supportcatholicsisters.files.wordpress.com/2012/04/schneiders-womenspirit-_3_-rtf.pdf.

77. Bridgit Bowden, "'Nuns on the Bus' Roll into KC," *Flatland*, September 13, 2015. https://www.flatlandkc.org/uncategorized/nuns-bus-visit-kc/.

78. Carol Zimmermann, "LCWR Plans to Continue to Dialogue on Vatican Assessment," *Angelus*, August 14, 2012. https://angelusnews.com/news/lcwr-plans-to-continue-to-dialogue-on-vatican-assessment/.

BIBLIOGRAPHY

Allen, John L. "Exclusive Interview: Levada Talks LCWR, Criticism in the States." *National Catholic Reporter*. June 15, 2012. https://www.ncronline.org/blogs/all-things-catholic/exclusive-interview-levada-talks-lcwr-criticism-states.

Blair, Leonard interview by Terry Gross. "Bishop Explains Vatican's Criticisms of U.S. Nuns." *Fresh Air*. July 25, 2012. https://www.npr.org/transcripts/157356092.

Boorstein, Michelle. "U.S. Nuns Seek 'Open Dialogue' with Rome Over Disputes." *The Washington Post*. August 10, 2012. https://www.washingtonpost.com/local/us-nuns-seek-open-dialogue-with-rome-over-disputes/2012/08/10/64ab2534-e31b-11e1-98e7-89d659f9c106_story.html.

Bowden, Bridgit. "'Nuns on the Bus' Roll into KC." *Flatland*. September 13, 2015. https://www.flatlandkc.org/uncategorized/nuns-bus-visit-kc/.

Brachear, Manya A. "Nuns on the Bus Protest Campaign Rolls into Chicago." *The Chicago Tribune*. June 20, 2012. https://www.chicagotribune.com/news/ct-xpm-2012-06-20-ct-met-nuns-on-the-bus-20120620-story.html.

Brigham, Erin. "Women Religious and the Public Voice of Catholicism." *The Journal of Feminist Studies in Religion* 31, no. 2 (Fall 2015): 109–126. https://doi.org/10.2979/jfemistudreli.31.2.109.

Browning, Melissa and Emily Reimer-Barry. "Preaching, Sexuality, and Women Religious: Listening to Prophetic Voices at the Margins of Religious Life." *Theology & Sexuality* 19, no. 1 (2013): 69–88. https://doi.org/10.1179/1355835814Z.00000000020.

Calhoun, Ada. "Radical Habits." *The New York Times*. October 26, 2012. https://www.nytimes.com/2012/10/28/magazine/sister-florence-deacon-the-rebel-nun.html.

Chittister, Joan. "Wanted: Women of Spirit in Our Own Time." *National Catholic Reporter*, August 11, 2010. https://www.ncronline.org/news/global-sisters-report/wanted-women-spirit-our-own-time.

Coburn, Carol K. "An Overview of the Historiography of Women Religious: A Twenty-Five-Year Retrospective." *U.S. Catholic Historian* 22, no. 1 (2004): 1–26. http://www.jstor.org/stable/25154889.

Coburn, Carol K. "Uneasy Alliance: A Look Back at American Sisters and Clerical Authority." *Global Sisters Report*. July 13, 2015. https://www.globalsistersreport.org/column/trends/uneasy-alliance-look-back-american-sisters-and-clerical-authority-27881.

Cogan, Marin. "Sister Act: The Nuns on the Bus Come Home to D.C." *GQ*. July 3, 2012. https://www.gq.com/story/sister-act-the-nuns-on-the-bus-come-home-to-dc.

Congregation for the Doctrine of the Faith. "Doctrinal Assessment of the Leadership Conference of Women Religious." The Holy See. April 18, 2012. https://www.vatican.va/roman_curia/congregations/cfaith/documents/rc_con_cfaith_doc_20120418_assessment-lcwr_en.html.

Dambroski, J. Lora et al. "Public Statement from the LCWR Officers." LCWR. Statement, April 23, 2009. https://lcwr.org/media/april-23-2009-lcwr-officers-statement-doctrinal-assessment-lcwr.

Darsey, James. *The Prophetic Tradition and Radical Rhetoric in America*. New York: NYU Press, 1997.

Deacon, Florence. Interview by Gayle King and Anthony Mason. CBS This Morning. March 11, 2013. www.cbs.com/shows/cbs_this_morning/ video/2342231215/rebel-nuns-talks-female-priestswomen-in-church/.

de Aviz, João Braz. "Apostolic Visitation Final Report." US Council of Catholic Bishops. September 8, 2014. https://www.usccb.org/beliefs-and-teachings/vocations/consecrated-life/apostolic-visitation-final-report.

Farrell, Pat interview by Terry Gross. "An American Nun Responds to Vatican Criticism." *Fresh Air*. July 17, 2012. https://www.npr.org/2012/07/17/156858223/an-american-nun-responds-to-vatican-condemnation.

Fortier, Anne-Marie. "Re-Membering Places and the Performance of Belonging(s)." *Theory, Culture & Society* 16, no. 2 (April 1999): 41–64. https://doi.org/10.1177/02632769922050548.

Fredericks, Andrew. "Sister Simone Campbell on What Drives 'Nuns on the Bus.'" *Moyers on Democracy*. June 27, 2012. https://billmoyers.com/2012/06/27/sister-simone-campbell-on-what-drives-nuns-on-the-bus/.

Gazette Editorial Board. "Nuns' Shared-Sacrifice Pitch Rings True." *The Gazette*, June 22, 2012. https://www.thegazette.com/2012/06/22/nuns-shared-sacrifice-pitch-rings-true.

Gibson, David. "New 'Nuns on the Bus' Tour to Highlight Pope Francis' US Visit and Agenda." *Washington Post*. August 26, 2015. https://www.washingtonpost.com/national/religion/new-nuns-on-the-bus-tour-to-highlight-pope-francis-us-visit-and-agenda/2015/08/26/116628de-4c0d-11e5-80c2-106ea7fb80d4_story.html.

Goodstein, Laurie. "National Nuns' Group Dodges Showdown with Vatican," *The New York Times*. August 10, 2012. https://www.nytimes.com/2012/08/11/us/national-nuns-group-seeks-dialogue-with-vatican.html.

Goodstein, Laurie. "The Nuns Spoke Out, but the Archbishop Listened." *The New York Times*. May 15, 2012. https://www.nytimes.com/2015/05/15/us/the-nuns-spoke-out-but-the-archbishop-listened.html.

Halloran, S. Michael. "Aristotle's Concept of Ethos, or If Not His Somebody Else's." *Rhetoric Review* 1, no. 1 (1982): 58–63. http://www.jstor.org/stable/465559.

Hart, Roderick P. "The Rhetoric of the True Believer." *Speech Monographs* 38, no. 4 (1971): 249–261. https://doi.org/10.1080/03637757109375718.

Henderson, Katharine Rhodes. "The Content of our Character." *The Hill*. August 4, 2016. https://thehill.com/blogs/ballot-box/290406-the-content-of-our-character.

Heyer, Kristin. "A Feminist Appraisal of Catholic Social Thought." Speech delivered as part of Fall Lecture Series, Lane Center for Catholic Studies and Catholic Social Thought, University of San Francisco. November 9, 2007. https://www.academia.edu/4433442/A_FEMINIST_APPRAISAL_OF_CATHOLIC_SOCIAL_THOUGHT.

Hinze, Bradford. *Practices of Dialogue in the Roman Catholic Church: Aims and Obstacles, Lessons and Laments*. New York: Continuum International Publishing, 2006.

Horowitz, Jason. "Biden, a Catholic School 'Kid,' Praises Nuns Under Fire from the Vatican." *The New York Times*. September 14, 2014. https://www.nytimes.com/2014/09/18/us/politics/biden-drawing-on-his-past-expresses-common-cause-with-activist-nuns.html.

Jablonski, Carol J. "Aggiornamento and The American Catholic Bishops: A Rhetoric of Institutional Continuity and Change." *Quarterly Journal of Speech* 75, no. 4 (1989): 416–432. https://doi.org/10.1080/00335638909383888.

Jaffe, Sarah. "Nuns of the Bus Take Capitol Hill by Storm." *Bill Moyers*. July 25, 2017. https://billmoyers.com/story/nuns-bus-take-capitol-hill-storm/.

LCWR. "About LCWR." Accessed June 1, 2021. https://lcwr.org/about.

LCWR. "April 23, 2009—LCWR Officers Statement on Doctrinal Assessment of LCWR." April 23, 2009. https://lcwr.org/media/april-23-2009-lcwr-officers-statement-doctrinal-assessment-lcwr.

LCWR. "LCWR Mission Statement." Accessed June 1, 2021, https://lcwr.org/about/mission.

LCWR. "Leadership Conference of Women Religious Assembly Explores Concerns of the Global Community." Statement, August 19, 2013. https://lcwr.org/sites/default/files/calendar/attachments/lcwr_2013_assembly_press_release_-_8-19-13.pdf.

Lisee, Chris. "Catholic Nuns' Bus Tour Concludes in Nation's Capital." *Religious News Service*, July 2, 2012. https://religionnews.com/2012/07/02/catholic-nuns-end-bus-tour-in-washington/.

Manson, Jamie. "LCWR's Annual Meeting: Some Reflections and A Little Backstory." *National Catholic Reporter*. August 15, 2012. https://www.ncronline.org/blogs/grace-margins/lcwrs-annual-meeting-some-reflections-and-little-back-story.

Mastrofini, Fabrizio. "'Rebel' Nuns Receive Religious Freedom Award." *Vatican Insider*. November 19, 2012. http://vaticaninsider.lastampa.it/en/world-news/detail/articolo/usa-stati-uniti-estados-unidos-suore-nuns-monjas-19867/.

McCauley, Bernadette. "Nuns' Stories: Writing the History of Women Religious in the United States." *American Catholic Studies* 125, no. 4 (2014): 51–68. https://doi.org/10.1353/acs.2014.0067.

Miller, Arthur B. "Aristotle on Habit (εθō) and Character (ηθō): Implications for the Rhetoric." *Speech Monographs* 41, no. 4 (1974): 309–316. https://doi.org/10.1080/03637757409375855.

Miner, Barbara. "The Nuns are Here! The Nuns are Here!" *Milwaukee Journal Sentinel*. June 20, 2012. http://archive.jsonline.com/blogs/purple-wisconsin/159706575.html.

Mongoven, Anne Marie. "We Did What the Church Asked Us to Do." *National Catholic Reporter*. August 7, 2009. https://www.ncronline.org/news/global-sisters-report/we-did-what-church-asked-us-do.Network.

"Network History." Accessed June 1, 2021. https://networklobby.org/about/history/.

Network. "Networks' Nuns on the Bus is Coming to Madison!" Flyer accessed July 2, 2021. https://networklobby.org/wp-content/uploads/2016/06/madison-flyer.pdf.

Network. "Nuns on the Bus." Accessed June 1, 2021. https://networklobby.org/nunsonthebus/.

"Nuns Hit the Road Again for Real Immigration Reform." *Angelus*. June 18, 2013. https://angelusnews.com/local/california/nuns-hit-the-road-again-for-real-immigration-reform/.

"Nuns on the Bus 2015: Bridge the Divides, Transform Politics." *Network Nuns on the Bus*. Accessed July 2, 2021. https://bus.networklobby.org/bus2015/?fbclid=IwAR1dJKzq6ksmV3z1qm6k30aPw3_Btesee_xG19kRsqd0qx-QM9WaHsxRBYM.

O'Loughlin, Michael. "Paul Ryan Defends Poverty Reform Efforts to a Catholic Nun." *America: The Jesuit Review*. August 22, 2017. https://www.americamagazine.org

/politics-society/2017/08/22/paul-ryan-defends-poverty-reform-efforts-catholic-nun.

Reynolds, Nedra. "Ethos as Location: New Sites for Understanding Discursive Authority." *Rhetoric Review* 11, no. 2 (1993): 325–338. http://www.jstor.org/stable/465805.

Rodé, Franc. "From Past to Present: Religious Life Before and After Vatican II." Transcript of speech delivered at Stonehill College. Delivered September 27, 2008, https://www.ewtn.com/catholicism/library/from-past-to-present-religious-life-before-and-after-vatican-ii-9851.

Ryan, Kathleen J., Nancy Myers, and Rebecca Jones. "Introduction: Identifying Feminist Ecological Ethē." In *Rethinking Ethos: A Feminist Ecological Approach to Rhetoric*, edited by Kathleen J. Ryan, Nancy Myers, and Rebecca Jones, 1–22. Carbondale, IL: Southern Illinois UP, 2016.

Schenk, Christine. *To Speak the Truth in Love: A Biography of Theresa Kane, R.S.M.* Maryknoll, NY: Orbis Books, 2019.

Schneiders, Sandra. *Prophets in Their Own Country: Women Religious Bearing Witness to the Gospel in a Troubled Church*. Maryknoll, NY: Orbis Press, 2011.

Schneiders, Sandra. "'That was Then, This is Now': The Past, Present, and Future of Women Religious in the United States," Woman & Spirit Lecture, Saint Mary's College and the University of Notre Dame, September 24, 2011. https://supportcatholicsisters.files.wordpress.com/2012/04/schneiders-womenspirit-_3_-rtf.pdf.

Schneiders, Sandra. "We've Given Birth to a New Form of Religious Life." *National Catholic Reporter*. February 27, 2009. https://www.ncronline.org/news/global-sisters-report/weve-given-birth-new-form-religious-life.

Steenland, Sally, Hannah Moser, and Elana Leopold, "An Overview of the Nuns on the Bus Tour." Center for American Progress. Last modified July 17, 2012. americanprogress.org/issues/religion/news/2012/07/17/11924/an-overview-of-the-nuns-on-the-bus-tour/.

Thompson, Margaret Susan. "Circles of Sisterhood: Formal and Informal Collaboration Among American Nuns in Response to Conflict with Vatican Kyriarchy." *Journal of Feminist Studies in Religion* 32, no. 2 (2016): 63–82. https://doi.org/10.2979/jfemistudreli.32.2.06.

Valente, Judith. "A Ride with The Nuns on the Bus." WGLT. July 14, 2016. https://www.wglt.org/post/ride-nuns-bus.

Wincek, Jean and Nancy Reynolds. "Tracing the Apostolic Visitation through a Chronology of Primary Sources." In *Power of Sisterhood: Women Religious Tell the Story of Apostolic Visitation*, edited by Margaret Cain McCarthy and Mary Ann Zollman, 47–64. Lanham, MD: University Press, 2014.

Zagano, Phyllis. "Ministry by Women Religious and the U.S. Apostolic Visitation." *New Blackfriars* 92, no. 1041 (September 2011): 591–606. https://www.jstor.org/stable/43251556.

Zimmermann, Carol. "LCWR Plans to Continue to Dialogue on Vatican Assessment." *Angelus*, August 14, 2012. https://angelusnews.com/news/lcwr-plans-to-continue-to-dialogue-on-vatican-assessment/.

Index

accountability, 119, 123–25, 128, 139, 140, 143–49; as acknowledging women, 145–46; exigence for, 143–45; as listening and justice, 146–49
achieved ethos, 27, 38, 39, 41
activism, 56, 61, 81–83, 88, 91, 92, 100, 102, 207, 214, 215
Acuña y Rossetti, Elisa, 211
advocacy, 47, 48, 119, 126, 230, 231, 233, 235–37; ecological perspective, 240–43; incompatible, 237–40
agency, 25, 30, 39, 101, 105–7, 110, 175, 178, 179
Agricultural Labor Relations Act, 205
alternative ethos, 270
Althaus-Reid, Marcella, 195
Amazon Grace: Re-Calling the Courage to Sin Big, 173
American Catholics, 6, 10, 156–58, 166
American women, 287, 289, 293, 294
Angelica, Mother Mary, 13, 249–51, 253–63; background and history, 250–52; ethos, 250, 262; feud with Cardinal Mahony, 258–61; financial support, 256; God needs dodoes, 257–58; monastery and fund, 255; rhetorical beginnings, Birmingham, 253–54; rhetorical style, 254–55; rhetorical tactics of, 249–64
Angels Monastery, 253
Annalen der Verbreitung des Glaubens, the Annals of Spreading the Faith, 33
Annals, 49, 50, 52
annual report genre, 160–61
Anzaldúa, Gloria E., 206, 208
Aponte, Barbara, 120, 121
Applegarth, Risa, 25, 157
archbishop, 32–35, 68, 258, 276, 293, 301
Aristotelian conceptions of ethos, 13, 199
Aristotelian ethos, 236, 237
Arroyo, Raymond, 251, 252, 254, 260
ascribed ethos, 38–41
Aslakson, Kenneth, 64, 70
Assmann, Jan, 51, 54, 57
associations, 65, 66, 69, 73, 209
authentic ethos, 13, 268, 272, 280, 281
authenticity, 190, 193, 269, 276, 278

Babenroth, A. Charles, 160, 161
Baird, Peggy, 195
Baker, Ray Palmer, 161
Baker, Stephen, 122
Bakker, Jim, 257
Balboni, Jennifer, 125
Barnette, Sean, 55, 196
Batterham, Forster, 196

Bay, Jennifer, 7, 13
Beagle, Christine, 208
Beare, Zachary, 192
Belgium, 83
Bell, Caryn Cosse, 64
Bell, Marjorie, 169, 169n35
Bell, W. H., 169n35
Benedict, Pope, 11, 144
Bernal, Dolores Delgado, 209
Beyond God the Father, 173, 174, 180
Biden, Joe, 299
Biesecker, Barbara, 3
bishops, 32–36, 144, 146, 147, 163, 164, 260, 293, 294, 296, 297
Black Lives Matter movement, 48
Blackwell, Maylei, 212
Blaine, Barbara, 140, 144, 146–49
Blair, Bishop Leonard, 293
body rhetoric, 92
Boesen, Sister Mary Beth (Buffy), 87
Bonavoglia, 146, 147
Bonavoglia, Angela, 143, 144
Bonille, Cecile, 67
Booth, Wayne C., 175, 242
Boston Archdiocese, 139, 144
Boston Globe, 139, 144
Bourbon Orleans Hotel, 73
Bouvier, Bishop, 37
Brady, Ann, 100, 101, 106–10
Brereton, John, 229, 233
Britt-Smith, Laurie A., 187, 188, 200
Brown, Mary Borromeo, 28
Burke, Cardinal Raymond, 290
Burzynski, Joseph, 6, 13
business ethos, 157, 159, 164–67; developing, 159–60
business writing, 155–71
Buyserie, Beth, 13
Bynum, Caroline Walker, 2, 81

Campbell, Sister Simone, 297–300
Cano, Gabriela, 211
Carroll, Frank, 52
Catholic Church, 9, 10, 100, 102, 103, 110, 127, 143, 145, 149, 267, 269, 279, 287, 290; closures, 101, 102. *See also* Church
Catholic communities, 13, 99, 108, 110, 125, 128, 198, 200, 281
Catholic Diocese of Syracuse, 100
Catholic education, 2, 10
Catholic ethos, 164, 208–10, 270
Catholic faith, 11, 187, 214, 215, 262, 288, 293, 294, 298
Catholicism, 2, 4–6, 29, 30, 173, 174, 176, 177, 187, 196, 197, 207, 209
Catholic lay womanhood, development of, 157–58
Catholic laywomen, 10, 156, 165, 166
Catholic motherhood, 117–21, 128
Catholic mothers, 13, 117–22, 125, 127, 128
Catholic patriarchy, 8, 13, 14, 27, 28, 83, 173
Catholic schools, 1, 2, 210
Catholic sisters, 1, 2, 5, 13, 33, 82, 232, 287, 297, 298
Catholic spirit, 165
Catholic Women Confront Their Church: Stories of Hurt and Hope, 145
Catholic Women's League of Columbus (CWL), 159–67; *1919–1921 Year Book*, 162–66
Catholic Worker Movement, 187, 193, 197, 198
Charles, Josephine, 63, 67–68
Chávez, Alicia, 208
Chávez, César, 214
Chávez, Herculano, 208
Chernekoff, Janice, 82, 91, 189, 190
Chicana feminism, 205–22
Chicana rhetors, 205, 207, 211
Chicanas, 210, 211, 213, 214
children, 31, 32, 109, 110, 119–22, 124–28, 140, 216
Chittister, Sister Joan, 13, 267–69, 272, 274–81, 295; love, respect and acceptance, reframing, 276–80; questioning authority, 272–76;

reframing ethos, 270–72; rhetoric of acceptance, 267–84
Christianity, 7, 8, 173, 182, 291
Church, 9, 11, 13, 99, 102, 103, 107, 121, 122, 126–28, 145, 146, 174, 176, 181, 268, 280, 291; building, 13, 102, 103, 105, 107, 108, 110; closure, 99–113; communities, 99, 101, 102, 123, 274; hierarchy, 102, 108, 249, 255, 257, 259–61, 263, 296, 297, 300; teaching, 48, 209, 268, 288, 289
The Church and the Second Sex, 173, 174
Cisneros, Josue David, 122
classical rhetoric, 230, 243, 244
clergy perpetrated sex abuse (CPSA), 13, 117–28, 139, 140, 145; impact on Catholic motherhood, 121–28
clergy sex abuse scandals, 117–35
Clite, Brian, 119, 125–27, 130
Coburn, Carol, 1
coexistent ethos, 12, 156–60, 166; defining, 156–57; of professionalism, 160, 162, 166, 167
communal ethos, 57, 206, 207, 215
communication, 27, 31, 40, 229, 230, 234, 237, 243, 288, 289
communion, 90, 123, 207, 210, 218, 287
Community Service Organization (CSO), 214, 215
community's ethos, 55, 56
Conference of Major Superiors of Women, 289
conflict, 26, 37, 83, 119, 181, 260, 293, 297
confrontational ethos, 79
confrontational resistance, 79–95
Congregation for Institutes of Consecrated Life and Societies of Apostolic Life (CICSAL), 289, 290
Congregation for the Doctrine of the Faith (CFD), 288, 296–97, 301
Connors, Robert, 229
conscience, 84, 88, 90, 91, 145
Corbett, Edward, 229, 230, 237, 242
corporate body, 87–88
corporate embodied ethos, 88
correspondence, 32–34
The Correspondence of Catherine McAuley, 53
credibility, 12, 13, 38–40, 65, 68, 69, 92, 269–71, 274, 275, 278
Crosby, Richard Benjamin, 193
crossing the line metaphor, 85–87
culture, 128–30
curriculum, 233, 238, 239, 243
Czaplicka, John, 51, 54, 57

Daly, Mary, 12, 173–85; ethos, 174; rhetorical progression, 176–79; rhetorical stances, shifting, 179–82; silence, listening, and ethos, 182–83
Daniell, Beth, 140–41, 143
David Leigh, S.J., 235
Davis, Laura, 13
Day, Dorothy, 187–202, 258; embodied rhetoric, 188–90; ethos, reconsidering, 199–200; living rhetorically, 188–90; metanoia and transformation, 190–94; metanoias, 194–99
D.C. Nine, 88–91
Deacon, Florence, 296
Dear Joan Chittister, 270, 276
Deggs, Mary Bernard, 61, 62, 67–73
Degnan, Mary Bertrand, 53
Delille, Henriette, 62–65, 67, 70, 73
devotion, 67, 80, 81, 173, 209, 269, 290
Diocese of Syracuse, 101, 103–5, 107, 110
Dow Chemical Company, 89
Dow Chemical Property, 90
Downing, Jamie, 11, 13, 14
Duckworth, Angela, 101
dwelling places, 69–71
Dworkin, Andrea, 79

Eckenstein, Lina, 4, 8, 29
ecological thinking, 3, 4, 199, 250

Edmonds, Juliana, 12
Ellwanger, Adam, 190, 193
El Mundo Zurdo, 206, 214–15
El Santo Niño de Atocha, 209
embodied ethos, 14, 80–85, 92
embodied knowledge, 81, 89, 91, 189
embodied rhetoric, 12, 79–82, 84–87, 91, 92, 188, 189, 199, 200
Endres, Danielle, 69
environments, 29–31
epideictic rhetoric, 47–59
equity, 188, 271, 272, 278, 281
Eternal Word Television Network (EWTN), 249, 250, 260, 261
ethē, 2, 6, 12, 14, 27, 35, 37, 62, 213, 236, 240, 288, 290
ethics, 191, 211, 270, 271
ethos, 1–18, 25–44, 47–59, 140–42, 157, 191, 192, 205, 269, 270, 272, 275, 288; classical concepts of, 270; feminist accountability, 149–50; of interruption, 12, 175, 179; lay Catholic women's rhetorics, 139–51; practices, 288; as presence, 140–43, 149–50; of professionalism and Catholic lay womanhood, 155–71; of rhetoric, 262; Soeurs de Sainte-Famille's reconstruction of, 61–76; understanding of, 192, 270
ethos-building work, 156
ethotic claim, 141, 142, 146
etymological roots, 262
European American Catholic Sisters, 25–44
expansive queer ethos, 215–19
expansive queer faith, 215–19

Faranta, Signor, 71–72
Faranta's Iron Circus, Faranta's Theatre, 71–72
Farmer, Paul, 199
feminist ecological approach, 26, 37, 157, 199, 236, 270
feminist ecological ethē, 157, 236
feminist ecological ethos, 82, 83, 188, 199, 200
feminist ecological thinking, 62, 73
feminist ethē, 37
feminist ethics, 175
feminist protest rhetoric, 99–113
feminist resistance, 1–18
Feminist Rhetorical Practices, 251
feminist rhetorical resilience, 100, 101, 105–7, 109; agency, 106–8; Metis, 108–9; relationality, 109; of St. Mary's lay community, 106–9
feminist rhetorical studies, 101, 105, 140
feminist rhetoricians, 25, 66, 101, 205, 250
Ferder, Sister Fran, 290
Fernández, Alicia, 208
Fernández, Juan, 207
Fessenden, Tracy, 64, 68
Fitting, Ralph U., 161
Fitzgerald, Maureen, 5, 10
Flavin, Christopher M., 5
Fleckenstein, Kristine S., 81
Floyd, George, 48
Flynn, Elizabeth A., 100, 101, 106–10
Flynn, Maud, 165
Foucault, Michel, 34
Frey, Renea Carol, 25, 35, 41

Gaffney, Rev. Francis A., 164
Gameros, Sylvia, 120
Gannett, Cinthia, 229, 233
Gary, Elbert H., 159
Gaudin, Juliette, 63, 67
Gaum, Carl C., 162
González, Gabriela, 212, 260
good Catholic mothers, 117, 119, 121–23, 126, 127; children within institutional Church, 125–28; CPSA revelations and institutional Church, 122–23; (re)making of, 117–35; seek redress for CPSA, 123–25; themselves and families, life of Church, 121–22

Gould, Virginia Meacham, 71
Graves, Harold F., 162
Guerin, Mother Theodore, 26, 28, 29, 31–33, 37–39, 83
Guglielmo, Letizia, 140, 141, 143
Gutiérrez de Mendoza, Juana, 211

Habits of Compassion, 10
Haggard, Tim, 217
Halbwachs, Maurice, 51
Haller, Cynthia, 160
Halloran, S. Michael, 1, 190, 288
Hamill, Jimmy, 12
Handbook of Business English, 159
Hanh, Thich Nhat, *87*
happy-ending stories, resisting, 109–10
Harding, Vincent, 209
Harmon, Katharine E., 157
Haroway, Donna, 37
Hart, Borgia, 68
Hartley, Bishop, 162, 164
Hasson, Mary Rice, 117, 118, 128
Hauser, Gerard, 34
Heidenreich, Linda L., 85
Henderson, Gae Lyn, 34
Hollermann, Sister Ephrem, 29
Holy Cross Church, 105, 107
Hotchkiss, George Burton, 159
Hubbard, Phil, 66, 69
Huerta, Dolores, 12, 205–22; childhood matters, 207–8; ethos, 210, 213, 218; long line of rhetors, 210–13; prayer and girl scouts service, 207–8; theory, 213–14
Hughes, Archbishop John, 10
Hurricane Katrina, 102
Hyde, Michael J., 252

identity, 65–67
ignorance, 4–6
incompatible advocacy, 237–40
institutional Church, 119, 122–29, 209, 274
institutions, 2, 121, 122, 129, 140, 146, 147, 149, 235–37, 269, 274, 275, 294
interruption, 12, 174, 175, 179, 181–83
Ireland, 47, 49, 50, 53, 54

James Bond, 177
Jamesville, 99, 101, 104, 110
Jesuit rhetorical education, 233, 234
Jesuits, 9, 13, 229, 230, 233–36, 238, 239
Jiménez y Muro, Dolores, 211
John Paul II, Pope, 11, 144
Johnson, Nan, 5
Johnson, Wendy Dasler, 68
Johnstown, Altoona, 124
Jones, Cecily, 80, 84, 85, 87, 88
Jones, Rebecca, 2–3, 25, 37, 40, 54–55, 61, 62, 66, 188, 199, 206, 236, 240, 250, 254, 270, 272, 288
Joseph, Sister Miriam, 13, 230–41, 243, 244; ethé, 235–37; rhetorical advocacy, 229–46
Juárez, Benito, 217

Kane, Sister Theresa, 289
Kilduff, Edward Jones, 159
King, Martin Luther, 9, 29
Kirsch, Gesa E., 251
Knoblauch, Abby A., 80, 89, 91, 189
"Krone und Schleier," 2
Ksander, Margret, 103

The Lady and the Law: Notes on Protocol and Parliamentary Procedure, 155
La Mujer Moderna, 212
Landy, Thomas, 1
Las Hijas de Cuauhtémoc, 211
Lauer, Ilon, 57
lay Catholic activism, 99–113
Leadership Conference of Women Religious (LCWR), 13, 14, 287–90, 292–93, 295–98, 300–302
Leadership of Catholic Women Religious, 11
Leigh, David J., 197
Leo XIII, Pope, 209

Lester, Rebecca, 80
The Letters of Catherine McAuley, 53
Levada, William, 293
LGBTQ communities, 13, 80, 102, 215–19, 267–69, 274–76, 278, 280
liberal arts, 231, 233, 234, 239, 240
Lierheimer, Linda, 30
Life of Mother Catherine McAuley, 52, 53
limbo zone, 109–10
The Long Loneliness, 12, 187–202
Loretto Community, 12, 83–85, 88
Lottes, Mary Frances, 86
love, 90, 91, 147, 164, 165, 193, 194, 196, 268, 270, 275–77, 279, 280
Loveland, Matthew T., 103
Ludwig, Bavarian King, 32

MacLeish, Attorney Roderick, 147
Mahony, Cardinal, 249, 255, 258–61
Malone, Loretto Joann, 84, 88–91
Marina, Doña, 210
Martin, Reverend A., 36
Massingale, Father Bryan N., 274–75, 278–80
materiality, 65–67
Mattingly, Carol, 4
Maurin, Peter, 193, 198
McAllister, Anna Sharon, 162
McAuley, Catherine, 12, 47, 48, 50–57; circulating memory, 51–52; cultural memory, 53–54; memory through epideictic, 49–51; mercy ethos, 49–54; remembering, 47–59
McCort, Bishop, 124
McLaughlin, Eleanor, 5
McLuhan, Marshall, 230
McMorrow, Toni, 120–22, 124, 126, 127
McNamara, Jo Ann Kay, 6–8, 80
meaning, reconstruction, 71–73
memories, 47–59; theorizing phases of, 54–57
mercy ethos, 49–56; development of, 54–57
Mercy unto Thousands, 53
mestiza women, 211
The Metaethics of Radical Feminism, 173
metanoia, 188, 190–97, 199, 200
Metanoia: Rhetoric, Authenticity, and the Transformation of the Self, 190
metanoic faith, 187–202
metaphors, 85, 101, 177, 229
Meyers, Nancy, 2, 25, 54, 61, 188, 199, 288
Miller, Arthur B., 292
Miller, Jeanne, 119, 124–27
Minnesota, Riepp, 29
Miriam Joseph, 13
Modern Business English, 160
Moloney, Deirdre M., 6, 157, 158
monasteries, 7, 8, 30, 253, 255, 260, 261
Mongoven, Sister Anne Marie, 291
Moore, Mary Clare, 49
Moraga, Cherríe, 206
Mother McAuley. *See* McAuley, Catherine
Murphy, James J., 242
Myers, Kelly A., 191, 192
Myers, Nancy, 2–3, 25, 37, 40, 54–55, 61, 62, 66, 188, 199, 206, 236, 240, 250, 254, 270, 272, 288

Naming Our Truth: Stories of Loretto Women, 84
National Catholic War Council (NCWC), 164
National Council of Catholic Women, 155
Neisser, Ulric, 66
Nerinckx, Charles, 83
NETWORK, 297–98
Neuhaus, Richard, 260
Neumann, Mary Ignatia, 53
New Orleans, character redefining, 73
The Newsletter of the College English Association, 231, 237
New York Times, the *Washington Post*, 89
Nicomachean Ethics, 191

Niebauer, Allison, 11, 13
Nolan, Charles E., 71
"Nuns on the Bus," 297–300

O'Brien, Kevin J., 196
O'Connor, June, 197
O'Halloran, Ruth Libbey, 158
Okabe, Roichi, 27, 38, 39
O'Malley, John, 233, 235
Ong, Walter J., 229, 230, 237, 238, 241–43
oppressions, 5, 65, 207, 214, 271, 272, 296
orders of religious women, 48, 56
organizational ethos, 163, 302
Orwell, George, 231

Palmer-Mehta, Valerie, 79
parrhesia, 12, 25–44; rethinking, 39–41
parrhesiastic rhetoric, 26, 35
parrhesiastics, 26, 35, 39–41
Pastoral Care Area (PCA), 103–5
The Path of Mercy: The Life of Catherine McAuley, 53
patriarchy, 1–18
Pérez, Emma, 212
perpetual vigils, 100, 102–4, 106–10
Peters, Benjamin T., 196
Peynaud, J. B., 71
Peyton, Letitia, 117, 120, 121, 126, 127
Phillips, Kendall, 120
plaçage, 64, 66–71
Plaza del Zacate, 212
Poor Clare Nun(s) of Perpetual Adoration, 252, 253
Powell, Lawrence N., 65
power, 37–39, 128–30
preconstructed ethos, 55
The Preparation of Reports: Engineering, Scientific, Administrative, 161
Presenting Probation: A Study of Annual Reports, 169, 169n35
"Preserve Our Parishes," 103
Pritchard, Eric Darnell, 273
publicity, 117, 120, 125–29
public statements, 119, 121, 292
public work, 56, 57
"pulpitized spaces," 294
Purcell, Mary Teresa, 51
purposeful life, 6–11

Quadroom Ballroom, 69
queer, 218, 267–73, 275, 277, 279–81; ethos, 215–19, 268, 270, 278; faith, 215–19

radical ethos, 173, 175, 177, 179, 181, 183; as epistemic voyage, 173–85
Ratcliffe, Krista, 2, 177
reforms, 119, 120, 125, 126, 128, 140, 144, 145, 259, 291, 293, 295
Regles et Règlements, 63
religious communities, 7, 49, 51, 52, 82, 87, 118, 230, 252
religious orders, 5–9, 11, 12, 61, 62, 68, 83
religious women, 4, 8, 9, 11, 47, 48, 54–56, 85, 237
Report Writing, 161, 162
report-writing: manuals, guides, handbooks and textbooks, 161–62
resilience, 101, 106, 108, 110
responsibilities, 2, 9, 89, 125–28, 165, 198, 199, 275
Rethinking Ethos: A Feminist Ecological Approach to Rhetoric, 157, 199, 236
Retreat Instructions, 51
Review for Religious magazine, 253
Reynolds, Nedra, 2, 62, 66, 79, 82, 87, 175, 182, 191, 206
"Rhetoric, Paradox, and the Movement for Women's Ordination in the Roman Catholic Church," 180
rhetorical education, 1, 229, 232
rhetorical resilience, 110
rhetorical scholars, 104, 241–43
rhetorical work, 99, 101, 110, 237
Rhetoric at Rome or *Rhetoric in Shakespeare's Time*, 242

The Rhetoric of Rhetoric: The Quest for Effective Communication, 175
rhetorics of accountability, 140, 143, 144
rhetors, 25–27, 37, 38, 40, 41, 141, 143, 147, 157, 199, 210, 211, 236; ethos, 26, 183; long line of, 210–13
Richards, A., 237, 241
Riepp, Benedicta, 26, 28, 30–34, 36–39, 83
Rigney, Ann, 54, 57
Rizzo, Mae, 251, 252
Rizzo, Rita, 250–52
Rohan, Liz, 31
Roosevelt, Franklin, 205
Rose, Margaret, 214, 215
Ross, Fred, 214
Royster, Jacqueline Jones, 101, 251
Ruether, Rosemary Radford, 5, 200
Russett, Cynthia, 1
Ryan, Kathleen J., 2–3, 25, 37, 40, 54–55, 61, 62, 66, 188, 199, 206, 236, 240, 250, 254, 270, 272, 288
Ryan, Paul, 298

San Antonio, 212
San Francisco, 194, 195
Sartain, J. Peter, 293, 301
Schell, Eileen E., 105
Schier, Tracy, 1
Schneiders, Sister Sandra, 290–91, 293, 296–97
Scudder, Shana, 8, 12
Second Vatican Council, 291, 293
self-actualized ethos, 269, 272–74, 276, 278
Senda-Cook, Samantha, 69
Shakespeare's Use of the Arts of Language, 230, 232, 241
Shawn, M., 64
Sibley, David, 65, 66, 69
sidewalk services, 104, 107, 109
Sister Formation Conference (SFC), 294
sisterhood, 174, 181, 182, 277
Sisters of Color: habits and dwelling places, 61–76
Sisters of Loretto: case study, 83–84; Cecily Jones, 84; crossing the line metaphor, 85–87; embodied rhetoric of, 79–95; Joann Malone, 84
Sisters of Mercy, 47–51, 53, 55–57
Sisters of Providence, 28–30, 36, 83
Skinner, Carolyn, 157
Smith, Martha, 1
Smith, Michelle, 65
social justice, 83, 84, 87, 92, 145, 146, 187, 194, 268
Soeurs de Sainte-Famille (SSF), New Orleans, 12, 61–76; Henriette Delille and, 63–65
Soja, Edward, 65
solidarity, 48, 85–87, 292
Sotirin, Patricia, 100, 101, 106–10
St. Benedict, 34
Stempel, Frederick William, 71–73
St. Joseph Worker program, 276
St. Louis Cathedral, 69
St. Mary's Catholic Church, 99, 101, 104, 105, 107; closure to canonical first, 104–6
St. Mary's College, 229–46; trivium at, 230–35
Stolley, Amy, 12
structural change, 103, 275, 279, 280
St. Walburg, 30, 39
subject position, (re)making, 128–30
Sullivan, Mary C., 50, 53, 54
Survivors Network of those Abused by Priests (SNAP), 146–48

Tafolla, Carmen, 212
Tenayuca, Emma, 212
themes, 14, 119–23, 125, 129, 298
Thomas, Carlyle, 27
Thomas, Lynnell, 65
Thurstone Psychological Examination of the American Council of Education, 239
The Time is Now, 268, 271, 281
Tobin, Mary Luke, 86

traditional ethos, 269, 272, 274
Traditions of Eloquence: The Jesuits and Modern Rhetorical Studies, 229
transformation, 13, 101, 130, 176, 190, 192–94, 198, 200
trivium, 229–42
The Trivium in College Composition and Reading, 235
truth, 26, 27, 34, 35, 37–41, 234, 271, 277, 293, 294
"Tudor Writings on Rhetoric," 242

United Farm Workers (UFW), 85, 205, 207, 210, 214, 215
U.S. Catholic church closures, lay resistance, 102–4
U.S. women religious: contemplative dialogue, 292–93; eternal habits of, 287–306; hierarchical mindset, resistance, 293–95; immutable habits, 295–96; immutable laws, 295–96; nuns on bus initiative, 297–300; public faith, 296–97; public imaginary, revising, 300–301; re-membered habits, hope, 301–2; seeds of dispute, 289–90; subversion and incarnation, 290–91

Vatican II, 10, 83, 90, 100, 144, 145, 259, 261, 291, 295, 300
victims, 125–28, 144, 146–49, 292
Vietnam War, 80, 84–89, 187
visible habits, 67–68
Vogel, Elisa, 11, 13
voluntary poverty, 187, 196, 198, 216

Waite, Stacey, 270, 272, 278
Walzer, Arthur, 34
Weaver, Mary Jo, 158
Wenger, Christy, 140–44, 149
Wetzel, Dominic, 259
Wexler, Cecilia Viggo, 140, 143–46, 149
White-Farnham, Jamie, 11, 13
Williams, Terry Tempest, 61
Wilson, Woodrow, 195
Wimmer, Rev. Boniface, 32–34, 36, 37, 39, 40
Winsor, Dorothy, 160
Wise, Rhoda, 251–52, 254
women, 4–9, 28, 29, 55, 81, 120, 121, 123, 125–29, 140, 141, 143–47, 155, 156, 163, 164, 181, 211, 259, 260, 289; of color, 12, 61, 63, 64, 67, 70, 73; discourse, 4, 6, 27, 40, 182; equality, 48, 145, 146; ethos construction, 250; experiences, 14, 199; orders, 8; ordination, 100, 180, 289; report work, 160; rhetorical efforts, 149; rhetors, 3, 37, 55, 62, 66, 120, 182, 205, 207, 212, 250; rights, 211, 216; work, 80, 160
Women Physicians and Professional Ethos in Nineteenth-Century America, 157
women religious, 7–11, 287. *See also* U.S. women religious
"Women Uprooted and Scattered," 29
Wright, Elizabethada A., 50

young women, 49, 165

Zan Meyer Gonçalves, 143
zurdo ethos, 205–22

About the Contributors

Christina R. Pinkston is an assistant professor of English at Norfolk State University in Norfolk, VA. She earned her BA in English and French from Ohio Wesleyan University, her MA in English from the Ohio State University, and her PhD in Sacred Literature from Trinity Theological Seminary. Additionally, she earned an academic certificate for completion of advanced studies in French at the University of Dijon (Dijon, France). Dr. Pinkston specializes in African American studies and British literature (Medieval Period—Twentieth Century). Her research interests include the social-political-cultural voice of African and African Americans as well as the improvement of academic teaching initiatives both in and out of the classroom with a strong focus on student retention. Dr. Pinkston is the recipient of numerous national as well as international honors and special recognitions for her work as an outstanding educator and published writer.

Elizabethada A. Wright is professor at University of Minnesota Duluth and teaches in the Department of English, Linguistics, and Writing Studies and is a member of the faculty at the University of Minnesota Twin Cities' Literacy and Rhetorical Studies Program. She has published in *Rhetoric Society Quarterly*, *Rhetoric Review*, *College English Association Critic*, *Studies in the Literary Imagination*, as well as in a number of other journals and books.

Christiana Ares-Christian's scholarship and research interests are in black studies, contemporary ethnic studies with a focus on the intersections of historical imaginations of Asian Americans and Americans from the African diaspora, and womanist/black feminist thought. She has a forthcoming chapter in the collection *Futures of Cartoons Past: The Cultural Politics of X-Men: The Animated Series*, which will be published with University

Press of Mississippi. Her current book project is *Afrofuturism's Comic Imaginations: Independent Comics of the African Diaspora.*

Jennifer L. Bay is director of the professional writing program and an associate professor of English at Purdue University, where she teaches undergraduate courses in the Professional and Technical Writing major and graduate courses in Professional Writing, Community Engagement, and Rhetorical Theory. Her research focuses on community engagement and experiential learning, digital rhetorics, feminist rhetorics, and rhetorical theory. Her work has appeared in journals such as the *Journal of Business and Technical Communication*, *Rhetoric Society Quarterly*, *Technical Communication Quarterly*, *Computers & Composition*, *College English*, *Programmatic Perspectives*, as well as in edited collections. She is the recipient of Purdue University's Service-Learning Award, Faculty Engagement Scholar Award, and the Jefferson Award for Multiplying Good.

Jennifer Crosby Burgess is an assistant professor of English at Meredith College in Raleigh, North Carolina. In addition to teaching composition and professional writing courses, Dr. Burgess also directs the minor in professional writing. She researches and studies American Catholic women's rhetorical approaches and performances, American Catholic women's business writing practices, and the development of business and professional writing in nineteenth- and twentieth-century America.

Joseph Burzynski is an assistant professor of English in the Department of Literature, Composition, and Mass Communication at Texas A&M University-Texarkana, where he teaches courses in writing and rhetoric application, history, and theory. He earned his Ph.D. in English from Miami University and is the author of articles appearing in *Open Words: Access and English Studies* and *Spark: A 4C4Equality Journal*. His other research and publications investigate access issues, organized labor rhetoric, and the intersection of sustainability and composition studies.

Beth Buyserie is the director of composition and assistant professor of English at Utah State University. She earned her PhD in Cultural Studies and Social Thought in Education from Washington State University in May 2018. Her work focuses on writing program administration, composition and rhetoric, critical pedagogies, professional learning, and the intersections of language, knowledge, and power through the lenses of queer theory and critical race theory.

Laura J. Panning Davies is chief of staff at SUNY Cortland, where she served as and director of Writing Programs and professor of English. Her research on writing program administration and student composing and reading processes has been published in *WPA: Writing Program Administration*, *Composition Studies*, and *Composition Forum*. She is a contributor to the 5th editions of *They Say/I Say: The Moves That Matter in Academic Writing* and *They Say/I Say with Readings*, published by W. W. Norton & Co.

Jamie L. Downing is an assistant professor of communication at Georgia College & State University in Milledgeville, GA. Her research focuses on the rhetorical practices of minority religious communities. She is particularly interested in the intersections of critical regionalisms and the preservation of rural religious cultural identities.

Julianna Edmonds is an assistant professor of English and first-year writing coordinator at Valdosta State University in Valdosta, GA. She earned her PhD in Rhetoric and Composition from Florida State University. Her research interests include writing program administration, feminist rhetorics, and first-year composition.

Jimmy Hamill (he/him/his) is an instructor of English at Albright College in Reading, PA, and a doctoral candidate in English at Lehigh University in Bethlehem, PA. Jimmy specializes in composition and rhetoric, queer theory, and theology. His dissertation examines the rhetorical insights and strategies of LGBTQIA+ Catholics to understand how they help queer Catholics resist violent narratives constructed by the Catholic Church. Other research interests include multimodal composition, "ungrading" methodologies in the writing classroom, antiracist pedagogy, and Universal Design for Learning.

L Heidenreich is an associate professor with the Department of History at Washington State University, a PWI built on the lands of the Nimiipuu and the Palous peoples. They are author of *"This Land Was Mexican Once": Histories of Resistance from Northern California*, and *Nepantla^2: Excavating Transgender Mestiz(a) Histories in Times of Global Shift*. Dr. Heidenreich's articles have appeared in journals such as the *Journal of Chicana/Latina Studies*, *Aztlán*, and the *Journal of American Ethnic History*, while their poetry, sometimes under the name of onegangrygirlfag has been published in *Lean Seed*, *Sanctified*, and *Sinister Wisdom*. They continue to work with their friends and neighbors at Sacred Heart parish to keep the space queer friendly in times of political backlash.

Allison Niebauer is a postdoctoral teaching fellow at the Pennsylvania State University, where she earned her PhD in Communication Arts and Sciences. Her research rests at the intersection of rhetorical criticism, public memory, and communal conflict. Her work has also appeared in *Rhetoric and Public Affairs*, *ISA eSymposium*, and *Journal of Immigrant and Minority Health.*

Shana Scudder is a Lecturer in the First Year Writing Program at North Carolina State University. She earned her PhD from the University of North Carolina at Greensboro, and her research focuses on the intersections of feminist and embodied rhetorics. She has also taught writing in correctional facilities for 20 years and is passionate about providing educational and creative opportunities for persons who are incarcerated. She is the recipient of both a Diversity Grant and an Anti-Racist Fellowship at NCSU and is working to implement anti-racist pedagogy into writing curricula.

Amy Ferdinandt Stolley is an associate professor of Writing and director of First-Year Writing at Grand Valley State University where she teaches classes in first-year writing, style, and genre theory. Her scholarship focuses on the affective nature of writing program administration work and women's rhetorical history. She is the coauthor of *GenAdmin: Theorizing WPA Identities in the Twenty-First Century*, and her work has appeared in *WPA: Writing Program Administration*, *Peitho*, and numerous edited collections.

Elisa Vogel graduated from the Pennsylvania State University in 2020 with her bachelor's degrees in Communication Arts and Sciences and Economics, where she conducted a rhetorical analysis of political media bias for her honors thesis. She will be attending grad school next fall and hopes to study political media and communications

Jamie White-Farnham is an professor in the Writing Program at the University of Wisconsin-Superior, where she also serves as the director of the Teaching and Learning Center. Her research is concerned with feminisms and rhetorics in the material conditions of women's lives, and she is a coeditor of *Women's Health Advocacy: Rhetorical Ingenuity for the 21st Century.* Her work has appeared in *College English*, *Rhetoric Review*, *Computers & Composition*, among others.

www.ingramcontent.com/pod-product-compliance
Lightning Source LLC
Chambersburg PA
CBHW050628280326
41932CB00015B/2561